B. J. Rockliff was born in the north of England. Illness and a lengthy convalescence meant that most mornings were spent reading or listening to the wireless and inventing stories to tell her favourite toys. She trained as a secretary and worked in the oil industry before getting married and helping to raise three stepsons. She began writing when she was forty and her first two thrillers, *Paydirt* and *Crackerjack*, were published by Headline in 1988 and 1989. She lives with her husband just outside Lymington in Hampshire.

Praise for *Paydirt*:

'A spirited and fascinating heroine . . . a minefield of deadly perils . . . fast-moving, intelligent and topical' *Look Now*

Praise for *Crackerjack*:

'Tough and tender is our heroine, Meryl, and I'd put my money on her any day' *Woman's World*

Also by B. J. Rockliff

Paydirt
Crackerjack

Firestone

B. J. Rockliff

HEADLINE

First published in 1989
by HEADLINE BOOK PUBLISHING PLC

First published in paperback in 1990
by HEADLINE BOOK PUBLISHING PLC

10 9 8 7 6 5 4 3 2

ISBN 0 7472 3375 6

Typeset in 10/12 pt English Times
by Colset Private Limited, Singapore

Printed and bound in Great Britain by
Collins, Glasgow

HEADLINE BOOK PUBLISHING PLC
Headline House
79 Great Titchfield Street
London W1P 7FN

Firestone

PROLOGUE

Traffic in the tunnel, running from the north to the south side of Hong Kong island, was relatively light. The driver of the ageing American Ford limousine slowed down and held back from the truck in front, in an effort to avoid the thick diesel fumes belching out from the exhaust. He rested his elbow on the window and tapped his fingers on the steering wheel. His companion took a packet of gum from his pocket and offered it to the driver. The driver shook his head. His companion unwrapped the gum, bit a piece off and chewed noisily. He glanced sideways at the driver. 'How long before we reach Aberdeen?'

'Not long.'

'Will she be there?'

The driver gave a short laugh. 'If she isn't, she's dead. She knows that.'

Aberdeen Harbour was originally a typhoon shelter and a one-time refuge for pirates. The town built up around it in earlier times by the British as an important boat-building port had been developed and modernised into a bustling tourist attraction, leaving little sense of its history and origins. The harbour itself was tightly packed with floating restaurants, but in the hour before dawn it was quiet; the diners and out-of-town tourists having long since left. The Ford limousine cruised past the restaurant piers towards the old boat-building yards. The driver switched off the headlights and rolled the car to a halt. His companion got out and walked to the edge of the harbour.

The woman sitting in the sampan pinched out her cigarette at the sound of a car approaching. She was dressed in traditional black tunic and baggy pants, with a black kerchief wrapped around her head. She stood up and walked to the rear of the sampan. In this section of the harbour there were not many lights and she strained to see in the darkness. A man appeared out of the gloom and called to her. 'You ready?'

'I've been ready for the last fifteen minutes.'

The man bent down by the side of the jetty and passed over a small roll of bank notes. 'You get the rest later.'

'Be sure I do.' The woman pushed the money into the pocket of her pants and moved back to the front of the sampan.

The sampan rocked from side to side as the driver and his companion carried a blanket-wrapped bundle on board. The driver called out in a low voice to the woman to move off. She unhooked the pole from its pinion and plunged it into the dark waters. With surprising strength she poled the sampan away from the jetty, skilfully avoiding the crowded rows of gently swaying junks, and out into the Aberdeen channel.

Midway across the channel and still a little way off the island of Ap Lei Chau, the driver of the limousine called out again to the woman; this time to tell her to stop beneath the bridge spanning the two islands. She drew the pole out of the water and leaned against it, grateful for the few moments of rest. The two men unwrapped the blanket from the body. For a moment they stared down at the mutilated body of a man in his middle thirties. The driver shook his head. 'Foolish to annoy Mr Song like that.' His companion laughed. The woman didn't turn around at the sudden sound of the body splashing into the water, but continued staring into the darkness. It wasn't her business to know why two men wanted her to ferry them halfway to Ap Lei Chau and back in the middle of the night, particularly when they were members of the Bear's Paw Gang.

The driver signalled to the woman to take them back to the harbour. She plunged the pole back into the waters and slowly swung the sampan round. When they reached the jetty, the driver pushed his hand into his trouser pocket and gave the woman another small bank roll. She flicked through it quickly.

'Don't worry, you old crone, it's all there.'

As the woman glanced up at him, he fingered his silver tie-pin fashioned in the shape of a bear's paw. 'And keep your mouth shut.'

She stared at the tie-pin for a moment then nodded. 'You can trust me.'

He laughed. 'I know.'

She watched the two men scramble out of the sampan and vanish into the darkness then moved into the covered portion of the boat and sat down. She took out a little tin of tobacco from her pocket and a packet of cigarette papers and rolled herself a well-earned cigarette.

A man pushed back iron shuttered gates at the rear of Song Automobile Rental Company as the Ford limousine turned into the narrow street and flashed its headlights twice. The car was swiftly driven into the yard and the man pushed the gates shut again. As the driver alighted from the car, the man jerked his thumb in the direction of an upstairs window. 'Mr Song's had to go out. You're to call him from the office. He's left the number on the desk.'

The driver gave an acknowledging nod and hurried up the stairs.

A single light had been left on in the office. The driver of the limousine scanned the top of the desk quickly then picked up the sheet of paper by the telephone and dialled the number on it. 'Hello, Mr Song?'

'Yes.'

'Mui Shenlu has just taken a trip up river.'

'Good. I trust there were no problems?'

'No, Mr Song.'

There was a sharp click as Song Enlai hung up. The driver switched off the light then stepped quickly out of the office and down the stairs.

PART 1

Marti Van den Fleet parked her car and got out. She glanced up at the sky and ducked back inside the car to collect her umbrella. Taking a short cut across Huidevetterstraat, into one of the small side-streets leading off, she reached the doorway of Van den Fleet & Co. just as the rain began to fall heavily.

In Antwerp, the business of buying and selling diamonds, the craft of cutting and polishing gems, were centred around a small area encompassing Pelikannstraat and the surrounding streets. Van den Fleet's was one of the oldest companies and the most respected. The trading base of the company was the buying and selling of industrial diamonds. It was not the kind of diamond dealing that inspires the glamorous images occasionally portrayed by the media, but it was highly profitable. The company had been founded by Marti's great-great-great-grandfather and was now headed by her father, Erasmus. Ill health had forced him into semi-retirement and he reluctantly left Marti to run the company on a day-to-day basis, virtually on her own. It was a task which she had come to relish.

When she left school with no more than average academic achievements, Marti had joined Van den Fleet's the very next day. Her first job was to learn how to make a good cup of coffee and how to file correctly. The office manager had given her a stern warning. A document misfiled is a document lost. The following year she had been allowed to stand at her father's side and give her opinion on the quality and value of the diamonds that passed through his hands. She had been trained from the age of six by her father to use an eyeglass; to see more than just a whitish lump of crystal; to appreciate the hidden qualities of an uncut diamond. Her second year was spent with Conrad Van den Fleet, her father's cousin. Conrad was considered to be one of the best cutters and polishers in Europe. With Conrad, she learnt the art of letting the diamonds speak to her; telling her the natural spot to engrave a notch, where the cleaving line will run, how the diamond will divide neatly into its desired shape. It was an art she never entirely mastered, but her knowledge was sufficient to enable her to value cut and polished diamonds with unerring accuracy. Her real talent lay in sharp-witted bargaining. Like her father before her, she had an almost uncanny knack of assessing clients' negotiating tactics; knowing when a display was being put on for her benefit; knowing how far or near a client was from their 'ceiling'.

The telephone rang out before Marti had even closed the door of her father's office. She hurried to the desk and picked up the telephone. 'Yes, Astrid?'

'I have Mr Daniel Schmidt of Tel Aviv on the line for you.'

'Thanks, Astrid. Put him on.' Marti drew the chair away from the desk and sat down.

'Marti, Daniel here. How are you?'

'I'm fine and you?'

'So so. So so. Look, I'm coming over to Belgium tonight. What have you got in the way of industrials that will interest me?'

'Whatever you can afford.'

'OK. I am interested in three maybe four parcels of "J" grades.'

'Can do.'

'Fine. Tomorrow morning suit? Ten o'clock?'

'Yes. See you then.' Marti put the telephone down and made a quick note in her diary.

Marti's secretary half opened the door and carefully inched herself through. 'Miss Van den Fleet.'

Marti looked up. 'Yes, Astrid.'

'There's a Mrs Schapper waiting outside. She insists on seeing Mr Erasmus.' Astrid spoke in an exaggerated whisper.

Marti ran her finger down the page of the diary. 'He's not due in the office until Friday. Has she got an appointment?'

'No. She's just turned up out of the blue.'

'Make an appointment for her to come back on Friday.'

Astrid raised an eyebrow. Mrs Schapper was not going to like that. She eased herself back from the doorway and went to impart the news to Mrs Schapper. Marti gave a loud sigh as the sound of a querulous voice demanding to see Mr Erasmus immediately filtered through from the reception area. She got up from her desk and went to investigate.

Mrs Schapper was a plump woman in her eighties. She firmly clasped the handle of a battered leather vanity case resting in her lap. She stared balefully at Astrid. 'This young woman is refusing to let me see Mr Van den Fleet.'

Marti held out her hand. 'I am Martina, Erasmus Van den Fleet's daughter, Mrs Schapper. He will not be in the office until Friday. Can I be of assistance to you, or would you prefer to make an appointment for Friday?'

Mrs Schapper stared up at her, as if thoroughly confused by Marti's calm authority. She looked down at the vanity case in her lap, her lips silently shaping her thoughts. She suddenly looked deflated; sapped of her earlier energy. Marti's initial irritation gave way to tolerance of the ways of the aged. She touched the woman's arm. 'Perhaps you would like to come into my office, Mrs Schapper.'

Mrs Schapper looked relieved by the invitation and allowed Marti to help her up from the chair.

The reason for Mrs Schapper's visit became clear when she was safely installed in a chair in Marti's office and she unlocked the vanity case and removed a brown paper parcel wrapped in a plastic carrier bag. She carefully removed the brown paper then several layers of tissue paper and finally revealed an old jewellery case. After fumbling a few moments with the catch, she opened the case and looked up at Marti expectantly. An expression of disappointment flitted across her face when Marti merely gave a polite smile. She cleared her throat. 'I want Erasmus to dispose of these for me. I no longer need them. I have more than enough jewellery.' An imperious note crept back into Mrs Schapper's voice as she spoke.

Marti groaned inwardly. She cast an experienced eye over the diamond necklace laid before her. Tact and discretion, Martina. Tact and discretion. The old lady was long on pride and short on cash. Mrs Schapper pushed the jewellery case further across the desk. 'The necklace is extremely valuable.'

Marti smiled politely again. The stones were of very poor quality. Without even taking an eyeglass to it she would gamble on having industrials in the vault of better quality. She drew her chair away from the desk and sat down. 'I'm afraid we do not buy and sell jewellery, Mrs Schapper. We are diamond merchants.'

Mrs Schapper straightened her back. 'I know that. My husband bought those diamonds from your father. He had them specially made up into a necklace for me.'

'Ah, I see.' Marti picked up the jewellery case and pretended to inspect the necklace while she quickly marshalled her thoughts.

Mrs Schapper shifted in her chair. 'My late husband was a very wealthy man.' She tried to laugh in a girlish manner. 'And, as you can see, a very generous man.'

Marti nodded. She removed the necklace from the case. But not when it came to giving diamonds, he wasn't.

'I have always kept it properly insured, you know.'

Marti glanced across at Mrs Schapper. 'When did you last have the necklace valued?'

'My late husband always attended to matters of that kind.' Mrs Schapper opened her bag and searched inside. 'The last valuation was about BFr650,000.'

Marti's eyes widened. The necklace was only worth half of that, including the gold setting. But then Mr Schapper was not the first husband to deceive his wife. She carefully put the necklace back into the case. 'Mrs Schapper, I'm not an expert on jewellery, neither is my father, but I think you may be a little disappointed by the sale value of the necklace. Insurance valuations are often based on replacement value only.' She stopped as Astrid came into the office bearing a tray of coffee.

By the time coffee had been served to Mrs Schapper, Marti had formulated a tactful way of getting rid of her. She helped Mrs Schapper carefully wrap the jewellery case back into the tissue paper. 'May I suggest, Mrs Schapper, that you get an up-to-date valuation from Kluger's in De Keyserlei. I should think that they would be more than happy to arrange a sale for you.'

'Oh, I don't trust jewellers. My late husband always said they were robbers. That's why I came to see Erasmus.'

Marti spoke politely but firmly. 'That is not the case with Kluger's. Simon Kluger is a man of the highest integrity. He is a close friend of my father's.' Marti glanced at her watch. 'I'll give him a call now and tell him to expect you. You will be in safe hands with Simon, I promise.'

Mrs Schapper received the news that Simon Kluger would be delighted to see her at her convenience, and would deal with the matter of her necklace personally, with immense satisfaction. Her dignity restored, she picked up her vanity case and allowed Marti to escort her out and on to the street. Marti puffed her cheeks out as she hurried back to her office. Astrid followed her and shut the door. Marti flung herself down in her chair. 'Spare me from any more foolish old ladies, please, Astrid. Now, what's on the agenda?'

'If you could look through the proofs of the newsletter, Miss Van den Fleet. I promised the printers we'd get the proofs back to them by tonight. It has to go out on Friday.'

'Why have we delayed so much?'

Astrid shot Marti a sideways glance. 'Er, I believe you were waiting for some figures from the IDE economic unit.'

'So I was. OK. I'll go through the proofs now and will you get Justus to make up four parcels of "J"'s for Daniel Schmidt tomorrow, please.'

'Right away, Miss Van den Fleet.'

Hong Kong was suffering more than usual from its late summer weather; a combination of torrential rainstorms and humidity hovering daily around ninety-five per cent. James Wu walked quickly down the steps of the building in Central district, where he rented a small suite of offices. He was a diamond dealer sufficiently successful to be able to afford to live in a luxurious condominium in Stanley, on the south side of the island. When he reached his car his shirt was already sticking to his back. He hurriedly started the engine and switched on the air-conditioning then nosed his way into the traffic, joining the evening logjam heading for the Aberdeen tunnel.

Anna Wu called out a cheery greeting at the sound of the key turning in the front door, and the arrival of her brother. She came out of the kitchen and announced that their evening meal would be ready in half an hour. James was already heading for his bedroom. He just had time to have a quick shower and watch the start of a kung-fu film on television before sitting down to his sister's excellent cooking.

'James, wait a moment, Mr Chan rang just before you arrived.'

James looked at Anna expectantly.

'He tried to reach you at the office, but you had already left. He said he would ring later.'

'OK. Did he say what he wanted?'

'No.'

James nodded. He went to his bedroom and stripped off. Another call from Chan Chunling. He usually dealt with Mui Shenlu. Strange. He shrugged to himself and stepped under the shower.

James, in common with other people of like mind in Hong Kong, had made two decisions when the British reached agreement with the People's Republic of China that Hong Kong should revert to Chinese rule in 1997. The first was to recognise Hong Kong's importance to the Chinese as a flourishing economic gateway to the West and that it was unlikely that Hong Kong residents, who met with the approval of the PRC, would be turned into rice-sowing peasants overnight. The second was to acquire an Australian passport, by investing a hundred thousand dollars in an Australian mining company. Implementing the first decision had required a little more subtlety.

Fortunately for James, acquiring PRC approval had been helped by an approach from a man called Mui Shenlu, who claimed to be a diamond dealer from Shanghai who knew some very important people in some very important places. The word Beijing loomed large in James's mind and he made his interest in Mui's proposition quite plain. At that first meeting they had done little more than talk around the idea of doing business. The following week, Mui requested James to buy a substantial quantity of industrial diamonds on the open market. Payment was prompt. At the end of the month Mui contacted James again and asked him to sell a small parcel of 'H' grade cut and polished diamonds that were now surplus to his clients' requirements. James had no difficulty in selling the diamonds and he was assured that Mui's clients were very pleased with his efficiency. James could most certainly expect further business from him.

The following month James was asked a second time to

dispose of a small parcel of polished diamonds. The transaction was carried out promptly and James believed he had
earned his seal of approval from the PRC when Mui confided to James that he had an assignment for him that
required absolute discretion, but would be equally rewarding. Mui had been instructed to sell a large collection of cut
and polished diamonds. James was more than a little surprised at the nature of the assignment. He had believed that
anything of any value in China had either been sold or
destroyed by Mao Zedong's cultural revolutionaries in the
1970s, and said so. Mui stared at him blankly and James
immediately regretted airing his opinions. Mui emphasised
yet again the need for absolute discretion, but did think he
could say one word to James. Kampuchea. James stared
bemusedly at Mui for several seconds, his mind racing in
rapidly decreasing circles around the word. Mui shot him a
meaningful look. James reciprocated with an equally
meaningful look to confirm his complete understanding,
although he was experiencing great difficulty in compre-
hending why the PRC should be involved in the disposal of
ancestral diamonds of the ancient Kings of Cambodia.
What *was* clear in his mind was that the PRC would not be
assisting the present rulers of Kampuchea, the Vietnamese.
James was an opportunist and not a man to ask too many
questions of his clients and ruthlessly banished further
questions from his mind. He quickly reassured Mui that he
could rely upon James's absolute discretion in the matter.

James rubbed at his hair with a towel as he went into the
living room. He switched on the television and slumped on
the sofa. He rubbed at his hair again. The call from Chan
Chunling was nagging at him. The first telephone call had
been earlier in the week. Chan had introduced himself as
Mui's partner. A fact that came as some surprise to James
because Mui had never mentioned having a partner. Chan
explained that Mui was regrettably indisposed. Nothing too
serious, but it did mean that for the moment James should

refer any queries about what Chan called their little transaction directly to him. James stretched his legs out in front of him. Mui's indisposition was probably nothing more than his powerful people in powerful places using Chan to do some checking up.

Anna popped her head around the living-room door then burst into laughter. 'James, you're not watching the *Dragonhead* again! You've seen it twice.'

James stretched his arms. 'I'm not *watching*, I'm just winding down. Fix me a whisky on the rocks, will you?'

Anna crossed to the sideboard, but stopped halfway as the telephone rang out. 'That's probably for you, James.'

James flicked the sound-control button on the television remote control, then picked up the telephone. 'James Wu.' He shot a quick glance at Anna. 'Good evening, Mr Chan. I believe you rang earlier.'

Anna tiptoed out of the room.

James kept half an eye on the images on the television screen as he listened to Chan Chunling explaining that Mui was still indisposed, and that Chan himself would bring the diamonds to Hong Kong the day after tomorrow. James stood up and paced the carpet. 'As I explained to Mr Mui, I have sold the previous parcels to my own private clients based on my own authentication, but this – er – assignment will most certainly be beyond the capacity of my clients and the diamonds will need to be sold internationally if they are to achieve their best price.' He paused for a moment, allowing Chan to respond, but continued after several seconds of utter silence. 'Unless you can provide me with the necessary documentation yourself, these diamonds will require authentication as to classification and value etcetera by someone other than myself. It would be expected in the international market. You understand me?'

'Yes. Do what you consider is necessary to obtain such authentication, Mr Wu.'

'OK. Discretion tells me that these diamonds should be

split up into small parcels. One large offering of diamonds would attract too much attention, particularly from the Intercontinental Diamond Exchange. You understand that questions would most definitely be asked about their origins. So,' James scratched the back of his head, 'as they are to be offered internationally, I would suggest four parcels each to be authenticated by Erasmus Van den Fleet in Antwerp, Tony Bergman in New York, Chaim Eichler in Tel Aviv and,' James paused for a moment, 'probably Mark Singh in Bombay. All of them have excellent reputations. Authentications by them will increase the value of the diamonds considerably.'

'Good. I will be at your office at ten on Thursday, Mr Wu. Goodnight.'

James raised one eyebrow as he put the telephone down. Chan was not a man to waste words, unlike the affable but indisposed Mui Shenlu. James went to the sideboard and poured himself a drink. Important people had obviously had second thoughts about using Mui. He gently swirled the whisky around the ice-cubes. Perhaps the need for discretion was greater than he had realised.

Erasmus Van den Fleet opened the envelope with care and withdrew the monthly newsheet from the Intercontinental Diamond Exchange. He quickly glanced through it then snorted with disgust. He called to Marti. 'Here a minute, take a look at this.'

Marti hurriedly wiped her hands and came out of the kitchen. She gave a sigh of irritation when she saw the untouched bowl of soup by her father's side. 'Father, you've let your soup get cold.'

'Don't like vegetable soup. Why can't I have a slice of ham or two, a little sausage?'

'Father, you know what the doctor said. You must cut down on red meat and salt. You don't want another heart attack, do you?'

'Oh, never mind. Look at this.' Erasmus waved the newsletter at her. 'The IDE are informing us that they are confident of further growth in turnover by the end of the year. The North American Diamond Merchants' Association report diamond sales in America and Japan up by twenty-seven per cent in the last three months. What good is that kind of news to us in Antwerp? I ask you?' He flung the letter down on to the table. 'I shall write to Christian Debilius personally. He is confident? Well, I am not.'

'What is happening in America and Japan is reflected in Europe too, Father. We have been doing very good business with the Israelis recently.'

'You mean the Israelis have been doing good business, period. We are forced to purchase from the IDE on a cash-only basis, in American dollars. We sell on pay-when-you-feel-like-it terms. We are not diamond merchants, we are credit brokers. And more fool us for allowing it.'

'Father, please do not lose your temper. Too much stress is bad for you. The Israelis are good customers. Payment is made every month, without fail. I wouldn't encourage business with them if they weren't prompt payers.'

'Hmm. I still intend to write to Christian Debilius. As chairman of the European Diamond Merchants' Association, it is my duty to make our opinions heard.'

'Yes Father, and will you please eat your lunch.'

'Stop fussing. I'll eat it in a minute. Shouldn't you be getting back to the office? It is almost two.'

'I'm on my way.' Marti bent down and kissed the top of her father's head. She crossed the room, picking up her raincoat and briefcase as she went. Father was fretting about nothing. Trading over the last two months had been exceptionally good. She carefully shut the front door of the apartment behind her. But then Father fretted about everything these days. As much as she was devoted to him, sometimes it was a relief to go to work and escape for a few hours.

Erasmus waited until the front door of the apartment opened and closed, then got up and took his luncheon tray into the kitchen. He tipped the bowl of soup into the sink then went to the refrigerator and took out a piece of boudin blanc. He cut off three thick slices. He muttered to himself as he put the sausage back into the refrigerator. No salt. No beef. No animal fats. Boiled chicken and salad. Salad and boiled chicken. Life wasn't worth living. He took the plate back to the sitting room and reread the newsletter while he ate his illicit lunch.

Chan Chunling looked idly out of the window as the taxi hooted its way through a maze of workers cycling home. The calm expression on his face belied his anxious thoughts. He was rather more than the diamond dealer James Wu of Hong Kong had supposed him to be. Chan was the head of the Shanghai Technical & Research Corporation and a man with a particularly delicate mission to undertake. He fumbled in his pocket and withdrew a crumpled packet of cigarettes. With luck, he could manage to catch the last flight back to Shanghai. Even spending one night in Anshan was to be avoided. He lit up a cigarette and settled back more comfortably into the seat. Meetings with Li always left him feeling like a schoolboy of doubtful ability.

Anshan's huge steel-production plants belched out thick black smoke non-stop, filling the air with a strong sulphurous odour. Chan signalled to the taxi driver to stop, and paid him off. He glanced up at the smoke-filled sky with distaste, then quickly walked the couple of hundred yards to his meeting place with Professor Li at the Sound and Vibration Institute.

Professor Li, as head of the institute, had his own office although it was little used. He ushered Chan in, proffered a chair and the obligatory bowl of tea and sat down himself, all within the space of a minute. He glanced quickly at Chan to satisfy himself that his *politesse* had reminded Chan that he was dealing with a man of peerless refinement.

Chan lit up a cigarette, knowing that Li couldn't stand cigarette smoke and to indicate that he was neither to be rushed nor intimidated. Li gave a sigh of irritation and looked at his watch. 'The diamonds are packed and ready for you to collect, Director Chan.'

'Thank you, Professor Li.'

Li stared at him as if expecting Chan to leap to his feet at once. Chan drew on his cigarette.

'Have you heard from Mui yet?'

Chan slowly shook his head. 'No, and that might be a problem.'

Li stared at him again. 'Might be. There is no question of might be. It is a problem. Where is he? What has he been doing?'

'I don't know.' Chan examined the tip of his cigarette. 'The last time I saw him he was going to visit James Wu in Hong Kong. That was eight days ago. There has been no communication from him since which, even for Mui, is a little unusual.'

Li pushed his chair back from his desk and stood up. 'He must be found. You realise that?'

'Indeed. Those in the PSB who are sympathetic to our needs are searching for him.'

Li began pacing agitatedly up and down.

'He may have met with an accident, of course.'

Li stopped pacing. 'And he may well have been kidnapped by those in the PSB who are *un*sympathetic to our needs. Have you considered that possibility?'

Chan flicked the ash from his cigarette. As always, Li was kind enough to express his own anxieties for him, without his having to suffer the embarrassment of airing them.

Li continued his pacing. 'If anyone should find out, we would both face more than disgrace.'

'Neither of us is so stupid to allow that to happen, Professor Li.'

Li ignored him. 'If Mui has been forced to divulge information about our' – he gestured nervously with his hand – 'our arrangement, we will have lost everything.'

Chan drew on his cigarette. 'You mean you will.'

Li clenched and unclenched his hands in agitation. 'You don't seem to appreciate that I have devoted almost a lifetime to my work. I am within sight of the goal which will –' He stopped and bent his head, as if despairing of Chan's ability to comprehend his predicament. 'You must understand. To lose everything now. It would be a total disaster. Total.'

Chan drew the ashtray to him. 'With respect, Professor Li, you worry too much.'

Li continued staring down at the small piece of carpet he was standing on. 'It was a mistake to have sent Mui to Hong Kong. He is unreliable. It was a bad mistake.'

Chan shifted in his chair, suddenly angry at the blatant attack on his own competence. 'Mui has his faults, gambling being one of them, but there was no alternative. I sent Mui to Hong Kong because he is one of the very few people left in the People's Republic of China who is an expert on authenticating diamonds. James Wu would have seen through him if he wasn't. Mui has worked well. He has gained Wu's confidence. Do not describe the achievements of my department, Professor, as a bad mistake. Mui has forged our link with the West. The only mistake being made, Professor, is being made by you, in doubting.' Chan pushed the chair back and stood up abruptly. 'You said the diamonds were ready?'

'Yes, yes, I'll have them brought in. You must excuse me, I am extremely worried about Mui's disappearance. Extremely worried, Director Chan. It would be a disaster if –'

Chan interrupted him curtly. 'There aren't going to *be* any disasters, Professor. I am taking the diamonds personally to Hong Kong.' Li gave a reluctant nod and rang for his assistant.

* * *

The call from Simon Kluger was brief and not unfriendly, but he did warn Marti that if she sent another customer to him like Mrs Schapper he would have to seriously consider speaking to her father about her.

Marti chortled when he confided that the woman had almost reduced him to tearing out what little remained of his hair. Out of pity and against his better judgement he had made her a very generous offer for the necklace, whereupon she had burst into tears and accused him of robbing her. He did concede, however, that after an excellent lunch the memory of Mrs Schapper was mercifully receding and Marti was forgiven, but just this once.

Marti put the telephone down and buzzed through to Astrid. If there were no further interruptions, she could clear the paperwork that appeared to grow more mountainous every time she looked at it, and still leave the office on time this evening. Astrid pushed her way through the door clutching a bundle of computer printout to her chest. Marti grimaced and pointed to a clear space on her desk.

'Last year's accounts, Miss Van den Fleet. And, Mr Witt called while you were on the other line.' Astrid paused and flicked open her notebook. 'He's been asked to supply six cut and polished heart-shaped diamonds for a necklace. He asked if he could come and look at some roughs tomorrow. I said you would call him back.'

'I'll call him from home this evening. Now, Astrid, let's get this paperwork out of the way.'

Erasmus suddenly straightened up in his chair, unaware for a moment that he had dropped off to sleep after his lunch. He went to the kitchen to fetch himself a glass of water and take another of the wretched tablets the doctors had given him. He leaned against the side of the kitchen unit, reassuring himself that the heavy, vice-like pressure in his chest was just the sausage at lunch time. He bent his head and stared down at the floor tiles, as if contemplating their simple design. He mustn't delay any longer. He must speak to Hendrik. Who knows, he could be dead by tomorrow?

Erasmus walked slowly back into the sitting room and went to stand in front of the telephone. He hesitated for a few moments then shook his head at himself. The decision had been made for him. Hendrik must come home. He picked up the telephone and placed a call to Zaire. He swore under his breath when he was told that the lines to Zaire were all engaged and to try again later. He sat down in his chair and leaned his head back. When he had spoken to Hendrik then he would speak to Marti.

Erasmus had put off the idea of marriage until he was in his middle thirties. It was not because he hadn't found the right woman, but because there was so much in life to be experienced, to be enjoyed, unencumbered. He had at one stage believed himself to be in love with a Filipino girl, but eventually made a marriage of which his parents thoroughly approved. Clarice was a distant relative of Erasmus and while there was nothing about her that could ever remotely excite him, she would make a good wife. Her family were decent, hardworking farmers from the Brabant region and, although Erasmus was fifteen years her senior, Clarice was happy enough to accept a proposal of marriage and leave the dull countryside for the excitement of life in the city.

When they had been married for five years, Erasmus accepted the fact that Clarice was never going to bear him a child, although the doctors had assured him that physically there was nothing wrong with her, and they adopted a baby boy who had been named Paul Hendrik. They decided to call him Hendrik after Clarice's grandfather. The same year that Erasmus celebrated his fiftieth birthday, Clarice discovered that she was pregnant and presented him with a baby daughter the following Christmas Eve. He was overjoyed and purchased the finest diamond he could afford for Clarice. His joy dimmed a little when the daughter, whom they christened Martina, turned out to be a restless, colicky baby.

After a few weeks, he began to insist that he take Hendrik

out each weekend. Walking. Boating. Cycling. He was happy to do whatever Hendrik wanted, provided it kept them out of the apartment for as long as possible. Anything was preferable to listening to Marti's constant wailing. He told Clarice that it was important, now that they had at long last produced a child of their own, that Hendrik should not feel neglected by his father. Clarice, as patient as ever, would nod as she paced up and down the sitting room trying to soothe the distraught baby in her arms. Almost as soon as Erasmus and Hendrik left, as if by magic, the crying would cease. Sometimes Clarice swore that little Marti knew when they had gone; knew that she had her mother all to herself. Clarice would sit in the armchair by the window and soon both mother and baby would fall into an exhausted sleep.

The clock chiming the quarter-hour awoke Erasmus from his disturbed dream. He rubbed at his eyes then checked the time on his watch. The clock on the mantelshelf always ran five minutes fast. He got up from his chair and went to the telephone. This time he got through to Zaire with minimal delay. He had to shout above the crackling noises to make himself heard, but managed to make the voice on the other end of the line understand that Hendrik Van den Fleet's father wished to speak to him. He swore under his breath when Hendrik's secretary told him that Hendrik was out of the office and would he like to leave a message. He asked that his son call him without delay. It was very important. He put the telephone down and went into the kitchen to make himself a cup of coffee. While he waited for Hendrik to return his call, he would compose his letter to Christian Debilius, ready for Marti to read when she came home.

A plain-clothes policeman from the Shanghai Public Security Bureau leaned against the desk in the entrance to Hong Kong's main mortuary. He flipped open a fake identity card which declared him to be a member of the Hong Kong police force. The attendant gave it a cursory glance then told him to follow him down the corridor.

The attendant glanced back over his shoulder at the policeman. 'Who are you looking for?'

'Won't know until I see him. Missing husband. Wife is convinced he's dead. Never been late for his evening meal since they were married.'

The attendant shrugged. 'Always the first time, though, isn't there?'

The attendant switched on the light and began pulling out metal drawers encased in the wall. 'These are all we've got at the moment.' The policeman nodded and took his time examining each corpse. The attendant leaned against the wall and lit up a cigarette. The policeman stopped near the end of the row and stared down at a body that had obviously spent some time immersed in water. The shape of a bear's paw had been crudely etched with a knife on the dead man's forehead. The policeman pulled a dog-eared photograph from an inner pocket and studied it. The attendant sauntered up and jerked his thumb at the mutilated body. 'Reminder to pay your gambling debts, eh?'

The policeman laughed. He glanced around. 'Is this all?'

'Yes. No luck?'

The policeman shook his head. 'Doesn't look like it.'

'Come back at the end of the week. Sure to have more in by then. If you like, leave the photograph and if he turns up I'll give you a call.'

'Er – no, I've only got this one on me and I need that. I'll have one sent round.'

'OK.' The attendant slammed the drawers shut as he walked back to the door.

The policeman waited patiently in the main post office, until there was a public telephone free. He quickly placed a call to the PSB headquarters in Shanghai. 'Hello, is that you Cao? Listen. Missing person. One Mui Shenlu. Deputy head of the metals and minerals export department of the Shanghai Technical & Research Corporation. Found him. He's lying in a mortuary with the mark of the Bear's Paw Gang gouged on his face. What do you want me to do? Stay here and wait for further instructions? Pity. I haven't had a chance to sample the night-life here, yet. OK. I'll get the next flight back to Shanghai.' The policeman put the telephone down. He turned round and smiled at the pretty young girl who stepped forward to use the telephone.

Hendrik Van den Fleet was a tall, heavily built man. He always made a habit of standing just a little too close to women, either to dominate them or to charm them. He came to stand by the side of his secretary's chair and put his hands on his hips. 'Jane, I thought I said that whenever my father called, I was to be told immediately.'

Jane drew her body in defensively, as if shielding herself from his bulk. 'I am sorry, Hendrik. I did try to reach you. I tried the Diamond Register, your club, your apartment, the compound.' She omitted to mention that she hadn't tried to call the apartment of the French commercial attaché where Hendrik spent a couple of afternoons a week with the French commercial attaché's wife.

'All right, all right. Try and get my father now.' He sat on the edge of the desk and lit a cigarette.

She reached across the desk to the telephone, careful to avoid accidental contact with his thigh.

Contact with Antwerp was established at the third attempt and Jane handed the telephone to Hendrik, but failed to avoid the brush of warm, stubby fingers.

'Father, hello? You'll have to speak up. The line is faint.'

Jane went to push her chair back from the desk and stand up, but Hendrik clamped a hand on her shoulder and motioned to her to stay where she was. 'That's better. I can hear you now. How are you?'

Jane clasped her arms across her chest as pale

expressionless eyes casually roved over her body. Hendrik
swivelled round and flicked the ash from his cigarette into
an empty coffee cup. 'My secretary said you wanted to
speak to me urgently. Is anything wrong?'

Jane glanced up at Hendrik as he slowly rose to his feet.

'Well, Father, I think you have made the right decision.
You might as well enjoy a happy retirement while you still
have your health and strength intact. No, no, there is no
change of mind on my part. I said I would always be willing
to take over Van den Fleet's when the time came. You have
nothing to worry about. My partner, Gerry, knows my
situation. I'll obviously have a few things to tie up here, but
I can probably be in Antwerp by the end of the week. Good.
That's settled then,' Hendrik paused for a moment. 'You
have mentioned this to Marti? I see. Well, I think you
should tell her without delay. You know what she is like.
She has always resented my position in the family. No, no,
don't start worrying, Father. There won't be any trouble, at
least not from me. If there is, you can place the blame fairly
and squarely at her feet. OK. I'll get in touch with you
tomorrow and finalise everything. 'Bye.' Hendrik put the
telephone down. A slow smile crossed his face. He dropped
his cigarette end into the coffee cup. He glanced across at
Jane. 'What are you doing tonight?'

The answer was well rehearsed and swift. 'Washing my
hair.'

'Afterwards.'

She looked down at her typewriter, while she tried to
formulate a reply that didn't include words which Hendrik
would find provocative; like bed, or an early night.

He brushed his fingers under her chin. 'This is your last
chance. I'm going back to Belgium. My father is retiring.
I'm taking over the business.'

She looked up at him. 'Permanently?'

'Permanently.'

'Who'll be taking over from you?'

He shrugged. 'Roger, perhaps. Although Gerry might try managing on his own for a while. I think the idea of complete power will be irresistible.'

Jane looked at him anxiously. Gerry already had a secretary and a junior. 'What about me, if he does?'

He gave her a knowing smile. 'Well, if you promise to wash your hair another night, I might, just might, put in a good word for you.'

She hesitated for a moment, then reluctantly nodded her head. He gave a low laugh. 'Always knew you were more intelligent than you look, Jane.' He turned on his heel and went out of the office. He rubbed his hands together as he walked along the corridor. The telephone call from his father was just what he had been waiting for. The only fly in the ointment was Marti, but he would soon sort her out.

Hendrik had trained as a diamond merchant in his father's business in Antwerp. His decision to leave Belgium and work in Zaire was prompted by the death of his mother and a need to establish his independence. The palpable, crushing sorrow at home nearly drove him mad. Neither his father nor his sister seemed aware that he was grieving. He, too, had watched his mother suffering, growing weaker by the day, until she finally faded away. He was glad she was dead, for her sake. But they couldn't understand that. He had also needed to step out of his father's shadow. His father never allowed him to take a business decision without first consulting him. For as long as his father was alive, he would always be number two at Van den Fleet's. He would inherit the business one day, but his ambitions wouldn't wait that long.

Erasmus had accepted Hendrik's need to work abroad, the need to get away from everything, without too much argument. It was a good sign in a man that he should want to fulfil his own ambitions, amass his own wealth. And, in truth, Erasmus wanted to grieve alone. Sounds of youthful activity wearied him. The death of his wife had touched him

more deeply than he had expected. Now, his only wish was
to return to the apartment after the day's business was
finished and sit by the window, with Marti opposite him in
her mother's chair, each content to sit in the twilight,
watching the encroaching darkness, until Marti, as her
mother had done before her, would get up and prepare his
cup of hot chocolate.

Having secured his father's agreement, Hendrik lost no
time in consolidating his plans. With the assistance of
Christian Debilius, head of the Intercontinental Diamond
Exchange, Hendrik secured himself a job with a mining
company in Zaire. Quality controller of diamond production offered ample opportunity for promotion and, as
Hendrik was already aware that Christian Debilius had
marked him down as good 'IDE material', it further
strengthened his ties with the powerful IDE. On Hendrik's
last day at the offices of Van den Fleet's, Erasmus had
placed his hands on Hendrik's shoulders and made him
promise that when the time came for Erasmus to retire,
Hendrik would return. Erasmus had always treated him as
his own flesh and blood. Hendrik must promise to return.
Hendrik put his arms around his father and hugged him. He
had only one father. He would return.

Hendrik had discovered he was adopted when he was
nineteen. An arch remark by one of his mother's friends
had set him thinking. Having shaken hands with him when
he returned home from work, she had remarked to Clarice
that Hendrik was growing up into such a handsome young
man, so blond and so tall. Taller even than his father.
Clarice had smiled nervously and hastily changed the subject to Marti's schoolwork.

The more Hendrik thought about it the more obvious it
became. He didn't resemble either of his parents, if he was
honest with himself. He asked his mother first, but she
appeared upset and said he must wait until his father came
home and then ask him. When his father returned from

work Hendrik was sat down on the sofa, his mother one side of him, his father the other. Both Erasmus and Clarice had always said they would tell Hendrik that he was adopted when he was twenty-one and capable of understanding these things, and they had their gentle, caring explanation word-perfect.

The news made Hendrik feel strange, alienated at first, but he was of a pragmatic mind and quickly reconciled himself to it. Both his parents had been genuine in expressing their love for him. His mother had even wept a little when she told him how she had felt the first time she had been allowed to hold him in her arms. As for his father, he had always been very good to him. Hendrik had been taken straight into Erasmus's business and had enjoyed the many privileges of being his only son. He had no intention of giving up everything just for the dubious honour of knowing who his biological parents were. There was a further reason why he accepted the news of his adoption with equanimity. Marti. Now he didn't have to go on pretending any affection for the fat little brat. She wasn't his sister.

Marti watched Justus, the office manager, check that each individual drawer of diamonds was safely locked. He stepped out of the ceiling-high safe and swung the heavy door shut. Marti nodded to him and pressed a combination of buttons on the wall-mounted, computerised time-clock. The door could not be opened again until nine-thirty the following day.

Justus wished Marti goodnight and she hurried back to her office. She pushed a cash-flow report into her briefcase, to show to her father when she got home, and slipped her coat on. She would just have time to stop off at the hypermarket. The prospect of a piece of steak, although it would have to be a very small piece, would take her father's mind off the newsletter from the IDE. She sighed to herself. No doubt he would complain because the steak would not be topped by a lavish pat of butter.

Marti had never known a time when her father was young. He was already grey-haired when she was born. Until his first heart attack she had simply not noticed that he was becoming frail and, she was forced to admit on occasions, downright cantankerous. There were days when nothing that she did was right. Yet he refused to have any-one else take care of him.

When her mother died, their shared and silent sorrow had brought Marti and Erasmus closer together. Marti's grief had been eased by trying to relieve her father of his. She would ensure that there were always fresh flowers on the table, the newspaper carefully folded on the table by Erasmus's chair, a glass of white port poured out as soon as she heard his key being turned in the door; all the things that her mother had done to ensure his comfort. If continuing these rituals somehow helped to stem her father's sense of loss, she considered it little to ask of her. Sometimes, Erasmus would laugh and call her 'little mother' and say that he didn't know what he would do without her. She would kiss his cheek and say that he didn't have to. She would always take care of him.

Erasmus's second heart attack left him feeling fright-ened. Once again he was reminded of his own mortality. A persistent fear would take hold of him in the night that the next attack might be the last. Sometimes it was so strong he would call out to Marti, just to reassure himself that he was not entirely alone. Whatever hour of the night, she would come to him. He would make some excuse for waking her. He was thirsty. He couldn't breathe properly. He was too hot. He was too cold. Whatever the reason, she would sit by his bed until he fell asleep. Sometimes, she was so tired herself she would fall asleep in the chair.

When Erasmus was finally allowed to return to work by his doctors it was obvious, even to himself, that he needed to reduce his workload. Without ever actually discussing it, he and Marti evolved a work pattern that suited them both. Erasmus would come into the office for a couple of hours two or three times a week. Marti took on the responsibility of running the business, ostensibly under his guidance, but very much with a free hand. Erasmus's friends, who had also known Clarice when she was alive, were open in their admiration of Marti. They would tell Erasmus he was a lucky man to have such a fine daughter. They would quietly confide to Marti, out of his hearing, that she was doing too much. She had her own life to lead. She should get out more. She would only be young once. Marti would smile and say she was happy enough as things were. That wasn't always true, but she enjoyed her work at Van den Fleet's. Responsibility had given her budding business acumen a chance to flourish. Within twelve months she had established a strong working relationship with all of Van den Fleet's customers. So much so, that sometimes her father would complain that even his oldest clients seemed to prefer to do business with Marti rather than with him. It was a complaint that was not meant to be taken seriously. Although he never actually said so, Erasmus was relieved that day-to-day business was conducted by his daughter. Someone whom he could trust. Someone who would never try to usurp his authority. He may not now be the man he once was, but he was not ready to hand over that authority to anyone. The living death of retirement was not a prospect he chose to dwell on.

The Sound & Vibration Institute in Anshan was housed, like many of the other research laboratories, in a drab, concrete building that gave little hint of its true purpose. Its funding was primarily for research into sixth-generation superconducting materials.

Professor Li waved his hand dismissively as his assistant came to his side. 'Away, away. Can't you see I am busy?'

His assistant cleared his throat. 'It is urgent, Professor Li.'

'What is urgent?'

'One of the men unloading the new ultrasonic equipment has been injured.'

Li turned his gaze away from the computer screen. 'The equipment hasn't been damaged, has it?' He got up from his seat. 'Well, has it or hasn't it?'

'No, Professor Li, but one of the men has been injured.'

'Then if the generator hasn't been damaged, why are you bothering me? What can I do if some stupid peasant has injured himself?'

The assistant cleared his throat again. 'They think the man has broken his back, Professor Li. The truck from the railway depot had to have a wheel changed, because of a puncture. The jack started to slip. When the driver got down to brace the jack, the truck slipped off the jack and fell on him.'

'Mmm.' Li sat down and turned his attention to the computer again.

'He is in a very serious condition. They cannot stop him screaming.'

'Mmm. Listen, read that report on what the French are doing. It is very encouraging. They are at least twelve months behind us in their experiments in ultrasonic sound levitation.'

His assistant sighed heavily. 'Yes, Professor Li.'

'And I must have that sound generator set up by tonight.'

'Yes, Professor Li.'

Li waved his hand at his assistant. 'Go on, go on. You are not paid to stand around watching me.'

The assistant bowed his head and went to the door.

Li swivelled around in his chair and picked up the scientific journal that had been sent to him by a sympathetic fellow scientist in Holland. He reread the article entitled 'Comparative Studies of Amorphous and Crystalline Glasses'. He stroked the end of his chin. They were at least twelve months ahead of the French. A fact which needed to be brought to the attention of the Leading Group for High Technology. A fact which might encourage the Group to recognise the logic of his request for further funding, if he was to succeed in his experiments. He gave a disdainful sniff. They were nothing but a bunch of corrupt bourgeois intellectuals. They were incapable of recognising anything except what brought them material wealth.

The table had been laid for dinner and six potatoes had been clumsily peeled and left in a bowl of water when Marti arrived home. Erasmus had not only had the time to draft his letter to Christian Debilius of the IDE, but also to rehearse his speech to Marti. Hendrik had been right. He must tell Marti as soon as she came home.

Marti's coat was hung up, the meat put into the refrigerator, then she was instructed to sit down and share a glass of port with her father. Marti good-humouredly promised to do as she was told, but first she had to make a quick telephone call. Johannes Witt wanted to look at some uncut diamonds the following day. Erasmus was content to wait until she had finished her telephone call. Her need to speak to Johannes had given him an idea.

Marti spoke briefly to Johannes then, as promised, sat down opposite her father. Erasmus clasped his hands between his knees. 'I have been thinking, Marti. It is time that you and I discussed your future. I know I am old-fashioned. You tell me often enough. However, you are twenty-seven. It is more than time enough for you to think of marriage, of children. I realise that I have become a selfish old man. I am denying you the opportunity of these things.'

She laughed. 'Father, what are you talking about? Of course you're not selfish.'

'I am. It is selfish of me to allow you to give up so much for me. Running the business. Caring for me. It leaves you with little time, with little opportunity, to see more of Johannes.'

She laughed again. 'That was just a business call. I don't

want to see more of Johannes. If I did, I would. Father, what are you going on about? What is all this?'

'I mean, Marti, that I do not wish anything to stand in the way of your future happiness. It is time you and Johannes were married. You know I care about you. Johannes is a good man. I trust him. He will make an ideal husband. There is obviously no doubt in Johannes's mind that he considers you to be the ideal wife.'

Marti raised an eyebrow.

'Listen to me, Marti. All that I wish as I near the end of my life is –'

'Father, stop talking like that.'

'Listen to me. It is true. I am almost seventy-eight. I have had two heart attacks. I have had a good life, a full life. I am not complaining. Now all I want is to see you happily married. My dearest wish would be to hold my grandchild in my arms before I die. To see the next generation of this family safely born. You and Johannes will make a perfect couple. His parents speak of you very highly, you know that.' Erasmus glanced at Marti. His carefully rehearsed speech was not being received as warmly as he had anticipated. In fact it was not being received at all. Her face had settled into an all-too-familiar mulish expression.

Marti placed the glass of port she had been clutching on the table by the sofa. 'Father, I really don't know what has brought all this on, but I cannot marry a man who I do not love. One day I suppose I will marry, but it will not be Johannes. I don't know who it will be, but it won't be him. He is a good friend. Nothing more.'

Erasmus's forehead creased in irritation. 'It is a mistake for a woman of your age to be too choosey.'

Marti rolled her eyes. 'Thank you, Father, thank you. You may be right, but I will take that risk.'

Erasmus got up from his chair and walked to the window. 'Now it is you who is being selfish. How can I settle my affairs unless I can be sure that your future will be assured?'

'I will look after my own future, Father. You have nothing to worry about.'

'Hmm. That remains to be seen.' He turned his back on her and stared out of the window. 'Well, you might as well know. I have decided to retire.'

She gave a sigh of relief. Now she understood what the conversation was really about. 'Father, please don't worry about the future. I am perfectly capable of handling things. I shall carry on the business just as you have taught me.'

He pushed his hands into his trouser pockets. 'I spoke to Hendrik this afternoon. He is coming home at the end of the week.'

'What for?'

He looked down at his shoes. 'To take over the running of the company.'

'*What?*'

'I have asked him to and he has agreed.'

She stared at him disbelievingly. He shrugged. 'I know you and your brother haven't always seen eye to eye, but you must put all of that behind you.'

'Father, do you know what you are saying?'

'Yes.'

She got to her feet as sudden anger swept through her. 'I don't think you do. Hendrik has never shown the slightest interest in the company. He has been too concerned about himself for that. And you are suggesting that he should run Van den Fleet's. I think you must have taken leave of your senses.'

He spun round to face her. 'And you must have taken leave of your senses even to dare speak to me like that.'

She passed a hand across her brow. 'I'm sorry, Father. If you feel it is time for you to retire, of course, I understand. But the idea of Hendrik returning to run the business in your place is ridiculous. Half of our customers don't even know him.' She picked up her glass. 'I'll put the steak on to grill. When we have eaten we can discuss this properly.'

'I don't want anything to eat and there is nothing to discuss. I have made my decision.'

She gripped the glass between her fingers. 'Without consulting me?'

'I do not need to consult you.'

'I think you do.'

'Then you are mistaken.'

Her patience snapped. 'It is you who are mistaken. Who has done all the work while you have been ill? Who has almost doubled the turnover of the business in the last twelve months? I have the right to be consulted, at the very least.'

He looked up above him, as if trying to control his growing exasperation. 'I do not deny what you have done, but I have made my decision. Hendrik will run the company.'

'Why him?' She couldn't stop her voice from rising. 'Why?'

'I have told you, Marti. I have made my decision. Let that be the end of the matter.'

She gave up all pretence of controlling her anger. 'No, Father, it is not the end of the matter. Why him? Why not me? Why shouldn't I run the company? I practically do just that already. Why him?'

'Because he is a man.'

She laughed sarcastically. 'Is that the only criterion for running Van den Fleet's? Why bother asking Hendrik to come home? Why not go out on the street now and ask the first man you meet?'

Erasmus's face flushed. 'How dare you speak to me like that? I am your father.'

'And I am your daughter. The daughter you taught to grade diamonds at the age of six. The daughter you profess to have taught everything you know. The daughter you have entrusted with the running of the company.'

Erasmus raised his voice. 'I know all of these things and

you also know as well as I do that as a woman you will not be accepted by the IDE. You will not be granted option-bearer status. Hendrik is the only other Van den Fleet apart from myself who has option-bearer status. Who else will be allowed to view diamonds from the Exchange, let alone buy them? Van den Fleet's will be out of business within the year, unless Hendrik takes over when I retire.'

'That just isn't true, Father.'

'It is and you know it. All that you have done is to sell from our existing stocks. What you have not done is to trade actively with the IDE. I allowed you to run the business until now, because I knew that our stockpiles were more than sufficient to carry us through. Now they must be replaced. The time has come for me to make a decision and I have made it. I will not see one of the oldest and most respected diamond merchants in the world cease to exist. You must understand that.' He rested his hand briefly on her shoulder before going to sit down in his chair. The conversation had left him exhausted and the painful constriction in his chest seemed to grow by the second. He rested his hands on the arms of the chair and took in a deep breath. 'Hendrik must take over from me. There is no one else. No one.'

Marti came to the side of his chair and knelt down. 'Father, listen to me. Things have changed. The IDE cannot prevent women from becoming option bearers. It is sexual discrimination. It is against the law. I will *make* them appoint me.'

He shook his head slowly. 'Don't be foolish, Marti. No one makes the IDE do anything it doesn't want to do.'

'I will. Listen to me, Father. I will make them. Just give me the chance of proving that to you. Give me the chance to show you that I can run the company. You don't need Hendrik. You have me.'

He shook his head again. 'It is not enough. Hendrik is my son. He will be accepted by the IDE without question. He is a Van den Fleet.'

Marti stood up abruptly. 'Your son? What are you talking

about? He is not your son.' Her voice rose in anger. 'He is not a Van den Fleet and never can be. What are you talking about?'

Erasmus shut his eyes. His face crumpled, as if he was overtaken by some sudden anguish. Marti clenched her fists. At any other time she would have contained her anger, remained silent, rather than upset her father, but a tidal flow of frustration broke down the self-imposed barriers. 'Is a bastard superior to a woman? Is that what you are telling me?' She banged her fist on the table. 'Are you trying to tell me that the IDE will accept a man without a drop of Van den Fleet blood in his veins, in preference to me?'

Erasmus's head sank to his chest. A tear rolled down the side of his face. Marti drew in a shuddering breath. One part of her wanted to rush and put her arms around him, the other remained aloof, coldly determined that the truth of her argument would be recognised.

Erasmus brushed the tear from his face. 'You must never say that again. No one outside this family must ever know that Hendrik was adopted. It was your mother's wish.' He spoke quietly, as if talking to himself.

'It was my mother's wish that I received as good an education as Hendrik. It was my mother's wish that I choose my own career.' Marti gave a bitter laugh. 'Since when have my mother's wishes ever been of any importance to you?'

Erasmus leapt up from the chair and raised a shaking finger at Marti. 'You wicked girl. Do you hear me? Wicked. How dare you say such a thing.'

Marti's mouth tightened. 'I do dare.'

He jabbed his finger in the air. 'You will obey me, young woman. I am still the head of this household and you will obey me.' His face suffused with rage. 'You will marry Johannes and Hendrik will run the company. I will not stand by and see you fling yourself at some scoundrel whose only intent is getting his hands on my company.' Anger gave power to his voice. 'Hendrik may not be a Van den Fleet, but he is his own man. Always has been. He is the only man fit to run the company.'

Marti nodded her head very slowly. 'Ah, I see. You prefer the scoundrel in the family to one that I may bring home.' Her voice was filled with heavy sarcasm. 'Of course, I should have known. All this talk of Johannes, my future happiness. You just want me tidily out of the way for when Hendrik comes home. Marry Marti off to someone then she won't be a nuisance to us. You don't care about me. I am just a willing workhorse. A stopgap. All you care about is Hendrik.'

Erasmus went to speak, but instead his mouth widened as he gasped for breath. He clutched at his chest as crucifying pain swept over him. He reached out to grasp the arm of the chair, but lost his balance and fell to the floor. Marti let out a horrified cry.

Two attendants leapt out of the private ambulance and slid the stretcher out of the back, pulling down the front and rear wheels at the same time, then raced through the already opened doors of the cardiac arrest unit. Marti scrambled out of the ambulance and hurried after them. The paramedics shouted out clinical details of Erasmus's condition to the nurses running towards them, then Erasmus was wheeled into an examination room. Someone held on to Marti's arm and held her back. She let herself be taken to a small waiting room and be sat down.

Some time later, a nurse opened the door of the waiting room, looked around, then smiled encouragingly at Marti before closing it again. Marti glanced up only half aware that the door had been opened and closed. The quiet, measured sounds outside in the corridor were more frightening than the frenzied rush accompanying her father's arrival. She leaned her head back against the wall. He had been swallowed up by the hospital, taken away from her; numbered and listed as just another being who may or may not live. She buried her face in her hands. If he died, it would be her fault. She had caused the heart attack. She had said things she should never have said. She had driven him to anger and to death.

The doctor nodded at Marti as the nurse accompanying him motioned to her. 'This is Mr Van den Fleet's daughter, Doctor.'

Marti got up from the chair. 'My father, is he going to –' She paused.

'His condition is stable for the moment. We will know more when we have received the results of our further tests.'

'Can I see him?'

'Not to talk to and only for a minute or so.' The doctor gestured to the nurse. 'Take Miss Van den Fleet to see her father, will you.' He gave a brief smile to Marti. 'If you will now excuse me.'

Marti pressed her face against the glass partition in the intensive-care room. The nurse sitting at the monitoring console glanced round and nodded to Marti, as if to confirm that everything was all right.

Marti's eyes filled with tears. Erasmus lay as if asleep, his arms stretched out by his sides, his face tinged with a greyish pallor. Marti turned at the sudden hand on her arm. The charge nurse spoke quietly. 'Go home and get some rest, Miss Van den Fleet. We will call you if there is any change in his condition.'

Marti shook her head. 'No. I'm not leaving.'

'There is nothing you can do. You would be far better off at home.'

'No. I'm staying here.'

The charge nurse nodded. 'Very well. There is a rest room just along the corridor. I will get someone to show you where it is.'

The rest room was simply furnished with twin beds and a

small bedside table. Marti removed her shoes and swung her feet up on the bed. She looked at her watch. It was almost two o'clock in the morning. She leaned back against the bedhead and stared at the picture on the wall opposite until her eyelids began to droop.

Chan Chunling signalled to the driver to stop half-way along Suzhou Creek and paid him off. He walked briskly along the river front oblivious to the activity around him. Mui was dead. The simplest explanation was that his insatiable appetite for gambling had caused his downfall. The simplest explanation, but not necessarily the truest.

Chan pulled up the collar of his raincoat, as if trying to shield his face from any curious glances. Mui's disappearance had pushed him into unwelcome limelight. He must now visit Hong Kong himself. He would have preferred his role to have remained anonymous, as had been promised. He checked his watch as he approached the yellow outer walls of the Jade Buddha Temple and joined the throngs of tourists.

A bejewelled, white jade Buddha was the centrepiece of the temple. Chan held back from a group of tourists who stopped to admire it, then, when they had passed on, stepped forward as if taking a closer look. A quick glance at his watch showed him that he was still a little early for his meeting with the 'faceless one'. He walked slowly towards the three gold-plated Buddhas in the main hall. He stepped to one side as a procession of monks made their way across the hall then went to stand by the side of the statues. He turned his head slightly as a voice spoke to him from behind the statue nearest him.

Chan referred to Fang Ka-Shing as the 'faceless one' because he never saw him; not even the briefest of glimpses. All that he knew or assumed about Fang was that he was a member of a high-ranking cadre in Shanghai. Secrecy was a precaution that Fang considered sensible. He was chairman

Chinese People's Association for International Trade in Hong Kong. A position of growing importance as the PRC's tentacle-like grip on the economy of Hong Kong spread. The company was wholly owned by mainland China and Fang had direct communication with the Central Committee of the Chinese Communist Party. He also had direct communication with his cousin, Pa Jiaming, head of the Central Military Commission for Scientific Advancement. Family loyalty and greed persuaded Fang unhesitatingly to join his cousin in what Pa described as a small, private business venture. Corruption was not a word that Fang even considered. One's duty to one's family was paramount and if the individual happened to benefit as well, all to the good. The business venture, dubbed 'Bright Mountain' by Pa, required the cooperation of more than just Fang himself, but Fang was a careful man and he took great care to ensure that if one of the weaker links in the enterprise should break, his own position would remain safeguarded.

Fang glanced around the hall. No one appeared to be watching the man standing in front of the statues. He leaned his head forward. 'It is regrettable that we have suffered this disruption, but a squad from the PSB "A" department has been sent to Hong Kong to track down and eliminate the Bear's Paw Gang. What information they might have discovered from Mui will die with them.'

Chan brushed the back of his hand across his mouth. 'It is important that matters are dealt with discreetly, respected Comrade. It would jeopardise my position with James Wu if Mui's death becomes public.'

'It won't. What other news do you have for me?'

Chan cleared his throat. 'I am pleased to report that the quota of diamonds is complete. I had a meeting with Professor Li in Anshan and everything is going according to your plan, esteemed Comrade. I am delivering a further batch of diamonds to Wu on Monday. He recommended, without much prompting, that they should be split into small and therefore discreet parcels, and authenticated by four of the West's top diamond dealers. Each of them also is an option bearer at the IDE.'

Fang nodded to himself in satisfaction. 'You have done well. The treasures of Bright Mountain will bring us all good fortune. Yes?'

'Indeed, esteemed Comrade.'

Fang laughed quietly. 'Enjoy your trip to Hong Kong.'

Chan glanced quickly to his right as a group of tourists entered the main hall. 'I think I should leave now. There are people coming this way.'

'Very well.'

'I will report to you as soon as the diamonds have been authenticated.'

Fang didn't reply and Chan moved away from the statues as the group of tourists gathered around. When he got outside again, he wiped his hands on his handkerchief. The visits to the Temple made him uncomfortable. He could never understand why there were times when Fang would conduct conversations over the telephone, and others when he insisted that they meet at the Temple. He suspected it was a ruse to ensure his continuing fear and continuing obedience.

The cocktail party at Christian Debilius's apartment had reached the level of noise indicative of people determined to enjoy themselves. The valet carefully picked his way to where Christian was standing, and waited. Christian glanced round and excused himself to the woman who had been earnestly endeavouring to persuade him to go and see the stunning new production of Verdi's *Ernani* at the Met.

'Yes, Samson?'

'A Mr Hendrik Van den Fleet on the telephone, sir.'

'I'll take it in the study, thank you.' Christian flashed a smile at the woman who still stood in the frozen pose of one who has been stopped in full flight. 'Rose, dearest, I shan't be a few seconds. Don't go away.'

She smiled flirtatiously. 'Promise.' She cocked her head slightly to one side as she watched him walk swiftly across the room. He was everything her husband was not. Handsome. Rich. And, from what she had heard, sexually competent. The corners of her mouth turned down as she dwelt on that fact. She signalled to the waiter to come and refill her champagne glass.

Christian had an abundance of old-world money and old-world charm. His consciously erect bearing gave the impression that he was taller than he actually was. What was not merely an impression was his power. He had headed up the Intercontinental Diamond Exchange since its formation following the diamond crash in the early 1980s. Now, the names of Debilius and the IDE were synonymous with success. Although always coy about its true financial status, the IDE was now widely believed to have outstripped even the successes of the De Beers' Central Selling Organisation.

Christian waited until the valet had closed the door behind him then picked up the telephone. 'Hendrik?'

'Christian, how are you? I hope I haven't interrupted anything important?'

Christian gave a gentle laugh. 'It is a little early in the evening for that. What can I do for you?'

'Nothing really. I just thought I should let you know that my father is retiring. I am returning to Antwerp to take over the business.'

'Excellent. My congratulations, Hendrik. May I say that it is long overdue. I have absolute respect for Erasmus's work in the past, but there comes a time, does there not?'

'Indeed. It has to be a blow to him to give everything up, but he is being very sensible about the whole thing.'

'Good, good. He will be staying on in a consultancy capacity, I presume?'

'Oh yes. It was the first thing I suggested to him. Nothing

too taxing. A visit to the office and lunch once a month. Something along those lines.'

'Excellent. The IDE always places great importance on continuity of business. Well, Hendrik, we must see you and celebrate. Any chance of you being in New York?'

'Actually, I was thinking of making a brief visit before I return to Antwerp. I have a couple of things to tie up with my partner, Gerry, in Zaire first.'

'I understand. Look, Hendrik, call me when you reach New York. We can discuss the future of Van den Fleet's over lunch, or dinner, whichever is convenient.'

'Thank you, Christian. I shall look forward to it.'

'Good, good. I am sure we shall be doing excellent business together in the future.'

'So am I.'

Christian put the telephone down and nodded to himself. Hendrik's telephone call had neatly resolved a problem that he had intended to put to the governing committee at their next meeting. The non-appearance by Van den Fleet's on five consecutive option days had been overlooked, because of Erasmus's known health problems, but the situation could not be allowed to continue. Option bearers were either active or they were replaced by the next name on the five-year waiting list.

Christian picked up the telephone again and punched in a local telephone number. 'George? Christian here. Just a quick call. Erasmus Van den Fleet is retiring. His son, Hendrik, is taking over. Yes, that does resolve the problem for us. Hendrik Van den Fleet is an able man. I think we can have every confidence in him. Good, good. I'll say good-night then.'

When Christian returned to the living room he paused for a moment by the door and scanned the room. He eased himself behind a knot of people standing in the centre, carefully shielding himself from Rose's view, then headed for the window and to the girl who had caught his eye half an hour ago. He touched her elbow and gently manoeuvred her into the corner. He deliberately turned his back on the rest of the room to deter interlopers. She stared up at him as if mesmerised by his warm, inviting gaze. He lightly brushed his fingers along her forearm. 'I'm Christian Debilius.' The explanation was unnecessary. She knew exactly who he was.

The nurse gently shook Marti's shoulder. Marti opened her eyes instantly. She struggled up from her semi-sitting position, propped up against the bedhead. The nurse gave a reassuring smile. 'Your father is awake, Miss Van den Fleet. Doctor said you can see him for a few minutes.'

Marti got to her feet. 'How is he?'

'He's still stable.'

Erasmus turned his head on the pillow and gave a weak smile at the sight of Marti at his side. She scanned his face anxiously. Some of the greyish pallor had gone. 'How do you feel?'

He swallowed, then spoke softly in a husky voice. 'Feel as if I've been kicked by a herd of horses, but I'm all right.'

She sat down on the chair by his bedside and took his hand in hers. 'Oh, Father, I was so worried about you.'

'Don't worry. I'm not going to die just yet. Doctor says I'm as tough as old boots.'

'I'm sorry, Father, about what happened.'

'Your mother always used to say to control one's anger was a sign of maturity. Neither of us seem to be able to do that, do we?'

She looked at him pleadingly. 'Forgive me.'

'Sshh. There is nothing to forgive.'

'Yes there is. I said things I can't forgive myself –'

'No, no. There is nothing to forgive. Just promise me that we will never quarrel again.'

'I promise.'

'And promise that you will accept Hendrik as head of the

company.' He gently squeezed her fingers. 'For me, Marti, do it for me. It is all that I ask.'

She bent her head. That was the most difficult promise to make. 'Yes, Father, I promise.'

He turned his head away on the pillow and shut his eyes.

A nurse appeared at Marti's side. 'You must leave now. Mr Van den Fleet must have his medication.'

Marti got up and leaned over her father and kissed his cheek. 'I'll be back in a few minutes.'

'No, no. Don't stay. Go and open up the office. The staff will be expecting you. I shall be all right.'

'I am *not* leaving you, Father. The staff can cope very well on their own.'

Erasmus raised his hand from the bed. 'No. Leave me. I shall be all right. Besides, I want to be on my own. I want to have a chat with my nurse. Have you noticed how pretty she is?'

The nurse smiled cheerfully at Erasmus in acknowledgement of his spirited attempt to behave as if he was not a very ill old man. The will to live was the best medication of all. She rolled her eyes at Marti. 'I think we are definitely feeling a little better.'

Marti gave a relieved smile. 'Looks like it.'

Erasmus waved his hand again. 'Go on, off you go. Stop fussing. I'll be all right.'

When Marti left the room she looked back through the glass partition to give a final wave. Erasmus managed to raise his hand and wave back. When she had gone, he let his head sink back against the pillows. The effort to appear alert and bright in front of Marti had taxed him considerably. He looked up at the nurse. 'She worries too much, you know.'

The nurse placed her hand under his head and smoothed his pillow. 'Now no more talking, Mr Van den Fleet. You must rest. Is your oxygen supply comfortable? Just nod or shake your head.'

He raised his hand to his nose and adjusted the tiny oxygen tube clamped to his nostril, then nodded. As the nurse fitted a fresh pouch of fluid to the saline drip by the side of the bed, she chatted to him. She had seen a most beautiful sunrise on her way to work that morning. Erasmus closed his eyes. A feeling of calm swept through him. Hendrik would be home soon.

Marti stepped out of the shower and quickly dried herself. She tried not to think of how silent the apartment was. She went into her bedroom and pulled out the first suit nearest to hand from the wardrobe. While taking a shower she had reconsidered her original decision to call Hendrik and tell him Erasmus was ill. Perhaps she should wait until she had visited the hospital again. There might be better news. As she hastily dressed, she argued with herself that she should, on second thoughts, telephone Hendrik. If the worst did happen and he hadn't been told, he would blame her for ever. She picked up the hairbrush on the dressing table and brushed her hair away from her face. No. Perhaps it was better to wait. He wouldn't thank her for making alarmist calls. She rested the brush on the dressing table and looked at herself in the mirror. For God's sake stop it. Call him. She spoke out loud to herself. Do it. Call him from the office. Satisfied that she had resolved her dilemma she straightened the front of her jacket and picked up her bag from the bed.

As Marti grew up, dislike had replaced her fear of Hendrik. The first clear memory she had was of him shaking her so hard she had bitten her own tongue. She had been almost three and a half. She had tried to scramble up on to a chair at the table in the playroom, wanting to see what he was doing. With her favourite doll tucked under her arm, the manoeuvre proved difficult. She had reached out to clutch at the edge of the table with her free hand. Instead she had clutched at the wing of the model aircraft he was making. The wing had snapped off from its plastic mounting. She had ruined hours of careful work.

The occasions when Erasmus and Clarice went out for the evening and Hendrik was left to look after her, were spent lying in bed rigid with terror until she heard the reassuring sounds of her parents' return. Hendrik waited only for them to shut the door of the apartment behind them before ordering her to bed. Her Snoopy night-light would be taken away and she would be left in total darkness with the knowledge that if she was not a good girl, rats would come in under the door, creep under the sheets and gnaw at her body. Rats ate naughty girls. Just to make sure she knew what a rat was, he had brought in a dead one and held it up by its tail in front of her face. Her fear was compounded by the fact that, should the rats try to eat her, there was always so much noise coming from the living room that Hendrik wouldn't hear her cries for help.

A desperate need to visit the bathroom one night had forced her to make the perilous journey in the dark from her bed to the door. On her return she had lingered for a moment by the open door of the living room, reluctant to have to return to the blackness of her bedroom. The record player was blaring out the latest rhythm and blues song, an empty bottle of wine lay on the floor, and Hendrik was lying on top of his girlfriend on the sofa. They appeared to be fighting with each other and she felt scared. She went to call out to Hendrik, but remembered the rats. Being a good girl meant staying in her room and not being a nuisance. It was a little over six years later that she became sufficiently informed about the facts of life to realise what Hendrik had been doing to the girl on the sofa that night.

When she was thirteen she learned to lock the bathroom door. Hendrik had come into the bathroom while she was stepping out of the bath. His silent stare both embarrassed and frightened her. He threw a towel to her and declared the rest of her to be as ugly as her face. By the time she was fifteen, their quarrels had taken on a frequent and regular pattern. She refused to do anything he said on principle. He would harry her to the point of tears until she did. Efforts to get her mother to champion her cause would only result in Clarice sighing and rubbing at her brow. She had long since given up trying to control her warring children.

When Hendrik left home to work in Zaire, Marti felt free for the first time in her life. She willingly helped the maid to clean out his bedroom. She scrubbed and polished until her arms ached, only stopping when the room was free of his rank, masculine smell. The next time she saw him was five years later. She was twenty and had long since shed her fear of the dark. She had also discovered, through tidying up a bundle of old documents at the back of her father's wardrobe, that Hendrik had been adopted. It gave her new-found confidence to deal with him. He wasn't her brother. He was just a stupid pest. Her confidence increased at the sight of a very subdued Hendrik returning home. He was now thirty and had been married and divorced, and was looking to his father to provide a loan to meet his divorce settlement. Her plan to have an obliging boyfriend present in the apartment, as moral support, didn't appear to be necessary. Most of the time Hendrik appeared not to notice she was there. He did take notice of her when she couldn't resist making sly reference to his adoption. She received a hard slap on the face that left her eyes stinging. The pain was worth suffering just to glimpse the momentary hunted expression in his eyes.

Astrid looked anxiously at Marti when she arrived at the office. 'Something wrong, Miss Van den Fleet?'

Marti nodded wearily. 'My father has suffered another heart attack.'

'Oh, I am so sorry. I'll make you some coffee. You look as though you need a cup. How is he?'

'All the hospital will say at the moment is that he is comfortable.'

'Well that's cheering news.'

Marti nodded again.

'Er, Miss Van den Fleet, if you want to go back to the hospital I can look after things here, except two things I should mention. Mr Erasmus's lawyer rang to say that the documents Mr Erasmus asked him to prepare are ready for signature.'

Marti glanced at her quickly. 'Did he say what the documents were?'

'No, he didn't.'

Marti pulled the chair away from her desk. The documents could only be to transfer control of the company. She had quarrelled with her father for nothing. He had already done what he had set out to do.

'And Mr Hendrik called from Zaire. I explained you were delayed. He said he would try the apartment.' Astrid automatically reached for the telephone as it rang out. She put her hand over the mouthpiece. 'Mr Hendrik is on the line now.'

Marti took the telephone reluctantly. 'Yes?'

'I am pleased to see you have decided to open for business. What the hell's going on? I called the office an hour ago.'

Marti gripped the telephone at the sound of the familiar rasping voice.

'Hello? Are you there, Marti?'

'Yes, Father has had another heart attack. I spent the night at the hospital.'

There was a shocked pause on the other end of the line. 'Has he told you I'm coming home?'

'Yes.'

'Has he had the papers drawn up for him and me to sign?'

'I believe so.'

'Oh well, that's all right then. How long is he going to be in hospital?'

'I don't know. The doctors won't commit themselves.'

'Well, get the lawyer to take the documents to the hospital straight away. They must be signed.'

Marti drew in her breath. 'Father is in no fit state to sign anything. He is a very sick man, Hendrik.'

'Do it. On second thoughs, don't bother. I will speak to the lawyer myself. That way I know it will be done.'

Marti looked at the telephone in disgust as Hendrik hung up on her. He hadn't even asked how Father was.

Astrid returned to the office and placed a coffee tray on the corner of the desk. Marti hesitated for a moment then decided there was nothing to be gained in keeping back the news. 'Astrid, although it is confidential for the moment, I think I should mention that my father has decided to retire.'

Astrid looked at her questioningly, but didn't seem unduly surprised.

'My brother will be taking over the company.'

'Will I still be working for you, Miss Van den Fleet?'

'For the moment. I don't know what plans my brother has, as yet. Presumably you won't have any objections to working for both of us initially?'

'Not at all. I've never met Mr Hendrik, but he sounds a very nice gentleman on the telephone.'

Marti nodded. 'What's on the agenda for this morning?'

'Not much. There's a letter for you from the IDE.'

Marti took the letter and glanced through it. It was a politely veiled rejection of the application she had made almost three months ago to become an option bearer. She tossed it into the waste-paper bin in anger.

'And Mr Schmidt has an appointment at ten o'clock. It's almost that now.'

Marti clapped a hand to her forehead. 'God, I'd completely forgotten about him.'

'Justus can see him, if you want?'

'No. I'll see him.'

Daniel Schmidt arrived exactly at ten. He bounded

towards Marti with outstretched hand. 'Marti, good to see you again. Busy?'

'Very. We have done some excellent trading this quarter.' Marti clapped her hands together. 'Well, if you'd like to come through to the viewing room, you can see what we've got for you.'

Four trays of 'J' grade diamonds were already laid out on the table in the viewing room. Although too imperfect to be cut and polished and sold to the jewellery trade, they were still of considerable commercial value and destined, eventually, to be used in many industrial processes. Daniel took out his eyeglass and carefully examined the contents of each tray. He pulled out three of the trays towards the edge of the table. 'Price?'

'$200,000.'

He sucked in air between his teeth. 'Say again?'

'$200,000.'

'Come on, Marti. I can buy cheaper in London.'

'Then you should have checked your boarding ticket before you left Tel Aviv.'

He bent down and examined one of the trays again. 'Someone's been very generous in grading these as "J"'s.'

'They're top quality "J"'s, Daniel, and you know it, and you won't buy them cheaper in London.'

'I can do $100,000.'

She gave a faint smile. 'Not like you, Daniel, to make a wasted journey. $200,000.'

He pushed his hands into his pockets and rocked gently back and forth on his heels. Marti waited impassively. Daniel would reach middle ground in his own good time. He half turned away from the table to look at her. '$150,000?'

She shook her head. He breathed out through his nostrils sharply like a horse. 'I am a good customer, you know.'

'Amongst others.'

He turned back to the table and studied the diamonds again. 'What would you say to $200,000 if I take the fourth tray?'

'I would say only for you, Daniel. Only for you.'

He grinned. 'If I was an impressionable man, I would believe you, but you say that to everyone, Marti.' He held out his hand to her to shake on the agreement. 'Payment at the end of the month, as usual?'

'Fine.'

They returned to Marti's office for coffee and ten minutes of the latest business gossip. Marti was happy to let Daniel dominate the conversation with his tales of woe. It avoided having to fend off too many questions about her father. Daniel puffed on his cheroot. 'Ritzer's are closing down at the end of the month, you know?'

Marti raised an eyebrow. 'No, I didn't. I suppose it leaves you with a bigger slice of the cake.'

He laughed. 'What cake? When you can get stones cut and polished in India for a tenth of the cost in Tel Aviv, you're fighting over crumbs, Marti.'

'Get your stones cut in India on an out-take basis.'

He laughed again. 'And my mother would see me put half of my family out of business?'

'Forget I said that. Actually, we have the same problem here. A friend of mine, and I don't think I'm being too biased when I say he is one of the best cutters in Antwerp, says the same thing. Johannes Witt. You've heard of him?'

'Sure I have.'

'Well, he says he just can't match the Indians on price. His overheads simply won't allow it.'

Daniel nodded his head vigorously. 'My cousin reckons he has to quadruple his turnover just to match his profit margins of two years ago.' He glanced at his watch. 'Well, must be going. Want to catch the afternoon flight back to Tel Aviv. Time away from the office is business lost.' He held out his hand. 'Good to do business with you again, Marti.'

Marti accompanied Daniel to the front door of the building and they shook hands again. She watched him walk

down the street. Daniel Schmidt was one of the nice guys.
Knowledgeable and well respected. Although he was an
option bearer and could trade with the IDE, once he had
sold his strictly limited quota of diamonds he had no other
choice but to purchase from dealers like Van den Fleet's. At
a price Van den Fleet's were prepared to sell. He could only
squeeze out a profit for himself after they had taken theirs.
She went back inside again. Daniel may see life as a basket
of woes, but at least he could trade as an option bearer. She
had no hope of ever becoming one. The IDE always claimed
that women were welcome to join, provided they met the
stringent financial requirements that were designed to
ensure they were permanently denied access. She walked
slowly up the stairs. There was no real argument to mount
against her father's decision. They needed to trade with the
IDE. Hendrik could. She couldn't.

Astrid met Marti at the top of the stairs. 'Miss Van den
Fleet, Mr Yasim just called. He said he would ring you
back.'

Marti frowned in annoyance. 'Why didn't you come and
tell me he was on the telephone. He is my most important
customer. You know that, Astrid.'

'I'm sorry, Miss Van den Fleet, but Mr Yasim was calling
from Geneva airport. He couldn't hold.'

'Did he leave a number where he could be reached?'

'No, but he did promise to call back. He told me to tell
you that he was looking forward very much to a long-
overdue meeting with you.' A mischievous smile flitted
across Astrid's face.

Marti looked sternly at her. 'Don't misinterpret things,
Astrid. It is a bad habit of yours.'

'Sorry, Miss Van den Fleet.'

Marti suppressed a smile at Astrid's suddenly crestfallen
expression. Beni Yasim was undeniably a very attractive
man and knew it, but he was much more than that. He only
appeared twice maybe three times a year to purchase

diamonds, but he was a quality buyer on behalf of Arab interests and represented big business to Van den Fleet's.

Bar Tango Tango was a gay brothel in the Mong Kok district of Kowloon. The red neon sign over the door cast a garish glow in the alleyway. The owner threw his cigarette into the gutter and went back inside. He glanced around the half-empty bar. Business was slack apart from the four men who had paid double the going rate for a back room upstairs. The four men hadn't expressed any interest in the custom sitting around the bar. The fourth man hadn't expressed interest in anything. He had been dragged in drunk as a prawn by the other three men. The owner went behind the bar and into a small office. He sat down and glanced through the two-way mirror before settling down to read the racing results in the newspaper.

The three men from 'A' department of the Shanghai Public Security Bureau watched impassively as the man tied down on to the bed slowly regained consciousness. 'A' department concerned itself with anything that the PRC considered alien activity. The three men also concerned themselves, at a price, with what Fang Ka-Shing considered troublesome. The men were extremely efficient in the retrieval of information. Whether from a spy, a rioting student or, as in this case, someone suspected of being a member of the Bear's Paw Gang. The man had so far not told them anything of significance, except that his name was Jimmy, that he had never heard of a man called Mui Shenlu, and that he didn't know what they were talking about. One of the men stepped forward and grabbed a handful of his hair and shook him. Jimmy whimpered as recognition of his dangerous predicament returned. The man shook him again. 'Who is your leader?'

Jimmy turned his head. The man swung the butt of his pistol across his face. Jimmy uttered a long drawn-out wail. The man shook him again. 'Who is the leader of the Bear's Paw Gang?'

Jimmy's head lolled on to his shoulder. 'Kill me, just kill me.'

Jimmy had been picked up by the PSB as he plied his usual trade of drug-pushing in the side-streets off Nathan Road. At first he thought they were members of the Hong Kong drugs squad, but he soon realised, to his terror, that they weren't interested in what he was carrying in his pockets. They were more interested in the information he carried in his head. An hour in their company had proved to be excruciatingly painful. Now he just wanted to die. If he told them what they wanted to know, he would die anyway. Song Enlai would see to that.

Jimmy gasped as cold water was thrown over him. He saw, through half-closed eyelids, the man leaning against the wall straighten up and approach the side of the bed. He slowly lit up a cigarette.

Jimmy shuddered. The man was the devil of all devils. Jimmy moved his lips. He spoke the words without realising that he had done so. 'Song. Song Enlai.'

The man by his head shook him again. 'Speak up.'

Jimmy moistened his lips. 'The leader of the Bear's Paw Gang is Song Enlai.' He turned his face to the wall. It didn't matter now. Nothing did.

The third man, who had remained silent throughout, gave a brief nod of his head. He turned on his heel and left the room. The two men pressed a pillow over Jimmy's face.

Astrid popped her head around the door of Marti's office. 'Excuse me, Miss Van den Fleet, I wondered if you would mind taking these flowers to Mr Erasmus for me. I wasn't sure what to get him. I hope he will like these.'

Marti pushed the files in front of her to one side and stood up. 'Oh, Astrid, that's very kind. Thank you.'

'Anything else I can do for you, Miss Van den Fleet?'

'No. You might as well go, Astrid, it's almost five-thirty.'

The telephone rang out. Marti gestured with her hand.
'I'll get this. See you tomorrow.'

'Thank you, Miss Van den Fleet. Goodnight.'

Marti picked up the telephone. 'Yes?'

'Marti, it's Hendrik here.'

She leaned back in her chair and shut her eyes. Not again.
Please.

'Yes, Hendrik.'

'The lawyer's just been on to me. Father has signed the
documents. It just needs me to add my signature when I
return.' Hendrik paused for a moment. 'Aren't you going
to congratulate me?'

'Congratulations on whatever you think you are celebrating, Hendrik.'

'Don't be clever, Marti, you're not very good at it. And
shouldn't you be showing more respect for the new head of
Van den Fleet's?'

'And shouldn't you be showing more concern for
Father's health. You haven't even asked how he is.'

'I don't need to. I already know. I took the trouble to
have a long conversation with his specialist. Something you
obviously didn't think was necessary.'

She pressed her lips together and counted slowly to three.
'I had fully intended to. For your information I have been
trying to run the office, Hendrik, as well as having been up
all night.'

'All right, all right, stop moaning. When are you going to
see Father?'

'Straight from the office.'

'Get some flowers, some fruit for him, from me. And tell
him not to worry. Tell him I'll be with him as soon as I can.
Oh, by the way, get my room ready for me as well.'

Marti gripped the telephone. You promised. You promised. She spoke as politely as her anger would allow. 'I'll tell
the maid when she comes in tomorrow. And Father has
nothing to worry about. I have been running the company

quite well on my own for the last twelve months.'

'You'd better. There'll be trouble if you haven't. Listen, I haven't booked my flight, but I'll call you with a time to pick me up at the airport when I have. See you, little sister.'

Marti put the telephone down. She was neither little, nor his sister. She buried her head in her hands. Hendrik was insufferable. She was not sure if she could keep her promise to her father.

Song Enlai and senior members of the Bear's Paw Gang had gathered in a back room of Song Automobile Rentals. Their business was to discuss the message someone was taking great pains to deliver. They had lost four of their members in the last few days. Each had been tortured then suffocated.

The Bear's Paw Gang was one of the secret Triad societies that ruled the Hong Kong underworld. Each of the senior men operated perfectly legitimate businesses as cover for their individually assigned operations. Extortion. Prostitution. Heroin. Generations of tradition and ritual bound them in life-long loyalty.

Song Enlai cleaned beneath his thumbnail with a nail file. 'Are you certain it is the work of the Third Moon Gang?'

The man sitting by his side nodded. 'No question. They have been trying to expand their operations for some time.'

Song nodded. He placed the nail file down on the table. 'So. They think they can expand at our expense, by frightening us.' He glanced around the table. 'They are mistaken. And we will prove to them how mistaken they are.'

The men around the table murmured their agreement. Song looked at his personal chauffeur and bodyguard. The man gave a quick nod. 'We can take eight of them out, Mr Song, for starters.'

Song glanced around the table again, and again the men nodded their assent. He pushed his chair back and stood up. 'If the Third Moon Gang want war, they will get it.' He gestured towards a man leaning against the wall at the far end of the room. 'In the meantime, you take Jimmy's place.' Song walked slowly to the door behind him and returned to his private office. The men around the table stood up and filed out of the room.

Song lit a cigarette then went to the safe. He unlocked it and removed a small chamois leather pouch. He opened it and shook out a handful of diamonds. He selected one and held it up to the light then slipped it into his pocket. He had a ready buyer for that. He returned the rest of the diamonds to the pouch. He drew on his cigarette. It was a pity Mui Shenlu had to die. He had been useful.

Mui had been a compulsive gambler. Always believing that the next throw, if not earning him a fortune, would at least get him out of trouble. A frequent visitor, when in Hong Kong, at one of the illegal gambling dens run by the Bear's Paw Gang, he had quickly discovered the house rules on credit after a particularly bad run of luck. A knife had been held at his throat until he had convinced them that he could pay. He promised that he could get his hands on sufficient diamonds to settle his debts.

Song put the diamond pouch back into the safe. Mui had been foolish. He had failed to pay up, despite a forceful reminder that had left him doubled up on the floor, screaming in agony. Song slammed the safe shut. Mui had the effrontery to plead for time. There were no more diamonds. His source had dried up. Song walked back to his desk and carefully stubbed out his cigarette. No one lied to Song Enlai and everyone paid their debts one way or another. He picked up the telephone and quickly punched out a number. 'Is Joey Heung there yet? OK. Tell him Mr Song wants to buy him a drink.' He put the telephone down and reached across to the intercom and buzzed down to the garage. 'Bring the limo round in five minutes. The Cortina Club.'

* * *

Chan Chunling was greeted by Anna Wu with all the respect due to one of her brother's most important clients. She humbly apologised for James's lateness in arriving home at the appointed hour and offered Chan the choice of four different kinds of beverages. He accepted a glass of genuine Scotch whisky.

James arrived home just as Chan was settling himself down on the sofa and Anna was apologising profusely for the humbleness of their home. James slung his jacket over a chair and signalled to Anna to leave. She hastily escaped into the kitchen. Chan drained his glass of whisky then pulled out a package from his raincoat pocket and handed it to James. James picked up his jacket and searched in the pockets for his eyeglass. He took the parcel to a table by the window and rolled it out flat. He stared at the diamonds for a moment. They were of very high quality. He glanced back at Chan.

'How is Mr Mui?'

'Still indisposed, I'm afraid to say.'

James nodded and picked up one of the diamonds. He examined it, put it down and picked up another. 'I shouldn't think we will have much problem getting authentication for these. In fact, no problem at all as far as I can see.'

'Good.' Chan picked up his raincoat and slung it over his arm. He took a piece of paper out of his breast pocket and placed it on the table. 'Call me on that number when you have received authentication.' He was already moving towards the door as James turned round.

Anna waited behind the kitchen door until she heard the front door slam shut. She stuck her head out. 'When do you want to eat, James?'

'Give me five minutes. I've got a telephone call to make.' His brow puckered into a frown.

'Is there something wrong, James?'

'No, I'm just trying to work out a plan of action. I need to visit four dealers. Logically, as far as travelling is concerned, my itinerary should be Bombay, Tel Aviv, Antwerp, New York, but . . .' he scratched at his ear. 'But, I think I will visit Antwerp first. If Van den Fleet's authenticate the diamonds, so, theoretically, will the others. If they don't, then I have saved myself the trouble of travelling halfway around the world.'

'Why Van den Fleet's, James?'

'Because they are the most respected diamond merchants in Europe, Anna, that's why.'

Her expression became subdued. James had considered her question to be a foolish one. 'I will leave you to your work and go and prepare the vegetables.'

He frowned, as if in very deep thought, and consulted his filofax. He dialled Van den Fleet's number and it was answered almost immediately. 'I wish to speak to Mr Erasmus Van den Fleet, please. Oh, I see. Very well. I will speak to Miss Van den Fleet then.' He tapped his fingers on the table while he waited to be connected.

'Martina Van den Fleet. Can I help you?'

'Miss Van den Fleet, my names is James Wu. I am calling from Hong Kong. I did actually wish to speak to your father.'

'I'm afraid he is away from the office for a few days. Can I be of assistance?'

James chewed at his lip. 'Er – yes, possibly. I wish to have a parcel of diamonds authenticated.'

'Certainly. We can do that for you.'

'Miss Van den Fleet, my client does wish to remain anonymous. I –'

'I quite understand, Mr Wu. You will have the benefit of our usual discretion.'

'Ah, yes, of course,' James scratched at the back of his head. 'I can be in Antwerp in two days' time.'

'That will be convenient, Mr Wu. Let me know when you arrive and I will see that you are given a firm appointment.'

'Thank you, Miss Van den Fleet.' James put the

telephone down and went to pour himself a drink.

Anna came into the sitting room and looked at him expectantly. James nodded to her. 'A-OK, as the Americans say.'

Anna's face broke out into a smile. James was a very clever man. Perhaps they would never need to go and live in Australia.

Pa Jiaming stubbed out his cigarette as his limousine sped towards Zhongnanhai. A roughly rectangular area due west of the Imperial Palace in Beijing, it derived its name from the two lakes within. It had once been part of the ancient Imperial City, but now housed members of the Central Committee of the Chinese Communist Party. Pa gathered up his raincoat lying on the seat beside him as the limousine drove through the south gate, past the armed guards. The perception of power in Beijing was as tenuous as the changing images of a cloud and even Fang Ka-Shing was unaware that his cousin, Pa, besides heading up the Central Military Commission for Scientific Advancement, was also the vice-leader of the Leading Group for High Technology. Leading groups were the Chinese attempt to harmonise the overlapping activities of ministries that, by tradition, clung to their secrecy and isolation. It gave Pa access to information to which he would otherwise not have been privy and a degree of power that his cousin Fang would have envied.

The young girl sitting in the outer office briefly lowered her head in polite acknowledgment. Pa gave a friendly smile in her direction which brought sudden colour to her cheeks. Her gaze followed his retreating back in awe and admiration. Vice-leader Pa was a man of great authority. One could tell immediately that this was so, by the excellent cut of his clothes. He was also very handsome. She shook her head slightly, as if reprimanding herself for indulging in foolish daydreams.

Pa lit up another cigarette and walked slowly to the

window. He stared up at the bright blue sky. Days like this would become fewer. Soon, winter would encroach bringing bitingly cold northern winds that would whip up the dry dust of summer, covering everyone and everything in its yellow cloak. He drew on his cigarette and inhaled deeply. Profits from Bright Mountain were securely deposited in an Austrian bank, whose discretion outweighed that of the Swiss. It was time to arrange an overseas trip for himself. Did not Confucius say, 'one should learn and employ one's knowledge at the appropriate season'? He walked across to his desk and picked up the telephone. 'Connect me with Chairman Fang Ka-Shing in Hong Kong immediately.'

PART 2

The offices of the Shanghai Technical & Research Corporation were situated on the Bund. Chan Chunling's office had a clear view of the Huangpu River across the wide avenue. He stood looking out of the window with a telephone clamped to his ear, waiting for Professor Li to be found.

A rather breathless and irritated voice eventually came on the line. Chan turned away from the window and sat down at his desk. 'You are to receive some visitors from Beijing, Professor Li. They are most interested in seeing your process for themselves.'

There was a strangled hissing sound on the line. 'Do not make jokes with me, Director Chan. What does this mean?'

'Compose yourself, Professor Li. They simply wish to see for themselves your process for making diamond film using ultrasonic sound.'

Li gave a sharp sigh of relief. 'Ah, I see.'

'And it is up to you to ensure that they only see what you wish them to.'

'Do they suspect anything?'

'Of course they do not suspect anything. Just make sure they do not discover Bright Mountain. That is for our eyes alone.'

'Indeed, indeed. Do not worry, Director Chan, I will see that they are suitably entertained. When are they coming?'

'You will be informed from Beijing.'

'Very well.' Professor Li hung up, then paced slowly up

and down his office. He must make arrangements to welcome his visitors. Immediate arrangements.

Success by Western scientists in producing a new generation of high-temperature superconducting ceramics, a technology that the Americans had prevented the Chinese from sharing, had forced the Chinese to concentrate their research in other areas to produce new forms of carbon electronics. Li and his team in Anshan had been conducting research into the application of ultrasonic sound techniques for more than two years. Li's failure to match the achievements of the research centre in Shenzhen, where scientists had developed diamond film carbon using plasma, a highly ionised gas, had prompted a reprimand from the vice-leader of the Leading Group for High Technology, Pa Jiaming. Practice is the sole gauge of theory. Li was to always remember that. His funding would be redirected to other research centres if his theories remained just that. Anxious that his funding should not be abruptly terminated and determined to outshine his rivals in Shenzhen, Li successfully developed a method of producing artificial diamond crystals using ultrasonic sound techniques. The result was industrial diamond film, of remarkably high quality; capable of being used as a superconductor in microelectronics.

When Li demonstrated the technique to Pa Jiaming, he was justifiably proud of his achievements and in a moment of careless boasting claimed he could even produce a solid diamond crystal. Many crystals. A complete diamond. Pa had looked at him as if he believed he had suddenly taken leave of his senses. Li became more insistent. A diamond that was indistinguishable from a real stone. The only difference being that real diamonds mined from the earth took millions of years to develop. His took twelve hours. Pa was an avaricious man with a taste for high living. The idea of producing perfect diamonds at a fraction of the cost of the real thing was immensely appealing. He laughed at Li and said he couldn't believe such a thing. Diamond film, yes. A whole diamond, no. That was fantasy. Craftily enraging Li to the point of Li demanding that he should examine for himself the proof of his words, Pa found himself staring, in a state of excitement, at a sizeable uncut diamond. Li watched him in triumph. Pa looked as if he had just witnessed a miracle. Li casually enquired if Pa wished a further test; to see the rough diamond cut and polished. It would not take very long. Computerised cutting using lasers made little work of the task. A matter of ten minutes later, Pa was holding in the palm of his hand one of the most beautiful diamonds he had ever seen. His usually bland expression became alive with excitement. He looked up at Li and demanded to know who had guided the laser to cut the diamond. The art of diamond cutting was known only to the few. Li had smiled. Coordinates calculated from stereoscopic imaging of a diamond had been fed into the computer operating the laser. The art of the few was no longer.

Having made the diamond, Li was now rather bored with Pa's preoccupation with it. He was more anxious to demonstrate the need for more funding for his latest research into ultrasonic levitation to create energy wells. Pa nodded occasionally and made non-committal noises as he continued staring at the diamond. His mind had automatically noted the inevitable plea for funding, but was focused firmly on the vast potential for a little private enterprise that now lay open to him. He informed Li that he would of, course, require the diamond to be examined by experts before he could be entirely convinced of Li's demonstration. Li had shrugged, as if to indicate that Pa could do what he liked with the diamond.

Four days later, Pa made a return visit to Professor Li. He had secretly requested the scientists at Shenzhen, as a special favour to him, to test the diamond, if necessary to destruction. When they completed their investigations, they informed him that all the tests had proved conclusive.

The diamond was genuine. Over a pot of tea in Li's office, Pa confessed to being extremely impressed with Li's work, but there was one small problem. The research centre in Shenzhen required extra funding to continue its work and it was likely that, to meet this need, funding for the Sound & Vibration Institute would have to be similarly downgraded. Li protested vehemently that his institute was on the verge of creating glasses that would revolutionise the making of capsules for nuclear fusion reactors; all without grovelling to the West and their corrupt and exploitative methods. Pa quickly pressed Li for evidence of his new research and Li was forced to admit that they had only reached the stage of ultrasonic levitation, but he insisted that the time was not far away when the whole world would recognise the institute's work. Li trusted that the Leading Group for High Technology would take note of that. Pa had shrugged. He was only the vice-leader of the group. He could not speak for everyone. Li must be aware of the power struggles in Beijing. The institute at Shenzhen was strongly favoured by some of the conservatives.

Pa allowed Li to wallow in his miseries for a few moments then informed Li that he would require more diamonds. Li stared at him in bewildered silence. Pa took the diamond Li had made for him from his pocket and rolled it around the palm of his hand. He would require a lot more. If Li could meet such a requirement, it was possible that some way could be found to ensure the continued funding of the Sound & Vibration Institute. Pa's insinuations took a little time to sink in, but when they did, Li felt rooted to the spot by fear. Fear of being involved in what was pure theft against the State, the penalty for which was probably death, and fear of the man standing in front of him. It was not true that Pa Jiaming lacked influence in the Leading Group for High Technology. He was a most significant influence, particularly when it came to allocation, or more importantly non-allocation of funds for research.

Li swallowed several times to clear the suffocating tightness in his throat, before nodding his head in agreement. Pa smiled. He hadn't doubted for a second what Li's answer would be. Scientists were all the same. Their needs must be met whatever the cost. Pa rubbed his hands together. Now, at least one of them would pay for the intellectual arrogance that had been meted out to him on every possible occasion, since his appointment as vice-leader of the Leading Group. Li would build him a bright mountain of diamonds that would provide Pa and his family with everything that they could desire and more. A state of family harmony for which his wife and children would be continually grateful.

Pa stepped outside the laboratory to have a cigarette in the corridor. An action which was expressly forbidden anywhere in the institute. When he rejoined Li a few minutes later, Li had overcome his initial terror and had adopted a purely pragmatical view of Pa's proposal. If Pa was consumed by greed, that merely confirmed his lack of education and personal refinement. There was nothing Li could or should do about it. He agreed to supply Pa with artificial diamonds, but did make one request. His name must be protected. Pa must ensure his anonymity. Pa had laughed. It was, under the circumstances, a not unreasonable request. There was nothing for Li to fear, provided he fulfilled his part in the scheme of things. Pa had already decided on a suitable go-between to oversee the transfer of diamonds from Anshan to their destined point of sale. He knew just the person.

The Shanghai Technical & Research Corporation had only recently come under the umbrella of the Leading Group for High Technology, but Pa gambled that its director, Chan Chunling, was taking advantage of his status to supplement his salary by accepting 'gifts' from Western companies eager to participate in Sino-foreign trading ventures. It was not uncommon. Even if it were not the case, Pa had the wherewithal to make it so.

At very little cost, Pa arranged delivery of a consignment of colour television sets and video recorders to certain members of the Shanghai police. They, in turn, lost little time in informing Chan Chunling that his financial misdemeanours, real or otherwise, would be reported to one of the special teams set up personally by the Secretary-general of the Chinese Communist Party to rout out corruption and the menace of racketeers such as himself, unless he was prepared to cooperate with a nameless but esteemed comrade.

Pa's gamble paid off. Chan was gripped both by the inherent Chinese fear of public shame and disgrace, and fear of an abrupt termination of the good life. The prospect of being shot in the back of the head at a mass gathering of grinning peasants, or many years spent in a prison in Qinghai Province being 'reformed through labour', was too much to contemplate. He declared himself willing to cooperate with anyone. He was told his esteemed comrade would be in touch. Two days later he was contacted. His esteemed comrade was Pa's cousin, Fang Ka-Shing. Chan was relieved to discover that his task appeared to be less potentially dangerous than he had imagined. On the instructions of his esteemed comrade he was to collect diamonds from Professor Li in Anshan and send them by a courier of his own choosing to Hong Kong. It was taken for granted that Chan, for his own protection, would elect the most suitable person. The courier would then discreetly make contact with James Wu & Co. Chan had little hesitation in choosing his courier. Mui Shenlu could be relied upon. He was married to Chan's niece.

Marti carefully balanced a sheaf of flowers and a basket of fruit in her left arm, then shut and locked the car door with her free hand. She recognised one of the nurses coming out of the cardiac unit and managed a brief wave in her direction.

The receptionist ran her finger down the appointment list. 'When did you say you had an appointment with Dr Rensburg?'

'Actually, he said to come any time after four o'clock.' Marti looked up at the clock on the wall. The hour hand had just ticked on to four. She hoped she wouldn't have to wait. 'I have to get back to the office by five. I have a client to see.'

'I'll page Dr Rensburg now. Would you like to sit over there? He won't be long, I'm sure.'

Marti sat down on one of the chairs. She averted her eyes from the sight of a nurse escorting a woman, who was openly weeping, along the corridor. At least she had received one piece of good news that afternoon. Hendrik had called her again to say that he was stopping over in New York for a couple of days. He had some business to tie up. It was only putting off the fateful hour, but she was glad of the extra time. The last two days had felt like a nightmare. First, the shock of Hendrik's return. Then, her father's collapse.

Dr Rensburg wasted no time in making it clear that in his opinion Erasmus's recovery was being undermined by his business worries. It was not helping his condition and he must stay in hospital for an enforced period of rest. Marti shifted uncomfortably in her chair. Something about Dr Rensburg's manner gave her the distinct impression that he believed she was somehow responsible for her father's anxieties and she felt obliged to explain that her father's worries had no real material basis. She had been running the company for the last twelve months. Business, according to their latest figures, had improved substantially. There was no need for him to worry. Dr Rensburg stood up and pushed his hands in the pockets of his coat. What was very important was that his patient believed that. Marti sighed. She found it difficult to say, because she didn't want even to consider it herself, but she reluctantly explained that her brother, Hendrik, was returning from Zaire to take over the family business. It was what her father wanted and that would no doubt put his mind at rest. Dr Rensburg gave a quick nod, as if to indicate that he wholeheartedly approved of the idea and said that if she now wished to see her father, she could do so. Her father might appear somewhat drowsy, but there was no cause for alarm. He had been sedated.

Erasmus opened his eyes as Marti bent over him and planted a kiss on his cheek. He blinked and looked at her for a couple of seconds before smiling and grasping at her hand. Marti pulled the chair away from the bed and sat down. 'How are you?'

'I'm all right. How are things at the office?'

'No problems. We have just done some very good business with Daniel Schmidt.'

He turned his head on the pillow to look at her. 'Who?'

'Daniel Schmidt. From Tel Aviv. You remember him.'

'Oh yes, I remember. Have you heard from Hendrik? When is he coming?'

'Soon. He rang earlier to say he would be delayed for a couple of days. He's stopping off in New York. Apparently he's got some business there.'

He nodded and turned his head again on the pillow, and closed his eyes.

'Dr Rensburg says you have been worrying. You mustn't, Father. We've just had an analysis of last year's figures. They are very good.'

Erasmus didn't reply. Marti studied his face. His colour had improved. He had lost that frightening greyish pallor. But all that he was really concerned about was Hendrik. When was he coming home? That was all that mattered to him.

A nurse appeared and placed the flowers Marti had brought with her on the table at the foot of the bed. She nodded in the direction of Erasmus. 'I think you should leave now, Miss Van den Fleet. Your father needs his rest.'

Marti got up from the chair and kissed her father again. His eyelids fluttered briefly. She glanced at the flowers. 'I forgot to tell my father that the flowers and fruits are from my brother.'

'Ah, yes, that will be Hendrik, won't it. Don't worry. When your father wakes up, I won't forget to tell him.'

'I bought a mango for him. I wasn't sure what he could eat.'

The nurse smiled brightly. 'What a good idea. He can have a couple of slices for his breakfast tomorrow. I'm sure he will enjoy it.' She went to Erasmus's side and adjusted the pillow beneath his neck.

Marti picked up her bag and walked quietly out of the room, filled yet again with the awful sense of being an intruder; of not really being needed. She checked her watch and quickened her pace. She had promised to arrange a viewing of their finest uncut diamonds for Johannes at five. It was that now.

Johannes Witt suffered from male pattern baldness at his temples and a rapidly growing bald spot on the top of his head. His habit of frequently feeling his head to check that both sections had an equal covering of hair created an air of nervousness about him.

Marti stood to one side of the viewing table, while Johannes carefully examined the diamonds laid out for him. She shut her eyes as his hand unconsciously strayed to the top of his head. She wished he would stop doing that. It was getting on her nerves.

'Marti, are you feeling all right?'

She opened her eyes to find Johannes staring at her anxiously. 'Yes. Just a little tired, I suppose.'

He came to her and put his arm around her shoulders. 'You mustn't worry about Hendrik, you know.'

She nodded.

'I mean it. He's probably changed more than you think.'
He squeezed her shoulder. 'Just give things a chance
between the two of you.'

'Let's not talk about it now. I know it's my fault you have
been kept waiting, but Justus will be anxious to lock up for
the night.'

'OK. I was just trying to help.'

'I know. Thanks.'

He returned to the table and picked up one of the diamonds. She placed her hands behind her back and leaned
against the wall. Johannes was a good friend. A very good
friend.

They had known each other since they were children, but
it wasn't until they were both in their twenties and found
themselves alone after a late-night party that, as Marti later
recalled, they drifted into bed together. They had a brief
affair although, as Marti was again to recall, affair was too
strong a word to describe matters. A mundane 'coming-
together' was a phrase she thought more suitable. She discovered that Johannes had the irritating habit of forgetting
the layout of her anatomy from one occasion to the next,
and found his continual asking of what pleased her off-
putting and eventually boring. He never, as he put it,
imposed upon a woman and she found to her relief that,
without encouragement, he seemed content to revert back
to a purely platonic relationship.

Johannes picked up one of the diamonds and rested it in
the palm of his hand. 'I think this one will be perfect for the
centrepiece.' He ran his fingertips almost lovingly over the
uncut surface of the diamond.

Marti gave a quiet smile. Diamonds were more arousing
than women to Johannes. With a diamond Johannes was
confident. Knew exactly what he was doing. Knew instinc-
tively how to draw out the hidden fire within.

Johannes placed his eyeglass down on the table. 'These
will do splendidly. I think I will get matching heart-shaped

gems from these without too much trouble. Thank you, Marti. You have chosen well for me.'

'Who is the lucky recipient going to be, or shouldn't I ask?'

He shrugged. 'No doubt a woman whose ugliness will be magnified by their beauty.'

She gave an irritated laugh. 'Johannes, you sound positively bitchy.'

He shrugged again. 'Maybe, but it is often the way. Can I discuss the price tomorrow? I have yet to work out my own costs on this.'

'Surely.'

'Useful business for both of us, eh, Marti?'

'Indeed.' Marti reached out to the bellpush in the wall and rang for Justus, then walked back to the table and gathered together the diamonds Johannes had selected. Beni Yasim had not called back as quickly as she had anticipated, but when he did, his business would make Johannes's pale into insignificance.

Johannes cleared his throat nervously. Marti was in a strange mood. She didn't seem particularly impressed by the importance of his purchases. He smoothed his hair across his head. She was tired. That was the reason. Understandable. He reached out and touched her arm. 'Marti, I know you're worried about your father, but don't spend the evening alone at home. When you have been to see him, come along to my place and have dinner with me.'

'Thanks, Johannes, but I don't want to be a nuisance. I'm not very good company for anyone at the moment.'

'Nonsense. And you wouldn't be a nuisance. My mother stopped by this afternoon and left a casserole of beef. We can share it.'

'Well, if you're sure.'

He ruffled her hair then stepped quickly away from her as Justus opened the door, as if fearful the gesture might have been seen.

* * *

As Song Enlai walked out of the Cortina Club, his limousine pulled up smoothly a few feet ahead of him. He stiffened as two men from the Shanghai PSB appeared out of nowhere at his side. A gun was pressed into his ribs and he was escorted to the car. A third man from the PSB had replaced Song's usual chauffeur in the driving seat.

The gates at the rear of Song's Automobile Rental Company were opened and as soon as the limousine entered the yard the man at the wheel leapt out and stood by the rear door. Song needed no warning to behave as if nothing was untoward. He stepped out of the car and walked unhurriedly with the three policemen to his office. The receptionist, who had a sawn-off shotgun lying across his lap, looked curiously at the three men accompanying Song. Song gestured to them. 'Business. I'm not to be disturbed.'

'Yes, Mr Song.' The receptionist returned to the girlie magazine he had been flicking through, as the four men climbed the stairs.

The man who had acted as chauffeur pointed to Song's leather, executive-type chair. Song sat down in it and rested his hands on the arms. Out of the corner of his eye he saw one of the other men walk around to stand behind the chair. The chauffeur perched himself on the corner of the desk. 'Business doing well?'

Song nodded.

'We have a mutual friend. Mui Shenlu. He gave you something that didn't belong to him, Mr Song.'

Song shifted in the chair. Under his weight the seat emitted a soft, sighing noise. He looked across at the man standing by the door. He had not spoken one word. They weren't members of any gang that he knew of and they weren't police either, but experience told him that they were good at their type of business. Very good. He gestured to the wall safe. 'I didn't know that, but they are in there.'

'Open it.'

Song got up and slowly moved towards the safe. He

didn't need instructions to avoid sudden movements. He opened it and withdrew the pouch containing the diamonds given to him by Mui Shenlu.

'Bring it to the desk.'

Song walked back to the desk and dropped the pouch on to it.

'Sit down.'

Song did as he was told.

The chauffeur shook the diamonds out of the pouch and quickly counted them. He raised his head and looked at Song. 'Where are the other twenty?'

Song gripped the arms of the chair. 'I'm not –'

A hand was clamped over his mouth and Song let out a muffled scream as the man behind the chair pulled his arm back at an angle and broke the bone in his little finger. He slumped against the side of the chair, gulping in great breaths of air. The chauffeur nodded to the man behind the chair. Song raised his free arm. 'This isn't necessary. I will tell you.'

The chauffeur nodded.

James Wu glanced idly about him as he sat in the gloomy, wood-panelled office. Four generations of Van den Fleets stared down on him from the walls with stern, disapproving eyes. He turned quickly as the door opened and Astrid came in. 'So sorry you have been kept waiting, Mr Wu. Miss Van den Fleet has just finished on the telephone. She will be right with you.'

'Thank you.' James drew his briefcase closer to him. He would have preferred to have dealt with Erasmus Van den Fleet personally, but a quick check with business contacts in New York was reassuring. They had dealt with Martina Van den Fleet. They reckoned she knew what she was about.

Marti held out her hand as she came through the door. 'Good morning, Mr Wu. My apologies for the delay.'

James stood up and took her hand. She was a vast improvement on her forebears. Friendly, sparkling eyes. He drew himself up to his full height. She was an inch smaller than he was and he drew comfort from it. He always felt instantly dwarfed when visiting Europe.

'Would you like to come to our viewing room, Mr Wu, and we can get down to business. I'm sure you do not wish to be further detained.' A fresh flower smell wafted over him as she turned and held the door open for him.

The cut and polished diamonds were laid out neatly in a single row. Marti drew her chair up to the table and removed a low-power magnifying glass from a leather case. Her first impression was favourable. Mr Wu was a dealer in quality merchandise. She didn't lift her head as Astrid came into the room carrying a tray of coffee. Astrid glanced at her then put the tray down on a table by the side of James's chair. She bent down and whispered to him. 'Milk and sugar, Mr Wu?'

'Plain black for me. Thank you.' He, too, whispered.

Astrid poured him a cup of coffee then tiptoed out.

Marti picked up the first diamond in the row and examined it through the eyeglass. Diamonds are graded by the letters of the alphabet, beginning with 'D'. All in all there are 5,000 given classifications to which gems can be assigned, depending upon their quality and colour. Marti raised her head and adjusted the eyeglass to ten-power magnification. She looked down again at the diamond. She turned it slowly through 360 degrees and nodded to herself. No inclusions were visible. She made a quick note on the pad at her side. 'D'. Flawless. She dropped the stone into the pan of a small pair of brass scales, weighed it, and made a further note on the pad. James picked up his coffee cup and took a sip. He flushed as he slurped the hot coffee. The sound seemed to echo around the room.

Just under half an hour later the last stone had been examined and weighed. Marti slipped her eyeglass back into its leather case. 'We concur with your assessment of the stones, Mr Wu. We will have a certificate of authentication ready for you by tomorrow, if that is convenient.'

James stood up and discreetly flexed his shoulders. His neck felt rigid with tension. 'Thank you, Miss Van den Fleet. I am grateful for your assistance.'

She picked up one of the diamonds and looked at it again. It had been skilfully faceted to reflect the greatest amount of light. 'This is superb, Mr Wu.'

He smiled. 'In Hong Kong we call diamonds like that "firestones". An old name, but apt, I think.'

She nodded and put the diamond back on the table. She smiled to herself. A quaint, but not inaccurate description of the flawless, white fiery light. 'Er, Mr Wu.'

James tensed his shoulders. Now for the questions of the curious. This was what he had been anticipating.

'You have an altogether exceptionally fine parcel of gems here. I must tell you that if your client should ever consider their sale, he or she will not find a shortage of buyers.'

'I have no instructions for sale at the moment.'

'Well, if you do, I for one have a client who would be most interested in them.' She held out her hand to him. 'Thank you for seeking our assistance, Mr Wu. It has been a pleasure dealing with you.'

James relaxed his shoulders. His contacts were right. She was super discreet. No questions as to the origin of the diamonds. No sly probing. He took her hand and shook it heartily.

The door of the room was swung open with some force. Marti turned round, startled by the sudden noise, then her heart sank as Hendrik appeared in the doorway. She stared at him nonplussed. 'What are you doing here?'

Hendrik gave a short bark of laughter. 'What a question to ask your loving brother?' He nodded affably at James then walked swiftly to Marti's side.

She tried to dodge a roughly planted kiss on the side of

her face and grimaced at sudden aromas of sweat, cigarette smoke, and stale cologne.

'I managed to get away from New York earlier than I had anticipated. So I thought I would come straight here.' Hendrik stared at James then at Marti. 'Aren't you going to introduce me?'

'Yes, of course. Mr Wu, this is my brother, Hendrik. Hendrik, James Wu of Hong Kong. Mr Wu asked us to authenticate a parcel of diamonds for him.'

Hendrik pushed out his hand. 'Nice to do business with you, James. I assume my sister has told you that I have taken over the company. My father is retiring. Now, are these they?' He gestured to the diamonds on the table.

Marti stepped in front of him. 'I have just finished examining them, Hendrik.'

Hendrik ignored her and sat down at the table. He looked back at James. 'This won't take long. Now, let's see what we have here.'

Marti pressed her lips together and counted to three. 'Hendrik, they have been examined.'

Hendrik glanced up at her. Pale eyes held her gaze. 'Mr Wu will presumably not decline a second opinion from the head of the company.' He shifted his gaze and glanced at James.

James shook his head in a bemused way.

Unlike Marti, Hendrik kept up an almost running commentary as he examined each of the diamonds. Asking James their origin. Convincing himself, but not James, that they had met some years previously. Promising, if things hadn't changed too much while he had been away, that Antwerp night-life was really hot; if you knew the right places, which he did.

Marti stared pointedly at the ceiling. Hendrik was behaving as if she had just disappeared into nothing. And nothing had changed. She glanced at the splayed thighs and bulging waistline. Fat slob. If anything, his time in Zaire

had made him worse. She watched him in growing anger as
he ostentatiously marked each of her assessments with a
large tick. Hendrik slipped his eyeglass into his pocket and
pushed his chair back. 'Nice collection you have there,
James. Find you a buyer for those tomorrow.'

Marti intervened. 'I have already told Mr Wu that we
would be interested if they were for sale.'

Again, pale eyes stared at her, as if reminding her that
once again she had spoken without permission. James
cleared his throat. 'I do not have instructions to sell –
er – Hendrik, but I will bear what you have said in
mind.'

Hendrik pushed out his hand again to James. 'Fine,
fine.' He looked over his shoulder at Marti. 'Get an authentication prepared right away, will you.'

Marti glared at him then went to the bellpush on the wall
and pressed it.

James shook hands with Hendrik, at the same time cast-
ing a curious glance at Marti. If he was not mistaken, she
looked as if she was about to self-ignite. Marti walked pur-
posefully to where Hendrik and James were standing and
managed to place herself between them, with her back
almost completely turned on Hendrik. She smiled sweetly
at James. 'So nice having done business with you, Mr Wu.
As I mentioned earlier' – she gave heavy emphasis to the
word *earlier* – 'I will arrange for the authentication certificate to be ready for you tomorrow morning.'

'Thank you very much, Miss Van den Fleet. I hope we do
business again sometime.'

Hendrik moved towards the door and Marti squealed as
he stepped on the side of her foot. He gripped her arm to
steady her. She bit her lip, not knowing which was worse,
the pain in her foot or the painful pressure on her arm. She
shook herself free from Hendrik's grasp. If she didn't know
him better she would have believed that had been an accident. He made a somewhat sketchy apology then gestured

with his hand to James to precede him to the door. As James went out he turned back and smiled sympathetically at Marti. She waited until both men had left the room before bending down to rub at her foot. Hendrik really was the limit. Treating her like a minion in front of her own client.

Astrid was smiling too brightly and her eyes shone in a way Marti was unaccustomed to seeing. Marti glanced at Hendrik, who had already taken possession of his father's office and was sitting back with his feet up on the desk. She never, never could see what women found remotely interesting in Hendrik.

'Oh, Miss Van den Fleet, Mr Hendrik has asked me to be his personal secretary.'

Marti nodded. 'I hope you know what you are letting yourself in for.'

Astrid laughed gaily. Hendrik swung his feet off the desk and stood up. 'Don't listen to my sister, Astrid. When I left Zaire, my secretary out there wept.'

Marti nodded again. 'With relief.'

Hendrik managed a half smile at the sharp retort. He hitched his trousers higher up around his waist. 'Enough of my sister's badinage, Astrid. You and I have work to do. Bring me a printout of our mailing list, will you?'

'Right away, Mr Hendrik.'

'And bring some coffee.'

'Yes, Mr Hendrik.'

Hendrik watched Astrid's retreating figure with a lustful gaze until she shut the office door behind her. He swept the jacket of his suit back and stuck his hands on his hips. 'What do you make of our oriental friend, then?'

Marti shrugged. 'Difficult to say.'

'Come on, Marti, where's this feminine intuition you are supposed to have been blessed with? Wu was as coy as a twelve-year-old virgin.'

'Well, if it's Hong Kong, it has to be a wealthy

Chinese thinking of taking a permanent vacation.'

Hendrik nodded his head slowly. 'I think you've got it in one, little sister. Do you think there's a sale to be had?'

'Doubt it. Those diamonds are somebody's insurance policy.'

Hendrik stretched and yawned loudly. 'Christ, I feel terrible. When I've given the desirable Astrid a letter to send out about my return, I think I'll get off home and try to get some sleep.' He yawned again. 'My brain is still in Zaire and my stomach feels as if it is floating around New York somewhere.'

Marti raised an eyebrow. It was news to her that he even owned a brain.

He collected up his briefcase and raincoat. 'Bring last year's accounts home with you, will you? I'll look at them tonight.'

She raised her hand and gave a mock salute behind his back as he left the office.

The three men from the PSB, having completed their business with Song Enlai, arrived separately at Kai Tak airport to board a flight to Shanghai. Mui Shenlu's indiscretions had been eradicated. Song Enlai had been blown up in his own car. His unfortunate purchaser of the diamonds, Joey Heung, leader of the Thousand Clouds Gang, had been shot and the mark of a bear's paw gouged on his forehead.

The man who had acted as chauffeur the previous night kept his briefcase, containing the missing fifty diamonds, close to his side. He sipped at a cup of coffee and watched the morning news on the television screen behind the counter with apparent disinterest. The newscaster gave a brief outline of the main news stories then reported in detail on a fresh outbreak of warring between the Triads the previous night. The newscaster was replaced by a shot of the remains of Song's car. The voice-over continued with the tally of deaths as the scene changed again to show a corpse being removed from an ambulance. The sheet had been partially drawn back to show the bloody sign on his forehead. The newscaster then announced that they were going over to police headquarters for a live interview.

The spokesman for the Hong Kong police spoke in firm and reassuring tones. A major crackdown on gangland violence was already in operation. The remains found in the burnt-out car had been identified as Song Enlai, leader of the Bear's Paw Gang. Two members of the Third Moon Gang had been arrested and charged with the murder of Song Enlai. The Bear's Paw was known to have been in serious conflict with the Third Moon. Four members of the Bear's Paw Gang had been detained on suspicion of murdering, or having caused to have been murdered, Joey Heung, the leader of the Thousand Clouds Gang. A gang known to have close connections with the Third Moon Gang. The police spokesman reiterated that the matter was firmly under their control and further arrests were likely to be announced during the day. When questioned as to the whereabouts of the leader of the Third Moon, the spokesman said that too was under close investigation.

The flight to Shanghai was called and passengers were instructed to report to the embarkation gate. The man at the coffee bar drained his cup and picked up his briefcase. He glanced casually behind him. His companions had moved ahead of him. He tucked the briefcase under his arm. An expression of contempt flitted across his face as he glanced again at the television on the bar. The Hong Kong police had given themselves more credit than they deserved.

Erasmus was sitting up in a chair, watching television, when Marti and Hendrik arrived. Marti felt hurt at the expression of relief and delight on Erasmus's face when he caught sight of Hendrik.

Hendrik grasped Erasmus's hand. 'You're doing all right

for yourself, I see. That nurse out there is a real little cracker.'

Erasmus laughed. 'You should see the one who comes on at night.'

Hendrik gave him an affectionate punch on the shoulder. 'How are you?'

'I'm fine. They tell me they're going to get me up on my feet very soon.'

'Good for you.'

Erasmus turned his head. 'Hello, Marti. Come. Sit down here. Opposite Hendrik.'

She began to speak, but Erasmus turned back to Hendrik. 'It's good to see you home. Have you been to the office yet?'

'Went straight from the airport. And don't worry about a thing. Everything is under control now.'

Marti glanced sourly at Hendrik. Everything had been under control before he had arrived. Hendrik slung his arm over the back of his chair. 'Had a rather interesting client today. James Wu. Heard of him?'

Erasmus stared in front of him for a few seconds. 'Hong Kong?'

Hendrik laughed. 'On the button, Father. You certainly haven't lost your touch.'

Erasmus gave a quiet smile of pride.

'He had an interesting parcel of diamonds he wanted valuing. Top quality. Could be a sale there, if I'm not mistaken.'

Marti spoke up. 'I arranged the authentication, Father. I was very impressed, but I don't think James –'

Hendrik forcefully interrupted her. 'As I was saying, I think there's a possible sale there.'

Erasmus straightened up in the chair, his attention captured by Hendrik's conversation. 'Now that I come to think of it, I met him once at the IDE. Sure I did. I remember him telling some story about his grandfather being Scottish or something.'

'Talking about the IDE reminds me, Father. Dined with Christian Debilius when I was in New York. Asked me to send you his very good wishes. He was very sorry to hear you've been ill.'

Marti clasped her hands in her lap as Erasmus and Hendrik fell into deep conversation. She flicked at the tab on the plastic box resting on her lap. Father hadn't even asked her what she had brought for him. She glanced away in disgust as Hendrik told Erasmus a joke about a girl from Hong Kong with an extraordinary and vulgar talent. Erasmus laughed so much, it almost left him devoid of breath. Marti was relieved when the nurse appeared and said it was time for visitors to leave. She got up and kissed her father on the cheek. 'I've brought you some grapes, Father. They're seedless.'

'Oh, good. Hate seeds.'

Hendrik shook his father's hand again and promised to visit again the next day. Marti tightened her lips in irritation when he reminded Erasmus that everything was under control. There was nothing to worry about. Marti turned when she and Hendrik reached the door and gave her father a cheery smile and a wave, but Erasmus was already engaged in animated conversation with the nurse. The charge nurse got up from her desk as they passed. 'Good evening. How did you find Mr Van den Fleet today?'

Marti was about to speak, but Hendrik cut in. 'I don't think the old fellow's doing too badly, by the look of things. He seems very lively. But then I know who we have to thank for that.' Hendrik gave one of his rare open smiles.

The nurse returned his smile graciously. 'We do our best for all our patients, Mr Van den Fleet, but I think he has just received the best tonic of all. He talks about you such a lot.'

Hendrik laughed. 'All good, I hope.'

The nurse smiled mischievously. 'Mostly, Mr Van den Fleet, mostly.'

Marti slung her bag over her shoulder. 'I'll try to come in

again and see my father tomorrow morning, before I go to work.'

The nurse gave a brief nod. 'Very good, Miss Van den Fleet.'

All ten lanes of the ring expressway were crowded with fast-moving traffic. Marti checked her mirror and swung the car into the inner lane. Hendrik gave a sharp sigh of exasperation. 'What *are* you doing?'

She answered slowly and deliberately. 'I'm getting into the correct lane for the tunnel. I would have thought that was perfectly obvious.'

'Jesus. You could have overtaken the next six trucks before getting into lane. Now we have to sit and inhale diesel fumes.'

She pressed her lips together and gripped the steering wheel.

Hendrik rested his elbow on the edge of the car window. 'Old man's not looking too bad, is he? When he gets out, I think we should send him on holiday for a bit. You can go with him. Take care of him.'

'What about you taking care of him?'

Hendrik glanced at her disparagingly. 'Don't be stupid. Anyway, he prefers you to look after him. He always has.'

When they exited from the tunnel and drove towards the centre of the city, the road narrowed to a single lane. Marti slowed down and stopped behind an illegally parked truck and waited for a gap in the oncoming traffic.

'For God's sake, Marti, what's the matter with you? You could drive an armoured truck through that gap.' Hendrik stared at her in irritation.

Marti swung the steering wheel sharply and pulled out. As she passed the truck there was a sound of crunching metal.

'Jesus Christ, what are you doing?'

She jammed on the brakes then leapt out of the car to

survey the damage. She shut her eyes for an instant at the
sight of a jagged dent running the entire length of the passenger door. She took a deep breath and walked round to
the driver's door again, got in, and pulled over to the side, a
few feet ahead of the truck. Hendrik went to speak, but she
turned on him. 'Shut up, Hendrik. Just shut up. That was
your fault. I knew there wasn't enough room.'

'Don't you tell me to shut up. That was your own fault.'

'It wasn't.'

'It fucking well was. Hasn't anyone ever told you, when
you overtake a vehicle you are supposed to drive around it,
not through it.' He pulled out a packet of cigarettes and lit
one. 'If I remember correctly, you couldn't ride a tricycle,
even with trainers, without falling off.'

She gripped the steering wheel. 'And if I remember correctly, I wouldn't have fallen off and broken my nose, if
you hadn't pushed me.' She glanced in the side mirror. Her
heart sank as the burly driver of the truck approached the
car with a decidedly unfriendly expression on his face.

Marti and Hendrik arrived at the apartment in tight-lipped
silence. She went to the kitchen and poured herself a glass
of wine. She leaned against the refrigerator door. Hendrik
had sat with a smug expression on his face while that creep
of a French truck-driver had verbally abused her. She
couldn't understand what he was complaining about. He had
only suffered a smashed tail light. She would probably need
a new door fitted and the whole side of the car resprayed.
She went to the sitting room and switched on the television.

Hendrik came into the sitting room, strode across to the
television and switched it off, before slinging a briefcase,
containing the company reports, on to the table by
Erasmus's chair.

Marti stared at him. 'What are you doing?'

Hendrik sprawled out in the chair and unzipped the briefcase. 'What does it look like?'

She got up and switched the television on again.

'Switch that off. I can't concentrate with that thing blaring away.'

'*I* am watching the news.'

'Watch it later. I want you to go through these accounts with me.'

Her mind quickly scanned the obvious scenario. No way was she going to be treated like some low-grade employee by him. She stood up. 'If there is anything you don't understand, make a note of it. I'm going to wash my hair.'

Hendrik stared after her as Marti swept out of the living room. He lit up a cigarette. She'd always believed she was better than him. Never let him forget for a second who he was, or, more precisely, who he was not. She never tired of playing that game. She was a genuine Van den Fleet and that placed her somewhere near the left hand of God, or so she thought. He flicked the ash from his cigarette. It was time little sister learned a few overdue lessons. He picked up the company report and carefully read through it.

Marti looked around the bathroom in disgust. Two soggy towels had been dumped on the floor. A pair of underpants half hung out of the laundry basket. She kicked the towels to one side and went to the washbasin. He really was a slob. Within four hours he had the place looking like a rubbish dump.

Hendrik pushed the bathroom door open. Marti held the tangle of wet hair up from her face. 'What do you think you're doing.' She stared angrily at him. 'Get out.'

Hendrik leaned against the side of the door. 'Excuse me. I hadn't realised you were carrying out some private and intimate ablution. I thought you said you were washing your hair.'

Marti flipped a towel around her hair and twisted it tightly.

'What's for dinner?'

She stared up at him. 'What do you mean, what's for dinner?'

He made gestures of eating with a knife and fork. 'You know, that stuff you put on a plate. I think it's called food.'

She turned away and began rubbing at her hair. 'Don't know why you are asking me. I'm not your servant. If you want something to eat, get it yourself.'

His mouth tightened in anger. 'Look, I'm not putting up with this. This is my first day back home and all you have done so far is to make me feel as unwelcome as possible. I mean it, Marti, I'm not going to put up with all of this.'

She carefully screwed the top back on to the bottle of shampoo. A little twinge of guilt crept over her. Perhaps she had been a bit childish. Besides, she wasn't in the mood to face one of Hendrik's tempers. 'What do you want to eat?'

'Don't mind. Whatever you are having.' Mollified by her sudden change in attitude, Hendrik backed out of the bathroom. 'I'll pour some drinks while you're drying your hair.'

Fang Ka-Shing, making his regular twice-weekly visit to his mistress, carefully negotiated the hairpin bends leading to the Peak. The stately houses built on the steep hillside had originally been constructed for the British in their efforts to escape from the heat and humidity of Hong Kong. Two thirds of the way up, Fang swung the limousine into a small driveway leading to one of the mansions. The electronically controlled gates swung open and he drove up to the house.

Lai Chunxia called herself Candy. On deciding to adopt a Westernised first name, it seemed eminently sensible to follow the advice of the American businessman, to whom she had been loaned, who told her she was sweet as sugar candy. Two Americans later, she had acquired enough gifts to afford an operation to reshape her eyelids. Americans were generous, but smelt vaguely of the cleanser her maid sprinkled in the water closet every morning. But Americans were things of the past. Now she was the delight of Fang Ka-Shing. It was a delight that showed no signs of ebbing and further fuelled her ambitions to become part of the wealthy Chinese set in Hong Kong.

Fang's heart skipped a beat as he entered the hallway. Candy was wearing a black negligee, loosely tied at her bosom, and she had made herself up in the Western fashion. It was a style she adopted with frustrating infrequency. It depended much on whether she approved of the gifts he had sent. He proffered a bunch of flowers and was rewarded with a brush of moist lips against his cheek. 'Did you receive my gift, Candy?'

She kissed his cheek again. 'Of course, Big Bear.'

He sighed with pleasure. The use of the nickname foretold her willingness to participate in acts of Western decadence. 'Why are you not wearing it, then?'

She gave a shrill laugh. 'No one wears a fur coat in the house.' She slipped her arm through his. 'You must take me somewhere special, then I shall wear it for you.'

He glanced around to make sure the maid was no longer in the hall, then buried his face into Candy's enticing, shadowy cleavage. She sighed contentedly at his silent acquiescence. The Jockey Club restaurant. That was where she would wear her new fur coat. She frowned slightly as she considered the problem of how to show off to maximum effect the inside label of the coat, which proclaimed it to be genuine Russian sable. There was little point in wearing it if others were left in ignorance of its quality. Fang raised his head from her bosom and looked pointedly up at the staircase. Her perfume had heightened his ardour.

Fang had not hesitated in accepting Pa's invitation to join his private business venture. The reward for keeping a close watch on Chan Chunling's activities, both in Hong Kong and Shanghai, was substantial enough for Fang to afford Candy's extravagances in return for her deeply yearned-for favours. His wife, as he continually complained to Candy, was no wife at all. What wife could consider herself loyal when she refused to grant her husband's desires? Candy would gently smooth his hair and listen patiently to the litany of complaints until he eventually lasped into silence, then she would tell him what a stupid woman he had for a wife. She should consider herself very, very lucky to be married to such a very clever and very important man. Was he not the chairman of the Chinese People's Association for International Trade? He would nod his head, as if grateful for the reminder. Candy would then reach out for the bottle of aromatic oil on the bedside table and proceed to give him a massage that a hankering tourist in a back-street Tsimshatsui 'girlie' bar would envy. His groans of ecstasy would be interspersed with Candy's gentle questioning as to what her very clever and important man had been doing that day. The information gleaned from him provided her with another useful source of gifts.

The summarily executed Joey Heung, head of the Thousand Clouds Gang, was distantly related to Candy by marriage. His legitimate business had been a thriving legal practice. Fang's 'pillow-talk', faithfully reported by Candy, had provided Joey with useful insider knowledge when acting on behalf of Western companies negotiating with the Chinese People's Association for International Trade, for which they paid handsomely.

To many of the inhabitants of Hong Kong the various Triad Gangs were a way of life: an expensive way of life if it involved paying protection money; a fearful way of life if one had the misfortune to incur their displeasure. Joey's gift to Candy, in return for her information, was a salary that appeared on his company's payroll as PR consultancy fees, together with his personal protection as a member of his family.

Fang stirred slowly from his slumber as the little bird on the gaudily enamelled, musical clock rotated slowly as its song heralded the approaching hour of six o'clock. He rubbed at his eyes then leapt out of Candy's fur-covered bed. He looked down for a moment at his limp penis then glanced at Candy. To awaken her would be to awaken his flesh. The little bird on the clock whirred to a halt and ended its song, closing its beak with a faint click. Fang sighed and bent down to pick up his underpants from the floor. Discretion required that he should leave the house while the Peak road was still deserted. Candy rolled over on her back and stretched her arms above her head. Her eyes snapped open quickly. She did not usually rise until midday, but today was an important day.

Astrid placed a cup of coffee on the desk, by Hendrik's side. She glanced at him, unsure whether it was wise to speak. Yesterday's fascination with his sexually charged persona was now tempered with some caution. Hendrik had arrived in the office in a black mood which was directed at everybody. 'Er, Mr Hendrik, the printers have just delivered copies of the newsletter.'

He glanced up from the file in front of him. 'Bring them in. Is my sister in yet?'

'No, Mr Hendrik.'

He glanced at his watch. 'Tell her to see me as soon as she comes in.'

'Yes, Mr Hendrik.'

Hendrik pulled a bottle of indigestion tablets out of his pocket and gulped two of them down with a mouthful of coffee. Two helpings of Marti's special Indonesian curry and too much alcohol the previous night had left his insides feeling like a cement mixer. He had woken up late with a splitting headache to find that Marti had already left, taking her car with her. He had spent twenty minutes trying to get a taxi, was then held up for a further fifteen minutes in heavy traffic, and arrived at the office with a strong urge to kill anyone or anything that stood in his way.

Marti stuck her head around the door of Astrid's office. 'Good morning. Any mail for me, Astrid?'

'Yes, Miss Van den Fleet, and good morning. Oh, and Mr Hendrik said he wanted to see you as soon as you came in.'

Marti gave a brief nod of acknowledgement. Astrid hesitated, not knowing whether she should say anything further or not. 'Er, hope you don't mind my saying, Miss Van den Fleet, but I don't think Mr Hendrik finds it a particularly good morning.'

Marti smiled in amusement. 'Don't worry, Astrid, you'll soon get used to it. My brother never has good mornings.'

Hendrik glared at Marti when she walked into his office. She pretended not to notice and sat down by the desk. He rubbed at his brow, then fumbled in his pocket for a bottle of aspirin. The piledrivers had started up in his head again. 'These accounts for last year. At most, I suppose I have to be grateful that you haven't managed to plunge the company into insolvency.'

'What –'

'Shut up and listen. I haven't got time to repeat myself. As far as I can see, while Father has been ill, you have just been on one extended ego trip.' He picked up one of the copies of the monthly newsletter. 'Is this the kind of bullshit you send out to our clients?'

She started to speak, but he didn't give her chance. 'Quote. We have been doing good business. Unquote. Who are you trying to fool, Marti? Yourself?'

'What are you talking about?' Her mouth tightened. His hangover was his problem. She wasn't going to be spoken to like that.

'I am talking about the fact that I do more business in one day than you have done in a fucking year.' He lit up a cigarette. '*Good* business. What the hell do you know about good business? You wouldn't recognise it even if you discovered it between your legs.'

Marti stood up, her face flushing in anger. 'Don't you dare speak to me like that. Who do you think you are?'

The telephone rang out and Hendrik snatched it up. 'Yes.'

'Mr Debilius is on the line and Mr Wu has arrived to see Miss Van den Fleet.' Astrid spoke timidly.

'OK.' Hendrik put his hand over the receiver. 'Wu's here. Go and deal with him.'

Marti's colour deepened at his peremptory instruction. She clenched her hands and spoke with icy dignity. 'I have every intention. He is my client, in case you have forgotten.'

James Wu leapt from the chair as soon as Marti appeared, and held out his hand to her. 'Good morning, Miss Van den Fleet.'

She took his hand briefly. 'Good morning.'

He studied her face curiously. She had that same look as yesterday. Agitation. Temper. Something had upset her.

'Astrid is bringing the authentication document. She won't be a moment.' Marti turned at the sound of hurrying footsteps. 'Ah, here she is now.' She took the papers from Astrid and scanned them briefly before handing them to James. 'I think you will find everything in order, Mr Wu.'

'Thank you.' James sat down again and carefully checked the document, then put it into his briefcase. He smiled. 'As you say, everything in order. Shall I settle your fees now?'

'That won't be necessary, Mr Wu. We will send you a note at the end of the month.'

He stood up again. 'Well, thank you for your assistance. I –' He stopped and turned as Hendrik swept the door open.

'James, nice to meet you again.' Hendrik pumped James's hand vigorously. 'You have received the authentication documents?'

'Yes, thank you.'

'No problems?'

'No, no.'

Marti cut in to prevent Hendrik from dominating the conversation. 'Thank you for coming in to see us. As I mentioned, Mr Wu, we will send a note of our fees on to you.' Marti edged towards the door making sure she didn't have to pass within spitting distance of Hendrik. 'How long are you staying in Antwerp?'

'Just until tomorrow morning. I was going to –' James was interrupted again, this time by Astrid popping her head around the door.

She raised a hand in supplication. 'Forgive me interrupting, but there's an urgent call for Mr Hendrik from Zaire.'

Hendrik rolled his eyes. 'Are they ever not urgent.' He pushed his hand out to James again. 'I'll be in touch, James.' He turned and quickly followed on Astrid's heels.

James watched Hendrik rush back along the corridor. Brother and sister had managed, if he was not mistaken, to avoid even looking at each other, let alone speaking to each other. Odd. Very odd. He turned and smiled at Marti. 'I was wondering if you and your brother would join me for lunch.'

'That is very kind.' Marti took less than a second to seize the opportunity of spiking Hendrik's guns. 'I'm afraid my brother is terribly busy, as you can see, but I think we can probably muster one Van den Fleet to join you.'

James laughed. 'If lunch isn't convenient, may I suggest perhaps dinner? I would very much welcome your company.'

She thought for a moment. She had seen her father. A dinner engagement would excuse her from cooking dinner for Hendrik. 'Why not? That sounds a lovely idea.' She walked with James to the front door and hurriedly opened it and ushered him out, at the sound of Hendrik's voice in the corridor. If there was the remotest chance of James Wu selling the diamonds, she was going to be the one to handle it. It was most definitely not going to be Hendrik. She knew more about striking a bargain than he ever could.

Astrid collided with Hendrik as she rushed out of her office. Her eyes widened in surprise as hands, in a pretence of helping her regain her balance, gripped her sides, reaching high enough to press against her breasts. She stepped back quickly, embarrassed by the coarse physical contact. 'Sorry, Mr Hendrik, I thought you were Miss Van den Fleet.'

'Can't you tell the difference yet? I'm the good-looking one.'

She edged her way past him. She caught sight of Marti climbing the stairs and hurried to her. 'Miss Van den Fleet, Mr Yasim is on the line for you. I told him you were just taking leave of a client. He said he would hold.'

Marti's face brightened. 'Good. I was beginning to think he had changed his mind.' She ran to her office and grabbed at the telephone. 'Beni, hello. Marti here.'

'Ah, Marti, how lovely to hear your voice. I was beginning to think you were avoiding me.'

'Would such a thing ever cross my mind?'

'I trust not. How are you?'

'Fine. You?'

'Very well, thank you. Listen, Marti, my business has taken longer to finalise than I had predicted. I am leaving Geneva today, but I shall be returning again at the end of the month. Have you come across anything that will be of interest to my client?'

Her face clouded with disappointment. She had been expecting a firm order. She decided to keep her options open. 'I may have by the time you get back.'

'Splendid. I have left my telephone number with your secretary. I must say goodbye for the moment, Marti, my flight leaves in an hour. Let us hope that we meet soon.'

'Yes, of course. 'Bye.' She put the telephone down. If. If.

She chewed at her lip. The diamonds she had authenticated for James Wu were the kind of merchandise Beni would buy on sight. If there was a possibility of Wu selling, she could turn the diamonds round so fast Hendrik would be left out in the cold. She gave a grim-faced smile. Seriously out in the cold.

Frankie Heung slung his travel bag over his shoulder and strutted into the main concourse of Hong Kong's international airport. His nickname was derived from his passable imitation of Frank Sinatra singing 'My Way': a trick he had acquired through his predilection for gambling in Las Vegas, when business permitted. His detractors referred to him as Eggroll Heung because, as the Number Two in the Unicorn Gang based in San Francisco, he was responsible for overseeing the collection of insurance from Chinese restaurateurs.

The girl at the reception desk raised her head as Frankie dumped his bag on the counter. Her gaze took in the strongly patterned, checked jacket, the gold watch, and the diamond-studded cufflinks. No doubt about it. American and wealthy. She smiled brightly at him. 'Good morning, sir, can I assist you?'

'Why not? I was supposed to have been met when my flight landed. My name is Heung. Frankie Heung.'

Something in his tone of voice indicated that he was a man to be taken very seriously. She smiled at him again. 'One moment, Mr Heung, and I will see what I can do for you.' She bent to speak into the public address system, but glanced up as a gauntly thin man hurried to the desk.

He lightly touched Frankie's arm. 'Sorry to keep you waiting, Mr Heung. If you'd like to come this way, Mr Heung.'

Frankie ignored him and glanced at the receptionist. He leaned forward to read the name on her lapel badge. 'What does the ''J'' stand for?'

She smiled again. 'Just call me Jojo.'

'OK. Jojo. When do you get off from this place?'

'Five.'

'Ever been to the Club Manhattan?'

She shook her head and looked at him expectantly. The Manhattan was the most expensive nightclub in the city.

'Be there for happy hour and I'll buy you a drink.' He flashed a quick smile, displaying two gold fillings.

'Thank you, Mr Heung.'

'That's OK. You tried to be helpful. I like that.' He picked up his travel bag and tossed it to the man waiting by his side. He followed the man to the doors. He spoke quietly, but with menace. 'Keep me waiting just one more time, buddy, and I'll have you cemented into the fucking parking lot. Read me?'

The man clutched the travel bag to his chest. 'Yes, Mr Heung. Sorry, Mr Heung. The traffic was –'

'I don't want to hear about the goddam traffic. OK?'

'OK, Mr Heung.'

Candy ran the tip of her tongue over her lips and smoothed the sides of her skirt. The way Frankie had looked her over signalled a strong possibility that her greatest ambition could be fulfilled: to go and live in the United States. Uncle Joey had provided her with a passport and a visa for Australia, but America was her preferred destination.

Frankie stuck a cigar in his mouth and waited for the man standing at his side in constant attendance to light it for him. Frankie leaned back in his chair. His father, Joey, had been united with his ancestors, his mother consoled, and a quick look through the accounts showed that the Thousand Clouds Gang needed some reorganisation – with no disrespect to his father. The clientele must believe they were living in Disneyland. Frankie puffed on the cigar. 'I'm taking over from my father.' He flicked an imaginary piece of fluff from the lapel of his jacket. 'Prepared to do for me what you did for him, Candy?'

She gave a sultry smile and rested a long, pointed finger-nail lightly on his knee. 'Whatever you want, Frankie.'

He jerked his knee away. 'Get one thing straight. I don't sleep with whores.'

She jerked her hand back, as if the offending finger had been burnt. 'No need to talk like that to me, Frankie.'

'OK, just wanted you to know where you stand. This guy Fang. I want something personal on him.' He jabbed his cigar at her. 'You provide it. OK?'

'OK, Frankie.'

He got up from the chair and signalled to his aide to follow him out of the room.

Candy picked up her bag. She frowned to herself as she got to her feet; her dreams of living in the United States fading rapidly. Frankie was a bad-mouthed man and vicious.

James Wu stopped and stared up at the Cathedral of Our Lady. He craned his neck back to take in the towering vista. 'That is magnificent. When was it built?'

Marti pursed her lips. 'About the middle of the four-teenth century, I think. It's supposed to have two towers, but we didn't get around to building the second one.'

James laughed. He was beginning to enjoy the company of his attractive guest and her dry sense of humour.

'I'm going to have to drag you away, James. The restaurant gets a bit fussy, if people are late.'

'Yes, of course.'

They quickened their pace across the square. Marti pulled her raincoat more firmly around her shoulders. The quick shower of rain had left the evening air refreshed, but rather chilly. She glanced around her. A few tourists were brave enough to sit at outdoor tables drinking beer. A feel-ing of well-being washed over her. The day's traumas were beginning to recede. She hadn't even had to think of an excuse to keep Hendrik firmly out of the way. The earlier telephone call from Zaire had left him still closeted in his office when it was time for her to leave.

James stared with great concentration at the menu as Marti gave a running commentary on each of the dishes. He had shyly professed always liking to sample the food of the country he was in, much to her relief. She had intended to take him to a restaurant serving Chinese food, although she herself was not overfond of it. She insisted he tried the mousse of woodcock. It was delicious.

Their choice of meal decided upon, James thought it time for a little gentle probing. She still looked rather tense and he suspected that it had a lot to do with her brother's arrival the previous day. Until he had showed up, she had appeared to behave in a perfectly normal way, then her manner changed. There was a certain tautness, a forced brightness, that wasn't there before. He picked up his glass of vermouth and took an experimental sip. 'I'm sorry that your brother couldn't join us. He must be very pleased to return home after such a long stay in Zaire. Ten years wasn't it?'

'Yes, almost ten.'

He took another sip of the vermouth. 'Your father must also be pleased to have his family reunited once again in the business.'

She suppressed a smile. He was fishing. Very discreetly. She picked up her own glass. He might as well know. He would sooner or later. 'Actually, my father is retiring, James.'

'Ah, I see, and you and Hendrik will be jointly running the business from now on?'

She took a sip of vermouth. Hendrik's letter would be on James's desk by the time he got back to Hong Kong. 'Actually, Hendrik is taking over the business from my father.'

James stared at her, then quickly covered up his surprise. 'Will that not make him the sixth generation to run the business? When I was at your office I admired the paintings of your ancestors.'

She twirled the glass between her fingers. 'Yes, I suppose it will be the sixth generation.'

The waiter brought the first course to the table. James decided to let the conversation lapse for the moment. He had learned enough already to give much food for thought. He sampled the mousse and nodded his head vigorously. 'Excellent.' He dabbed at his mouth with his napkin. 'I wish Anna was here to try it.'

She propped her chin on her hand. 'Forgive my curiosity, but who's Anna?'

'My sister. We share an apartment together. Accommodation in Hong Kong is very scarce. Fortunately, Anna and I get on very well together. She is a very successful jewellery designer. She, I think you say, housekeeps for me, and I, in return, pass on any commissions that I get to know of.'

'I think that's called good teamwork.'

'Like your brother and yourself?'

Marti hastily put a piece of food into her mouth to avoid answering.

'People always say that Anna and I are very alike, but neither of us can see it. We think we are very unalike. Do people say the same thing about you and Hendrik?'

'No, not really. He is ten years older than me; I suppose, because of it, we haven't had much in common.'

Marti glanced across at the waiter and signalled him to come and remove their plates. Talk of family relationships had brought on a cold feeling of depression, sweeping away her earlier cheerfulness. She picked up her glass. 'Do you travel a lot, James?'

'It depends. Obviously, New York. The IDE option days.'

'What do you think of New York?'

'Wonderfully exciting place, provided you have a good friend to guide you around.'

She laughed. 'It can be daunting if you are on your own. I know.'

The conversation was interrupted by the arrival of the meat course. James inspected it with great interest. 'Now you said this is roast veal's heart, yes?'

Marti smiled. 'Kidney; and veal is just very young cow.'

'Ah, yes. In the PRC they have many such exotic dishes. Braised bear's paw with brown sauce is a great delicacy, although scarce.'

Her eyes widened. 'Bear?'

'Yes.' He cut into the veal and chewed slowly. 'This is very good. Very tender.'

'Do you like the flavour?'

'Oh yes. Very aromatic.' He carefully cut into the veal again. It was time to pick up the threads of their earlier conversation. 'Do you go to New York frequently too?'

'No. I've only been there once. I went with my father. He was visiting the IDE and took me along as well.'

'It is quite a place, isn't it?'

'I don't know. I've never been inside.'

He glanced at her questioningly.

'I am not an option bearer, James. I know of no woman who is.'

He nodded. He studied the food on his plate. Of course. He had been stupid. That was why Hendrik Van den Fleet had taken over the company. He carefully speared a piece of veal on to his fork. 'And how is business? In Hong Kong we have been doing some very brisk trading over the last twelve months.'

'Same here. We have been doing a lot of good business with the Israelis.'

He sighed. 'Sometimes I think too much business can be a bad thing. My volume of trading is expanding faster than I can cope with. What we lack in Hong Kong is high-calibre people. So many have left.' He laid his fork on the side of the plate. 'I hope you do not mind my asking, but if you know of anyone interested in working with me in Hong Kong, I would be grateful. I would be prepared to consider a consultancy position if necessary, with a share in the profits. Naturally, it would have to be the right type of person. Someone like yourself, for instance.'

'I'll see what I can do.'

He pulled out a business card from his jacket and quickly wrote his private telephone number on it. 'Please, have this. If you want to get in touch, don't hesitate to use that number. If I'm not there, Anna will take a message.'

She slipped the card into her bag. She would ask around. Although no one immediately came to mind, somebody might be interested, and a favour done never hurt business relations. She picked up her wine glass and studied it. 'I must say, James, after seeing the diamonds you brought in yesterday, you certainly deal in quality. I am not pressing the point, but if they ever do come up for sale I have a definite buyer.'

He gave a wry smile. 'I would, too.'

She laughed. 'Come on, I had to try. Just once.'

'Please, don't apologise. Business must be created.' He glanced around the restaurant and noticed a man light up a cheroot. 'Would you mind if I smoked?'

'Not at all.'

He lit up a cigarette and relaxed back in his chair. Martina Van den Fleet was a very attractive woman and had made the first part of his task easy enough to complete.

A Red Flag cadre limousine swung into the entrance to the Sound and Vibration Research Institute in Anshan. Professor Li peered out from the corner of the window in his office. An expression of distaste crossed his face as three smartly dressed men, in well-tailored business suits, got out of the car. He gave a quiet snort of disgust and drew back from the window. Wasting time. That was all it was. Wasting time. They would understand little if anything, but would consider themselves competent to question his work when they returned to Beijing.

The lecture room contained Li's first line of attack on visitors. Twelve time chairs: chairs so uncomfortable to sit on, that within a very short space of time, even the most keenly interested visitor would quickly be made aware of his physical discomfort. His second line of attack was a deliberately lengthy and boring account of how diamonds are produced naturally. After that, visitors were usually grateful to be invited to move along to the laboratory. There, they would be made to stand for fifteen minutes watching and hearing absolutely nothing happening. Rarely, a visitor would pluck up the courage to ask exactly what was going on and would be instantly silenced by a stream of technical gobbledegook. Sensible visitors contented themselves with maintaining an expression of deep understanding and interest. They were rewarded by an invitation to lunch.

Li's glance swept over his audience of three. He placed the wooden ruler he had been using as a pointer down on to the table by his side. 'Diamonds are nothing more than an allotropic form of carbon, as we have clearly demonstrated.' He clasped his hands behind his back. 'So, to recapitulate our findings. Number one: carbon. Number two: heat. Number three: pressure.' From the corner of his eye, he noticed one of the men shift from one haunch to the other. He gestured to the picture of a diamond on the screen behind him. 'Now you know how to make diamonds. Simple, isn't it?'

More appreciative visitors would, at this juncture, have tittered quietly at his joke. The three men sitting in front of Li remained silent. He stared at the screen for a moment. One of the chairs creaked as its occupant shifted slightly. He would punish them by continuing the lecture for a further ten minutes. 'There is one further essential component to carbon, heat and pressure that we have not mentioned.

Time. Around three thousand million years is the norm. If you have the patience to wait that long, you will produce a diamond.' Li pressed the button on the side of the slide projector and a new image appeared on the screen. 'But first we will consider the molecular structure of diamonds. From this diagram, you will see the orderly structure of carbon atoms. Each atom is the centre of a tetrahedron, linked to four further atoms at its corners.' He turned and stared balefully at the person who had just lit up a cigarette. He pointed to the no-smoking sign on the wall.

One of the other two men got up from his chair. 'Professor Li, my colleagues and I have found your lecture most interesting. Unfortunately, our time here is limited. May we please see how your process actually works.'

Li stared the man out, but he refused to be intimidated and stared back just as coldly. 'Very well.' Li snapped off the projector. 'If you will follow me.'

Li's assistant was waiting in the laboratory. Li nodded to him, then made a semi-circular movement of his arm at his visitors. 'If you will please stand here.'

The three men did as they were bid.

'The process which I have invented to produce diamond film coating uses exactly the same elements as the earth itself. Carbon. Heat. Pressure. But there is one exception. Time. In this laboratory we can produce in a day what has taken the earth three thousand million years.' He looked around at his visitors, allowing them time to digest his startling piece of information. Satisfied that they looked suitably impressed, he continued. 'By using ultrasonic sound waves we recreate the implosive effect of the earth's natural forces.' Li turned and pointed to a ceramic-clad furnace in the centre of the room. 'This is an ultrasonic sound matter stabiliser.' He bent down. 'Here, is a generator. The source of the ultrasonic power. It emits sound waves at a frequency of 40,000 cycles per second.' He straightened up again. 'And up here is the furnace.'

The three men moved in to take a closer look at the equipment. Li clasped his hands behind his back. 'I will now, for your benefit, explain as simply as I can something of the process itself. When the apparatus is activated, criss-crossing beams of sound bombard carbon atoms. The energy with which each atom collides with another is sufficient to create instant fusion. You will remember I explained the crystalline nature of natural diamonds, that no natural diamond is totally flawless?'

The three visitors nodded dutifully.

'Very well. Flaws, however minute, can be detected where crystalline domains meet. The diamond film that we create here, although the carbon atoms fuse together, are of an amorphous nature. Unlike experiments to produce film using natural diamond grit, our diamond film does not have the orderly crystalline structure of natural diamonds. We therefore produce what can be accurately described as the perfect diamond film. Denser. Harder. Without flaws.'

The man who had previously lit up a cigarette in defiance of the no-smoking sign, cleared his throat. 'I trust that we are to see a demonstration of the – er – matter stabiliser, Professor Li.'

'Indeed.' Li nodded to his assistant. 'Switch on.' He folded his arms against his chest.

There was complete silence for just over four minutes, before one of the men shuffled his feet impatiently. 'Professor Li, why is there no sound coming from the matter stabiliser? I thought you said you used beams of sound.'

Li gave him a withering look. 'You thought correctly, but the range of human hearing is limited to 16,000 cycles per second. You are incapable of hearing ultrasonic sound.'

The man unconsciously let his head droop and cast his gaze downwards, as if in disgrace. His shameful ignorance had been observed by everyone in the room.

The other two men glanced at each other and remained silent, until ten minutes later when Li's assistant opened a small hatch in the side of the furnace. The men leaned forward.

'There, gentlemen, is our diamond film.' Li permitted himself a modest smile.

The men straightened up again and glanced at each other. Li looked at them contemptuously. Peasants. They had not understood even one word.

One man cleared his throat. 'This has been very interesting to observe, Professor Li.'

Li pushed his hands into the pockets of his white coat. Interesting. That was all they could say. Interesting. His limited patience worn out, Li announced it was time for lunch. After they had filled themselves from the trough, perhaps, they would go back from where they came.

Hendrik stopped in mid-speech as Marti opened the sitting-room door. He gave a quick wink at Johannes. She stared at them both. Hendrik had obviously been in the middle of telling one of his boring and no doubt vulgar jokes. Marti stared at Hendrik pointedly. He drained his whisky glass and got to his feet. 'Time to throw myself out.'

Johannes gave an embarrassed laugh. 'Look, stay if you want to. I wouldn't like you to think –'

'Would never dream of ruining one of my little sister's dinner parties. Know my place.' He slapped Johannes on the shoulder. 'Enjoy yourselves and remember, if you can't be good be careful.' Marti raised her eyes to the ceiling. If Hendrik made one more sexual innuendo, she would hit him. Johannes gave a half-hearted laugh. 'And you, Hendrik.'

Marti stepped back into the hall to let Hendrik pass. 'When will you be back?'

Hendrik gave a lewd grin. 'If this girl-friend of yours is all she's cracked up to be, not at all.'

Marti heaved a sigh of relief at the sound of the front door being shut with a bang. At least Hendrik would be out of sight and mind for a couple of hours. She experienced a twinge of guilt at what she had let an old school-friend in for, in persuading her to go out on the town with Hendrik. She consoled herself with the thought that Berenice had done the same thing to her a few years previously. Berenice's cousin had come complete with bad breath and hot, clammy hands, and had talked about nothing except computers.

Johannes got to his feet when Marti returned to the sitting room. 'Can I help in the kitchen?'

'No thanks, dinner is almost ready.'

He pushed his hands into his pockets and glanced down briefly at his shoes. He supposed he should say something, although she was in one of her brittle moods. 'I suppose it's not really any of my business, but you should have let Hendrik stay if he wanted to, you know. I certainly wouldn't have minded.'

'I would.' She spoke firmly. 'You forget, I have to work with him all day. He then expects me to come home and wait on him hand and foot. I need *some* respite, Johannes.'

He drained his glass. 'You need a holiday.'

She shot him a warning glance. 'What does that mean?'

'It means you need a break, that's all. You've worked like a slave over the last year. This business with your father is very worrying. You're tired. Dare I suggest, as a good friend, Marti, that it's easy to get things out of perspective. Hendrik isn't a bad fellow, you know. Just try to avoid antagonising him.'

'Who's antagonising him?'

'You know what I mean, Marti. You two have been fighting ever since I can remember. OK, so he's a macho type of a guy, but he's always been like that. Just ignore him.'

She gave an abrupt laugh. 'Hendrik is a bullying wimp.'

'I don't know about that. I remember once, he saved me from getting a beating from some kids across the river. As a boy I used to look up to him. Even envy him, I suppose.'

'You! Envy Hendrik! What could you possibly envy about Hendrik?'

'He was good at everything. Learning. Sport. Girls. Everything I wasn't good at, I suppose.'

She linked her arm through his. 'You are very good at being a friend, Johannes. That's what really matters.'

'So, listen to what I'm saying. Do you know when your father is coming out of hospital?'

'A couple of days, if he keeps on making progress.'

'Well then, when he's settled back at home again.' He squeezed her arm against his side. 'You take a holiday. You need one.'

She shook her head. 'I can't, I really can't. If I went away, when I got back I would probably find Hendrik had given my desk to somebody else.'

'Come on, that's ridiculous.'

'Don't you be so sure. He goes on and on about all the changes he's going to make. I suspect I am one of them.'

'Your father wouldn't let that happen, you know that.'

'I don't know that. Father is happy with anything Hendrik wants to do.' She shot him a sideways glance. 'I was just the stopgap, remember.'

Johannes sighed inwardly. It had been right for the business, but wrong for Marti. 'Let me replenish your glass. Where is it?'

'Think I left it in the kitchen and changing the subject won't, unfortunately, Johannes, change the situation.'

'I know, I know. What your father did was tough, very tough on you, but he had little choice, if you look at things logically.'

She rubbed a hand across her eyes. 'I am tired of always being the one to have to look at things logically. Looking at things logically just means agreeing to what Father and Hendrik want for themselves.'

'Look, sit down here and I will go and fetch your glass.'

When Johannes returned from the kitchen he replenished

both their glasses and came to sit down beside her on the sofa. 'Marti, I know we said we would never discuss this again, because neither of us felt it was important to us, but if you would like us to get married, I wouldn't mind.'

She frowned in puzzlement. 'Why should we get married?'

'I just thought that might be what you want. I thought, perhaps, you felt it was time to lead a life of your own. Away from Van den Fleet's. We have always been good friends, I'm sure we could make a go of things.'

She looked down at the glass in her hands. If she married, she would need more from a husband than friendship and would need more than just to make a go of things. She raised her glass to her lips. The conversation reminded her of the one she had had with her father.

Johannes shifted slightly away from her and stared around the room. He didn't really know why he made the offer. He was more than content with his life as it was.

Marti took a sip of white port. She couldn't communicate her true thoughts to Johannes, that would be wounding. She sighed to herself. Johannes glanced round at her. She gave him an affectionate smile. 'I think we make better friends than marriage partners.'

He reached out and squeezed her hand. 'As a matter of fact, so do I, but what are you going to do?'

'Do?'

Johannes twirled his glass between his fingers. 'I think you need to come to terms with what has happened. You are unhappy. I can see that.' He took a mouthful of whisky. 'I think part of the problem is maybe that the anger you feel for your father, you are directing towards Hendrik.'

'I didn't know you had been taking amateur psychology lessons.' She spoke humorously, but there was a certain edge to her voice.

'No, I am just saying what I think should be said. I don't like to see you like this, Marti, but only you, I suppose, can do anything about it.'

She raised her arms and clasped her hands behind her head. 'All right, Professor Freud, go on.'

'Seriously, Marti, you need to make up your mind. Are you prepared to accept things and work with Hendrik, or, if you feel you cannot do that, strike out on your own?'

She unclasped her hands from behind her head and stared at him. 'You mean leave Van den Fleet's?'

'It is a possibility to consider.'

She continued staring at him, as if his words had not fully sunk in. She set her glass down on the table by the sofa arm. 'You are a strange person sometimes, Johannes. You say the most extraordinary things.'

'What is so extraordinary about what I have said?'

She thought for a moment, then broke into a peal of forced laughter. 'Nothing, when I come to think of it.' She grabbed at his hand. 'Come on, let's eat.'

He allowed himself to be pulled up from the sofa. 'And while we are eating, we will plan a holiday for you.'

'Johannes, I am getting this curious feeling that you are trying to get rid of me. First you tell me to leave Van den Fleet's, now you are packing me off on holiday.'

He groaned. 'Stop twisting my words. I am not telling you anything, but a holiday would give you a little breathing space to think things out, wouldn't it?'

She nodded. By the time they had reached the door a thought suddenly occurred to her. She spoke almost as if to herself. 'I suppose when Father comes home I could always mix a little business with pleasure, as they say. I could take a weekend break in Geneva and hopefully do a little business as well.'

He grinned mischievously. 'Ah, Mr Yasim is back in town is he?'

'That would be telling, wouldn't it?' She opened the kitchen door, then turned around to confront Johannes. 'You don't like him, do you?'

He shrugged. 'I find conspicuous wealth and arrogance an ugly combination.'

She smiled wryly. Not when it was mixed with a hefty measure of sex appeal it wasn't.

Christian Debilius raised an eyebrow in the direction of the waiter, and the waiter quickly came to the table. Christian gestured to the two brandy glasses on the table. 'Same again, Royston, if you please.'

'Certainly sir.'

Christian looked across at his dining companion, Beni Yasim. 'What do you think of this place?'

Beni inclined his head. 'I'm impressed. I didn't know you could get such polite service in New York.'

Christian laughed. 'You can't. I confess I just happen to own the place, lock, stock and barrel.'

'Aha, so that is your secret.' Beni gently moved his cigar to the edge of the ashtray and allowed the ash to fall in to it. 'Are you making restaurants a hobby, or should one read more into your confession?'

Christian laughed again. 'I have no intention of taking early retirement, if that is what you have in mind.'

'You would be a sad loss to the IDE if you were.'

'It would survive. No one is indispensable.'

The waiter returned to the table. 'Your cognac, Mr Debilius.' Christian gave a brief nod in the waiter's direction. Beni slid two fingers around the stem of his glass and tilted it slightly, allowing the liquor to warm to his hand. 'You come pretty close to the definition, Christian. You have made the IDE what it is. Your members would not argue with that, even if they did feel that it has at times been at their expense.'

Christian leaned back in his chair with an amused expression on his face. He drew on his cigar and blew a perfect smoke ring into the air. 'No one is forced to stay if they don't want to. They know that.'

Firestone

'The trouble is, my friend, that they have nowhere else to go.'

'Quite. By the way, you know Van den Fleet's of Antwerp?'

'Indeed. We do regular business together. They have the most attractive diamond dealer I have ever come across.'

'Ah, the young daughter. Yes, she is quite a looker, I must say. Her brother, Hendrik, is back from Zaire, you know. Taking over the business. The old man is retiring. Not before time, if I may say so. Good man in his day, but well past it now.'

Beni looked at him in surprise. It was a piece of news he would have naturally expected Marti to have mentioned; but then perhaps not. She rarely spoke of her brother.

'You seem surprised, Beni.'

Beni shrugged. 'A little, maybe. You say taking over the business. I would have assumed it would have been run by both the two children.'

'I expect it will to some extent. I imagine Hendrik will leave the administrative side to Martina. Would seem a sensible solution.'

'He's an option bearer in his own right, isn't he?'

'Yes.' Christian leaned forward across the table. 'Off the record, that is a side of Van den Fleet's business that needs to be expanded without delay. Hendrik knows that, of course. A good man. Like his father in many ways.'

Beni dropped his cigar butt into the ashtray. The topic of business having been raised, it was time to acquaint his companion with the dissatisfactions of his own clients.

Beni's business cards proclaimed him to be a director of an international business consultancy based in Paris. It was an active and legitimate company, which also provided the façade for his activities as personal negotiator for the Arab Trustee Corporation. The organisation had originally been set up by a group of leading families in Kuwait, specifically to conduct clandestine investment in leading Western ventures; they believed that secrecy was an integral part of success. Although maintaining friendly relations with certain Western countries, the Kuwaitis held to the belief that knowledge was a powerful weapon: your friends can hurt you more than your enemies.

Beni rarely figured personally in direct negotiations with Western companies – that was left to more prominent members of the Arab Trustee Corporation – but there were few captains of industry in Europe and North America who did not believe that a seemingly chance meeting with Beni Yasim heralded rapid stake-building in their corporations.

Beni picked up his brandy glass and inhaled the rich aroma. 'I am delighted to hear you are interested in expanding business, my friend.'

Christian's eyes narrowed a little. Beni was never one to allow the slightest of opportunities to pass him by.

'My clients are concerned that negotiations with you have not reached a mutually agreeable conclusion.'

'They will. Both sides need a little more time.'

Beni adjusted the signet ring on his little finger. 'How little is little?'

'Couple of months. It depends.'

'On what?'

'On your clients, Beni, coming to terms with the fact that they are not going to be given special treatment by the IDE at the expense of others.'

'Would that necessarily be the case?'

'Come on!' Christian gave a sigh of irritation. 'Look, your clients want the IDE to upgrade the direct supply of uncut diamonds to them by thirty per cent. They already enjoy a contract ten per cent higher than other members.'

'Is that not, my friend, because they can sell more than other members? My clients feel that they are being penalised for creating a bigger market. To meet the shortfall in supply from the IDE, they have to buy on the open market. Good news for the delectable Martina

Van den Fleets of this world. Bad news for my clients.'

'It isn't all good news for dealers, Beni. Your clients know that very well. So, they take their profits, but when business slackens, as it sometimes does, do you hear them screaming because they are left with large stocks of diamonds on their hands? Let your clients take a lesson from them, Beni. They must learn to take the rough with the smooth. This is not a game for the faint-hearted. Your clients should know that.'

Beni swirled the remains of the cognac in his glass. He was content to sit back and be lectured by Christian if ultimately it answered an important question.

Christian pulled the ashtray towards him and angrily ground the stub of his cigar into it. 'I do get tired of hearing these constant, whingeing complaints.'

Beni nodded. 'You understand that I only pass on these things to you.'

'Yes, yes, of course. No offence taken.'

'My clients do not ordinarily act purely on rumour, but they are concerned at what seems to be substantiated rumour that the IDE is intending to increase the quota of the Israelis.'

Christian glanced sharply at Beni. 'Substantiated? If your clients have proof, then I want to know about it. As far as I am concerned, no way is the IDE going to increase the quota of the Israelis. Why do you think the negotiations with your clients must proceed with due caution? If the IDE gave your clients what they wanted on a plate, the Israelis would be up in arms.'

Beni relaxed his shoulders against the back of his chair. He had just heard precisely what he wanted to know; his trip to New York and dinner with Christian had been arranged for precisely this reason.

Christian locked his fingers together with some force. 'I wish people would concentrate more on fact and less on rumour. Without control in supply, without fixed pricing, the diamond market would collapse tomorrow. The IDE ensures that prices are sustained. That is the protection we give.' He rocked his clasped hands back and forth on the table. 'If anyone wishes to go back and re-experience the disasters at the beginning of the decade, they are welcome. Otherwise, they will abide by the decisions of the IDE. We are, after all, working in everybody's interests. Although sometimes members have a habit of forgetting that.'

Beni nodded again, as if in full agreement. He ran his thumb down the side of his brandy glass. The IDE did occasionally work in the interests of some more than others, but it was good that the Israelis would appear not be getting all their own way. His clients would not wish that and would make known their anger if it was so.

Beni enjoyed a relationship with Christian that many members of the IDE would have envied. Although Beni was not an option bearer, he had acquired special status with Christian through his useful business dealings when the IDE was in its infancy. Neither man would describe the other as being a true friend, but each recognised the other's worth. Beni's worth was that he also carried out purely personal tasks for the head of the Al Jalal family; the leading stockholder in the Arab Trustee Corporation. Khalid Al Jalal was a generous man to his adored wife and three daughters, and each of them had a penchant for fine diamonds. A fact for which Christian, before his rise to power, had reason to be grateful. In return, when Beni was buying 'big', as he sometimes did, Christian would grant the favour of discreetly indicating the resources of the dealer concerned; thereby giving Beni important leverage in bargaining.

Beni checked his watch. 'My friend, if you will forgive me.'

Christian signalled to the waiter. 'Of course, Beni. When's your flight?'

'Midnight.'

'I'll drive you to the airport.'

'Thank you.'

The waiter hurried to the table and drew out Beni's chair, then Christian's. 'I hope everything has been to your satisfaction, sir?'

'Excellent meal, Royston. My compliments to the chef.'

As Christian and Beni walked to the front door, the receptionist was already handing their coats to the assistant manager.

The two men stood for a moment on the steps of the restaurant. Christian looked up and down the quiet street. 'Ah, transport has arrived.' As he spoke, a metallic grey Cadillac pulled up in front of them and the chauffeur leapt out to open the rear doors. Christian gestured to Beni to go ahead of him. 'By the way, Hendrik Van den Fleet will be buying big at next month's viewing. If you are interested, I will mention it to him.'

'I would much prefer if you would express my interest to his sister. I don't find him as attractive as her.'

'Have you ever got anywhere with her?'

'I intend to.'

Christian chuckled. 'I wish you luck. I tried it once with her but, I must confess, without much success.'

'My friend, with women it is a question of timing, not luck. The right time and the right place is all one needs.'

Christian ducked his head and followed Beni into the back of the Cadillac. 'I prefer to make sure I've got the right woman, first.'

'You don't believe in working too hard, eh?'

'I work hard only at my job.'

Beni carefully draped the ends of his overcoat over his knees. 'It would make my job a little less hard if I could advise my clients that the cartel has given its word that the Israelis' quota will not be increased.'

Christian turned his head and looked out of the darkened side-window. 'You know I dislike that word, Beni.'

'I beg your pardon. That the *IDE* will not increase the Israelis' quota.'

'You may tell your clients just that.'

'Thank you, my friend. I owe you one.'

'I have already made a note.' Christian swivelled around on the seat to half face Beni. 'Off the record, it would be of assistance to everyone, you know, if your clients would keep their petty nationalistic squabbling to themselves. It beats me why the Kuwaitis feel obliged to make suitable Islamic noises at the Israelis from time to time. Or do I offend?'

'As a Christian Lebanese of French extraction, you do not offend me in the least; but, my friend,' Beni paused to give weight to his words, 'when rumours abound that our friends from the Promised Land are buying and selling outside the IDE's jurisdiction, then my clients will most certainly make, as you say, Islamic noises.'

Christian's mouth narrowed to a thin, straight line. 'If I find any member, repeat any member, whether from the Promised Land or not, trading in diamonds outside the IDE, they will be instantly expelled. I do not say that it never happens, but it doesn't happen for very long. May I draw your attention to what I did to Zaire and Australia?'

'Issued a world-wide ban on trading with either of them, until they were forced to close down half of their diamond mines.'

'Precisely.'

'Then you all kissed and made up.'

Christian smiled grimly. Marketing gurus were fond of saying that his methods of doing business were outmoded, while marvelling at how he outperformed other commodities. He shifted in his seat and faced forwards again. What they failed to realise was that the carrot and stick routine, old fashioned as it was, never ever failed.

The diamond district of New York was centred between Fifth and Sixth Avenues, on Forty-seventh Street. Tony

Bergman was one of its leading lights, as head of the American Diamond Merchants' Association. A burly, outwardly genial man in his early fifties, his reputation on the street was one of ruthless trading. He was fond of claiming that he had been a close acquaintance of Christian Debilius for many, many years. If asked why the acquaintanceship had never developed into friendship, he would grin broadly and say that Christian Debilius didn't have friends. It was a distinction that some dealers believed Tony shared and would sometimes point out. Tony would shrug his shoulders and say, who cares? His momma loved him.

James Wu looked up expectantly as Roz, Tony's personal assistant, reappeared and came to his side. 'Sorry Tony's call is taking so long, Mr Wu. Can I get you another cup of coffee?'

'No, thanks, I haven't finished this one yet.'

'No rush.' She sat down opposite him. 'How was your flight?'

'Not too bad, thanks.'

'Where did they set you down? Queens or Newark?'

'Newark airport.'

She groaned. 'Getting out of New Jersey can be absolute hell. How was the traffic?'

'Fairly light, actually.'

She smiled brightly and glanced across at the telephone on her desk. The red light was still flashing, indicating that the line was still engaged. She looked back at James and smiled again. Making conversation with the guy was like making up to a marble statue. She quickly got to her feet as the red light went out. 'I think Tony's free now, Mr Wu, but I'll just check.'

'Thank you.' James picked up his coffee cup and drained it. His insides felt awash with coffee. He put the cup back down on the table. His brain felt as if someone had been lightly tapping his skull with a sledgehammer.

Roz reappeared from Tony's office, with Tony rapidly overtaking her. He stretched out both hands. 'James. It's been too long. Must be three years. Good to see you. Has Roz been looking after you?'

James's mind reeled as he attempted to answer the rapid-fire questions in strict order. He gave up the battle and settled for just shaking hands. He gritted his teeth into a smile as he felt one of his knuckles crack under the hearty handshake.

'Apologies for the wait, James. Come along into the office.'

James picked up his briefcase and stepped swiftly after Tony's disappearing back. He was almost knocked backwards as Tony suddenly wheeled round. 'Lunch at the club suit you, James?'

'Er – yes. Thank you.'

Tony shot a finger towards the telephone. 'My usual table, Roz. Twelve-thirty.' He turned back on his heel and opened the door to his office, then stood back to let James go ahead of him.

The parcel of diamonds had been almost leisurely examined and now lay in a neat row in front of Tony. He looked across at James, as if asking himself a lot of questions and not being too happy with the answers. 'You've got quality business there, James.'

James gave a quick smile. 'Deal in nothing else.'

'Sure, sure. You're happy with the source?'

'Yes, of course.'

'Who is it?'

'Can't say.'

'Are you selling?'

'I have no instructions.'

Tony moved his lips, as if silently chewing. His instincts told him he should get a second opinion. The diamonds, unless he had accidentally flushed his brains down the john, were genuine, but these guys from Hong Kong could be tricky, and he had no intention of ending up as the fall guy. He pushed his chair back and stood up, hitching his trousers higher up around his waist. 'No objection, James, if a colleague takes a look at these? I like to give the goddam lazy youth of today every opportunity to gain experience.'

'No, not at all.' James tensed his shoulders. That was a lie. Bergman wasn't happy about something. His mouth felt suddenly dry. He knew Bergman would be trouble.

'OK, James, give me a few minutes. Roz will bring you some coffee.' James felt slightly nauseous at the thought of more coffee.

Tony bent down and whispered into Roz's ear. 'Get me the IDE, sweetheart, pronto.'

Her hand was reaching for the telephone before he had even finished speaking.

'And is Max free?'

'Got a client in five minutes, Tony.'

'Stall him. I need ten with Max.'

'You got it.'

Max was Tony's first cousin once removed, but usually referred to Tony as Uncle. He looked up as Tony barged through the office door.

'Is this going to be quick? I have a client in one minute, Uncle. The guy is very precise.'

Tony held his hand up. 'I know, I know. What would you say if a dealer from Hong Kong asks you to authenticate a parcel of diamonds and that same dealer has, according to the latest diamond audit at the IDE, disposed of his entire stock from last month's viewing already.'

Max raised his eyebrows. 'I would say, he should be so lucky.'

'Max!'

'OK. I would want to ask a couple of friendly questions.'

'I just did and got a couple of unfriendly answers.'

'Discretion is the name of the game, Uncle. What's bugging you?'

'Can you remember where you left your head last night? What do you mean, what's bugging me? Look, my name on an authentication certificate adds fifty per cent to the sale price, or am I being too modest?'

'Make it sixty.'

'It also means that Debilius is going to splash his shoes, if these diamonds suddenly appear on the open market without having duly passed through the IDE pipeline. Maybe he'll splash on my shoes too, if my name is on the certificate.'

Max propped his hands behind his head. 'We are told seventy per cent of cut and polished diamonds are accounted for and documented. After the breakdown of the IDE's computers, perhaps we should make that fifteen per cent. Whatever. So you're looking at part of the undocumented thirty per cent. That's not your problem. That's the IDE's.'

Tony ran his fingers through his hair. 'It's everybody's problem. If those diamonds are Chinese, are there more? We have enough problems with the Russians trying to flood the market with polished stones. Max, as head of the Association, I have to be seen to act responsibly.'

'Do you want me to authenticate them?'

'Nah, I'll let the guy sweat a little. It might help his conversational skills. If you want to take a look at the diamonds, I wouldn't say no, though.'

'Sure. Give me twenty minutes and I'll be right with you.'

'That's fine.'

James twiddled his thumbs in a clockwise direction, then anti-clockwise. He brushed the cuff of his sleeve back and checked his watch. If, for any reason, Bergman refused to issue a certificate of authentication, it would be a severe blow to his reputation. His face reddened with nervous tension, as he imagined telephones already ringing around the world and a red line being drawn beneath the name of James Wu. He jumped in his seat at the sound of the office door opening.

'James, sorry I've kept you. My colleague is detained longer than expected. Shall we take an early lunch?'

'I – er – would like to conclude our business as soon as possible.'

'Sure, sure. Let's take a break. My colleague, Max, will be free by one o'clock. I want him to see the parcel you've brought.' Tony's easy-going manner became tinged with a certain forcefulness.

James admitted defeat and rose reluctantly from his chair; to insist on finalising matters now would arouse suspicions. He smoothed the front of his tie flat and straightened his jacket. Tony was a man who needed to work hard for his information before he would believe it.

Max took his time in examining the diamonds. He returned to one or two a second time, but made no comment. When he was finally satisfied, he looked up at James. 'Nice merchandise you have here.'

'Yes, not bad.'

'Chinese?'

'I haven't been told anything about them.'

'Wouldn't have thought there was much left in China nowadays, anyway. Not after Mao Tse-whatsit's little revolutionaries had their fun.'

'You mean Mao Zedong?'

'Whatever.' Max replaced his eyeglass into its leather case.

James swallowed twice to ease the burning sensation that had started in his chest and was now attacking his throat. The main course on the luncheon menu had been a choice of meat or fish. Disliking the enormous steaks the club served, James had opted for the fish and regretted the decision. Not even an elaborate sauce could disguise the fact that the fish must have been caught the day before. He felt a pang of homesickness. In Hong Kong, people shopped for food three times a day to ensure perfect freshness. Tony caught Max's eye and Max gave an almost imperceptible nod.

After returning to the office with James, Tony had

quickly briefed Max on the conversation at the club. He had had to work hard to break down James's oriental reticence, but he had finally got him to express his personal opinion. The diamonds could possibly be Russian. Just as possibly, a one-off. The Russians were notorious for slipping polished diamonds on to the open market, without the IDE's knowledge, but James had a feeling someone was just checking that their insurance was still valid. It happened from time to time.

The brief nod from Max meant that he concurred with Tony's opinion. The diamonds were genuine and it was not their business to write the owner's name in blood on the walls of the IDE. Tony clamped a hand on James's shoulder. 'The certificate of authentication can be ready in half an hour. Even sooner, if the girl from Registry isn't late back to her desk.'

James held out his hand. 'Fine by me, and thanks for your assistance.'

'Any time. Just say the word.' Tony gripped James's hand and shook it several times. 'Don't forget what I said, now. If you want to sell, we want to buy. First offer to me, right?'

'You'll be the first to know, Tony.' James placed his hands behind his back again and discreetly massaged the hand that had been shaken in Tony's crushing grip. Two down and two to go. Tel Aviv and Chaim Eichler. Bombay and Mark Singh.

Candy Lai swept into Fascinations Jewellery Boutique and stared arrogantly at the young shop assistant. Sin-Mei hurried forward. 'Good morning, it's Miss Lai, isn't it?'

'It is.'

'May I take your coat, madam.'

'No. Where is Anna?'

'She is in the workshop, Miss Lai. She is very busy at the moment. She is working on a special commission.'

'Really?' Candy glanced around her, as if she found the news of little interest.

'If you will wait just one moment, Miss Lai, I will go and fetch her.'

'Thank you.' Candy waited until the girl left the shop, then slipped off her sable coat. She carefully draped it over a chair so that the inside label was visible. She took several steps backwards to make sure that the wording on the label could be clearly seen.

Anna pushed up the safety goggles from her face as Sin-Mei popped her head around the door of the workshop. 'Excuse me, Miss Wu, but Miss Lai is in the shop.'

Anna frowned in irritation. 'Boutique, not shop. How many times do I have to tell you.'

Sin-Mei flushed. 'Sorry, Miss Wu.'

'Can't you deal with her? I am very busy. Who is she anyway?'

'You remember, Miss Wu, the one with the sable coat.'

'Oh *her*. She is just a time-waster. The last time she came in she spent half an hour examining everything in the boutique, then left without buying a single thing.' Anna sighed and pushed back her chair. 'I suppose I should see her. Tell her I'll be out in a moment, when I've washed my hands.'

'Yes, Miss Wu.'

Anna pulled off the goggles from her head and smoothed her hair back. Candy Lai was unlikely to buy anything, but if she was treated well, perhaps her friends could be potential clients.

Anna Wu had originally wanted to be an artist, but there were few, if any, wealthy artists in the world and she turned to studying the craft of a goldsmith and jewellery designer. Her original designs sold moderately well, but her skill in copying jewellery designs faithfully, even if they were simply torn-out advertisements from a magazine, earned her sufficient money to open her own jewellery boutique.

After three years, Fascinations had gained a reputation

for high-quality jewellery at a fraction of the price to be paid in Paris or New York. Anna had also gained a reputation for discretion. She always ensured that favoured clients would never meet each other wearing an identical piece of jewellery.

Candy adjusted the bracelet of her diamond-studded watch so that Anna would notice how expensive it was. Anna smiled politely. 'Good morning. Can I help you?'

Candy plucked a silk dress from a bag and tossed it on the chair, as if she was in the act of discarding it. 'I bought this from Jooles, but now I'm not sure about it. I just wanted something simple to wear at the Jockey Club.' She paused to allow the information to sink in. 'We always have a party to celebrate the first race of the new season.' She glanced sideways at Anna and was a little disappointed to find that Anna seemed unimpressed. She flicked at the hem of the dress. 'None of my jewellery will go with it.' She gave a little high-pitched laugh. 'I have so much, I surely should have something suitable, but –' She flicked at the dress again.

Anna picked up the dress. 'May I see it against you? I think I have something that will be perfect with it.'

Candy held the dress to her body. She smoothed the ruffles of the plunging V-neckline. Anna nodded to herself. 'Yes, I have a pearl choker with an extremely fine, pink diamond clasp.' She snapped her fingers at Sin-Mei. 'Fetch the Eternal Rose necklace.'

Sin-Mei scurried away to do Anna's bidding.

'Would you like to come and sit down at the mirror, Miss Lai.' Anna smiled sweetly. She was determined to make a sale, to make up for the time-wasting previous visit.

The pearl choker was draped around Candy's neck and both Anna and Sin-Mei held the dress up to her shoulders. Candy looked at her reflection. Her heart gave a quick beat. It was perfect. The colour of the diamond was a tone paler than the dress. The pearl choker was unclasped and removed and placed on the table in front of Candy. Anna smiled again. 'We also have a bird of paradise brooch, which would look equally good with the dress, but pearls are so flattering to the complexion, aren't they?'

Candy glanced down at the discreetly small price tag on the choker and quickly averted her eyes in shock. It cost more than the new car Fang Ka-Shing had bought her the previous month.

'It is the only one of its kind. If you will be wearing it at the Jockey Club, I can assure you, Miss Lai, no one else will have anything remotely like it.'

Candy looked at her reflection again and pouted. Surely Big Bear wanted to be proud of her at the Jockey Club. Her finger travelled compulsively across the diamond clasp. 'I will have this.' She pushed the chair back from the table and went to collect her coat. 'Have it delivered tomorrow.'

Sin-Mei hurried forward to help Candy slip the fur around her shoulders. Anna smiled sweetly again, not daring to believe her luck. 'We can deliver it this afternoon for you, Miss Lai.'

Candy's eyes flicked open wide for a moment. She needed to see Fang Ka-Shing before she could pay for the necklace. 'Er – no. I shall be out with friends. Tomorrow will be better.'

'Very well, Miss Lai.'

Sin-Mei rushed ahead of Candy to the door and opened it.

Candy's ears rang with the pleasing sound of respectful goodbyes as she stepped out on to the street. She checked her watch and decided to lunch at La Traviata, the new Italian restaurant on Lan Kwai Fong. She didn't much care for Italian food, but it was the newest and best place to be seen. After a few further paces the oppressive humidity forced her to remove her fur coat and carry it over her arm. She turned quickly at the sight of a metallic gold Mercedes rolling to a halt a few feet in front of her. The rear side window slid down. Frankie Heung pushed his head through the open window. 'Something tells me you look hungry, Candy.'

She giggled nervously.

'Get in.'

The rear door was opened and she slipped into the car. Frankie rested his arm across the top of the seat. 'When do you see that boy-friend of yours?'

'Er –' She smoothed the fur with her fingers.

'You remember our little conversation, Candy.' His hand slid up to the back of her neck and squeezed it hard enough to make her wince.

'Oh yes, Frankie. I remember every word. I'm seeing him tonight.'

'Good.' He withdrew his hand. 'I'll buy you a burger at the Rib Shack.'

'There's a new Italian –'

'I said the Rib Shack, Candy. Get me something on Fang and I'll think about going up-market on the foodstakes. OK?'

'Yes, Frankie.' She pouted her lips and stared down at the fur coat on her lap. After a few moments, she settled back in the seat; cheered by the thought that if she could blackmail Fang he would have to buy her anything she wanted. She was growing tired of his stupid fantasies.

Hendrik hunched his shoulders and stared angrily out of the window. What he had naïvely believed could be a sensible conversation with Marti had turned into one of her full-scale tantrums. All he had asked her to do was to move out of the apartment for the sake of their father. He searched in his pockets for his cigarettes and lighter. She had behaved as if she had been summarily sentenced to live in Siberia.

Marti sat in angry silence on the sofa. She threw a disgusted glance in his direction. Hendrik always had perfectly logical reasons why people should do what he said; logical reasons that cleverly disguised his real intentions. She twisted the dress ring on her finger until it bit into her flesh. She was more angry with herself than with him. She had allowed him to completely wrong-foot her.

According to Hendrik, the specialist looking after Erasmus had laid down strict conditions for his return home. He must return to a calm and reassuring atmosphere. There must be someone in attendance at all times. The fear, not so much of dying, but of dying alone was common in someone of his age and in his condition. In a calm and reassuring atmosphere Erasmus, by the grace of God, would spend what time was left to him in peaceful contentment.

Marti twisted the ring back and forth around her finger. Of course, it would have to be Marti who must move out to provide accommodation for a housekeeper. It couldn't be Hendrik. Hendrik was needed to give moral support. Father must be made to feel he still had a useful contribution to make in the running of the company. If Hendrik moved out, it would serve only to make Father feel isolated. Marti scowled at Hendrik's back. Of course, if she wasn't so selfish, she would understand that it must have cost Father much to give up control of the business. It had been his life.

Hendrik turned away from the window and looked around for an ashtray. He went to the coffee table and stubbed out his cigarette. 'What's it to be? Do I tell the specialist everything is prepared for Father's return, or do I tell him to keep him in hospital?'

Marti glared at him mutinously. 'I still don't see why this is necessary. Why not get a bigger apartment? Father needs me just as much as he needs you.'

He shook his head. 'Don't you listen to anything I say? Moving would be too unsettling for Father. He has lived in this place since God knows when. He would be leaving not just the apartment, he would be leaving memories. Some of them, I hope for his sake, have been happy ones. It's asking too much of him.' He began pacing up and down the room. 'It's for your good as well, you know. You can't cope with a full-time job and look after Father the way he needs looking after, as well. Unless you think you're Superwoman, or something.' He stopped and lit up another cigarette. 'I'm not very good at understanding women. Perhaps you enjoy playing the role of martyr.'

'I leave that to you, Hendrik. You play the noble son returning to the homeland, to perfection.'

'Come on, don't be childish.'

She adjusted the strap of her wristwatch. She was losing the battle of logic hands down. Father's needs did come first. She couldn't argue with that. 'I will be given time to find somewhere to live, or is that a rash assumption on my part?'

A look of relief flashed across his face. The climbdown was abruptly swift. 'Johannes knows of a place that's going on the market. A friend of his is getting married, I think. Sounds a nice place. Got a little private balcony.'

She stared at him. 'Johannes? What's he got to do with this?'

'I told you. He knows someone who wants to get rid of his apartment.'

'I meant, Hendrik, have you been discussing this with Johannes, behind my back, before consulting me?'

'No, course not. I just asked him if he knew of any accommodation available. He asked if it was for me and I just explained about Father coming home, that's all.'

Her eyes roved restlessly around the room. Another of Hendrik's little *faits accomplis*. She stood up. 'Well, I suppose I'd better start packing.'

'Don't be stupid. Go and see Johannes. Take a look at the apartment. The housekeeper isn't coming until Friday.'

She sucked her cheeks in. 'So what's been the point of this so-called discussion we were supposed to have, if everything has been arranged over my head?'

'Look, Marti, Father is anxious to get home. It's where he wants to be. Not stuck in some hospital surrounded by strangers. If he's to come home at the weekend, I don't have much time to arrange things. Show some sense, will you.'

She turned on her heel and swept past him. Hendrik had a happy knack of always leaving her in the wrong. Always making her look like an empty-headed schoolgirl. Always.

James Wu sat down on the bed and opened his filofax. He pressed his lips together as he stared at the telephone number for Chaim Eichler. He sighed to himself and picked up the telephone. Two down and two to go, as they say. He gave another sigh, this time in exasperation, on hearing an engaged signal. He rapped his fingers on the open pages of his filofax. At least it proved that someone was at home in the Eichler residence.

Chaim Eichler was one of the few remaining old-established diamond merchants in Tel Aviv. Speculative hoarding in the late 1970s had left many diamond merchants too vulnerable to the effects of the worldwide slump in diamond prices at the beginning of the 1980s. Their place was now taken up by young men more than twenty years Chaim's junior, who brought the philosophy of supermarket selling into Ramat-Gan's fortified skyscrapers: rapid turnover; low profit margins.

James straightened up as he heard a rather querulous voice answer him. 'Good evening, is that Mr Eichler?'

'Which Eichler do you want? We have many here.' The voice gave a throaty, rasping laugh.

'Er – I would very much like to speak to Mr Chaim Eichler, please. My names is James Wu.'

'Who? Speak up. Can't hear you.'

'Wu. *W. U.* Wu.'

'Got it; hold, will you?'

James twined his fingers around the telephone flex. He sat to attention at the sound of a softly spoken voice.

'Chaim Eichler here, Mr Wu.'

'Ah, good evening Mr Eichler. I am James Wu from Hong Kong. I believe we have met a couple of times at the IDE in New York. My apologies for ringing you in the evening, but –'

'Don't apologise. I should apologise to you. My father-in-law is, unfortunately, rather deaf. We do not usually allow him to answer the telephone. It is bad for business, you understand.' Chaim chuckled softly at his own joke.

'I understand. My aunt has the very same problem. Mr Eichler, I have a parcel of diamonds that require authentication. As you are extremely highly respected by myself and my colleagues, I wonder if you would oblige me?'

The flattery worked and Chaim answered without hesitation. 'Sure. When?'

'Whenever is convenient to you, Mr Eichler.'

'Bring them round now if you want.'

'Thank you. I can be with you in, say, fifteen minutes?'

'See you then.'

James let his breath out as he replaced the handset. He glanced around the plainly furnished hotel bedroom, mentally rehearsing the answers to as yet unspoken questions. He winced as a stabbing pain shot through his abdomen. He should not have eaten that fish at the IDE. It had made him ill.

Mrs Eichler was plainly fat, but it couldn't disguise the fact that in her youth she had been extremely attractive. She greeted James effusively and plied him with offers of coffee and cake. James looked around him. Two particularly fine bronze statues, shown off to perfection in a niche in the corner wall, caught his eye. The Eichlers were wealthy. He allowed Mrs Eichler to take his arm and lead him to the sitting room, but was rescued by the appearance of Chaim.

Chaim immediately took charge of the situation by telling his wife that Mr Wu was on business and business required something stronger than coffee and cake. He took James to his study.

'I make no apologies for my wife, James. She is the finest hostess in Tel Aviv.'

James smiled politely, relieved to have escaped from the prospect of eating any food.

'And call me Chaim.' Chaim studied him carefully for a moment. 'I remember you. I couldn't remember your face when we spoke on the telephone, but I remember you now.'

James opened his briefcase and removed a small oilskin-wrapped parcel. 'I am sorry to trouble you at this hour.'

'Not at all. Now. Let's see what we have.' Chaim took an eye glass from his pocket. 'Bring them to the desk, James.'

Chaim took his time in examining each diamond. He lingered over one. Although smaller than the others, even under ten-power magnification, he could find no inclusions. He raised his head. 'This is very fine. Very fine.'

James nodded quickly. 'Yes, I thought so too.'

Chaim lowered his head again and continued his examination. James took a small sip of the whisky that had been poured for him.

'How is business, James?'

'Excellent, I am pleased to say.'

Chaim laughed to himself. 'With diamonds like these, I should ask you how business is?'

James cleared his throat. 'How are things with you?'

'Terrible, terrible. You know what they are doing to us now?'

'The IDE?'

'No, no. Our government. Biting the hand that feeds them. That is what they are doing. They have just told us that they are increasing taxes based on our annual turnover, by ten per cent. Ten per cent. I ask you, *ten* per cent. They will be telling us next that they expect us to work for no profit at all.'

James took another sip of the whisky. While Chaim was talking, he wasn't asking questions. 'You don't do too badly, do you, Chaim?'

Chaim raised his head. 'I don't do too badly. You are telling me I don't do too badly. We are taxed to the hilt. The IDE refuse to increase our quota on directly imported diamonds. We are ripped off by Antwerp when we buy from them.' He shook his head, as if in despair of his situation then picked up the last of the diamonds and focused his eyeglass on to it. 'When do you want the certificate of authentication, James? I could have it ready by tomorrow morning.'

'That would suit very well, thank you.'

Chaim removed his eyeglass and put it into his pocket. 'Are you selling?'

'I have no instructions.'

'When you do, come to me. We can do excellent business together.'

'Thank you.'

'I have a buyer who would take them up straight away.'

'So do I.'

Chaim laughed. He carefully put the diamonds back into the bag. 'What do you know about these?'

'Nothing.'

'Of course, of course, but just between you and me, eh?'

'Truthfully. I don't, to be honest, even know the identity of the client. He acts through an agent.'

Chaim shrugged. 'A man is entitled to his secrets.' He picked up the bag of diamonds and handed them back to James. 'I bet they have an interesting history.'

James gave a non-committal smile.

'I would guess they have been out of circulation for a while.'

James nodded. Chaim looked at him quizzically and James unconsciously shifted from one foot to the other. James put the bag back into his briefcase. It was time to feed information to the hungry. 'Off the record, Chaim, the thought did cross my mind that they are Russian. The cut is very old fashioned.'

A gleam came into Chaim's eyes. 'So, the Kremlin appears to be short of a rouble or two.'

James raised a hand in protest. 'I didn't say that.'

''Course you didn't. I said it.' Chaim pushed his hands into his trouser pockets. 'Let us hope that it is no more than a rouble or two. There is nothing the IDE can do if the Russians start flooding the market with polished stones. And that would be bad business for everybody.'

The muscles in James's stomach tightened. His face reddened slightly as his insides rumbled. 'I – er wouldn't think that is the case.'

Chaim dropped his voice to a whisper. 'Heard about the head-crash at the IDE?'

'Head-crash?'

'Sure. I have good friends in New York. They tell me.' Chaim moved closer to James. 'Don't spread this around, but you know the IDE are cataloguing everything in the diamond pipeline?'

'Did hear something about it.'

'Last week their computer blew up and two back-ups as well. New York think the IDE has lost half of its data.'

James raised his eyebrows. 'I certainly didn't know that.'

Chaim tapped the side of his nose with his finger. 'Keep it to yourself, James.'

James checked his watch. 'Well, I must be on my way.' He held out his hand. 'Thank you for your assistance.'

Chaim pumped his hand vigorously. 'Any time, any time. You going to New York next month to view?'

'Very probably.'

'See you there. Hey, even better, I'll buy you the best hot pastrami on rye in New York.'

'I look forward to that. Thank you.'

When James finally managed to escape from Mrs

Chaim's goodbyes, by promising that whenever he came to Tel Aviv he would call by without fail, he quickly left the apartment block and took in several deep breaths as he walked back to the main street. He pressed the briefcase, tucked under his arm, tightly to his side. Three down. One to go. The next name on the list was Mark Singh.

Astrid placed two new notepads on either side of the table. She stepped back, then, just as quickly, moved forward again and repositioned the tape recorder in the middle of the table. As a finishing touch, she placed a carafe of water and two glasses at one end. The room was normally used as a viewing room for visiting clients but, on Hendrik's instructions, it had been turned into a conference room. His policy meeting with Marti was scheduled for three o'clock.

Hendrik stuck his head around the door. 'Everything ready, Astrid?'

'Yes. I was just going to test the tape recorder to make sure it was working.'

'Good girl. Is my sister back yet?'

'Er, she should be here any minute now, Hendrik.'

'OK.'

Astrid picked at the plastic wrapping covering a new tape cassette. Over an enjoyable business lunch with Hendrik, she had been instructed to drop the *Mr* when addressing him. It had been deeply flattering to be taken into his confidence as to the changes that were going to be made. The change that was of most significance to her, was the upgrading of her position from secretary to his personal assistant with a corresponding rise in salary. Hendrik's ploy of expressing his respect for her intelligence had charmed her into doing his bidding. She bit at the plastic covering, trying to make an opening at one corner. Her first assignment had been to assist Hendrik in drafting a future policy agenda for the meeting with his sister. The proposals were sweeping and wide-ranging, particularly where his sister was concerned. Astrid broke open the plastic wrapping and placed the cassette into the recorder. However politely couched, the changes were little short of a total down-grading of Martina Van den Fleet's authority. Astrid spoke a few words into the recorder then played it back. Satisfied that all was working efficiently, she switched the recorder off. She stood for a moment and looked around the room. Her promotion, as welcome and exciting as it was, required a switch of loyalties from sister to brother. Hendrik had made it plain that he needed an assistant he could trust; loyalty mattered more to him than anything else. She pressed her lips together as doubt turned to a vague feeling of guilt that Martina Van den Fleet knew nothing, as yet, of the changes she would face. She turned and walked swiftly to the door. What went on between the management was their affair, not hers.

Marti stared down suspiciously at the red cover of the pro-posed policy document. The in-house printed cover and binding would have looked more at home in some global conglomerate: so would the American conference-style meeting planned by Hendrik. She glanced up at him. His delusions of grandeur were showing slightly. They could just as well have had a meeting in his office.

Hendrik pulled his chair away from the table and sat down. He laid his cigarettes and lighter neatly by the side of the ashtray, thoughtfully provided by Astrid. 'Seen the apartment with Johannes yet?'

'No. He won't be back until this evening.'

'When are you going to see it then?'

'Tonight.'

He drew his chair up closer to the table. 'Right. Let's get the show on the road.'

Marti clasped her hands in front of her. She would listen patiently to what Hendrik had to say. It would be selfish to deprive him of one of his pleasures in life; listening to the sound of his own voice.

It took Marti less than ten minutes to decipher Hendrik's convoluted business-school jargon and realise that she was expected to agree to being relegated to a status lower than Justus, the office manager. She drew in an unsteady breath to quell the rising anger that was threatening to propel her up out of her chair, demanding to know what the hell Hendrik thought he was doing. She shut the file in front of her and concentrated on the cover. Very professional. She ran a finger over the printing. Astrid should be commended. She had mastered the art of operating the newly-purchased printing and binding machine better than expected.

Hendrik stubbed out his cigarette. 'Marti, are you listening to me? This is important.'

Marti stared across the table at him. Her tongue seemed inexplicably to fill the whole of her mouth, making speech suddenly difficult. She articulated her words slowly and carefully. 'I am listening and the importance of what is going on is not lost on me.'

'OK. It just leaves me to say that I have agreed this package of changes with Christian Debilius and he has virtually promised the upgrading of Van den Fleet's box at next month's option bearers' viewing. And, as a matter of courtesy, I have discussed the details with Father. I think my expansion plans for the company cheered him up. He has been very worried by the way the company has drifted into stagnation.' Hendrik closed the folder in front of him. 'Like some coffee, before we go over the finer points?' He didn't wait for an answer and got up to buzz through to Astrid. 'Coffee please, Astrid.' He came back to the table and sat down again.

She watched him with a mutinous expression. He had an irritating bouncy step to his walk when he was feeling very, very confident. He lit up another cigarette. 'Astrid's a good girl. Got a lot of potential. She was a great help in drafting this policy document.'

'What!'

'I said she was a great help in –'

'I know what you said, Hendrik.' Marti's control over her angry feelings was ebbing dangerously fast. 'What I want to know is why you appear to have discussed these so-called plans of yours with Christian Debilius, Father, and even my secretary, but not with me.'

'I am discussing them with you.'

'After you have discussed them with everyone else? I know what you are trying to do, Hendrik, but I am not going to let you get away with it.'

'Don't know what you are talking about.' Hendrik spoke in a flat, obstinate voice.

'Then let me tell you.' She gripped at the edge of the table. 'You think you can push me aside, get rid of me, under the guise of this – this expansion plan. This is what it's all about, isn't it? You think you can present me with one of your little *faits accomplis* again. Like getting me out of the apartment, so that you can influence Father. Well, let me tell you something, Hendrik. It won't work. Not this time.' She swallowed quickly to clear the huskiness from her voice. 'Not this time, you won't.'

Hendrik looked over her head at the wall opposite. 'I don't know what you are talking about, Marti, and I would appreciate a little more maturity and less emotion. This is supposed to be a business meeting, not a kindergarten squabble.'

She went to open her mouth in swift reply, but Astrid entered the room with a tray of coffee.

Astrid took one look at Marti's angry expression and glanced away. She quietly placed the tray on the table. 'Shall I pour the coffee, Hendrik?'

'I think you'd better leave it for the moment.'

Astrid shot him a questioning look, but he ignored her and looked down at his file. She gave a brief smile in Marti's direction and left the room almost on tiptoe, quietly shutting the door behind her.

Marti stood up and moved to where Astrid had left the tray. Her movements brought a quick release of tension, leaving her legs weak and shaky. She picked up the coffee pot and one of the cups. The humiliation of receiving a pitying smile from her own secretary, burned in the back of her throat. She carefully filled one cup and then the other, using the quiet time allowed by her actions to marshall her thoughts. She passed a cup to Hendrik then returned to her own side of the table and sat down again. 'I would like to ask one simple question, Hendrik. Why is it, after running this company single-handedly for over a year, I am now presented with a new job description that leaves me with as much responsibility as a junior filing clerk?'

Hendrik held his hands in front of him and examined the palms, as if inspecting them for any trace of dirt. 'I dispute your interpretation of the job description, but the answer to your question is change. Change, Marti. It is something we all have to get used to.'

'Why have you promoted Justus virtually to do my job?'

'Because he has potential, given half an opportunity to show it, but I don't expect any man to do any job lacking the appropriate status and salary. I cannot afford to pay him *and* you senior-dealer salaries. I intend to make this business more successful than it has ever been, and Justus is the man who can help me do that.'

'Meaning I can't?'

He sighed loudly. 'We have been through this once already. The facts of the matter are there.' He jabbed his finger at her file. 'There.' He ran his fingers through the front of his hair. 'No one is saying you don't have something to contribute to the future of Van den Fleet's. No one is saying that you don't have a part to play. What I am saying is that things must be changed if we are to meet market demands and if we are to profit from them. To put it bluntly, it is simply not enough to go on doing what you have been doing. It is not good enough to content ourselves with selling the odd parcel of diamonds from the stockpile to any itinerant who happens to stop by. We must make inroads into the Japanese market. The Americans are making more money than they know what to do with from the Japanese, and the market shows no sign of diminishing. I have no intention of seeing us left out in the cold.'

'Neither have I. You seem conveniently to forget the new business I have brought in during the last year.'

'Not international business, you haven't. All you have done is to dig us deeper into one single market. Sure, you have expanded business with the Israelis by something over sixty per cent, but if their market collapses so do we. And don't claim it can't happen. They are under pressure. The Asians are undercutting them every way they turn.'

She momentarily shut her eyes to block out the flat-sounding voice; relentless, in its pragmatism. 'Very well. We deal with the Japanese, as you suggest.'

His pale eyes finally focused on hers. 'Not *we*, Marti. You couldn't do it. You would be out of your depth.'

She laughed derisively. 'Who says?'

'I say, Marti. They don't know you. They don't like doing business with people they are not used to. It even took me a couple of years of very hard work to gain their confidence. Besides, I know this is going to sound offensive, but it has to be said. They would feel uncomfortable dealing with a woman.'

She nodded to herself. 'I see. So you are conveniently using the Japanese as an excuse to write me out.'

'No. As I have said, you will play a valuable role in the administrative running of the business. I couldn't do without you, even if I wanted to.'

Her mouth tightened. 'Don't patronise me, Hendrik. I am a trained dealer, not a filing-cabinet supervisor. And you are much mistaken, if you think I am going to be quietly shunted to one side. All you have done is twist and distort the facts to suit your own purposes. Well, I'm not accepting any of them. I don't know what methods you used to get Father to agree to all of this, but I will speak to him myself and –'

'You will do no such thing.' He reached out and switched the tape recorder off. 'If you upset Father, you will have to answer to me and I mean it.' His eyes momentarily flickered with an angry warning.

'Listen to me, Hendrik, don't you dare threaten me. If I –'

He raised his voice and drowned out her words. 'No, you listen to me, Marti. I have had as much of you as I can stand. I thought when I returned from Zaire things might have changed. I admit I made a mistake. I don't usually make mistakes, but I have this time. I imagined you would by now have grown out of your self-centred, self-seeking, brattish ways. Obviously, you haven't.' He jabbed his forefinger at her. 'You still expect to have everything your own way, don't you? Doesn't matter about any fucking one else. Just as long as you get what you want.'

An angry flush came to her cheeks. 'Just who do you think you are, Hendrik?'

He folded his arms against his chest; a bitter smile hovering around his mouth. 'Ah, I thought it would come down to that sooner or later. It usually does. You have always resented me, haven't you, Marti? Ever since you were old enough to know what the word means.'

'That is rich, coming from you. It is you who has resented me,' she shouted back at him. 'Your obsessive jealousy. Your foundling complex. You –'

'My what?' He pushed his chair back and stood up.

She glanced away from him. He reached across the table and pulled her upright by her arm. 'My what, Marti?' His neck reddened, the colour spreading like fire to his face.

His expression warned her that she had gone too far. 'I'm sorry. I didn't mean to say that.'

He stared at her, his face stiff with anger. 'You had better be. My God, you had better be.'

'I am. I am.' She spoke appeasingly. When Hendrik felt he was losing ground, he would think nothing of lashing out. It didn't matter who it was. He had been sued for divorce on the grounds of physical cruelty.

Hendrik released his grip on Marti's arm so abruptly that she momentarily lost her balance, and almost toppled forwards. He pushed his chair up to the table and picked up his folder. 'I've got a couple of telephone calls to make and some dictation to give to Astrid. I will be out all evening. Don't cook for me.' He spoke mechanically, as if issuing daily orders to a houseboy. 'I have a meeting at nine tomorrow morning until about eleven. I shall be free for half an hour, after that. Let me know then what you have decided.' He leaned across the table, removed the cassette from the tape recorder and slipped it into his jacket pocket.

Marti watched him go out, closing the door behind him with exaggerated carefulness as he did so. She silently thumped her fist on the table. She had allowed her temper to get the better of her and had just scored an own goal. She picked up the red file and flicked open the page setting out her job description. Chief Administration Controller. She closed the file. An impressive title for someone reduced to making sure they didn't run out of coffee and sugar and that the linen hire company returned the same number of towels they had taken away the previous week. She passed a hand across her eyes. And every member of staff would know it.

Fang Ka-Shing stared moodily into a glass of whisky and soda. The fingers that had crept along the inside of his thigh to his crotch did not stir him. Candy lolled back on her heels. She gave an exaggerated sigh. Big Bear was being very disagreeable. What was the cost of a pearl choker to him? She hung her head back and scanned the ceiling above. Sometimes she wondered why she bothered to please him, if in return all he could do was to accuse her of being ruinously extravagant. She glanced at him out of the corner of her eye. She was not going to be humiliated. It was unthinkable to have to cancel the order with Fascinations Jewellery Boutique. Candy pulled the front of her robe more firmly over her knees. She would not be made a fool of in front of that contemptuous, self-important Anna Wu.

Fang drained his glass and waited for Candy to leap to her feet and offer to replenish it. He sighed to himself when she made no sign of moving, and stood up. 'You must understand, Candy, I am not drowning in money. I have a wife and family to support.'

Candy smiled in quiet triumph. He was softening up. She knew he would. 'I know, I know, I just thought you would want to be proud of the way I looked, when we went to the Jockey Club.' She let her mouth droop into a discontented pout. 'But, what does it matter if people see that the Chairman of the Chinese People's Association for International Trade is a poor man? That he cannot even afford to buy a little trinket for a loving friend.' She gave a little shrug of her shoulders and lapsed into silence.

A flush of shame spread through Fang at the thought of such a thing, but was quickly stifled by the thought that what she wanted was no mere trinket. It represented a fortune to any man. He dropped a couple of ice cubes into his glass and splashed a generous double measure of whisky over them. Good fortune had brought Candy to him. If he had not stopped off to buy chocolates for his wife on the way home; if the rain had not become a deluge just as he was leaving the shop; if Candy's heel of her shoe had not caught in a crack in the pavement; if she hadn't tumbled straight into his arms. He nodded in silent agreement with himself. Without good fortune, they would never have met. If he caused her to leave him, he would appear to scorn the benefits of good fortune. He swirled the whisky around the glass. To scorn good fortune was to invite bad fortune. Very bad fortune. He walked slowly back to the sofa. He simply couldn't afford to buy the pearl choker for her. Not this month certainly. His commission from Pa Jiaming was not due for another six weeks. He sighed aloud again, then a shiver of excitement shot through his body as he thought of the answer to his problems. A handful of diamonds from Anshan would cost less than a taxi ride to the Jockey Club. His face relaxed, smoothing out the lines on his forehead. He would think of a way of obtaining them. Any back-street jeweller in Kowloon would make the diamonds up as desired, in less than twenty-four hours. Candy and good fortune would be kept at very little cost.

Candy glanced suspiciously out of the corner of her eye, as Fang placed a hand on her knee. He gently stroked the silken outline. 'I have a secret that I must tell you.'

'If it isn't a happy secret, I don't want to hear it.'

He massaged her knee, as if believing that was the physical centre of her discontent and could be rubbed away. 'It is a very happy secret. I did not want to tell you yet, but I had planned a special present for you to celebrate the three months of good fortune since we first met. It is very expensive.' He gave a loud, sorrowful sigh. 'But, regrettably, I cannot afford such a gift as well as the pearl choker you ordered.'

She inclined her head to one side as if carefully considering his words. 'Are you telling the truth to me?'

'You know I never lie to you. Never.'

'Then what is this present that you talk about?'

'Come.' He bent forward and slipped an arm around her waist. 'Sit on my lap and I will tell you.'

She eased herself on to his lap then folded her hands primly. Ordinarily she would have swept her arms around his neck, but further information had to be revealed before further affection was displayed. He drew her close to him.

'Diamonds. Only diamonds are worthy of your beauty, Candy.'

She turned her head quickly to look at him full face.

'I have had one of the best jewellers design a diamond necklace for you, my beautiful one. There will be nothing like it. Anywhere in the world, you will not find a more beautiful necklace.' He licked at the lobe of her ear. 'Or do you still want this pearl choker?' He gave contemptuous emphasis to the word pearl.

She didn't hesitate in her decision and slid her arms around his neck. 'Little Bear has been a stupid girl, hasn't she? How could she think Big Bear was being unkind to her?'

He removed one of her arms from his neck and guided her hand down to the buckle of his belt. He rested his head on the back of the sofa. Good fortune had been protected. He closed his eyes. Now he could enjoy it.

Johannes moved about methodically between the kitchen and the dining room, listening to Marti pouring out her troubles. She unconsciously followed him back and forth between the rooms. 'First, I'm talked out of my own home. Now, I'm being talked out of my job.'

He returned to the kitchen and removed a plate containing two veal cutlets from the refrigerator. 'I must admit, it must seem like that.'

'Seem!'

'Well, I understand how you feel, but I can also see what Hendrik's problems are with the business.' He dropped a knob of butter into the frying pan and shook it until it began to sizzle. 'I know both of you. I suppose that makes it easy for me to see both sides of the problem.'

'What do you mean?'

He dropped the cutlets into the pan. 'Hendrik needs to expand the business. You feel pushed out.' He turned the cutlets over to sear the other side. 'I think he has a point about opening up trade with the Japanese, but why not let you continue with the business you have been building up in Europe, where being a woman isn't a hindrance?'

'Because, Johannes, don't you see? He wants to get rid of me altogether.'

Johannes wiped his fingers on a tea cloth and flipped it over his shoulder. His forehead creased into a troubled frown. Marti's business activities were limited, although she would never admit it. If Van den Fleet's were to survive, Hendrik had to broaden their marketing base. But. Johannes bent down and lowered the heat beneath the pan. But, Marti and Hendrik were embroiled in one of their power-struggles that had nothing to do with the business. He picked up his wine glass and gazed at the pale straw-coloured liquid. It was inconceivable that two grown-up people should still be battling out what should have been left behind in the nursery.

'What do you think?'

Johannes inclined his head. 'Maybe you're right, but if Hendrik is trying to get rid of you, you are helping him to do it.'

'What do you mean?' She grimaced to herself. She had spoken more sharply than she intended.

'You should have seen it coming. Consider the basic facts. The company needs another option bearer now that your father is retiring. Hendrik is an option bearer. You are not and, bluntly, because you are a woman, are unlikely ever to become one. It must have occurred to you at some time, Marti, that Hendrik would rejoin the business when Erasmus retired, simply because there is no one else whom the IDE recognises. You undermine your own position by expressing naïve shock and horror that Hendrik has returned.' He spoke slowly to give emphasis to his words. 'You should have planned, beforehand, a course of action to meet that eventuality.' He shot her a sympathetic glance. 'I know that sounds tough talk, Marti, but you have to face facts. You won't get the better of Hendrik, if you don't.'

'I know, I know.' She bent her head and stared down at the floor. 'I know what you are saying is right, but, I suppose I just didn't want to have to think about it.' She smiled wryly. 'I am my own worst enemy, right?'

He gave an affectionate grin. 'Only sometimes.'

She wrapped her arms around her body. 'But that doesn't change what Hendrik is trying to do. I didn't think I needed to plan anything. I thought we would run the company jointly. Equal status.' She hugged herself tightly. 'I don't understand why Hendrik won't do that.'

'Maybe he sees you as a threat to his authority.'

'How so?'

'Because, Marti, you fight him. You are not prepared to negotiate with him. Hendrik needs to believe he has everything and everyone under control. He is that kind of man. Perhaps it is why he has been so successful in his own right.'

She rolled her eyes upwards. She was not in the mood for Johannes's psychoanalysing. He turned to give the pan a quick shake. 'I think these are almost ready.' He turned round to face her again. 'You see, Marti, what is really happening is that you and Hendrik, despite a lapse of ten years or more, are still fighting an old battle. Both of you have picked up the threads so quickly, it is difficult to imagine that you haven't seen each other for ten years. To an innocent bystander, it is almost fascinating to watch.' He picked up a spatula and deftly lifted the cutlets out of the pan and on to a serving dish. 'I'll just put these in the oven to keep warm while I make the sauce.' He bent down and opened the oven door. 'You know, Marti, I can almost date when you and Hendrik started this personal war between you.'

'When?'

'After your mother died. That first time he came home from Zaire. It started then.'

She took a sip of wine. She could date it more accurately

than that. It was the day she discovered that Hendrik was adopted.

'I am trying to be objective, Marti. You do understand that, don't you?'

She nodded.

'Good, because I think that this time, someone could get hurt and that someone could be you.'

'I can look after myself where Hendrik is concerned. I give as good as I get.'

He gave a muffled groan. 'I sometimes get the feeling that you both enjoy this in-fighting. You know, I can almost guarantee that if you and Hendrik are together for more than five minutes, it starts and it doesn't stop until you have both aired every conceivable misdemeanour perpetrated by the other. As a friend to both of you, I am sometimes tempted to tell you how ridiculous you both sound.'

'You make us sound like a couple of neurotics.'

'From where I stand, you are. I don't know why the two of you don't just stop it and call it quits. Why waste your energies on this continual, stupid quarrelling?'

She pursed her lips doubtfully. 'We don't quarrel all that much. Only over important things.'

'Oh, sure. Look, you remember the night before last, when I dropped round to ask how your father was?'

'Mmm.'

'If I remember correctly, you informed me that it was Hendrik's night to cook. Somehow, we all ended up having a drink in the kitchen, and I suddenly found myself in the middle of a paprika war.'

She smiled sheepishly.

'It's true, Marti. You said Hendrik had put too much paprika in the goulash. He said he hadn't. You said it would be too hot. He said it wouldn't. You said he had spoilt it. He said you didn't know what you were talking about and should be grateful he took the trouble to cook for you. You

said he was the one who didn't know what he was talking
about and you weren't going to eat it. He said suit your
fucking self and banged the spoon down on the worktop.
What appeared to me to be a minute speck of paprika fell
on to the sleeve of your blouse. You said he had ruined your
blouse and screeched at him for being so clumsy. He said
don't be so bloody stupid, and it was your fault for inter-
fering and getting in his way. You said he had done it on
purpose. He said he hadn't. I thought to myself, Johannes,
here we go again. Within minutes we had traversed time to
the point where Hendrik had pushed you off your bicycle
and you had broken the wing off his plane. It is amazing,
Marti, truly amazing, how two supposedly grown-up people
can get from goulash to bicycles and planes in five minutes
flat.' He shook his head in bewilderment. 'It is some kind of
private game you both play and both relish.'

'That is just not true. Hendrik might play games, but I
don't.'

'Then why do you draw him, goad him, so much? You
know him better than I do, he's your brother. He has a very
quick temper. Why do you do it?'

She gave an audible gasp of astonishment. 'That's
unfair. I don't.'

'Marti, just the way you can look at him is enough to
wind him up. I will say this for you, you certainly know all
the wrong buttons to press with Hendrik.'

'And what about the things he says to me. What about
the way he criticises everything I do, even before I've done
it? What do you call that?'

Johannes shook his head again. 'I don't know, Marti.'
He picked up a small saucer of mushrooms and tossed them
into the pan. 'I just don't know. You behave like sworn
enemies instead of brother and sister, and you are both
equally to blame.' He reached out and touched her elbow.
'I am sorry, perhaps I shouldn't be so outspoken. I am an
only child and don't understand what it is like to have a

brother or sister. Perhaps I am wrong in what I say.'

She shrugged. 'And perhaps you are not.'

'Look, Marti, you are my dearest friend and I care about what happens to you.' He squeezed her elbow affectionately. 'Can't you just give a little? Just for once. Give him a chance, give him some leeway, particularly in the business. You have to admit there is genuine logic in what he is trying to achieve business-wise.'

'I know, I know. That, Johannes, is what makes it all the more maddening. Under the guise of logical action he is easing me out. I can't prove it, but I know it.'

'Do you? Do you really?'

'You think it is all a figment of my demented imagination, don't you?'

'No.'

'You do.' She set her glass down on the worktop. 'Johannes, there is something you don't know. It is supposed to be a secret, but,' she went to him and put her arms around his neck. 'You won't understand unless I tell you and I think I will go mad, if I don't have someone who does understand. Johannes, he isn't my real brother. My parents adopted him.' She stared into his eyes. 'It is true. I can prove it. He hates me, because I am their real flesh and blood and he is not.'

He lifted his head back and shut his eyes.

'You mustn't tell anyone, Johannes, what I have said. It would kill Father. He always wanted it kept secret.'

He gave a long drawn-out sigh. 'And it wouldn't be good for business, either. Not as far as the IDE is concerned. They like to know exactly who they are doing business with, don't they.' He wrapped his arms around her tightly. 'Oh, Marti, I'm sorry. If I had known, I wouldn't have said the things I have.' He rocked her gently from side to side. 'When did you find out?'

'Just before Hendrik came back after his divorce.'

'When did he know?'

'Years ago. When he was in his teens, I think.'

Johannes turned his head suddenly. 'Argh, the mush-rooms. They're burning.' He leapt to the pan and took it off the hob.

She groaned. 'I'm sorry. That's my fault.'

'No, no, don't worry. I'll cook some more.'

The veal was a little tough, having been kept warming too long while a fresh batch of mushrooms was cooked, but Marti ate enthusiastically. She felt almost ridiculously light-hearted after her confession to Johannes. He reached across to refill her wine glass. 'You and Hendrik need to sit down together and do some straight talking, Marti. It is important for both of you. It won't be easy, but you need to understand and accept how the other feels.'

She rested her knife and fork on her plate. 'Do you think that would work?'

He slowly put the wine bottle back on to the silver coaster. 'I don't honestly know. Perhaps you have both travelled too far down the wrong path, as they say, to retrace your steps and change direction.'

She picked up her knife and fork again. 'I don't think Hendrik and I know how to talk to each other. When I was a child, he was already an adult. I was just the kid sister he thought he could boss around and make my life a misery, whenever he chose.'

He picked up his wine glass. 'Don't you remember the happy times?'

'No.'

'Oh, come on, you must remember some of them.'

'Don't remember any.'

'I can. Do you want to know something?'

'What?'

'When Hendrik used to take you and I out when we were kids, I used to pretend you and he were my brother and sister.'

She stared at him in surprise. He laughed in embarrassment

at the fleeting look of pity on her face. 'Stupid, wasn't it? I suppose as an only child, I felt lonely at times and it helped to pretend I had brothers and sisters.' He leaned across the table to her. 'There were happy times, you know. Do you remember the time he insisted on taking us both to the circus? I can remember being so excited.'

'He only insisted on taking us to the circus, because he knew I was frightened of the clowns.'

Johannes's appetite suddenly deserted him. He had forgotten that. Completely forgotten. He put his knife and fork together on his plate. She had been terrified of the one with the cone-shaped hat and the whitened face. She had screamed and screamed when Hendrik held her up to shake the clown's hand. He looked across at Marti. 'I don't think Hendrik realised how frightened you were. He didn't do it deliberately, I'm sure.'

She shrugged. 'Doesn't matter any more. If I see a clown now, I just cross to the opposite side of the street.'

He gave a forced laugh. 'A lot of them about in our business, aren't there?' He glanced at her again. She too had laid down her knife and fork, as if no longer hungry. He edged his plate slightly away from him and rested his elbows on the table. 'What are you going to do, Marti?' His laughter of seconds before was replaced by quiet concern.

She twirled the stem of her wine glass back and forth. 'You said recently I must either accept the situation or make a clean break. I think Hendrik has made my mind up for me.'

'You sound almost resigned.'

'After talking things over with you, I suppose I am. I am a dealer, Johannes, not an administrator. I cannot accept Hendrik's terms. He knows that. He also appears to have Father's unequivocal support. To question that support would mean upsetting Father, and that I would never do. Hendrik knows that, too. So, it looks like the clean break, doesn't it?'

'Are you really sure? Jobs are not easy to find.'

'Not here, no.'

'You have something in mind?'

She leaned back in her chair. 'To be honest, it's only just occurred to me. A client of ours in Hong Kong is looking for a dealer. He's prepared to offer a partnership to the right person.'

'Presumably that would require money?'

'I think he's more concerned about personpower than an injection of capital. Anyway, I've still got money that my grandmother left to me, and what Mother left in her will.'

'Hong Kong is a long way away, Marti; what about your father?'

'I don't know. He has Hendrik back home to run the business. Van den Fleet's future is assured. Presumably, he will not object to what is now best for me, or do you think I am being selfish?'

'No, and I think it isn't a bad idea to be selfish at times. Self-sacrifice can turn one into a doormat.' Johannes pushed his chair back and collected up their dinner plates. Parents could be selfish; demanding more than filial duty. Marti had danced to the tune of attendance ever since her mother had passed on.

Anna Wu hastily slipped on a silk robe at the sudden burring sound of the doorbell and hurried out of the bedroom. She frowned to herself as she went into the hall. She wasn't expecting any callers and, having just bathed, was not properly dressed to receive them. She flicked the switch on the intercom. 'Yes?'

'Chan Chunling, Miss Wu. May I come up?'

Her eyes widened in horror. James's new and very important client was standing downstairs and she was half naked. 'Er, James is away, Mr Chan.'

'I know.'

She gave an embarrassed smile, as if speaking face to face

with him. 'Yes, of course, how stupid of me. Please come up straight away.'

'Thank you.'

She spun round and rushed headlong back into the bedroom.

By the time Chan had arrived at the front door, Anna was wearing a silk wrap-around dress and had her hair loosely coiled at the nape of her neck. She smiled and held the door open to him, careful to keep her neck straight; there had only been time to fasten the coil of hair with a single mother-of-pearl comb. She gestured with outstretched arm. 'Please, Mr Chan, won't you go into the living room.'

His eyes roved swiftly over her body then settled on her breasts. She hastily let her arm drop, realising that the action had revealed more to him than was polite.

'After you, please.' Chan smiled, revealing a gap between his front teeth.

Chan followed Anna into the living room, lustfully gazing at the silk rippling across her bottom with every step she took. She offered to take his coat and invited him to sit down. 'Please let me offer you a drink, Mr Chan.'

'Thank you.' He scanned the bottles on the sideboard. 'Whisky, if you have any.'

'Yes, of course.'

He leaned back in the sofa and enjoyed another opportunity of observing the movements of her body as she walked across the room. 'I hope you do not mind my calling upon you. I was in the area and I thought you might have heard something from James.'

'Yes. He called from New York. He was preparing to fly to Tel Aviv.'

'Did he leave any message for me?'

'No.' She turned around anxiously. 'Should he have done?'

He shook his head. 'Not necessarily, if everything is going according to plan.'

She brought a glass of whisky on a small tray to his side. He smiled again. 'You are certain that you do not object to my calling?'

'I am always pleased to welcome James's clients, Mr Chan.'

His eyes dropped to where the cross-over bodice of her dress divided her breasts. The opportunity to re-examine Anna Wu in leisurely privacy, without the hindering presence of her brother, had been worth the journey to Stanley. He picked up the whisky glass. She was as fragrant as blossom, with nipples like willow buds. He took a mouthful of whisky then set it down on the tray again. 'I am lucky you were in when I called. I had supposed you might have been out on the town, enjoying yourself.' He smiled again.

Anna sat down on one of the chairs, carefully smoothing the sides of her dress down to her knees, to avoid exposing too much flesh. 'I had to bring some work home to finish off.'

'Ah, I see. You design jewellery, don't you?'

'Yes that is correct. I also have opened a boutique.' A note of unconscious pride crept into her voice.

Chan nodded to himself, as if impressed by her information. 'I should be very interested to see your designs.' He leaned sideways and retrieved his glass from the tray. 'I have many important contacts that might be useful to you.'

'You are very kind, Mr Chan.' Anna struggled to banish a recurring thought from her mind. She didn't think that she liked him very much, if at all, but she must not dwell on such things, lest her discourteous thoughts were mirrored in her expression.

Chan smoothed the front of his tie. 'I think they may be very useful to you, Miss Wu. Let us have dinner together and we can discuss it.'

'That is a very kind invitation, Mr Chan.' Anna's expression remained blankly polite. Many men she met claimed to have important contacts that would be useful to her which necessitated dinner and further discussion.

Anna had lived with her brother, James, in Hong Kong
since she was four years old. Her story and that of her
family was monotonous in its familiarity. Her parents had
lived in Shanghai. Her father had been a professor of
music, her mother a theatrical designer. When it became
evident that the Cultural Revolution was to be a purge of
intellectuals by any other name, her father sent his wife and
children to the safety of Hong Kong. The bribery necessary
to ensure their safe passage exhausted his meagre finances.
He falsely promised his wife and children that he would
follow them within a few days, and they would all be safely
reunited, but in just as short a time he was paraded through
the streets by a local gang of Red Guards. He had been
severely beaten; had a crudely painted headband tied
around his head proclaiming 'art must serve the party'; was
sent into the countryside to labour in a farming commune,
and was never seen alive again.

Anna's mother waited patiently for five years for her
husband to join her and, when he didn't, quietly slipped
into an existence somewhere between life and death and
died three years later. Anna and James were taken to live
with an aged, distant relative of their father's. She exercised
her duty to the two children in a manner more suited to the
nineteenth century; imbuing Anna, especially, with the traditional Confucian sense of order and propriety. Like
James, Anna, in adult life, acquired the cosmopolitan,
sophisticated ways of Hong Kong Chinese, but never
entirely lost her belief in the delicacy of manner that protected one from the shame of appearing ignorant and
lacking in refinement.

Anna glanced at her watch discreetly. She had exhausted
her repertoire of small talk; had politely replenished Chan
Chunling's glass twice; yet he made no apparent sign of
leaving. She was startled out of her dismaying thoughts by
the sound of the telephone ringing. She hastily got to her

feet, fervently hoping that it might be James; if it was, he could speak to Chan, and Chan would then have no further excuse for lingering. 'Please excuse me, Mr Chan, while I answer the telephone.'

He nodded.

Anna's hopes that it might be James were dashed at the sound of a female voice asking to speak to him. 'I am sorry, he isn't at home. He is abroad. He will be back, I think, by the weekend.' She picked up the pen by the side of the telephone. 'Yes, I will be happy to take a message for him.' She carefully wrote Marti's name and telephone number down, then furrowed her brow in concentration. She was very aware that foreigners thought the inability of the Chinese to differentiate between the letters r and l extremely amusing. 'Miss Van den.' She pressed the tip of her tongue firmly against her front teeth. 'Fleet. Yes. Of Antwerp.' Satisfied that she had given sufficient trill to the troublesome consonant, she relaxed her grip on the telephone. 'Yes, it is Anna speaking. He has spoken to me of you and of your kindness to him when he visited you. I know he will want to return your call as soon as he returns. It is no trouble at all, I assure you, Miss Van den Fleet. Thank you.' She put the telephone down and carefully removed the top sheet from the note pad. She was about to excuse herself again to Chan, but she saw with relief that he was getting to his feet.

'I must go back to Shanghai tomorrow, Miss Wu, but I shall be returning to Hong Kong very shortly. I hope you will accept my invitation to dinner when I do.'

'Thank you for your gracious invitation, Mr Chan.'

'You must call me Chunling.'

She edged backwards away from him and then turned to open the door for him. 'I will tell James that you called and I am sure he will get in touch with you straight away.'

Chan followed her into the hall. When they reached the front door, she repeated her promise that James would call him and thankfully closed the door behind him. He had a strange way of smiling at her, as if he found something about her secretly amusing.

She was about to return to her bedroom to finish her toilet when the telephone rang out again. She sighed in exasperation at the sound of James's voice. If only he had called half an hour previously, he would have saved her the embarrassment of entertaining Chan Chunling alone. 'James, were you able to get in touch with Mr Singh? Oh, good. He did seem genuinely anxious that you knew in advance that he had to change the time of the appointment. By the way, a Miss Van den Fleet called from Antwerp. No, she didn't say much. She just said if you could call her when convenient, if you still had a staff shortage.' Anna bit at her lip. She had saved the most interesting information until the last. 'Mr Chan called round. Yes, he knew you were away. He – er, said he was interested in my designs.' Her face coloured. 'James! You are being horrible. My jewellery designs, of course. Yes, yes, he's gone. He left about five minutes ago. All right. See you soon.' She put the telephone down and chewed at her lip again. Dinner with Chan Chunling was not something that filled her with excitement, but he was a diamond dealer and business was business. She pulled the comb from her hair and let it fall loose. If he pressed the invitation, she would dine with him, but nothing more.

Marti woke up with a start to find the bedside lamp still on and the book she had been reading in an effort to send herself off to sleep still lying on her chest. She rolled over and picked up the telephone, looking at her watch at the same time. It was almost one o'clock in the morning. If it was a wrong number, she would kill whoever it was.

James Wu was apologetic. 'I hope, Miss Van den Fleet, that I am not calling at an incorrect time.'

Marti yawned. 'No, no.'

'Ah, I am very glad. I rang my sister and she gave me your message, so I thought I would contact you soonest.'

She struggled up into a sitting position. She hadn't expected James to reply so soon and hadn't fully rehearsed her intended speech. 'You er – mentioned you needed staff, Mr Wu.'

'Yes, yes, that is still the case. Have you found someone you think suitable?'

'Well, actually, I was thinking of myself, Mr Wu. I need a change of scenery and am interested in applying for the position.'

There was a short pause as James digested the unexpected news. 'Miss Van den Fleet, I am delighted by your offer. I am most sure that after discussion we can arrive at an amicable arrangement.' He paused again wondering how best to broach a delicate question. 'May I say, Miss Van den Fleet, that your departure from your family company must deplete its resources.'

She raised an eyebrow. How far from the truth could you get? 'Not really, Mr Wu. My father seems to have made an excellent recovery and will be returning home at the weekend. My brother, Hendrik, as I think you know, has returned to take over the running of the company. It is for me a welcome time to change direction. I see gaining international experience as a necessary stage in my career.' She wrapped the telephone cord around her fingers. She hoped the explanation sounded convincing.

'Ah, I see, I see. May I say that is the kind of thinking that denotes a high-calibre mind.'

'Thank you, Mr Wu. I have a slight problem in providing references. A reference from my father would not be exactly objective, but if you wish to speak to any of my clients, I should be happy for you to do so.' She gave a quick grimace. That had sounded positively grovelling.

'The name of Van den Fleet is more than adequate

reference in itself. Well, when and where shall we meet for discussion?'

'Actually, I am taking a few days' vacation before I leave the business. I could come to Hong Kong. It's a place I have always wanted to visit. Would that be convenient?'

'Indeed. I hope you will allow me also to be your guide. I think you will find Hong Kong a fascinating place. Most people do. I shall be returning home at the weekend. Can you travel then?'

'Yes, no problem.'

'When you have made your travel arrangements, let Anna know.'

'Thank you.'

'I am very happy to be making your acquaintance again, Miss Van den Fleet.'

Marti smiled to herself as she put the telephone down. He wasn't half as happy as she was. Hendrik might be pushing her out, but at least she intended to leave with dignity. She lay back against the bedhead, thoughts jostling in her mind. She flung the duvet aside and got up. Sleep was too far away now.

Marti paused outside Hendrik's bedroom. He must still be out. If he was in bed she would hear his snores loud and clear. She went into the kitchen and made a cup of camomile tisane. She clasped the cup with both hands and looked around her. She had lived here all her life. Hendrik had said one must adapt to change. Change had spurred her into making a potentially humiliating telephone call to Hong Kong, but James Wu's encouraging response had made the risk worth taking. She tensed her body at the sound of the front door opening and closing, then Hendrik's footsteps passed the kitchen. She let her breath out when she heard his bedroom door being flung open then banged shut. She didn't want a confrontation now. She would speak to him in her own good time when her plans were safely made. She sipped at the camomile tea. First, she must go and see Father. She drained the cup and rinsed it out. Reassuring Father was not going to be an easy task.

James strolled along the street leading to the offices of Singh & Co. It was not wise to tax the energies too much after an uncomfortable and embarrassing flight from Tel Aviv that felt, for the most part, as if it had been spent locked in the lavatory; his innards straining to rid themselves of the stale fish he had been obliged to eat. He glanced up at the skyscrapers. Nariman Point was to Bombay as Manhattan was to New York, albeit smaller and dirtier underfoot, but just as noisy. He checked his watch and quickened his pace.

Mark Singh was almost a foot taller than James and was dressed in a three-piece suit cut in the English style. He gave a brief smile and held out his hand to James. 'We are delighted to see you, Mr Wu. I trust you had a pleasant journey.'

'Not too bad, thank you.'

'Do sit down.'

James sat down in the proffered chair, glad to be removed from close contact with a spicy-smelling cologne that had swiftly brought on a bout of nausea. He glanced discreetly at Mark as he returned to sit at his desk. The man had a reputation for being coldly polite, and acting more British than the British.

Mark flicked at his trouser leg before crossing one leg over the other. He was well respected at the IDE in New York, but was judged to be a man who liked to keep himself to himself. His rather aloof, aristocratic manner made him the butt of the London dealers and he was jokingly referred to as 'the Viceroy'. Mark folded his hands in his lap and stared across at James. James gave a slight start, as he realised that Mark was waiting for him to speak. He drew his briefcase on to his knee and opened it. 'I am most grateful for your assistance, Mr Singh.'

'I am flattered that you seek my opinion.'

James looked over the lid of his briefcase for a moment. He wasn't sure if the inflection in the clipped tones did not contain a touch of irony. He removed the parcel of diamonds and laid them on the desk. 'You are regarded, Mr Singh, as one of the best dealers there are in the business.'

Mark nodded as if he was aware of that already. James pushed the parcel a bit further forward on the desk.

'May I offer you some tea, Mr Wu?'

James thought quickly. The water would probably be safe, having been boiled, and he was very thirsty. 'Thank you. That is very kind.'

A very dark-skinned and unsmiling young man placed a tray of tea on a side table. Without saying a word, he placed a cup of tea in front of James and a second cup at Mark's elbow. Mark didn't even look up or say thank you. James gave a quick smile of thanks to the young man then returned his gaze to Mark's bent head. The examination of the diamonds was conducted in complete silence, making James overly conscious of his own breathing. He stared at the glistening, carefully-groomed black hair that shone like patent leather beneath the lowered ceiling light. Mark Singh also had a reputation for being as cunning as a serpent. James quietly reached out and picked up the cup of tea, and looked at it in dismay. Milk had already been added without asking. He took a cautious sip and winced. It was boiling hot, very strong, and very sweet. He replaced the cup on to the saucer and set it down on the desk. Politeness required him to drink the evil brew at some stage. The thought made his stomach churn slightly.

The same unsmiling young man who had provided the tea, carefully packed up the diamonds. Mark picked up the spoon lying in his saucer and stirred his tea with great thoroughness. 'We will have a printout from the computer in a couple of minutes, Mr Wu.' Mark looked up at the sound of a knock on the office door. 'Ah, here it is now, I believe.'

James experienced a joltingly swift dislocation of time as he found himself simultaneously confronted with the parcel of diamonds, a certificate of authentication, and the out-stretched hand of Mark. He pushed the parcel into his brief-case, took a quick look at the certificate and pushed that into his briefcase as well, then quickly grasped Mark's out-stretched hand. The brief contact with warm, dry flesh, convinced him that he had not dreamt the last fifteen minutes.

'If you are selling, Mr Wu, then you may take it as having been read that we shall be interested.'

'Er – I have no instructions at the moment.'

Mark nodded, again, as if in precognition.

The door of the elevator slid open to reveal an empty cabin. James stepped in and leaned against the wall. He pulled his handkerchief from his pocket and mopped his brow. The authentication of the diamonds had taken less than twenty minutes, with no more than a handful of words spoken. He dabbed at his neck then pushed the handker-chief back into his pocket. No questions. A total lack of interest. Singh was a strange man. The door of the elevator slid open and James almost stumbled as he stepped out on to the ground floor. He felt almost lightheaded with relief, having braced himself for a grilling like the one he had got from Tony Bergman. He halted by the main doors of the building and glanced anxiously around him. It had been a mistake to drink the tea. He needed to seek sanctuary in the men's washroom urgently. He hastily approached a man entering through the revolving doors. 'Excuse me, is there a men's washroom?'

The man stared suspiciously into his face, as if unaccus-tomed to Chinese features. 'Second floor.'

'Thank you.' James hurried back to the elevator and let out a small cry of relief as the red light lit up and the doors opened again. He glanced back and flushed at the sight of the man still staring after him. He shut his eyes and willed the elevator to speed up.

The girl at the check-in desk smiled and handed James his boarding pass. 'Your flight leaves in just under an hour and three quarters, sir.'

'Thank you.' James tucked his pass into his inside pocket and went to find himself a seat in the departure lounge. He sat down on the end of a banquette running the length of one wall and tucked his briefcase safely between his legs. Home. He looked around him at the jostling noisy crowds. Home. It had never been so welcoming. He plucked his briefcase from between his legs and opened it. He carefully took out a postcard without opening the lid too much and exposing the contents to curious eyes. He pulled out a pen from his inside pocket and used the top of his briefcase as a desk. He flipped over the postcard, which bore a picture of the Gateway of India. He stared ruefully at the Victorian-style, turreted building. Yet another remnant of British colonial power. He reversed the postcard. A poorly printed legend at the bottom of the card proclaimed the Gateway of India to have been built as a triumphal arch to welcome royal visitors. He picked up his pen and wrote a few words to Anna. He would be home before the card reached Hong Kong, but she liked to collect postcards from wherever he had visited. He placed the cap back on his pen and stared yet again at the postcard. The British had managed to flee India with a little face, a little dignity still intact, although they had not been able to prevent the chaos that followed. He moistened his forefinger and ran it across two postage stamps. At least when they left Hong Kong, they would not leave chaos behind them. The PRC would see to that. He carefully stuck the stamps on the card and gently hammered them down with the side of his fist. His task was completed. After almost a week of criss-crossing the continents he now had four certificates of authentication safely locked away in his briefcase. He could now give his attention to the intriguing question of Martina Van den Fleet. He would gladly welcome a person of her calibre into the business, but he would also like to know the real reason behind her departure from the family firm.

Erasmus bore the nurse's attentions with ill-concealed impatience. He glared at her when she adjusted his hands so that they rested, lightly clasped, on top of the sheet. She gave a bright smile. 'Your daughter is waiting to see you.'

'And whose fault is that?' He glared at her again.

'Now, now, Mr Van den Fleet. There is no need for that kind of remark. You want to look your best for your daughter, don't you?' He glanced away in disgust. Hands and faced washed. Hair brushed. He was being treated like a baby again. If it wasn't for his damned blood pressure playing up, he would be out of here by now. He had been told that the tablets they had given him would cure it. Now they were saying he had to stay in hospital for another few days. He plucked at the hem of the sheet. Damned hospital didn't know what they were doing.

Marti got to her feet as the charge nurse approached. The news that her father had to spend more time in hospital had come as a blow to her plans. The news that she would be leaving for good would have to wait a little longer.

'Good morning, Miss Van den Fleet. Doctor has spoken to you, hasn't he?'

'Yes, I saw him a few minutes ago.'

'Good. There is nothing to worry about. We think your father got just a little too excited about going home. At his age, one must be cautious, but I'm sure he will be ready to leave us early next week.'

'I hope so. He was looking forward to going home very much.'

The charge nurse smiled sympathetically. 'I know. It has been a disappointment for him, but Doctor just wants another electro-cardiogram done. Just a precaution, you understand.'

Marti nodded. She was beginning to doubt if she should mention she was going to Hong Kong, or if she should even be thinking of going.

'Well, come along, Miss Van den Fleet, and I will take you to see your father.'

Erasmus caught sight of the two figures approaching out of the corner of his eye and stared straight ahead. He was in no mood to be consoled and fussed over. If he didn't know better he could easily believe it was all a conspiracy between Hendrik and Martina to keep him safely out of the way. He plucked at the hem of the sheet again. Perhaps he had been too hasty in handing over control of the business.

The charge nurse positioned herself at the foot of the bed. 'Good morning, Mr Van den Fleet. Your daughter has come to see you.'

'Have got eyes, you know. Can see.'

The charge nurse shot a warning glance at Marti as she turned away from the bed. She silently mouthed the words, '*Humour* him.'

'Hello, Father. How are you feeling?'

'Feeling fine. I would feel even better, if I could get out of this place.'

'Just a couple more days, you know what doctors are like. They never like to take chances, do they?'

'Don't know about that, but they certainly like to keep themselves in work.'

'I've brought you some grapes. Shall I leave them here, on the table?'

'Sick of eating grapes. Can't you think of anything more interesting? If I eat any more grapes, I will begin to look like one. Where's Hendrik?'

'At the office. He'll be coming in this evening to see you.'

'How's Hendrik getting on with things?'

'Doing very well. He always does, doesn't he?'

Erasmus inclined his head in acknowledgement. 'He's a good business man. One can't deny that.'

Marti laced her fingers together and flexed them, wondering how she should broach the subject of going to Hong Kong.

'What have you been doing?'

She gave a little shrug of her shoulders. 'Usual things.'

'Johannes came to see me, you know? Said he thinks you need a holiday. No reason why you shouldn't, you know. Hendrik knows what he is doing and I shall be out of here in a couple of days.'

She looked at him doubtfully.

'I mean it, Marti. Spend a few days in the country. Get Johannes to go with you. You both look as if you could do with some good, fresh air.'

She flexed her fingers again. Bless Johannes for paving the way for her. Bless him, bless him. 'Er, if you think it will be all right, Father?'

''Course. Why shouldn't it be?'

She nodded. She glanced around the flower-filled room. It wasn't a lie. It was more the sin of omission. She pressed her hands into her lap. 'Actually, I have had an invitation to visit Hong Kong. I think I might take it up.'

Erasmus blinked in astonishment. 'Hong Kong?'

'Mmm. I'd like to go, just out of curiosity.' She gave a forced laugh. 'Travel is supposed to broaden one's outlook, so they say.'

'Who invited you out there?'

'James Wu. He has a sister called Anna. She's a jewellery designer.'

Erasmus nodded and looked around him, as if he was already losing interest in the conversation.

Marti seized on his silence. 'I wouldn't go until you come home, of course.'

'Why not? I won't need you. Hendrik says he has found a very good housekeeper with excellent references. You go off and enjoy yourself, Marti. It's time you did. No one gets any younger, you know.'

'Well, if you are sure you don't mind, Father?'

He shook his head firmly, then gave a sigh of irritation as he caught sight of the charge nurse approaching. 'Can't tolerate that woman. Treats me like a half-wit.'

Marti suppressed a smile. 'Make the effort to be nice to her, Father, or she won't let you out at all.'

He shot her a meaningful glance in silent agreement.

The charge nurse stopped at the foot of the bed and gave a smile which belied the brusqueness in her voice. 'Time for Mr Van den Fleet to rest now.'

Marti got to her feet and kissed her father's cheek. He grasped her hand. 'Hendrik's coming to see me tonight, isn't he?'

'Yes, promise.'

The charge nurse smiled again and gestured with her arm, as if indicating the way out to Marti.

Marti paused for a moment on the front steps of the visitors' exit. There was still a faint warmth to be felt from the late summer sun. She walked with a spring in her step to the car park. She must invite Johannes around for dinner and cook him something special. He had made the meeting with her father easier than she had anticipated.

Hendrik refilled his whisky glass and took it with him to the kitchen. A little discreet questioning of little sister was called for. She was up to something, that was for sure. He had heard the news that she was going to Hong Kong from his father. When he arrived home from the clinic, the dining table had been set for two, complete with a bowl of flowers, and a waft of *carbonnade flamande* emanated from the kitchen.

Marti glanced around as Hendrik entered the kitchen. 'Dinner won't be long. Just a couple of minutes.'

'No rush. You needn't have waited for me. I could have helped myself.'

'I wasn't particularly hungry and it saves having to reheat the meat again.'

He leaned against the wall by the side of the door. 'Forgive me for asking, but what's all this about?'

'What's what about?'

'Flowers on the table, your devotion to culinary duties.'

'Johannes thinks that you and I behave like children, quarrelling all the time. I thought I would try and prove him wrong.'

'Johannes wants to mind his own business. I didn't know he had published a thesis on family life.'

She turned to look at him sharply. 'What do you mean?'

'What I say. His energies would be better spent on his own family.'

'He hasn't got one.'

'His mother counts as enough family for any sane person, surely.'

'That's not fair.'

'I know, I'm just glad I am not Johannes, aren't you?'

She pursed her lips. Fair question. Johannes's mother smothered him. Hendrik took a mouthful of whisky. 'Do you want me to do anything?'

She glanced around her. 'Er, you can do the dressing for the salad, if you like.'

He drained his glass and set it down on the work unit. 'Father seemed very bright when I saw him. He says you're thinking of going to Hong Kong for a holiday.' He cast a sidelong glance at her. 'Bit exotic for you, isn't it?'

She picked up a cloth and wiped her hands. 'I was going to talk to you about it over dinner.'

'Let's talk now.'

She looked around for her wine glass as she went through a last mental rehearsal of her words. A second telephone call from James Wu had increased her confidence and belief that moving on was the best thing to do. Although sounding very weary, James had pressed her to come to

Hong Kong as soon as she could, if she was still interested in joining his company. By the time their conversation was finished, she considered herself to be firmly in line for the post. She twirled the wine glass in her fingers. 'It's not really a holiday, Hendrik. I only said that to Father to stop him worrying. James Wu has practically offered me a job as a partner. I am going to Hong Kong to discuss the details.' She glanced up at him and felt a spurt of glee at his sudden and intent stare. She took another sip of wine. Caught you on the hop, haven't I, Hendrik? She watched his face give way to one expression after another. Cognisance of her words. Relief.

He reached across and took her glass out of her hand. 'Let me get you a refill.'

She suppressed the urge to smile in triumph. His last expression had been one of curiosity tinged with envy. She folded her arms across her chest and watched him walk to the refrigerator and remove a bottle of wine. His gesture was born not out of politeness, but a need to do some quick thinking.

Hendrik replenished her glass and put the bottle of wine back into the refrigerator. He hadn't really expected her to have the guts to leave, but it didn't matter if she did. He held on to the door handle of the refrigerator for a moment. Getting rid of her altogether had its attractions. She would be one less problem with which to contend. His mouth twitched into a secretive smile. All he needed to do was to smooth her path to make sure she went. 'Look, Marti, I don't want you to think that you are being driven out of the company. Can we just agree that Father's retirement has put us both between a rock and a hard place?'

She repressed the quick retort that she was the one between a rock and a hard place. She bit firmly on her lower lip. Remember what Johannes said, Martina. Give a little.

Hendrik handed the wine glass back to her. 'You know, Father would have done both of us a good turn if he hadn't waited until he became ill before deciding to retire.'

'What do you mean?'

'I mean that because of him, you and I have both been forced into a lot of hasty decision-making. I have to do what is right for the business. You have to do what you think is right for you. Neither is easy. If you take a job in Hong Kong, it's not going to look good in the eyes of the IDE, you defecting as it were.'

She twirled the glass between her fingers again. So. That was the reason for his attempts at conciliation. The IDE.

Hendrik lit up a cigarette. Little sister was ominously quiet. That must mean that she had everything sewn up to her advantage. He drew on the cigarette and inhaled deeply. 'If you are going to leave, I wish you every success, of course, but I think for both our sakes the leaving should be amicable, and also for Father's sake as well.'

'No reason why it shouldn't be.'

'What did you tell this guy, Wu?'

She looked up at him. Now they were getting down to what was really worrying him. 'Not much. He said business was multiplying so rapidly he desperately needed someone to join him. He was prepared to offer a partnership to the right kind of person. I offered myself for the position. He accepted.'

'Surely he must have asked why you were leaving Van den Fleet's?'

'Mmm. I said, now that you had returned home, it gave me the opportunity to spread my wings. Get some international experience.' Hendrik's shoulders visibly dropped with relief. He reached across and flicked the ash from his cigarette into the sink. She gritted her teeth. She wished he wouldn't do that. She was the one who had to clean it up.

'Well, don't think you have to rush into the first job that is offered to you. What do you know about him, anyway?'

'Not much.'

He examined his hand back and front. 'If you like, I can have a word with Christian Debilius.'

She looked at him quickly. Crafty, helpful Hendrik. That gives you the chance to put your own story to Debilius. 'Not necessary, Hendrik. I shall learn all I need to know when I go to Hong Kong.'

'I don't mind doing it. Forewarned is forearmed, as they say. And,' he jabbed a finger at her, 'you want to be careful when you get there. Very careful. Hong Kong is not a good place for a respectable young white woman to be alone.'

She burst out laughing. 'For heaven's sake, Hendrik, Hong Kong isn't Zaire, you know.'

'I know. It's much worse.'

'How do you know? Have you ever been there?'

'No, but I know someone who has.'

'Who?'

'Girl I once knew in New York. Her itchy feet had landed her in Hong Kong, and rapidly running out of cash. Ended up staying at one of these cheap travellers' hostels. Approached by what she described as a very nice, very charming man offering her some modelling work. Five hundred dollars was too good to turn down. She later found out she could earn another five hundred dollars if she would meet a friend of his one evening.' He reached out and flicked his cigarette into the sink again. 'When she refused, nice, charming man became very persistent and very nasty. She had to flee for her life.'

'Come on, Hendrik, you're making it up. You make it sound like the white slave trade.'

'It's true. She was one very frightened lady and she is not the sort to panic. She's travelled practically halfway around the world. So be warned. Going to Hong Kong on your own is not like going on a package holiday, you know.'

'I won't be on my own. James has a sister. I shall be well chaperoned.' She set her glass down on the table. 'Anyway, let's eat, otherwise the meat will be dried up.'

He stubbed out his cigarette in the sink. It never failed. Tell Marti not to do something and it was the first thing she would insist upon doing. He checked his watch. 'Just give me a minute to make a quick call.'

'Who are you calling?'

'Christian Debilius.'

'There's no need, Hendrik.'

'No trouble.'

She sighed audibly.

'Stop fretting. The food won't spoil for a couple of minutes.' He picked up the telephone and dialled Christian's number.

Marti removed the casserole dish from the oven and gave the contents a quick stir. Perhaps it wasn't such a bad idea to find out about James Wu's business. She smiled to herself. She couldn't imagine him being a secret white-slave trader at all. He looked as if he couldn't bring himself to hurt a fly.

Hendrik redialled the number. The line was engaged so it must mean Christian was at home. He leaned against the side of the wall when he heard a ringing-out tone. 'Hello? Christian Debilius, please. Hendrik Van den Fleet calling.' He gestured to Marti. 'He's coming on the line now.' He straightened up at the sound of Christian's softly measured tones. 'Hello, Christian, Hendrik here. Hope I'm not inconveniencing. I need a little piece of info.'

'Not at all, Hendrik. How are you?'

'Fine.'

'And your father?'

'Coming out of hospital in a few days. Look, my sister, Martina, is thinking of taking up a job with James Wu of Hong Kong.'

'Really!' A note of surprise sharpened Christian's voice. 'May I ask why? This is unexpected news.'

Hendrik gave a little laugh. 'I thought it might be. Seriously, Marti and I have had thorough discussions about the business since I got back and she feels she needs a change. She wants to build up more international experience. I have said that I won't stand in her way on this.' Hendrik glanced around at Marti and gave a reassuring wink. 'My time in Zaire has proved to be invaluable to me. Hopefully, it will prove to be the case for Marti in Hong Kong.'

'Won't her absence leave a difficult gap to fill, Hendrik?'

A frown creased Hendrik's forehead. It was not the response he had expected from Christian. 'As I say, we have thoroughly discussed this. I am bringing Justus up as a dealer, along with various other promotions that in fact are long overdue. We are all going to miss Marti very much, of course.'

Marti raised both eyebrows. She leaned against the kitchen sink and folded her arms. That was the over-statement of the century. Hendrik hunched one shoulder as if conscious of her gaze. 'I was going to have a more formal chat with you about the changes, but I am really ringing on Marti's behalf. Apparently Wu is offering a partnership and before she puts her money into anything I thought I should check things out for her.'

'Yes, of course. Just give me a minute, Hendrik, and I'll run him through the computer. My first reaction is to say, no problem, but let me verify that.'

'Thanks, Christian.' Hendrik placed his hand over the handset and turned round. 'He's checking Wu on the computer.'

She nodded.

He turned away again. 'Yes, Christian.'

'No worries, Hendrik. Wu is financially very stable. Very active option bearer. We really need seriously to consider upgrading his status. So, no problems in putting money into the company, I should say.'

'Fine. I'll tell Marti.'

'Er, Hendrik, presumably you will have already dis-cussed which clients she is taking with her?'

Hendrik paused. As far as he was concerned, Van den Fleet clients would remain Van den Fleet clients. 'That won't be a problem, I can assure you, Christian.'

'I hope so. Your sister certainly has her admirers, Hendrik. She is a very competent young lady and, if I may say so without causing offence, an extremely attractive young lady. I can think of one Van den Fleet client who will move with her. A most important client, if I am not mistaken.'

Hendrik cleared his throat. He was beginning to regret his impetuous telephone call. 'Sorry,' he gave a forced laugh. 'Not quite *au fait* with Marti's love-life.'

'Seriously, Hendrik.' Christian's voice became more authoritative. 'I am talking about Beni Yasim. I was speaking to him only recently. He thinks very highly of Martina. On all levels, if you take my meaning.'

'Oh, don't worry, Christian. Marti is very level headed. Knows where she is at.'

'So does Yasim. Very much so. He is the fixer for the Arab Trustee Corporation.'

'I didn't know that, I must confess. I have still to get back on stream with European matters, I'm afraid.'

'I advise you to do so as quickly as possible. Perhaps we should have had this conversation much earlier. Martina is not only much respected in Europe, but Wu has the capability to undercut you, Hendrik. The combination will prove irresistible to her faithful followers.'

A muscle flicked in Hendrik's face. Wu's file wasn't the only one Christian had just run through the computer. 'Don't worry, Christian, I –'

'I don't, Hendrik. It is for you to worry. One can see Wu's eagerness to sign Martina up on the dotted line. With her experience, she will place him in a stronger position in the European market place. Much stronger. I wonder, Hendrik, if it is wise of you to allow him to poach your sister from you, as it were.'

A dull flush crept up Hendrik's neck. He gave a short bark of laughter. 'Perhaps, but Marti is a free agent and I can assure you that there won't be a problem as – er – you have outlined.'

'Do I take it that Martina is there with you?'

'Yes. She's just dishing up dinner.'

'May I speak to her for a moment?'

Hendrik's mouth tightened. 'Yes, of course. Hold on.' He swore at himself mentally. He had made Christian nervous. He placed his hand over the handset. 'Quick, Marti. Christian wants to speak to you.' He lowered his voice. 'For God's sake be careful what you say to him. He can and will read anything into everything, then we'll all feel the fallout from the fan.'

Marti slowly walked to the telephone. 'What does he want?'

'I don't know, do I? He just said he wanted to speak to you.'

Marti took the telephone from Hendrik. 'Good evening, Mr Debilius.'

'Martina, please, Christian. I think we have known each other long enough, don't you? Now, Hendrik tells me you are thinking of working in Hong Kong.'

'Yes, I am going there at the weekend.'

'Hendrik tells me you feel ready for some international experience, and I am delighted you feel that way, but why didn't you contact me? You can get no better experience than in New York, you know. I could have lined up a job for you that would have been ideal.'

'How kind of you, Christian. As an option bearer?' She grinned to herself when she heard a slightly muffled sound on the end of the line, then winced as Hendrik pinched her arm and glared at her.

'Not exactly, Martina, I'm afraid that is not within my power. Applications, as you know, are dealt with in strict rotation and terms of priority by the governing committee.'

She smiled cynically. And you just happen to be the head of the governing committee. And applications from women were strictly relegated to the waste-paper bin.

'I have no doubt that the time will come soon when you are elected an option bearer, but in the meantime, what I had in mind, Martina, was an administrative position within the IDE. I think you would find it a challenging and useful learning experience.'

'Thank you very much for the offer. I shall bear it in mind.'

'Good.' Christian's voice registered a little irritation at her cool response. 'Good. Well, get in touch with me whenever you like and we will see what we can arrange for you.'

'Thank you. Would you like to speak to Hendrik again?'

'No, I don't think so.'

'I'll say good night, then.'

'Yes, good night.'

Hendrik grabbed at the telephone as Marti hung up, but was too late. The line had gone dead. He eyed her suspiciously. 'What did he say to you?'

'Offered me a job. I hadn't realised how popular I was.'

He went to speak, but changed his mind. He picked up his glass. 'Going to get myself a refill.'

'Can we eat now, please.'

'Sure.' He turned on his heel and went out.

Hendrik poured a double measure of whisky into his glass and lit up a cigarette. He took the glass and cigarette to the window and pulled back the curtain. He looked out into the darkness. He was liable to make a fool of himself, if he wasn't careful. He had pushed her too far, and underestimated Christian's reaction. He had intended to keep her in check, nothing more. He swallowed a mouthful of whisky. Instead he had ended up opening a can of worms. He should have known the first thing she would do would be to flounce off. Worse still, Christian was behaving as if Van den Fleet's would suddenly collapse if she left. He chewed on his thumbnail. He would have to sort things out with her. He shook his head to himself. His brain was seizing up. Christian, in his inimitable byzantine way, had provided him with an answer to the problem. He turned away from the window at the sound of Marti's voice telling him to come and eat. The job Christian had offered her was meant to keep her under wraps. He should have realised that straight away. He drained his glass and stubbed out his cigarette. It was just a question of persuading her to take it.

Marti had already begun to serve the carbonnades of beef on to two plates when Hendrik reappeared in the kitchen. She carefully spooned slices of onion and gravy on top of the meat. He put his arm around her shoulders and gave her a gentle hug. 'That smells fantastic. Just like Mother used to make it.' He clapped his hand to his forehead. 'Sorry. Didn't do the salad dressing, did I?'

'I've already done it.'

'Sorry about that. Here, let me take the plates to the table.'

She looked at him warily, then chided herself for being suspicious of his motives. She picked up the salad bowl. Trouble was, brotherly concern followed by brotherly affection was too much to absorb all on the same night. She followed after him with the salad bowl. She supposed that he could afford to exhibit both, now that he was getting rid of her.

Anna quietly closed her bedroom door and leaned against it. Her face was still flushed after exchanging sharp words with James. She placed the back of her hand over her mouth. She should not quarrel with her brother, he was older than her, but neither should he expect her to suffer embarrassment because of one of his clients.

James quietly tapped on Anna's bedroom door. 'Anna, I must speak to you. Please open the door.'

Anna pressed the palms of her hands to her cheeks to cool them, then turned around and opened the door. She felt shame at the sight of her brother's strained and tired face. 'I am sorry, James. I should not have spoken the way I did. It was very wrong.'

He ran his fingers through his hair. 'I was wrong too. If Chan Chunling is pestering you then you should not have to attend in his presence. I should respect the feelings of my sister.'

Anna blinked back tears of gratitude. 'You are so tired, James, I should not burden you with these things.'

'No, no, it is just jet lag. I will get over it.'

She clasped her hands in front of her. 'I am being selfish in not entertaining your important client, I know, but I do not like Mr Chan.'

'Do not worry, Anna. You are right to think that it is better that you do not see Chan at all than decline an invitation from him. That way, no offence can be caused.' He ran his fingers through his hair again. 'We have both had a difficult week, haven't we?' He gave a rueful smile. 'Although mine has been the more profitable. I am sorry Candy Lai cancelled the order for the necklace. I know the sale would have created more orders for you in time.'

'I am not worried, James. I half expected it. She is just a time-waster. Fortunately I have many clients who are not.'

The doorbell rang and both James and Anna jumped at the sound. James drew the door shut. 'That will be Chan now. Stay here. I will deal with him.'

Anna gave a grateful smile. She stayed by the door, listening intently to the voices in the hall.

Chan Chunling glanced around the empty sitting room, then at James. James ignored his enquiring look. 'I have the certificates of authentication ready for you, but first may I offer you a drink, Mr Chan?'

'Thank you.'

'Please sit down, Mr Chan.'

'Thank you.' Chan eased himself on to the edge of the sofa. 'I hope that you are well.'

'Yes, I am very well.'

'And your sister, Miss Wu?'

'She is well, too, thank you.'

Chan smoothed the front of his tie flat. 'I am sorry that I do not appear to have the opportunity of speaking to her myself on this occasion.'

James handed him a glass of whisky. 'Anna is working late.' Chan glanced around the room again, as if unsure of what to say next.

James went to the table by the window and took out the certificates from his briefcase. 'I think you will find everything in order, Mr Chan. Here are the certificates and the diamonds for your inspection.'

Chan put down his glass and took the certificates and examined them carefully. 'You have done well. Were any questions asked?'

James gave a brief smile. 'Curiosity is endemic in the diamond world, but there were no questions that I couldn't handle.'

'What questions?'

James shrugged. 'The usual. If the diamonds were for sale. Their origin.'

Chan looked up sharply. 'What did you tell them?'

'That I had no instruction in the former and I personally suspected their origin was Russian.'

Chan continued staring at him as though unconvinced by the explanation.

'Don't worry, Mr Chan, the theory is a very plausible one, but almost impossible to check out. The Russians are known for not always being straight in their dealings. They do not feel obliged to inform the IDE of their every action, so they get blamed for everything whether they are the culprits or not.'

Chan nodded. He placed the diamonds in his briefcase. His disappointment at not seeing Anna clouded his excitement about them.

Chan finished his drink and placed the glass on the table at his side. 'I am very pleased with your work. It is possible that I may have further instructions for you in the very near future.'

James quickly translated Chan's remark to mean a sale, and very soon. 'Of course, Mr Chan, do not hesitate to contact me at any time.'

Chan got to his feet and smoothed his tie again. 'Please convey my good wishes to Miss Wu. We had proposed to have dinner together sometime. I have some business contacts that might be useful to her. I hope you have no objection?'

James smiled politely. 'It is not for me to raise objections, Mr Chan. It is entirely a matter for Anna to decide.'

Chan nodded to himself in satisfaction. He moved to the door. 'I will be in touch with you again.'

Anna eased the bedroom door open when she heard James wishing Chan a very good night, and the front door being opened and shut. She hurried down the hall and looked anxiously at James. 'What did he say?'

James rubbed his hands together. 'My efforts look likely to bear great fruit, Anna. I think Chan's clients want to sell the diamonds.'

She looked at him, excitement brightening her face. 'That will mean much commission for you, James.'

He grinned. 'I knew luck would be with me. I felt it as soon as I touched the diamonds.' He touched her elbow. 'Let us celebrate. Oh, I almost forgot,' his eyes twinkled mischievously. 'Chan told me that you had agreed to have dinner with him.'

She gasped in shock. 'James, that is not true. I didn't.'

'I know, I know, I was only joking. He actually said dinner was proposed and did I have any objections.'

'What did you say?'

'I told him it was entirely up to you.' He gave her a little push towards the sitting room. 'Perhaps you should not ignore our Mr Chan, Anna, he might be useful to you as well as to me.'

She nodded in gloomy acquiescence.

James burst out laughing. 'Anna, you look as if dinner with Chan is worse than a night of a thousand tortures.'

'I do not like the way he looks at me. It makes me feel uncomfortable.'

'You may not have to suffer him looking at you for much longer. When Martina Van den Fleet arrives, he may lose interest in you.'

Her eyes widened at the possibility and also at the thought of entertaining James's honoured guest. 'We must arrange a banquet for her, James.'

'Yes, that is a good idea but first I thought she might come here. We can have a drink together and get to know each other.'

She gave another gasp of astonishment. 'Not here, James. Our humble home is not good enough to receive such a guest.'

'Stop it, Anna. You are so old fashioned. The Europeans don't worry about such matters. You are the only one who does.'

'What if she is offended? What if she does not find me to her liking?'

He sighed. 'She will, and you will like her too. She is very nice and is anxious to meet you. She said so.'

Anna bit her lip. She hoped that was true. 'What does she look like, James? You have not told me.'

'She is a little taller than you. Brown eyes and hair.' He paused for a moment. 'No, not brown. When the sunlight falls on her hair it looks like autumn leaves.'

Anna shot him a quick glance. James was becoming too fascinated by this Miss Van den Fleet.

Pa Jiaming hurried to his desk and snatched up the telephone on the last insistent ring. His secretary informed him that the chairman of the Chinese People's Association for International Trade was calling from Hong Kong. Pa told her to put Fang Ka-Shing through and pulled out a packet of cigarettes from his pocket.

'Jiaming, this is Ka-Shing here. Can we talk?'

'Yes, but be brief. I have a meeting in five minutes.' Pa pulled a cigarette from the packet and lit it.

'I have been informed by Chan that the certificates have been collected and are now in his possession.'

'Were there any problems?'

Fang laughed. 'I believe they were all too dazzled by the sight of Bright Mountain. The people contacted were more interested in whether the merchandise was for sale.'

'How typical of the barbarians, Ka-Shing.'

'Indeed.'

Pa drew on his cigarette and blew a perfect smoke ring into the air. 'Instruct Chan Chunling to dispose of the merchandise and to bank the results as agreed.'

Fang's voice rose with excitement. 'I will go to Shanghai straight away and speak with him.'

'Excellent. The sooner you do, the sooner we can share our interests in Bright Mountain. I must go now, but keep me informed.'

'Yes, Jiaming. I will call from Shanghai.'

Pa put the telephone down and leaned back in his chair. He drew on his cigarette again. The transaction of the diamonds would take perhaps a month. He stood up and stubbed out his cigarette. It was time to inform the Leading Group for High Technology of his need to attend a meeting of UNCTAD in Geneva. By that time funds from the Cayman Islands should have been deposited in his private account. He reached across the desk and pressed a button on the intercom and informed his secretary she was required to work late. He had a report from the Leading Group to prepare, for the Central Military Commission for Scientific Advancement.

*   *   *

Marti surveyed the clothes laid out on the bed and tapped at her mouth with her forefinger. James had said Hong Kong would be wet and very humid. She went to the chest of drawers and pulled out two cardigans. She might just be able to squeeze the cardigans in her suitcase, if she rolled them up and pushed them down the sides. She pursed her lips. Or perhaps not. If she felt cold, she could always buy something there. She checked her watch and pushed the cardigans back into the drawer. Stop dithering, Martina. Hendrik would be home soon and she hadn't even thought about dinner. She drummed her fingers on top of the chest. Dear brother had graciously suggested she took the afternoon off to prepare for her trip. Her fingers drummed a final tattoo before she returned to the task of packing her clothes. The strange peace between them was almost unnerving. She picked up a blouse and padded the collar and cuffs with tissue paper. Hendrik had even washed the dishes the previous evening.

The telephone rang out just as Marti had balanced herself on top of the suitcase and was struggling to close it. She puffed her cheeks out and reached across the bed for the telephone. 'Hello.'

'Marti, your secretary said you would be at home.'

She curled up on the bed. There was no mistaking the slightly husky voice of Beni Yasim. 'Hello, Beni, how are you?'

'Fine. You?'

'Yes.'

'Good. Ah, I've just got back home and got your message on the answering machine. I wasn't sure if it was urgent or not.'

'Oh, sorry, it isn't really. I am going away for a few days and thought I should let you know, in case you were trying to reach me. I checked at the hotel you usually stay at in Geneva, but they said you weren't there, so I thought I would try your home number.'

'Actually, I should have been back in Geneva two days ago, but business has kept me here in Paris. Anyway, may I ask where you are going?'

'Hong Kong.'

'You don't normally venture so far away from home, Marti.'

'It's obviously time I did, then. Actually I'm just taking a break from the office and –' She paused undecided whether to say further or not.

'And are you going alone, or with a party?'

'Just taking myself.'

'How long are you staying out there?'

'Two, maybe three days.'

He groaned. 'What a shame. I have business to conduct in Hong Kong. If I had known I could have brought it forward. We could have met up. Modesty forbids my saying that I am an excellent guide, of course.'

'Of course.'

'But we could have had fun, Marti. What a shame you didn't let me know earlier. Never mind, I shall not be deprived of seeing you. Can you come to Geneva when you return home? I have an order for you. Ten parcels of highest grade industrials at your best possible price.'

Her eyes widened. That was an order well worth coming home for. 'Yes, no problem. Will sometime next week suit?'

'Call me when you get back. I promise definitely to be in Geneva.'

'All right. See you there.'

'Marti, wait a moment, I have had a thought. If you are going alone to Hong Kong let me give you an introduction to a good friend of mine. You may find it useful. His name is, ah, yes here we are, Piers Paulinson. He's the head of Paulinson Pacific.'

'Beni, can you hold for a moment and I will write it down.' She searched on the bed for the old envelope she had used to prepare her packing list. 'OK, so that's Piers Paulinson.' She grabbed her washbag, balancing the envelope on top of it, and quickly made a note of the name and telephone number.

'I will contact Piers and tell him you will get in touch with him.'

'But not if it is inconvenient for him, Beni.'

'It won't be. He and his wife, Marietta, are both charming people. They will be delighted to show you around.'

'Thank you.'

'Enjoy yourself, Marti. I will see you in Geneva next week. By the way, I recommend the Mandarin in Hong Kong. The service is very good.'

She gave a faint laugh. 'Thanks for the recommendation, but it is rather out of my price bracket.'

'Where are you staying?'

'The Continental.'

'I'm afraid I don't know it.'

'I wouldn't expect you to. It is fairly modest by your standards.'

'Well, don't forget to contact the Paulinsons. They will be expecting you. By the way, he is English, but she is of French–Portuguese extraction.'

'Thanks for the warning.'

He gave a throaty laugh. 'See you again, Marti.'

Marti put the telephone down then carefully folded the envelope in two. The instinctive decision to call up Beni had paid off. She put the envelope into her bag and made a note in her filofax for the following week. Beni. Tuesday. Geneva. She tapped the pen against her teeth then drew a heavy line under the words. At least while she was away, Hendrik couldn't take the credit for a deal done with her favourite and most important client.

Chan Chunling looked around the hall of the golden buddhas. It was the middle of the week and, luckily for him, there were few tourists around. He slipped the package from his coat pocket and placed it at the side of the statues, by the foot of the reclining buddha. He looked around again. He stood back and waited.

Chan had been summoned by Fang, the 'faceless one', to attend the temple. There was nothing unusual in that, apart from the command to bring a small number of diamonds with him. No explanation was given. Chan looked around again. Perhaps the 'faceless one' was dissatisfied with his endeavours and had chosen to conduct his business with others personally. He licked his lips. Perhaps his services were no longer required and he could be free of the dangers imposed upon him.

Chan saw the package slowly withdrawn from the foot of the buddha. He heard a slight rustling and stepped forward to wait for his instructions.

'Tell Wu to sell the diamonds.'

'Yes, esteemed Comrade.'

'You know what arrangements to make for the payment?'

'Yes, esteemed Comrade. The money is to be transferred to the bank in Austria.'

'Excellent.'

Chan licked his lips again. 'Is everything to your satisfaction, esteemed Comrade?'

'Yes. Report to me when the diamonds have been sold. That is all.'

Once outside of the confines of the temple, Chan fumbled in his pocket for his cigarettes. He lit one up and inhaled deeply. These visits were a great risk to him. Many people could notice the regularity of them and ask questions. Damning questions to which, if his life was to be spared, he could give no answers.

Frankie 'Eggroll' Heung tapped at the glass of fruit juice in front of him with his pen. 'OK. Extraordinary General

Meeting of the Thousand Clouds Society now convened.
Turtle.'

The man with a wine-red birthmark shaped like a
turtle on his brow continued studying the papers in front
of him.

'Turtle!'

Turtle looked up. 'Sorry, Mr Heung.'

'The agenda, please, Turtle.'

Frankie unwrapped a cigar as Turtle slowly read out the
agenda for the meeting. When Turtle had finished Frankie
leaned forward. 'OK. First item.' He looked around at the
men seated at the table. 'We suffer at this moment in time,
due to tragic and unforeseen circumstances, a manpower
shortage. Ordinarily, we would recruit from our own ranks
to make up the shortfall, but I consider we should use the
opportunity to strengthen our position in the – ah – market place, in readiness for the night of power. As you know,
the island is being handed back to the PRC on the 30 June
1997. On that night, gentlemen, we must be ready to seize
new opportunities. This strategy depends on our having a
strong power base.' Frankie glanced down at the cigar and
realised it was unlit. A hand immediately appeared from
behind him with a cigarette lighter. 'Thank you.' Frankie
puffed on the cigar. 'I have had very constructive dialogue
with Ronnie Lee.' He glanced around the table. 'You all
know Ronnie?'

Turtle look slightly puzzled. Frankie glanced at him and
gave an irritated sigh. 'Ronnie Lee was/is the accountant
for the Brotherhood of the Bear's Paw. Maybe *was* is the
right word at this moment in time. Tragically, Song Enlai
suffered the misfortune of no sons and I am told by Ronnie
that leadership of the brotherhood is, shall we say, still in
dispute. I have therefore proposed to the relatives, through
Ronnie, that our two gangs merge operations.'

There was an audible gasp from the men listening to him.
Frankie raised a hand. 'Not so fast, not so fast. I have

agreed with Ronnie that the Brotherhood of the Bear's Paw will retain their identity, but that their operations will be merged and rationalised with ours. They will take seventy-five per cent of profits from the Tsimshatsui sector, where their members solely and exclusively operate, and where they do not, they will be paid a royalty of twenty-five per cent. Same percentages will apply to the Yaumati sector within the agreed boundary of the typhoon shelter to west of Nathan Road.' Frankie puffed on his cigar again. 'OK. That's Kowloon side. On Hong Kong side, again the same percentages apply to the Wanchai sector including Causeway Bay, but excluding Happy Valley Racecourse.'

Turtle cleared his throat. 'Excuse me, Mr Heung, but won't that take us into the territory of the Third Moon Gang?'

Frankie leaned across and jabbed a finger at the paper in front of Turtle. 'That is dealt with in Item Three.'

'Sorry, Mr Heung.'

'That's OK. Shows you're paying attention. I like that.' Frankie leaned back in his chair again. 'OK. New Territories. Same percentages again, but sector to include Shatin Racecourse, but excluding the Laufaushan oyster sector. Any questions? OK. Item Two.'

Frankie was aware of the uneasy expressions on the faces around the table, but his rank as leader of the gang ensured complete silence. 'I propose fraternal greetings are sent to the Golden Cockerel Gang in Macao.' He sniffed. 'Maybe something comes of it, who knows?'

Turtle, spurred on by Frankie's earlier praise, spoke up. 'They don't like people crowding in on their casino activities, Mr Heung.'

Frankie shrugged. 'So who's crowding them? OK. Item Three. Due to the lengthy vacation that the leader of the Third Moon Gang is enjoying, courtesy of the Governor –' A ripple of laughter ran round the table; Frankie allowed himself a quick smile at his own joke: ' – your chairman can report that he is undertaking negotiations with certain members of the Third Moon Gang to acquire a controlling interest in their operations. I am confident that we can reach agreement on control of the reclamation works at Causeway. Item Four. Update on information on the reasons for our manpower shortage. I am reliably informed by Ronnie Lee that on the night Song Enlai was murdered, his night porter at the garage saw him return to his office with three men. They all left within minutes and he was not seen alive again. Jimmy, Song's runner in Nathan Road, was found in a demised state in the Jade Market. He was last seen entering a bar in Mong Kok with three other guys.' Frankie gestured with his cigar at the men around him. 'Wait for it. The guys' description was similar to the ones seen by the night porter at Song's Automobiles and by my father's – ah – friend, before he – ah – left her to return home.' Frankie looked at each man in turn. 'I have reached solemn agreement with Ronnie Lee and those members of the Third Moon Gang I am in conference with, that these guys seen on these three occasions are not bona fide members of our associations.' He ground the stub of his cigar into the ashtray by his side. 'So, we figure someone thought they could make trouble on the island. The owner of the bar figures the guys might have been from Shanghai, from their accents. I don't know. He could be right. He could be wrong.'

'But we find out, Mr Heung.' The man sitting at the far end of the table spoke out for the first time since the meeting began.

'You got it in one, Busy.'

Busy nodded and flexed his fist. His knuckles cracked loudly.

Frankie looked around the table again. 'Any questions?' Turtle cleared his throat nervously. 'You got a question, Turtle?'

'No, Mr Heung, but maybe I could find something out

about these guys. I have family in Shanghai. Maybe they could ask around.'

'Why not? Who did you have in mind?'

'My uncle. Good man, Mr Heung. He ran four *flower boats* for the Lotus Brotherhood when he was only seventeen.'

Frankie's eyes glazed slightly. He picked up his glass of fruit juice. Holy Jesus. The guy had to be in his seventies. He took a sip of juice and smacked his lips. 'Those were the days, Turtle. Remember my grandfather saying they floated out the most beautiful girls in Shanghai. Hey, you tell this uncle to take it easy, OK?'

'Sure, Mr Heung.'

'OK. Final business, gentlemen. Your chairman's strategy is this: following on from my father, it is my intention to strengthen the power base of the Thousand Clouds Society to meet the demands that the night of power will bring. Whether by acquisition or merger, we shall become the lead brotherhood on the island.' He banged his fist on the table. 'What is not my intention is that those shits from Guangzhou will take over the island in 1997.' Frankie folded his arms across his chest. 'With fraternal ties established with our Golden Cockerel neighbours in Macao, we will drive those shits straight back across the border. If we don't, they're going to come at us and we are going to be as wide open as a whore's legs. Right?'

The men around the table nodded their agreement. One or two looked at each other as if in sudden understanding of what the meeting was really about.

'OK. OK.' Frankie unfolded his arms. 'Business concluded.' He clasped his hands in front of him and bent his head. 'We will observe the ritual of fire and blood for my father's spirit and his ancestors.' He turned to Turtle. 'You have always been loyal to my father.' He placed his hand on Turtle's shoulder. 'You will light the flame, Turtle.'

Turtle's eyes filled with tears. 'I don't deserve that honour, Mr Heung.'

'Sure you do, Turtle.'

Turtle rose to his feet and crossed to the table by the door. He struck a match and lit a small, ornately carved bronze lamp. He then unsheathed an ivory-handled knife. Frankie and the other men got to their feet and walked slowly up to Turtle. Turtle rested the knife on the palms of his hand and offered it first to Frankie. Frankie picked it up and flicked it quickly across the side of his wrist. He raised his hand over the lamp. Two drops of blood fell on to the flame. The flame sputtered for a second. Frankie returned the knife to Turtle's outstretched palms. Turtle waited for Frankie to join him at his side, then offered the knife to the next man.

Candy Lai pushed at her hair with her fingertips, then straightened the short tight skirt of her suit. She sat back in the armless, wooden chair and crossed her legs. She had collected her monthly salary from Heung & Co., but had been told to wait. Mr Frankie Heung was in conference, but he wanted to see her.

Frankie examined the wound on his wrist, then applied a clean bandage. Turtle leapt forward. 'Can I help you, Mr Heung?'

'No, I can manage. Wait a minute, is Candy Lai around?'

'Yes, Mr Heung. I told her she had to wait.'

'Go check if she is menstruating, will you?' Frankie pulled the end of the bandage tight with his teeth. 'If she is, tell her to come back when she is clean. It would be disrespectful to the blood of my father to see her.'

Candy looked at the birthmark on Turtle's face and averted her eyes. Ugliness made her feel frightened. It was the mark of misfortune. Turtle tapped her on the shoulder. 'Mr Heung wants to know if you are menstruating.'

Candy's mouth dropped open.

'If you are, he says to come back when you're clean.'

She raised her chin in an attempt at dignity. 'That is none of Mr Heung's business, but as it happens I am not.'

Turtle nodded and went back to Frankie's office.

Frankie picked up a file and opened it. He flicked through the pages. He looked across the desk at Candy. 'You've been on the payroll for some time now Candy.'

She examined her nails. 'Time flies doesn't it?'

'Don't get smart, lady.'

She widened her eyes. 'I'm not, Frankie.'

'OK. Let me ask you a question. Do you consider yourself a cost-effective part of the work going on here?'

She widened her eyes to their fullest extent. 'Cost-effective? Don't know what you mean, Frankie.'

'I mean cost-effective as in, we are paying you a salary, are we getting anything in return. So far, it seems to me that we have been getting a load of crap.'

She pouted. 'That's not fair, Frankie. I told you Fang Ka-Shing is giving out tenders next month for the computerised container terminal system at Lo Wu.' Her mouth worked itself into a tremor, as if she was about to cry. 'And I told you that Erwin Klein had given him a generous gift on behalf of the German consortium.'

'Yeah, yeah. Big deal. Show me a guy on the Island who doesn't take a gift home now and then.' He jabbed a finger at her. 'What you are not telling me, is something personal. *Personal*. Do you read me, Candy?'

'Sure, Frankie.'

'Fine, because if you don't come up with something good, your name isn't going to stay on the payroll for much longer.'

'Uncle Joey –'

'Stop calling my father "uncle".' His eyes glittered. 'You are not a blood relative. He never was your uncle. You're related by marriage, that's all.' He slung an arm over the back of his chair. 'So what's it to be, Candy? Do you want to start looking for alternative employment?'

She hung her head. 'It's difficult, Frankie. If I ask too many questions Fang will get suspicious. Un –' She bit her lip. 'The late Mr Heung always said a little information was better than no information at all.'

Frankie breathed out through clenched teeth, making a soft whistling noise.

'I'm seeing Fang tonight, Frankie. He's given me a special gift. He usually talks a lot when he has given me a gift and' – she giggled softly – 'I've given him his gift.'

He nodded wearily.

She nervously picked at the side of her thumb, wondering what to say that would please him. 'He's taking me to the Jockey Club at the weekend. I think he's really beginning to trust me, Frankie, I really do. He's given me a diamond necklace specially made for me.'

'Which night?'

She gave a little shrug of her shoulders. 'Saturday, I think.'

'Shit. Look, you do me a favour, OK? I'm entertaining some very important people at the Club on Saturday night. If you see me, you don't know me. Right?'

'Right, Frankie.'

'What's all this about a necklace?'

'A diamond necklace. He said there isn't another in the whole world like it. I just told you, he's had the diamonds specially made up for me. He's really cute, isn't he?'

He nodded. 'Real cute.' He stared at her quizzically. 'Are they genuine?'

'Sure, Frankie. I got them looked over. They're the real thing.' He nodded again and swivelled around in his chair to face the window.

'What's the matter, Frankie?'

'Shut up. I'm thinking.'

Candy sighed heavily to indicate that she was bored with the long silence that had developed. Frankie slowly turned back to face his desk. 'I must be going crazy or something, doing your work for you, but the diamonds would be loose. Right?'

'Er –'

'OK. Let's take it a step at a time. He didn't buy the necklace off the shelf. Right? So, he must have bought the diamonds loose. Right?'

'Oh! Right, Frankie.'

'Step two. Find out where the diamonds came from.'

She looked at him doubtfully.

'Come on, that's not difficult. When you're pillow-talking, find out the name of the jeweller who made up the diamonds, OK?'

'OK, Frankie.'

'Get that information to me on Monday and don't screw up. Shoot through now. I've got a couple of calls to make.'

She picked up her bag and slung it over her shoulder. She shot him a puzzled glance as she went to the door. He picked up the telephone. 'Get me Ronnie Lee. Try the Cortina Club.'

Hendrik heaved the suitcase into the boot of the car then picked up Marti's travel bag. 'How long did you say you were going for?'

'Three days possibly.'

He slammed the lid shut. 'Thank God you're not going for a month. You would need a truck to carry your luggage.'

'Could we just drive to the airport, please.'

'Don't panic. There's plenty of time.' He slung himself into the driver's seat and stretched across to unlock the passenger door. Marti settled herself in the seat, then craned her neck to look at the apartment block. Change. She looked away and busied herself with checking the documents in her bag. We all had to adapt to change.

As the airport lights twinkled into view, Hendrik swung off the autoroute on to the approach road. Marti bit her lip, suddenly filled with doubt. She really should have stayed until Father arrived home. 'Make sure the housekeeper doesn't bully Father, Hendrik. She appears very strict. Father is used to his own routine at home.'

He sighed heavily. 'Stop worrying. He needs someone strict. You know what Father is like. He will have a lesser person reduced to tears inside seconds.'

She gave a reluctant nod.

Johannes pushed his way through the crowded terminal. He caught sight of Marti and Hendrik, and waved frantically. Marti saw him and waved back. 'Hendrik, look, Johannes is here.'

Hendrik glanced over his shoulder. 'Must be glad to get rid of you.' He touched her arm. 'Sorry, sorry. I didn't say that.'

She gave him a disgusted look. When Johannes reached them she held out her hand to him. 'Johannes, you shouldn't have bothered to come and see me off.'

Johannes kissed her cheek. 'I wasn't sure I was going to make it. The traffic is really heavy.'

Hendrik bent down and picked up Marti's travel bag, as her flight was called over the PAS. 'Time to go.'

'Have a good trip, Marti.' Johannes squeezed her hand and shot her a confiding look.

'Thanks. I hope to.'

'I'll walk with you to the gate.' Johannes nodded to Hendrik. 'I'll take Marti's bag.'

Hendrik passed the bag to Johannes, at the same time bending down to give Marti a swift peck on the cheek. She raised an eyebrow in astonishment, but decided it had been done purely for Johannes's benefit. Hendrik slung his raincoat over his shoulder. 'I won't wait, Marti, I need to get back and finish some work.'

'Thanks for the lift to the airport.'

'You're welcome.' He pushed his hands into his pockets and watched Johannes guide Marti through the crowds; a protective arm around her shoulders. He shook his head to himself. If he watched them for much longer, he would begin to feel sorry for her. The guy was as gay as hell, but Marti could never see it. He checked his watch and walked swiftly out of the terminal. With the apartment all to himself, Berenice was in for a night to remember.

James Wu picked up the telephone, at the same time switching off the sound on the television. 'Ah, hello, Mr Chan.' He listened intently for a few seconds then gave a quiet, knowing smile. 'Of course, Mr Chan. No problem. The diamonds attracted much interest. Fine. Er – yes, she is here. I'll fetch her.' James got up from the sofa and went to the door. 'Anna, call for you.' He waited until Anna appeared then shot a finger at the telephone. 'It's Chan, he wants me to sell the diamonds and' – he grinned at her – 'he wants to speak to you.'

She rolled her eyes. He gave her a push into the sitting room.

Anna smoothed the hair from her face before picking up the telephone. 'Mr Chan, Anna Wu speaking.'

'Good evening, Miss Wu. I am glad you are at home, now we can arrange a date for dinner, perhaps. I have mentioned your name to a colleague. He has expressed great interest in your designs.'

Anna looked at James in desperation. He mouthed a few words, but she couldn't understand him. 'Will you excuse me for just one moment, Mr Chan?'

'Yes, but I will not excuse you our dinner date.' He laughed to indicate his words were partly a joke.

James scribbled a note on the telephone pad. Anna

squinted at the hasty scrawl then nodded. 'Mr Chan, my apologies for keeping you on the line. I'm afraid you *will* have to excuse me. James has an important guest arriving tomorrow and I must be here to help entertain her during her stay.'

Chan laughed again. 'Surely if it is a lady, your brother will prefer to entertain her alone.'

Anna raised her eyes to the ceiling. Chan Chunling always had swift and ready answers. James quickly scribbled another note on the pad and tugged at Anna's arm. She looked down at it and her face flushed with relief. 'Mr Chan, my brother James has just suggested that perhaps we should all dine together. Make up a foursome. Would that be possible?'

Chan paused. Four was a crowd, but better than nothing. 'I shall be honoured to be your partner, Miss Wu.'

She smiled, believing that it would bring genuine warmth to her voice. 'Thank you, Mr Chan.'

'May I speak to your brother again, please?'

'Certainly.' Anna handed the telephone back to James. She stood at his side and gazed at him in admiration. James was so clever. A foursome would prevent embarrassing advances from Mr Chan. James wriggled his finger in his ear. 'Look forward to it. I'll call you when our honoured guest arrives.' He burst out laughing. 'No chance. I'm afraid she is purely a business colleague.'

Anna looked at James disapprovingly, guessing the reason for his vulgar laughter to be lewd.

James put the telephone down and went to the sideboard to pour himself a drink. Anna followed him. 'Will it be difficult to sell the diamonds?'

He laughed again. 'No, I can sell them four times over, but it will be interesting to see if Martina Van den Fleet lives up to her words.'

'Do you think she will?'

'I'd be willing to gamble on it.' He tossed back the whisky. 'Don't cook for me, I'll eat at the club.' He picked up his jacket from the back of the sofa. 'And don't wait up.'

Anna cast her gaze downwards. James gambled too much. On everything.

PART 3

Kai Tak airport on the Kowloon side was one of the busiest airports in Asia. Marti searched the sea of faces around her and panicked for a moment, believing she might not recognise James amongst the oriental features that looked so similar. A middle-aged American who had struck up a conversation while they both waited for their luggage, tapped her on the shoulder. 'Hi, again. You having trouble locating your party, too?'

She looked at him with ever growing relief. He had told her he was a construction engineer with a smattering of Cantonese. If she couldn't find James Wu, at least she could rely on her fellow traveller to guide her to a taxi and her hotel. The American slung his travel bag on to his shoulder. 'Uhhu, I think I've just located my party.' He held out his hand to her. 'Guess I'll say 'bye.'

As Marti turned to shake hands she suddenly noticed a large piece of white card held up above someone's head bearing her name in large letters. 'Oh, thank goodness. I think I see my party, too.' She shook hands with the American. He smiled. 'See you around.'

Marti hurried to the white card slowly being moved from left to right. 'Mr Wu, Mr Wu.' James lowered the card from above his head and smiled broadly. 'Miss Van den Fleet, welcome to Hong Kong.'

'Thank you, and thank you very much for coming to meet me. I do appreciate your trouble.'

'My pleasure that you should make the journey to come and see me.'

The traffic in the cross-harbour tunnel leading from Kowloon to Hong Kong was reduced to a crawling pace. James smiled apologetically. 'I am afraid it is often like this.'

Marti looked out of the front window of the car. 'Home from home for me. The Kennedy Tunnel in Antwerp is just the same.'

James lit up a cigarette. 'You know, it is a pity that first-time travellers no longer arrive by ship. It is much the best way to enjoy the beauty of the fragrant harbour.'

'Fragrant harbour?'

'It is the translation of the words Hong Kong. Although, when you smell it, you might not agree on the accuracy of the translation.'

She laughed in amusement. 'Sounds like Antwerp again. So much industry has grown up on the left bank of the Schelde. The waters are becoming very polluted.'

James nodded and turned his attention to the traffic again as the vehicles ahead suddenly speeded up.

The Continental Hotel was situated in a fairly quiet side-street off Connaught Road in Central District. A very small, young boy in an immaculately laundered white shirt and dark trousers hurried to the rear of James's car. He gave a quick bow from the shoulders and collected Marti's luggage. She looked up at the grey, drab building. It would not be Beni Yasim's idea of a hotel, but it was all that she could afford. James looked at her anxiously. 'There is something wrong?'

She gave a quick smile. 'No, no.'

When she stepped inside the hotel, her spirits lifted. Everywhere was spotlessly clean with bowls of flowers dotted around the tiny foyer. The woman behind the reception desk stepped forward. 'Welcome to Hong Kong and the Continental Hotel, Miss Van den Freet. We hope you are very happy staying here.'

Marti suppressed a slight smile at the mispronunciation of her name. The young boy who had removed her luggage from the car, stood to attention by the desk, still grimly hanging on to her suitcase and travel bag. Marti turned to James and held out her hand. 'Thanks for the invitation to drinks. I'll see you later, then.'

James shook her hand enthusiastically. 'I will be here promptly at six. Anna is looking forward to meeting you very much.'

'Thank you. I am looking forward to meeting Anna, too.'

The receptionist handed the key to Marti's room to the young boy. James gave a brief salute as he went out through the door and Marti turned to follow the boy to the elevator. It was very small and she just managed to squeeze herself in alongside the boy and the luggage.

Marti took a quick glance around the bedroom then gave the boy a HK$10 note. He immediately put his hand into his pocket and pulled out a few coins.

'No, no, that is all for you.'

His face broke out into a huge smile and he gave a little bow again. 'Thank you, thank you.'

When he had closed the door behind him, she made a quick tour of inspection. Like the foyer downstairs, everything was neat and spotlessly clean and very cramped. She rubbed her eyes, feeling suddenly weary. She opened the door of a mini refrigerator-bar and took out a bottle of mineral water. The travel agent in Antwerp had said space was at a premium in Hong Kong and therefore hotel prices were extremely high. She poured some water into a glass and drank thirstily. She looked around her again, wishing she could be back in the airy spaciousness of her bedroom at home.

The telephone warbled softly and Marti reached across the bed to answer it.

'Miss Van den Freet? There is a call for you. A Mr Piers Paulinson.' The receptionist's voice spoke in almost awed tones.

'Thank you. Put him through.'

'Miss Van den Fleet, Piers Paulinson here. How do you do? We haven't met, but I believe we have a mutual friend, Beni Yasim.'

Marti's face brightened into a smile. James's departure had left her feeling slightly abandoned. 'Mr Paulinson, thank you for ringing.'

'No trouble. I know you will want to rest after your flight, but when can we meet? May I suggest this evening? Both my wife and myself are looking forward to meeting you.'

'That is very kind, but I'm afraid I have to meet a business colleague this evening.'

'Lunch tomorrow, then?'

'Yes, that would be fine.'

'Super. Shall we say twelve-thirty for one? The chauffeur will pick you up.'

She rubbed at her forehead, thinking she must have missed some of the conversation. 'Where are we meeting?'

'Sorry; home, if that's all right. We have a humble abode on the Peak.'

'Ah, I see. Well, look forward to meeting you, Mr Paulinson.'

'Piers, please. We tend to be an informal lot out here. May I call you Marti?'

'Yes, of course.'

'Fine. See you tomorrow. 'Bye.'

She put the telephone down and made a quick note in her filofax. She yawned and blinked her eyes a few times to shake off the feeling of incipient sleep. She would take a shower, then call Antwerp. Father should be comfortably installed at home by now.

Anna carefully smoothed the sides of her head, checking for any stray wisps of hair, as she heard James open the front door. She bent down and quickly rearranged the four little bowls of American-style roasted nuts and savoury nibbles.

James was laughing as he pushed the sitting-room door open. 'Anna, come and welcome our honoured guest.' He gestured with his arm at Anna. 'My sister, Anna. Miss Martina Van den Fleet.'

Anna bowed her head. 'How do you do, Miss Van den Fleet.'

Marti held out her hand. 'I am so glad to meet you at last, James has told me so much about you.'

James hurried across to the sideboard. 'Marti, what would you like to drink?'

Anna's eyes flicked open at James's casual use of Marti's nickname. She shot a quick glance at him. Such intimacy was impolite to a stranger. Anna bowed her head again and gestured towards the sofa. 'Please, Miss Van den Fleet, if you will sit here.' She clasped her hands together in front of her. 'James and I must apologise for the humbleness of our home.'

Marti stared at her in surprise. 'Please don't apologise.' She glanced around the room. 'I think it is a lovely room.' She gave a friendly smile. 'And please call me Marti.'

'Thank you.'

Marti sat down on the sofa. James had warned her that his sister had not travelled as much as he had, and was very reserved in the old-fashioned Chinese way. She was glad he had. His sister's reserve was bordering on coldness. Her thoughts were interrupted by James coming to the sofa and asking her again what she would like to drink. She turned her attention to the array of bottles on the sideboard. She spotted a bottle of semi-dry vermouth. 'May I have some vermouth, please.'

'With ice?'

She hesitated. The travel agent had warned only to drink mineral or boiled water. James guessed at her hesitation.

'We prefer to drink boiled water ourselves, and Anna uses it to make ice-cubes, don't you, Anna?'

'Yes, indeed. I make them every day.'

Marti laughed. 'Ice it is, then.' She glanced sideways at Anna, who was perched on the edge of a chair with her hands clasped in her lap. She appeared to be very tense.

James handed Marti a glass of vermouth then passed a glass of fruit juice to Anna. He gestured at the bowls on the table. 'Anna.'

Anna flushed and leapt to her feet. 'Forgive me, I am very rude.' She picked up a bowl of nuts and offered it to Marti. Marti thanked her and scooped a few nuts into her hand. She noticed that Anna's hand shook slightly and realised that for some reason or other the girl was terrified. She popped a couple of nuts into her mouth. James came to sit down beside her. For a moment there was an embarrassing silence. Marti gestured to the bowl of flowers on the table. 'What lovely flowers. They are beautifully arranged.' She looked at Anna. 'Did you do these?'

Anna nodded.

'I wish I was as artistic as you.'

Anna smiled warmly for the first time. Marti took a sip of her drink. She wished she had Anna's bone structure, too. Anna's face was sculptured as finely as any statue. Anna caught Marti's glance and smiled again. Marti carefully set her glass on a free corner of the table. 'James tells me that you are a jewellery designer, Anna. I do hope you will let me see some of your work.'

'Yes, of course, I shall be honoured to receive your opinion.'

'James says you own a boutique as well.'

'Yes. I am pleased to say that business is encouraging.'

Marti nodded, then stifled a yawn, making her eyes water. Again there was an uncomfortable silence. Marti picked up her drink and took a small sip. 'What kind of designs do you do, Anna? Do you create them entirely yourself, or do your clients tell you what they want?'

Anna thought for a moment. 'Both, I suppose. Usually clients will bring in a gown, if they are attending a special event; or, if they are making a gift to someone, they will describe the person.'

'Ah, I see, and you create something to suit each individual.'

'Yes.'

Marti rotated the glass between her fingers. Making small talk with Anna was very hard work. 'Where do you get your inspiration from, or is that an artistic secret?'

Anna laughed. The sound was as soft as wind bells. 'From everything around me. Flowers, birds, everything.'

'What are you working on at the moment?'

'I have been specially commissioned to produce a set of jewellery for a client.'

'What inspiration have you used?'

'The butterfly.'

'How unusual. What materials are you using?'

'I am working in silver and lapis lazuli.'

'Are they your favoured materials?'

'I am trained to work in gold and diamonds and they are my preferred materials.'

'Ah, I see.' Marti took another sip of vermouth. The question and answer routine with Anna was becoming rather tedious.

'I think diamonds are the most beautiful and perfect stones to work with.'

Marti glanced quickly at Anna, surprised by the sudden, unsolicited statement.

'Do you like diamonds, Miss Van den Fleet?'

'Please call me Marti, and this will sound very philistine of me, but I don't think I actually notice their beauty. I look for soundness of quality, value. I suppose my job doesn't give me much time to actually admire them.'

James suddenly broke his self-imposed silence and

gestured at the ring on Marti's finger. 'That is a beautiful diamond, Marti.'

Marti held up her hand, as if inspecting the ring for the first time. 'It is very small, but it is "D" Grade VVS.'

'That means, Anna, that it is very white with only a tiny inclusion.'

A flicker of irritation crossed Anna's face as James spoke. She bent her head and remained silent. James had humiliated her. Marti Van den Fleet would think her ignorant. Sensing a slight awkwardness, Marti struggled to say something polite. 'As a designer, Anna, I think you must be as good as anyone in judging diamonds.'

Anna raised her head. 'Yes, I am, and I think your ring is very beautiful.'

'Thank you. Actually, it's my mother's ring. My father gave it to her when I was born.' Marti paused as she noticed a quick exchange of glances between brother and sister.

'The ring must be very precious to you.' Anna got to her feet. 'If you will excuse me now, I will leave you and James to talk. I have enjoyed our meeting very much.'

'Me too.' Marti managed a brief smile. She still hadn't got over her astonishment at Anna's obedient response to a mere look from her brother.

James waited until Anna had left the room before springing to his feet and picking up Marti's glass. 'Let me refill that for you. I thought tomorrow we might go to my office and you can take a look round. See what you think of it.'

'I'd like to. Thank you.' Marti leaned back into the sofa. They were getting down to business after the excruciatingly polite small talk.

'I don't know what ideas you have about salary, but I had planned on a consultant getting approximately HK$200,000 plus a profit-sharing bonus, say fifty-fifty.' He glanced back at her. 'What do you think?'

She made a rapid calculation into Belgian francs. 'Sounds reasonable.' She crossed her legs and settled deeper into the sofa. It was more than she earned at Van den Fleet's and any commission that was earned had always been expected to be ploughed back into the company. But she must check on the cost of living and accommodation in Hong Kong.

'Obviously, in the first year, any new clients you brought into the business would be treated on an enhanced commission basis.'

'You're looking for new business, James?'

He came back to the sofa and handed back her glass. 'I need to broaden the base. I want to expand the European market. I do a fantastic amount of business with the Japanese, but, as I say, I would be happier with a broader marketing base.'

She smiled to herself. She was standing on the other side of the looking glass. Hendrik wanted to get out of Europe into Japan. James wanted to get out of Japan into Europe. 'May I ask a question, James?'

'Sure.'

'Are you in discussion with others about a partnership?'

'I shall be honest and say no.' He slowly rubbed his hands together. 'I have had opening negotiations with one or two people over the last few months, but they haven't come to anything. People, you see, are uncertain about Hong Kong after 1997.'

'What do you think will happen?'

'I think things will change, obviously, once the island reverts to the PRC, but I don't believe those changes will be for the bad. It would be a severe loss of face on the part of the PRC for the island's economy to run down. It would be bad face with the British, who are leaving a thriving and expanding economy behind them, for a start. There are those who also say, and I am one of them, that Hong Kong is the PRC's window on the trading world. They need us rather more than we need them.' He flicked open the cigarette box on the table. 'Would you like one?'

'No thanks, but you go ahead.'

He picked out a cigarette and lit it. 'What I have said, of course, is not to imply that I see you as a last resort. It is simply that I need someone now, and I respect your knowledge and experience very much. I couldn't believe my good luck when you called me.' He drew on the cigarette. 'Excuse me for asking, but have you reached agreement with your brother about distribution of clients between yourselves?'

'No. It isn't something that will arise.' She picked up her glass. 'Frankly, James, that is something that the clients will decide, not us. Clients are only concerned about two things. Quality. Price. Loyalty to one particular dealer doesn't arise.'

He pursed his lips in doubt. 'I think you are being very modest, Marti. A dealer's honesty and integrity also has a price tag, and yours comes pretty high.'

She smiled. 'That is kind of you to say so.'

'It is true. You are highly respected, particularly by the Israelis.'

'Ah, been checking up, have we?'

He gave a slightly embarrassed grin. 'Forgive me.'

'Not at all. I would do the same thing if our positions were reversed. I suppose clients' opinions are a dealer's best visiting card.'

'Indeed.'

'What kind of capital would you expect a partner to inject?'

He shrugged. 'That isn't particularly important to me. Not at the moment, anyway. Perhaps after a six- or twelve-month period, to see how things go, it might be a matter for negotiation.'

She nodded.

'Are there any other questions you want to ask of me?'

'Not for the moment, James. Can we leave it until tomorrow at your office? I might think of some then.'

'Yes, fine.'

She glanced at her watch. 'I'm sorry, I hadn't realised how late it is. I'd better be on my way.'

'Er, if you haven't any plans for the evening, shall we eat together and chew the fat, as the Americans say?'

'Thank you; and no, I don't have any plans.'

'Fine.' He drained his glass. 'I'll just get my jacket. There is an excellent place near the beach. They specialise in seafood.'

'Sounds interesting.'

'I'll just tell Anna we're going out. Won't be a minute.'

She too got to her feet. 'Could I wash my hands?'

'Sure, sure. Third door on the left in the hall. I'll show you.'

As Marti passed the kitchen she took a quick glimpse inside. Anna was standing at a table swiftly slicing vegetables into tiny shreds. James pointed to the door lower down the hall. 'That door there, Marti.'

'Oh, thanks.'

He stuck his head round the kitchen door. 'Don't cook for me, Anna, we are eating out.'

Anna laid her knife down. 'James, can I speak with you a moment.'

He pushed the door open wide. 'What is it?'

'The banquet, James. We need to make arrangements.'

He clapped his hand to his forehead. 'Forgot all about it. I'll mention it to Marti when she comes back.'

Marti stared in astonishment at the sanitary ware in the small closet. She stepped up to the lavatory and peered at the row of press buttons on the top. She pressed the first one marked with three wriggly arrows. Nothing appeared to happen and she pressed the second one marked with a musical note. She clapped her hand over her mouth to stop herself laughing when she heard the strains of a Viennese waltz. She shook her head in disbelief. She pressed the third button marked with a teardrop. Water jetted into the bowl. She raised her eyebrows in relief. At least she knew how to operate the most important function. She sat down then gave a startled gasp. She had discovered the function of the first button. It heated the lavatory seat.

James was still standing in the doorway of the kitchen talking to Anna, when Marti reappeared. She gave a discreet cough as she approached.

'Oh, Marti, Anna's just reminded me. We wondered if you would like to experience a Chinese banquet during your stay?'

'Love to, thank you.'

'Fine. Anna will be bringing a guest along as well. He also happens to be a business colleague of mine.'

'I look forward to meeting him.'

James rubbed his hands together. 'Er, Anna, we should be back for coffee in a couple of hours.' He turned to Marti. 'Well, shall we go?'

Marti nodded. She dutifully followed him to the front door. The man was a born organiser, especially of women; almost on a par with Hendrik.

Erasmus stared at the television, his eyelids occasionally drooping. He had been settled into a chair in front of it. A table had been drawn up alongside with everything he needed readily to hand: his reading spectacles, newspaper, glass of water, remote-control unit for the television. He shifted in the chair. He should not have encouraged Marti to go on holiday. He missed her cheerful chatter. The housekeeper did nothing but issue instructions. He scowled to himself. The old harridan. He peered at the clock on the sideboard. Hendrik had said he was going out for ten minutes to buy some cigarettes. That had been half an hour ago. He turned his attention to the images on the screen again.

The housekeeper came into the sitting room and bustled up to Erasmus. 'Time to go to bed, Mr Van den Fleet.'

'Where's Hendrik?'

'He'll be back very soon. Now, let me help you up.'

Erasmus shook off the hand on his upper arm. 'I'll go to bed when I want to.'

'Now come along, Mr Van den Fleet, you know what the heart specialist said. Rest is essential. You have only been allowed home on the condition that you take proper rest.'

Erasmus's eyes brimmed with helpless tears. He didn't know why they didn't just put him to sleep permanently and be done with him. The housekeeper crouched down by his side. 'What is the matter, Mr Van den Fleet?' She patted his hand. 'You mustn't upset yourself, you know.'

He snatched his hand away. 'I am not upsetting myself. You are upsetting me. Go away. I don't want you here.'

The housekeeper sighed loudly and got to her feet. 'Very well.'

Hendrik was greeted by the housekeeper when he returned. She looked at her watch. 'You said ten minutes, Mr Hendrik. Your father has been asking for you.'

'Sorry. I was delayed. Met someone I know. Couldn't get away.'

'Your father appears to be upset about something and he refuses to go to bed. He says he doesn't want me here.'

He rolled his eyes. 'Leave it to me. I'll go and have a talk to him.'

Erasmus glanced fretfully at Hendrik as he came into the sitting room.

'Sorry I took a long time, Father. Met someone.' Hendrik looked at the television. 'What are you watching?'

Erasmus shrugged his shoulders and didn't answer.

'Thought you were going to watch the match. Should be a good game.'

'When's Marti coming home?'

'Couple of days.'

Erasmus folded the edge of the blanket, covering his knees, into small pleats. 'She couldn't have been very concerned about me, going away like that.'

Hendrik looked at him sharply. 'Now, come on, Father. You agreed to her going.'

Erasmus sniffed. 'She didn't need much persuasion, did she?'

Hendrik pushed his hands into his pockets. 'I persuaded her to go. I insisted she took a break. Marti's been under a lot of pressure, what with work and everything. Now, if you don't want to watch television, how about me helping you to bed. I'll sit with you until the night nurse arrives. He should be here in half an hour or so.'

Erasmus shut his eyes. He was surrounded by strangers. Strangers who saw nothing but a tiresome old body that had to be serviced like a worn-out machine.

'Come on, Father, it's your first day home from the hospital. You need to take it easy. If you feel a bit stronger tomorrow and it's fine weather, I'll take you for a drive in the country.'

Erasmus nodded in wearied acceptance. He gripped the arms of his chair and raised himself up.

Hendrik slipped his arm underneath Erasmus's shoulders. 'Take it easy, Father, let me take your weight.'

The night nurse quietly opened the bedroom door and slipped into the room. Hendrik looked up from the bible he had been reading aloud to his father and glanced at Erasmus. He closed the bible and eased his shoulders back. The night nurse tiptoed to Hendrik's chair. 'Has he been asleep long?'

'Not sure. Probably not long.'

Erasmus opened his eyes. 'I'm not asleep and stop whispering.'

The night nurse smiled cheerfully. 'Good evening, Mr Van den Fleet, my name's Paul. I shall be with you throughout the night, so don't worry about a thing.'

Erasmus turned his head on the pillow and looked away from him. Paul bent down and whispered into Hendrik's ear. 'Leave him with me now. I'll get him settled down. The scriptures his favourites, are they?' Hendrik gave a quick nod. He stood up and flexed his shoulders again in relief. Nursing the old and the irascible was not his particular forte.

The housekeeper held out the telephone to Hendrik as he came into the sitting room. 'Your sister is on the line, Mr Hendrik.'

'Thanks.' Hendrik rubbed a hand across his eyes. That was all he needed. He picked up the telephone. 'Marti?'

'Oh, Hendrik, sorry I'm late in calling. I couldn't get through earlier. How's Father?'

'Fine. Very cheerful.'

'I'm so glad. Can I speak to him?'

'Er, he's just gone to bed. He's very tired. Understandable. It's his first day back home.'

'Yes, of course. I'm sorry I couldn't call earlier.'

'Don't worry. Everything is under control. How's Hong Kong?'

'Interesting.'

'How are you getting on with Wu?'

'No problems. He seems very keen to have me here. He says he wants to broaden his European base. He's offered a very good salary plus commission, which for the first time in my life I can actually keep.'

He gave an abrupt laugh. 'If you are trying to make me envious, you are succeeding. He doesn't need another dealer by any chance?'

'I'll mention it.'

'Well, glad you seem to be having a good time. Met any white-slave traders yet?'

'Not yet, but I'll keep trying. How are you?'

'Not too bad.'

'How is Father getting on with the housekeeper?'

He laughed again. 'I think that should be how is the housekeeper getting on with Father. She's spent most of the day going around looking as if she has been hit by a bomb.'

'Well it's good to know Father is back on form.'

'He's fine. Don't worry about a thing.'

'Well, I'll go now. Tell him I called, won't you?'

'I will. 'Bye.' Hendrik put the telephone down and let his breath out slowly. He went to the sideboard and poured himself a large glass of whisky. He had believed Marti was his main problem. Now it looked as if Father was going to be the real problem.

The Cortina Club was a topless bar with a rear room devoted to illegal gambling. Frankie Heung pushed his way into the bar, gave a perfunctory glance at two girls tiredly gyrating to disco music, then went to the door at the far end and rapped on it twice. He waited a few seconds, then the man who had inspected him through the spy-hole unlocked the door. 'Have a good evening, Mr Heung.'

'You too.' Frankie looked around. 'Ronnie Lee here?'

'At the middle table, Mr Heung.'

'Thanks.' Frankie strolled up to the table where Ronnie was playing fan tan and waited for a chance to catch his eye: when he did, he gave a slight jerk of his head.

Ronnie nodded and gathered up his winnings. He vacated his seat to a man standing behind him and went to join Frankie in the corner of the room. 'How are you doing, Frankie?'

'OK. Listen, you remember telling me about a guy who used to visit one of your clubs? Used to pay up with loose diamonds. The last time he showed, you had to get a little tough on him.'

Ronnie's forehead creased into a frown.

'You said he suddenly vanished into thin air. Never saw him again.'

'Oh yeah. Crazy guy. Would bet on two fleas on a dog being the first to bite.'

'What's his name?'

'Used to call himself Mui. Mui Shenlu. Why, what's the problem, Frankie?'

'Need to trace something back to someone. Do you remember what he looked like?'

Ronnie shrugged. 'Ordinary-looking sort. Difficult to pick him out in a crowd.'

'If you saw a photograph, would you recognise him?'

'Probably.'

'Was he a regular visitor?'

Ronnie gently rocked his hand. 'Not exactly. He was the kind of guy who went on a lot of business trips. Maybe a month would go by before you saw him, then he'd hang around for a couple of nights, then go off again.'

'You ever had a guy called Fang Ka-Shing in any of your places?'

Ronnie pursed his lips. 'Not that I know of. I'll check it out for you.'

'Thanks, Ronnie. I would appreciate that.'

'Want a drink?'

'Just a quick one – I've got to get back.'

'I'll get back to my losing streak, then.'

Frankie laughed.

The barman came to the end of the counter, as Frankie propped himself on one of the stools. 'Good evening, Mr Heung. Usual?'

'Thanks.'

The barman bent down beneath the counter and produced a bottle of bourbon. Frankie swivelled around on the stool and watched the two dancers. One of them inexpertly swung tassels attached to her breasts in a semi-circle. The barman placed a glass of bourbon and ice in front of Frankie. 'Good floor show tonight, Mr Heung?'

Frankie swung round to face him. 'Seen better nipples on a Beijing duck.'

The barman laughed nervously. Frankie picked up the glass of bourbon and studied it. According to that dumbhead he employed, her boyfriend went on monthly business trips. He took a mouthful of bourbon and rolled it around

in his mouth. And maybe he liked his friends to call him
Mui Shenlu.

Marti looked around James's office. She walked over to a
piece of artwork on the far wall and studied it for several
seconds before realising it was a bas-relief outline of Hong
Kong Island. James swept back into the office. 'Sorry to
abandon you like that. Some clients think they can drop in
any time they like, which, of course, they can.' He grinned
and rubbed his hands together. 'Anyway, it has given you
a chance to look at last year's accounts. What do you
think?'

'Very impressive, James.' She struggled for appropriate
words. Her confidence had shrunk to almost nothing. She
looked about her. Perhaps Hendrik was right; she had been
deluding herself. James had done more business in the last
quarter than she had done in over a year. She summoned up
a bright smile. 'I can see why you need assistance. Your
workload is immense for one person.'

He shrugged. 'I don't mind. The business is also my
favourite hobby.' He looked down at his hands. 'Is it possible to come to a decision? I think your joining the company on a consultancy basis would be ideal and I would like
to get something settled as quickly as possible.'

She glanced across at the artwork on the wall. She would
give anything to be back in familiar, secure surroundings,
but what was there to decide? She needed a job. There was
no question of staying at Van den Fleet's. No question at
all. She fidgeted with the ring on her finger. 'You said last
night that you would think about a partnership in six or
twelve months. Shall we agree on a trial period of six
months on both sides?'

His face split into a beaming smile. He stuck his hand
out. 'Welcome to James Wu and Company.'

She shook his hand. 'I hope I shall be able to add to your
successes, James.'

He released her hand and crossed to his desk. He pulled out a file from a drawer and brought it back to her. 'I've had a contract of engagement drawn up. Would you like to look through it, and if you are happy we can sign it now.'

She suppressed a quick smile. James really didn't waste any time. She took the file from him and carefully read through the document.

'If you want to consult a lawyer, feel free, Marti.'

'I don't think so. This looks very straightforward.'

'Happy?'

'Yes.'

'I'll just get my secretary to come in and witness our signatures.' He buzzed through to the outer office. Within seconds his secretary appeared and he took out a pen from his inside jacket pocket. 'If you will sign here, Marti, on the last page, I will add my signature beneath yours, and then it can be witnessed.' She took the pen, but hesitated for a moment before writing her name, as a bleak feeling swept over her. If it hadn't been for Hendrik, she wouldn't be doing this. She wouldn't even be here. She bent her head and quickly scribbled her signature.

James gave a brief smile to his secretary and she left the office. He gave one copy of the contract to Marti and placed the other into the file. 'One important question to ask. When can you start?'

'I will have to have a word with Hendrik, but I should think whenever is convenient to you and me. He already has people in place to fill my position.' She stopped, wishing she hadn't let the words trip off her tongue in such a reckless way.

'Now would be an excellent time, but have a word with your brother and let me know when you can start.' His face grew still. 'There is, forgive me, a second important question. It is a personal question and I hope you will not be offended, but if we are to work closely together we have to be honest with each other.' He bent his head and addressed the floor. 'I felt, perhaps wrongly, that there was a problem between you and your brother, and that is why you got in touch with me.'

'I'm not quite sure what you mean by a problem?'

He bent his head even closer to his chest. 'Forgive me, but when I visited your office, I sensed that you both seemed very angry with each other. I only mention it, because I would not want ill feeling in your family to be a problem to you in, what I know will be, our very profitable relationship.'

She made another rapid decision. James was a shrewd man. Little appeared to escape his notice. There was no point in lying. 'There won't be ill feeling, James, but I admit that there have been problems.'

He raised his head to look at her. For the first time since he had spoken, she realised how acutely embarrassed he was. 'Quite simply, James, my brother and I do not always see eye to eye over matters. So, to strangers, we can give a very good impression of constantly being at each other's throat. We have a friend who has known us both from childhood, who keeps reminding us of the fact. The real problem, however, has been that since my father retired it has left a gap that I now recognise I cannot fill. I am not an option bearer. I also now understand a rather painful fact of life. Although I have been running the business on my own for over a year now, without an active option bearer Van den Fleet's cannot survive. Apart from that, Hendrik feels there are other difficulties in having a woman dealer. He wants to expand the Japanese market.'

'Sorry, I don't quite follow. What difficulties would there be in the Japanese market?'

'According to Hendrik, they prefer to deal with men.'

He nodded slowly.

'And Hendrik has decided to upgrade our office manager, Justus, as a dealer. He says he cannot afford to pay senior-dealer salaries to both Justus and me, so I was faced with accepting an administrative position, or leaving the company.'

James slipped a hand into his pocket and withdrew a packet of cigarettes. 'I am sorry that both you and your brother have been faced with such a difficult dilemma.'

'I must admit neither of us handled it very well in the beginning, but I am a dealer not an administrator. I took the only option open to me. I think Hendrik understands that. In fact, since this has happened we seem to get on better than we have done in ages.'

He rolled the cigarette between his fingers. 'Van den Fleet's is not big enough for both of you.'

She gave a little laugh. 'You could put it like that.'

'I am glad we have discussed this, Marti. I thank you for your openness and honesty in discussing a personal and obviously painful matter.'

'Well, as you say, if we are to work together, we must be honest with each other.'

He nodded again. He lit the cigarette and pushed the packet back into his pocket. 'So, what is your next move, Marti?'

'I shall telephone Hendrik when I get back to my hotel. I think he should be the first to know of my decision. I shall pop back home for a couple of days, if I may, and see my father. He has been so ill, neither Hendrik nor I have discussed any of this with him. Hopefully, I can be back here by the end of next week, probably earlier.'

His eyes flickered over her face, as if doubting her confident tone of voice. 'Well, I'll leave matters in your hands, Marti. Obviously, I shall be delighted if you can return at the earliest opportunity.' He looked down at the floor again. 'As a matter of policy, I should inform the IDE of these changes I am making in the company.'

For a moment she was filled with a sense of raging impotence. James probably asked the IDE's permission before using his musical lavatory. 'Could you give me time to

speak to Christian Debilius, James? He offered me a job
and until I could speak to you, I left the option open.'

'Yes, of course. Forgive me, I didn't know you had been
offered a position with the IDE.'

She had the satisfaction of seeing his attention suddenly
fixed; his manner slightly less presuming.

A strange objectiveness pervaded her mind, as if she had
somehow become merely an observer of the scene. It had
been a mistake to approach James. He had obviously
thought she had no other options; which was true, but she
would not be patronised. She needed a job, but she would
not be patronised. She looked again at the artwork hung on
the wall. Change. A feeling of panic made her shiver
involuntarily. She glanced away. Change was another name
for facing the unfamiliar.

James checked his watch. 'How about lunch?'

'Oh, thanks, but I did promise to have lunch with friends
of a client.'

'Yes, of course.' Again he sounded suddenly reduced to
boyish uncertainty.

'It's rather difficult really, as I don't even know them,
but they insisted I lunched with them.'

'May I ask their name? I might know them.'

'The Paulinsons. Piers and –'

He let his breath out in a strange, almost inaudible, hissing sound.

'Is anything wrong, James?'

'No, no. I had no idea you had contacts with the
Paulinsons.'

She looked at him, puzzled by his reaction. He had
almost the same tone of awe in his voice as the receptionist
in the hotel. 'You know them?'

'I know of them, in fact I have met them a couple of times.'

'What can you tell me about them? I would be grateful.
Lunch demands concentrated conversation. Doesn't allow
much circulation and/or escape.'

He laughed. 'You only need to know two things about the Paulinsons. They are the wealthiest British family on the island, and Paulinson Pacific is the most successful of the British trading companies.'

'I see.'

He drew on his cigarette. 'You mentioned the introduction came from a client. May I ask who it was?'

She hesitated for a moment but then decided she could rightly claim Beni as her client. Normally, clients came via the recommendation of the IDE, but she had met Beni at a diamond auction, purely by accident. She had made the mistake of sitting in his apparently designated chair. 'His name is Beni Yasim.'

Again he stared intently at her.

She checked her watch. 'I think I'd better make a move, James. Mustn't keep these important people waiting, must I?'

'Indeed not.'

James slammed the door of the taxi shut and stepped back on to the pavement. 'Don't eat too much at lunch. You have a Chinese banquet to face tonight, remember.'

Marti laughed. 'I promise.'

'I will pick you up at six o'clock at the hotel, all right?'

'Fine. See you.' She gave a final wave as the taxi pulled away from the kerb.

James stood where he was for a few moments, watching the taxi weave its way into the mainstream traffic. An extraordinarily modest woman. He turned on his heel and walked back to his office. But a woman with powerful connections. He pulled out his cigarettes and lit one up. He knew the diamonds would bring him luck.

Astrid picked up the telephone on the first ring then quickly handed it to Hendrik. 'It's Miss Van den Fleet for you.'

Hendrik took the telephone, at the same time closing a

file and slinging it into the tray by his side. 'Yes, Marti.'

'I thought you should know, Hendrik, that I have reached a decision with James Wu.'

'I see. Look, hold on a moment, will you.' He put his hand over the receiver. 'Give me a couple of minutes, Astrid.'

'Certainly.' Astrid hastily gathered up her notebook and files.

Hendrik waited until Astrid had left the office before speaking again. 'Hello, Marti, sorry about that. Just getting rid of Astrid. You were saying?'

'I have accepted the job with James Wu.'

'That's a very hasty decision, isn't it? What about Christian's offer?'

'It was identical to yours. I am a dealer, Hendrik, not an administrator. Working with James I can continue doing the job I am trained to do.'

Hendrik puffed his cheeks out. 'OK, if that is what you want, I am happy to go along with it. What happens next?'

'I'm coming home tomorrow. I am dreading speaking to Father, but I must. How is he today?'

'Fine. Look, Marti, there is no need for you to come back just to speak to Father. I can explain things to him.'

'Thanks, but I should speak to him myself. In any event, I have to come back. I have an appointment with Beni Yasim. I understand he wants to place a big order.'

'Yasim? You didn't mention anything.' Hendrik sat upright in sudden irritation.

'Sorry, it slipped my mind. Anyway, it will be a fitting way to leave Van den Fleet's.' She gave a faint laugh. 'Bowing out on a high note.'

'What does he want?'

'I think about ten parcels of best-grade industrials.'

'Well, I'm glad you told me. I will get Justus on to it right away.' Hendrik picked up his cigarette and drew on it before stubbing it out. 'Actually, Marti, it might be a good idea to let me handle this. It will give me an opportunity to meet Yasim and also to introduce him to Justus and keep up some continuity. When's he coming?'

She laughed again. 'Beni doesn't come to us. We go to Beni.'

'Oh, I see.'

'Hendrik, leave this with me. Beni is my client and I haven't left Van den Fleet's yet. I want to tell him myself that I am leaving. He is after all my most important client. He should hear first-hand.'

'What do you mean? He is a Van den Fleet client.'

'No, Hendrik, he is my client. I found him. I introduced him to the company. I have always dealt with him.'

Hendrik's face flushed. He slowly counted to five. 'As far as I am concerned, any client on our books stays with us.'

'Isn't that for the client to decide?'

'Look, Marti, I think we had better discuss this when you get back. It's not really appropriate to discuss these things over the telephone. Let me know when your plane arrives and I'll come and pick you up.'

'Don't bother, Johannes is picking me up.'

'We've got to talk, Marti.'

'I'll call you when I arrive home.'

'Where are you staying?'

'At Johannes's. I told you.'

'You didn't.'

'Hendrik, I've got to go. I'll see you when I come to talk to Father. 'Bye.'

'Goodbye.' Hendrik slammed the telephone down. He lit up another cigarette, Damn, damn, damn her. He got up and went to stand in front of the window. He should have made more effort to get her to accept the new job at Van den Fleet's, or at the very least persuaded her to take the job with the IDE. He rubbed at his forehead. You are making too many stupid mistakes, Van den Fleet. He drew on his cigarette. Christian had warned him and the warning was coming true. He returned to his desk and snatched up the telephone. 'Get me Christian Debilius.' He slammed the telephone down again. She would walk away with clients over his dead body.

The Paulinson residence was about a mile away from where Candy Lai lived, but much higher up the Peak, and in a much more exclusive area. As the limousine drew up to the house, a servant hurried forward bearing a large umbrella. He opened the rear passenger door, carefully shielding Marti with the umbrella, as she stepped out. She looked about her curiously. If it were not for the heavy curtain of falling rain and dense cloud, she supposed the view across Hong Kong must be quite spectacular.

The butler inquired Marti's name and led her to where the Paulinsons were standing. Marti looked around her again. She couldn't think why, but she had incorrectly assumed she would be the only guest for lunch; there were about fifty other people in the room.

'Excuse me, sir, Miss Van den Fleet.'

Piers spun round and held out his hand. 'Miss Van den Fleet, how do you do? So glad you could come.'

'Thank you for inviting me.'

'Not at all.' His eyes made a quick top to toe inspection of her. 'Let me get you a drink.' He snapped his fingers at one of the waiters, who hurried across with a half-filled drinks tray. Piers picked up a glass of champagne and handed it to Marti. 'Now, come and meet Marietta. She is dying to meet you.'

Piers led Marti across to the windows to a tallish, immaculately groomed woman. 'Marietta, darling, come and meet Marti Van den Fleet.'

Marietta turned around and looked blankly at Marti.

'Beni's little friend, darling. You remember?'

Marti glanced at Piers. She didn't much like the slightly

patronising tone of voice. Marietta smiled politely. 'Yes, of course.' She held out her hand to Marti. 'Any of Beni's friends are always welcome here.'

Marti shook hands with Marietta, not quite able to shake off the feeling that she had suddenly been reduced to the level of a stray dog.

Piers touched the elbow of the man who had been talking animatedly to Marietta. 'Let me introduce you to a very old friend of mine.' He led the man away.

Marti looked at Marietta and found herself being scrutinised by very large, dark eyes. Marti took a sip of champagne. They didn't look too friendly by her reckoning. 'Thank you for inviting me to lunch, Mrs Paulinson.'

'Beni insisted.' Marietta tossed back long black curls. 'How long have you known him?'

'Few years, I think.'

'Really. Beni and I have been very dear friends for a very long time.'

Marti looked straight into Marietta's eyes. 'I understand Beni has many friends, Mrs Paulinson.'

Marietta's eyes flickered with a dangerous light. Marti glanced curiously at the back of Piers Paulinson, who was standing several feet away from them. Marietta had obviously shared Beni's bed at some time. She turned her gaze back to Marietta. But it must have been a long time ago. The woman was attractive, but well into her forties. Marti twirled the glass of champagne between her fingers. Beni liked them young. The blossom on the vine is always more delicate than the fruit. Her lips twitched in an amused smile. Poetic sayings tripped off Beni's tongue like honey.

'How long are you staying in Hong Kong, Miss Van den Fleet?'

Marti suddenly realised Marietta was speaking. 'Er, I'm leaving tomorrow.'

'What a pity you can't stay longer.'

'I intend to return shortly.'

Marietta put her head to one side like a bird. Again, Marti felt she was being minutely dissected.

'Piers did tell me what you did, but I'm afraid I have forgotten.'

'I am a diamond dealer, Mrs Paulinson.'

'Really.'

'What do you do?'

Marietta's eyes flicked wide open. 'Do?'

'Mmm.'

Marietta gave a rather harsh laugh. 'I don't do, darling, I am.'

Marti sipped at the champagne again. She couldn't think of a reply that was polite.

Piers moved to the centre of the room and clapped his hands. 'Chow everybody. Time for chow.'

The waiters pushed folding doors back to reveal yet another spacious room. A very long buffet table was positioned in the centre. Guests drifted through the opened doors, chattering animatedly. Marietta turned to stand in front of Marti, her back to the other guests. 'There is something I think you should know, Miss Van den Fleet.'

'What's that?'

'You are wasting your time with Beni.' Marietta's face hardened, making her look older, less attractive. 'You're not his type at all.'

Marti stared in astonishment at her, then burst out laughing. 'Thank you for the advice, Mrs Paulinson, but there is something that you should know, also. Beni and I are business colleagues. Nothing more.'

Marietta eyes bored into her.

'You really have nothing to worry about, Mrs Paulinson.' Marti spoke quietly and contemptuously, and had the satisfaction of watching a slow flush rise in Marietta's cheeks.

'I see.' Marietta looked away from her. 'You must think me rather stupid, Miss Van den Fleet.'

'No.'

Marietta flicked her hair back. 'Shall we go in to lunch?' She put her glass down and walked swiftly across the room without bothering to wait for Marti.

Marti drifted uncertainly towards the buffet table. Marietta had managed to get herself surrounded by four or five people in a tight group. A paunchy, middle-aged man appeared at Marti's side. 'We have not been introduced. My name is Erwin Klein.' He held out his hand.

'Martina Van den Fleet. How do you do?'

'May I get you something to eat?'

'Yes. Thank you.'

He shouldered his way to the table with little grace, bumping into people until they moved aside. Marti followed in his wake. He picked up a plate and handed it to her. 'Are you a business or personal friend of the Paulinsons.'

'Neither actually. I am something of an interloper. A business colleague of mine knew I was coming to Hong Kong and gave me their name.'

He looked at her curiously. 'May I ask who?'

Marti looked down at her plate. She hoped she wasn't going to get another unpleasant reaction. 'Beni Yasim. Do you know him?'

'Slightly.' He moved further along the table. 'Would you like some smoked salmon?'

'Just a little. I have been threatened with a Chinese banquet tonight.'

'Is it your first?'

'I'm afraid so.'

He shook with laughter. 'Let me give you a word of warning. It is best not to ask what you are eating.'

She rolled her eyes. She could have done without the warning.

'Tell me, Miss Van den Fleet, what do you do?'

'I'm a diamond dealer.'

'Ah.' He didn't elaborate further and helped himself to

enough smoked salmon to almost cover his plate. 'I saw you talking to Marietta before. She is an extraordinary woman, is she not?'

Marti twitched her mouth. 'Very.'

He glanced at her quizzically. 'I take it that you do not like her.'

'I don't know her.'

'But –'

She spooned a little dill sauce on to her plate. 'But, she and her husband have been very kind in inviting me here.'

He laughed again. 'But, of course, Piers does what Yasim tells him to do.'

'What do you mean?'

He bent closer to her. 'It is rumoured that Yasim owns forty-five per cent of Paulinson Pacific.'

She looked across the length of the table to where Marietta was deep in conversation. And owns one hundred per cent of Marietta as well.

The doors to the dining room were drawn shut again as the last of the diners filtered back into the drawing room. A waiter approached the corner where Marti was standing and offered to replenish her coffee cup, but she refused. She put the cup down and made her way into the hall. The servant who had shielded her with an umbrella when she had arrived was standing passively at the front entrance.

'Excuse me, could someone call a taxi for me?'

He stared into her face, as if trying to place who she was. 'Ah, madame come in the Paulinson car. I tell chauffeur. Wait just one moment please.'

'No, no, don't do that. If I could just get a taxi, please.'

'No problem, madame.'

She sighed to herself. She had obviously been invited here under sufferance. It was rather rude to expect a lift back to the hotel.

'Miss Van den Fleet, you look a little lost.'

She turned round to see Erwin Klein standing behind her in the hallway. 'Just getting a taxi.'

'I am leaving myself, can I give you a lift?'

She hesitated.

'I can assure you, it is no trouble.'

'Well, if you are sure, thank you very much.'

'Where is your hotel?'

'Central. Off Connaught Road.'

'That is on my way.'

She wasn't sure she believed him, but if he was prepared to go out of his way, that was his problem. 'Will you excuse me a moment. I should say goodbye to the Paulinsons.'

'My car will be at the door by the time you come back.'

Marti hurried to where Piers and Marietta were standing. He had his arm loosely draped around her waist.

'Excuse me interrupting, but I must be on my way, and I just wanted to thank you very much for inviting me.'

Piers blinked at her, as if unsure who she was for a moment. 'Oh yes, glad you could come. Our pleasure, isn't it, Marietta?'

'Of course.' Marietta turned away slightly, as if considering the conversation at an end.

Piers held out his hand. 'Are you seeing Beni soon? If so, give him our regards.'

'Yes, I will.' Marti glanced at Marietta. Although she appeared to be listening intently to the conversation going on between two men standing next to her, Marti was sure she was listening to every word that Piers was saying.

'Seeing him soon then?'

Marti looked up at Piers. 'In a couple of days, probably.'

He tilted towards her then steadied himself. His eyes looked glassy, as if he had drunk too much. 'Well, let's hope the weather is better in Antwerp than it is here at the moment.' He gave a sudden braying laugh.

Marti smiled politely. 'Well, thank you once again. Goodbye, Mrs Paulinson.'

'Goodbye, Miss Van den Fleet.' Marietta gave a cool smile then turned to face the two men at her side, and began talking in a deliberately ringing voice.

Marti slid into the front seat of the Mercedes and winced as she managed to catch a strand of hair on a spoke of the umbrella held over the door. Erwin Klein waved his cigar in the air. 'You don't mind cigar smoke?'

'No, not at all.' She grabbed at the door handle as Erwin accelerated forward, making the tyres screech on the gravel.

'What do you think of Hong Kong, Miss Van den Fleet?'

'I have hardly seen it.'

'You must come again, then, when you have more time.'

'I shall be returning next week. I am taking up a job here.'

He shot her a quick glance. 'With Beni Yasim?'

'No. I am joining forces with James Wu. Do you know him?'

He shrugged. 'The name sounds vaguely familiar, but I only do business with the Chinese. I don't socialise with them.'

'What do you do?'

'I represent German interests here. I am a business consultant.'

'Are you kept busy?'

He laughed. 'Very much so. I haven't taken a holiday in three years.' He dropped his cigar butt into the ashtray. 'Where will you be living when you return to Hong Kong?'

'I don't know. I have yet to think about finding accommodation.'

'You won't find it easy. Accommodation is at a premium on the island. Apartments are, if you will forgive the pun, as valuable as diamonds.'

'I was hoping to find somewhere. Hotel life is not very satisfactory.'

'You'd be better off looking at one of the smaller islands. Lamma has quite a few Westerners living there, and the ferries to Hong Kong are fast and cheap.'

'I'll bear it in mind.'

'Get in touch with me when you return. I may be able to help you.'

'Thanks. I would appreciate it.'

By the time they reached Central District, the rain had begun to ease. Erwin pulled up in front of the hotel and switched off the engine. Marti gathered up her bag and reached for the door handle. 'Before you go, Miss Van den Fleet, let me give you my card.' He fumbled in his inside breast pocket, before producing a heavily embossed business card. 'I look forward to another meeting, Miss Van den Fleet. May I say you will be a welcome and very attractive addition to the island.'

'Thank you, and thanks for the lift.' She got out and almost collided with the little boy from the hotel, struggling to reach up and cover her head with a large umbrella.

The Central Market was only a fifteen-minute walk away from the Continental Hotel, according to the receptionist. Marti looked at her watch. She had been walking for twenty minutes and still wasn't in sight of it. She stepped into the street, thinking she would make better time than inching her way through the teeming masses on the pavements. She was in two minds whether to abandon the idea of buying gifts to take back home with her. She felt suddenly weary and very alone. She squared her shoulders and tramped on. It was something she was going to have to get used to; along with the strangely stale, spicy smell that pervaded Hong Kong.

The old man at the basket stall instantly held up several of his wares when Marti stopped to take a look. 'Genuine Cantonese basketware. You buy, yes?'

She shook her head and quickly walked on, crossing the

tiny alley formed by the rows of stalls, and stopping to take
a closer look at a row of porcelain dolls. She smiled in
amusement at one of the little dolls dressed in Chinese
boy's costume. It looked just like Hendrik. Same fat cheeks.
Same quiff of hair brushed forward. She was tempted to buy
it but decided he would probably not appreciate the joke.
She moved quickly on and eventually reached a stall that
sold brassware. She pulled out her purse. An ashtray for
Hendrik and then something for Father. She glanced across
the alleyway and saw a stall stacked high with lamps of all
shapes and sizes. She stepped across to take a closer look.
There was one little lamp hanging on the corner of the stall
that looked exactly like Aladdin's lamp. That would do for
Father.

As Marti retraced her steps back to the hotel, her thoughts
drifted back to the uncomfortable lunch party at the
Paulinsons'. Marietta was a superbitch. Piers was a typically
British upper-class dolt. Marti tucked the two parcels into a
more comfortable position under her arm. Beni's description of his friends was a little off-line. They were neither
charming, nor glad to see her. What had been interesting was
Klein's observation that Beni owned a slice of Paulinson
Pacific. Beni was always a very secretive man with a happy
knack of talking business without revealing much about his
affairs.

Marti breathed a sigh of relief when she saw the neon sign
above the hotel. The journey back from the market had
taken much longer and every neon sign, illuminating unfamiliar Chinese characters, had looked alike. At one stage she
feared that she had taken a wrong turning. She quickened her
pace. She wriggled her shoulders to loosen the fabric of her
blouse from her back. Walking around Hong Kong was like
walking around in a bowl of lukewarm soup. The rain began
again and poured down suddenly in torrents. She ran the last
few steps to the hotel.

*   *   *

Chan Chunling remained by the door after James had greeted him. 'Before we go in, have you any news for me about the merchandise?'

James smiled reassuringly. 'Everything is going according to plan. I have ready buyers, but one has to choose the right time to make a successful sale, Mr Chan. That time will be the week after next.'

'That is the most auspicious time?'

'Yes. I went to the temple today. The fall of the *sing pui* confirmed it.'

Chan nodded. 'Good, good.'

'Now, Mr Chan, please to come and meet my new business partner-to-be.'

'Your new partner?'

'Yes. Martina Van den Fleet.'

'The woman you got to authenticate the diamonds in Antwerp?'

'Yes. The *sing pui* decreed that it would be so.'

Chan inclined his head sideways. 'Then so be it.'

Anna rose to her feet to greet Chan Chunling. He pressed a bouquet of flowers into her arms. 'I am delighted to have the honour of being your partner tonight, Miss Wu.'

She bowed her head. 'Thank you for the flowers, Mr Chan. They are beautiful.'

Chan looked around and stared at Marti. James leapt forward. 'Marti, this is Mr Chan Chunling. Miss Martina Van den Fleet.'

Chan hesitated for a moment, unsure whether it was proper to offer to shake hands with a Western woman. It wasn't proper to do so with a Chinese woman. Marti solved the problem for him by holding out her own hand. 'How do you do, Mr Chan.'

'How do you do, Miss Van den Fleet. I hear from James that you are joining his company.'

'Yes, I'm very excited about it. Looking forward to working with James very much.'

Chan stared at her, somewhat bemused by the choice of the gods. A Western woman was the last choice he would have expected. His eyes dropped irresistibly to her bosom. There was, however, much to admire in the choice of the gods. Much.

James went to the sideboard and busied himself with pouring drinks. Anna excused herself and went to put the flowers immediately into water. Marti smiled politely at Chan. 'Are you in James's line of business, Mr Chan?'

Chan looked momentarily startled. 'Er, yes. I do deal in diamonds, but purely as an agent.'

'Ah, I see.'

James handed a glass of vermouth to Marti and a glass of whisky to Chan. 'Mr Chan is not telling all, Marti.'

Chan looked at him in alarm.

'Mr Chan is one of my very important clients.'

Chan let his breath out slowly. He took a mouthful of whisky.

Anna returned bearing a large vase containing the flowers Chan had brought. Marti went to inspect them. 'What beautiful red roses.' James peered over Anna's shoulder at the flowers. 'In China, Marti, red is the colour of marriage.'

'Really.' Marti looked at Anna and felt a twinge of pity. The girl's face had gone almost as red as the roses.

Anna buried her face into the flowers, as if inhaling their perfume. 'Red is better known as representing festivity.'

James grinned at Marti and silently mouthed the word marriage. She suddenly caught on to what was going on. She glanced across at Chan. Surely Anna could do better than that. He was a rather horrible-looking little man. James went to take Marti's glass. 'Let me top that up for you.'

'No thanks. This is fine for me.'

James turned to Chan. 'Mr Chan?'

'Yes, thank you.' Chan held out his empty glass. 'Where are we eating, by the way?'

'The Central Royale. They do the best banquet, I think.'

Marti joined James and Chan. 'What is a banquet, exactly?'

'A great feast of many courses. Is that how you would describe it, Mr Chan?'

Chan nodded. 'Yes, usually ten or twelve. We start with a few cold appetisers. A little soup is served after the main course to cleanse the tastebuds.'

Marti glanced anxiously at James, remembering his liking for braised bear's paw in gravy. 'What will be the main course, James?'

'Beijing duck. It is a speciality of the Central Royale.'

'Oh, you mean roasted duck?'

'Yes, served with what you would call little pancakes, and vegetables and a plum sauce.'

'Sounds delicious.' Relief made Marti sound more enthusiastic than she normally would have been. She turned to engage Chan in further conversation, but watched instead in silent amusement. He was staring at her bosom, as if he had never seen the like of it before. She turned away from him. If he was Anna's intended, he was not being particularly discreet.

Hendrik paced up and down the sitting-room floor. The housekeeper popped her head around the door to ask him if he would like something to eat, but took one look at the stormy expression on his face and retreated. Hendrik checked his watch and went to the telephone. He had spent the better part of the afternoon trying to reach Christian Debilius only to be fobbed off by his personal assistant claiming that he would be in conference all day. Hendrik snatched up the telephone and dialled Christian's personal number. He had been invited by the PA in the office to leave a message, but a request that the IDE bring pressure to bear on James Wu to withdraw his job offer to Marti was not the kind of message Christian would thank him for leaving. He put the telephone down when he heard the engaged signal. He waited a few seconds then redialled and got through. 'Mr Debilius please. Hendrik Van den Fleet calling.'

'Mr Debilius is unavailable.'

Hendrik sucked in his breath at the blandly reassuring voice. 'Will you please tell him that Hendrik Van den Fleet is calling and it is very important.'

'Mr Debilius is away.'

'Where?'

There was a pause on the line while the voice considered the question. 'Mr Debilius has left for Washington. He will be back the day after tomorrow.'

'Have you got a number for him in Washington?'

'Yes.'

Hendrik gripped the handset until his knuckles showed white. 'Could I have it please?'

'I am not authorised to give out the number. You can leave a message and I will see that it is passed to him.'

'Don't bother.' Hendrik slammed the telephone down and cursed aloud.

Hendrik went to the sideboard and poured himself a shot of whisky. He leaned against the sideboard and glared at the telephone, as if somehow it personally was to blame for all his problems. He tossed the whisky back in one gulp and refilled the glass. Beni Yasim had proved as elusive as Christian. Mr Yasim was travelling and could not be contacted. Even his partner had claimed that he was not authorised to pass on a telephone number for Mr Yasim's destination. Hendrik drained the glass and set it down with a bang on the sideboard. He would have more success trying to contact the fucking Flying Dutchman. He rubbed a hand across his eyes. If he didn't get control of the situation soon, things would start to unravel fast when Marti got back.

The housekeeper tapped on the sitting-room door as she

entered. 'Excuse me, Mr Hendrik, but your father would like a word with you.'

'Hasn't he fallen asleep yet?'

'No, Mr Hendrik. I think he is still reading the notes you gave him at dinner time.'

'OK. I'll go and see him.' He turned and refilled his glass again then collected up his cigarettes and lighter and slipped them into his pocket.

Erasmus pushed his glasses up on his head as Hendrik came into the bedroom.

'Something you want, Father?'

'Just want a word with you. These expansion plans. They're very ambitious aren't they?'

Hendrik pushed his hands into his pockets. 'What do you mean?'

'You seem to be committing a lot of capital to buying-in.'

Hendrik reached into his pocket for his cigarettes, then remembered that his father wasn't allowed to smoke. 'We did discuss this when you were in the clinic, Father. You did agree to the plan.'

'Only in principle. I wasn't aware of the detail then.'

Hendrik sat down on the bottom of the bed. 'Father, the business has been allowed to slide, to drift. Matters need to be put right now, if Van den Fleet's are to return to their strong trading position with the IDE.'

Erasmus looked down at the papers in his lap and gave a doubtful shake of his head. Hendrik hitched one leg across the other and gripped his ankle. 'Marti has been selling, without buying-in. Our stocks are very low. We must break this vicious circle she has created. She –'

His father interrupted. 'That's another thing I want to talk to you about, as well. I will not have you criticise Marti at every breath. She is a good girl. She has worked hard. She has kept the company going while I have been ill, without a complaint from any single one of our clients.'

Hendrik ground his teeth. 'I am not criticising, Father. I

am stating fact. The company is in the grip of a vicious circle. If we don't regularly buy from the IDE, the quality of our boxes is immediately reduced. If we do not have quality merchandise to offer, we cannot attract, nor even hold, clients. If we make insufficient sales we do not have the funds to buy from the IDE.' Hendrik let his breath out in an exasperated sigh. 'I am sorry if that doesn't make sense to you, Father, but it makes sense to me.'

Erasmus removed his glasses and tapped them on the papers in front of him. 'I understand very well what you are saying, and I agree with your plans. What I disagree about is the extent of those plans. You are committing the company to too much, too quickly. Look, after the diamond crash in 1980, like everyone else, we had to stockpile diamonds to a dangerous degree, to counteract falling prices in low-volume trading. It wasn't until the IDE stepped in that –'

'I know, Father, I know.' Hendrik grimaced in irritation.

'Just listen to what I am saying. It is unwise to buy what you cannot sell, but it is lunacy to buy what you cannot afford to hold back until the market improves.'

Hendrik looked around him. If he couldn't have a cigarette soon, he would die. 'Father, you are overlooking one factor here. There isn't going to be a crash. The market is improving all the time. The IDE's massive marketing campaign in Japan has opened up vast sales potential. The Japanese can't get enough diamonds. They are insatiable. We need to be in there, Father, selling anything we can get our hands on. We cannot afford to limit ourselves to Europe, the Israelis.' Hendrik jabbed a finger towards the windows. 'There is a big world out there, Father, and Van den Fleet's must be part of it, if it is to survive.'

Erasmus rubbed at one eye, trying to shake off the sudden weariness clouding his mind. 'I understand what you are saying, Hendrik. I know you are right in what you say, but just be careful. Don't overcommit us.'

'I won't, Father. I promise that is the last thing I shall do.'

Erasmus rested his head back on his pillow and shut his eyes.

'You all right, Father?'

'Yes, yes, just a little tired.'

'OK. I'll leave you to rest. I'll be in the kitchen getting something to eat, if you want me.'

Erasmus nodded. He opened his eyes as Hendrik got up off the bed. He watched the tall, burly figure quietly leave the room. Hendrik wasn't his son, but he was a good man. Erasmus shut his eyes again. He had done the right thing in bringing him back. Van den Fleet's needed new blood, if it was to prosper.

Marti rested her elbows on the wall of the verandah. The night-time view from the Peak was, as James had promised, spectacular. It was too misty to see across the waters to Kowloon, but in the darkness the lights of Hong Kong illuminated the skyscrapers, turning their outline into a fairytale giant's castle. She breathed in the damp but cooling air. She had survived the banquet. Most of the things she had eaten, she had recognised. She glanced back to where Anna and Chan Chunling were standing and smiled to herself. Chan had positioned himself so that Anna was almost pinned against the wall, with no escape. She turned around and studied the view again, her thoughts occupied by the wonder of how the Chinese ever made it together. She had relaxed sufficiently during the banquet to quietly observe Chan and Anna. His conversation with her had been so politely obscure, Marti had difficulty in deciding whether he was making a come-on or not.

James stepped up to Marti's side. 'What do you think of the view?'

'Magnificent.'

'Thought you would be impressed.' He glanced over his shoulder.

'Actually, I think I should go and rescue Anna. She does not like Chan Chunling very much.'

'I had got the impression. Forgive me for asking, but if she doesn't like him why does she bother with him?'

'Partly for my sake and partly because he has possible business contacts that might be useful to her.'

She stifled an incipient yawn. 'Er, James, would you mind if I called it a night? I have to make a very early start tomorrow.'

'Sure. I'll take you back to your hotel.'

Marti turned back for a final view of the skyline. This was going to be her home for who knows how long? Perhaps it was for the best. She was twenty-seven. She had spent all of the years since leaving school working for her father. Her life had become narrowed down to the office, looking after him, and the occasional night out with Johannes. Working for James was an opportunity to broaden her outlook. She shrugged the jacket from her shoulders and pushed her arms through the sleeves. Hong Kong was not her first choice of place. The Hong Kong Chinese were as mystifying as any alien, but fortunately, James was very westernised and easy to get on with.

Candy parked the car as close to the wall as she could manage. She got out and carefully walked the few steps down the street, to the old-style apartment block where Frankie Heung was staying with his mother. She patted at the back of her hair. Frankie expected her to be his slave. How was she supposed to have the time to make herself look attractive for Fang Ka-Shing, when she was expected to rush over to Frankie's apartment with a stupid photograph?

Frankie opened the front door to Candy and jerked his thumb backwards to indicate that she could come in. 'Keep your voice down. My mother's watching television.'

Candy was about to ask what was the point, she could hear every word from the television just standing in the hall, but thought better of it. Frankie didn't look in a very good mood.

'Have you brought the photograph of Fang?'

'Yes, Frankie.'

'Want some tea?'

Her face brightened. Perhaps he was in a good mood after all. 'Only if it's no trouble, Frankie.'

'Making some for my mother.'

She followed him down the hall into the kitchen.

Frankie examined the photograph carefully then flipped it over. 'What's this crap on the back mean? Happy is the man who has good fortune and you.'

'Oh, it was just crazy the way we met. So many things happened on the day in question. Fang says if they hadn't happened we would never have met.' She giggled. 'I ended up falling into his arms. Honestly, I did.'

Frankie nodded. He flipped the photograph over again and stared at the face of Fang Ka-Shing. Kuan Ti, the patron god of the Triads, had ensured that they had met. He slipped the photograph into his pocket. 'Found out the name of the jeweller who designed the necklace?'

'Sort of.'

'What is that supposed to mean?'

'Fang seemed embarrassed when I asked him. Didn't want to talk about it. Eventually, he said it was someone in Tsimshatsui. He couldn't tell me the man's name, because he had done the job privately and he would get into trouble with his employers if they knew. He said what did it matter anyway, who the man was. I thought I should drop it, Frankie. He seemed to be getting angry.'

'OK. Leave it with me. I'll get it checked out.' He looked at his watch. 'You'd better split. I got business to attend to.'

She gulped down the tea and picked up her bag. 'See you around, Frankie.'

'You bet you will.'

Ronnie Lee stepped out of the elevator as Frankie was closing the front door. Ronnie gave Candy an appraising look as she swept past him. Frankie put his finger to his lips and Ronnie gave a quick nod of affirmation. Frankie drew him inside and shut the door. 'Thanks for coming round. I appreciate it.'

'No problem, Frankie. How's your mother?'

'She's OK. Wish I could get her to move to something more modern, but she says this is where she is going to die and this is where she has to stay. Come on into the kitchen, Ronnie. We can talk there.'

Ronnie looked at the photograph of Fang Ka-Shing doubtfully. 'I don't know, Frankie, this could be Mui Shenlu.'

'So how many guys do you get who pay their debts in loose diamonds?'

'The trouble is, I don't get to see every customer often enough to be certain about a particular face, but some of the other guys would know. Can I show this around?'

'Sure, but don't put it up on a billboard, all right?'

'Understand you, Frankie.' Ronnie rubbed the side of his face thoughtfully. 'Seven-toed Wing is the doorman at the Cha Cha Club. He's pretty good at knowing who's been in and who hasn't. I'll show him the photograph and let you know.'

'I'll see that as a favour to me, Ronnie.'

Ronnie gave a quick smile of satisfaction at the news.

The doorman at the Cha Cha Club wiped his hand across his mouth and swallowed the remains of a coconut dim sum. 'Good evening, Mr Lee.'

Ronnie glanced around. 'Where's Seven-toed Wing? He's supposed to be on tonight, isn't he?'

'Yes, Mr Lee. He's just gone inside to deal with a

customer complaint.' As the man spoke, Wing appeared hauling a struggling, smaller man by the collar of his jacket. The man staggered forward as Wing released his grip, then slumped into the gutter with a scream, as Wing booted him with his foot. Wing straightened his jacket. 'Good evening, Mr Lee.'

Ronnie beckoned to him. 'Got something I'd like you to take a look at.'

'Yes, Mr Lee.'

Ronnie pulled the photograph out of his pocket. 'You remember a guy called Mui Shenlu? Mr Song had to speak to him once. Started paying his debts with loose diamonds.'

Wing scratched at his ear, then dawning recognition spread across his face. 'Went missing, Mr Lee, didn't he?'

'Yes that's him.'

'You found him, Mr Lee?'

'No, but I want you to take a look at this photograph. Is that Mui Shenlu?'

Wing took the photograph and stared down at it. 'Could be, Mr Lee.'

'Mr Heung wants to know one way or the other.' Ronnie gave him a meaningful look.

Wing nodded thoughtfully. Mr Heung was a very important man. The photograph didn't look too much like Mui, but rumour on the street was that Mr Heung was taking over the Bear's Paw Gang and Seven-toed Wing would be out of a job, if he didn't tell Mr Heung what he wanted to hear. 'Yeah, I recognise him now, Mr Lee. That's Mui Shenlu. You can tell Mr Heung, Seven-toed Wing says so.'

Ronnie nodded and took back the photograph.

Marti transferred her weight from one foot to the other. She suddenly felt on edge. Perhaps it was worrying about what to say to Father. She looked around the airport terminal. She also had a headache coming on. The noise level was unbearable. That was something else she would have to learn to live with, besides the food. Why the Cantonese had to shriek at the tops of their voices when conversing with each other was another mystery. She transferred her folded raincoat from one arm to the other. She was being uncharitable. The people she had met had gone out of their way to be helpful, despite the language barrier. She glanced at James and Anna standing by her side; they, in particular, had been very kind.

James looked up at the massive digital clock as the figures clicked on to the full hour. Marti bent down and picked up her travel bag. 'James, I think I should join the queue for my flight. Please don't wait. I shall be all right.'

'Are you sure?'

'Yes. I'll be fine.'

James held out his hand. 'I hope to see you very soon, Marti. Have a good flight.'

'Thanks.' Marti shook hands then held out her hand to Anna. 'Look forward to seeing you again, Anna.'

Anna surprised Marti a little, by shaking her hand enthusiastically. 'I am sorry there was no time to show you my designs.'

'When I come back, that's the first thing I am going to do. You can't escape, you know.'

Anna laughed merrily. She was just beginning to get used to Marti's strange, Western sense of humour.

Marti slung her bag over her shoulder and gave a quick wave before threading her way through the crowd.

'Hi! I've heard of coincidence, but this is ridiculous.'

Marti whirled around and stared up at the man who had tapped her on the shoulder. 'Oh, heavens, we were waiting to find our contacts, weren't we? It's Mr – ah.'

'Joe. Joe Fielding. I'm in construction.'

'Yes, of course, I remember.'

'Are you going home?'

'Yes, just for a couple of days. Are you returning to the USA?'

'Wish I was. I am heading for Bangkok. Probably be there a month or so.'

'Well, have a good trip.'

He held out his hand. 'Thanks, and I'm afraid this really is hello and goodbye again. I haven't checked in yet.'

Marti shook hands with him, then caught sight of James and Anna through a small gap in the people around her. She raised her arm and waved to them. They waved back. She mouthed the words *don't wait*, but they just continued waving and smiling. She shook her head to herself and began forcing her way to the departure checkpoint. She raised a hand to the strap of her travel bag and hitched it up into a more comfortable position, as thoughts of home and its problems settled like an unseen burden around her shoulders.

Busy slipped the photograph of Fang into his inside breast pocket. 'What you want me to do with him, Mr Heung?'

'I don't want you to do anything to him. Yet.' Frankie leaned back in the chair and put his feet up on the table. 'Now, listen carefully, I'm going to say this once, OK?'

'Right, Mr Heung.'

'I want you to go to Kowloon side. Tsimshatsui. Check out every jewellery business in every goddam alley. I want the name of the guy who made up eight loose diamonds into a pendant-style necklace with a twist-effect gold chain. Diamonds provided by the guy in that photograph. Got it?'

'Sure, Mr Heung.'

'You can say that there is a reward for giving information and there's a reward for not giving information.'

An evil smile spread across Busy's face, as he fingered the flick-knife in his breast pocket.

'Start with the area around Nathan Road. You'll be in Bear's Paw Gang territory some of the time. Be discreet. Be polite. Offer condolences for Mr Song. Got that?'

'Yes, Mr Heung.'

'Show them the photograph. Say the guy don't pay his debts like he should. Someone may recognise him. OK?'

'Yes, Mr Heung. Er, this could take a little time, Mr Heung.'

'You've got it, but don't come back without the name of the jeweller. Right?'

'Right, Mr Heung.' Busy took that as his cue to depart.

Frankie pulled out a cigar from his pocket and lit it. Once he had got something on Fang, Candy could shoot through permanently.

Johannes looked anxiously into Marti's face. 'You look very tired.'

'I think I am more worried than tired.'

He loaded her luggage into the back of the car and closed the lid. 'You mean about your father?'

'Mmm. I am not looking forward to telling him I am going to Hong Kong.'

He rested his hand on her shoulder. 'I don't know whether I should say this or not, but when I went to see him he looked rather down, a bit depressed. He asked me when you were coming home, and apparently he wakes up in the night asking for you.'

She shut her eyes.

'Sorry, Marti, but I thought you should know.'

'Don't apologise. I'm glad you told me.' She pressed her fingers to her brow. 'Johannes, instead of going to your apartment, would you mind driving me straight home?'

'Of course not.'

'You don't have to stay. I know you're very busy. I can get a taxi back to your apartment.'

'I'm not all that busy and I think I should stay with you, Marti. I have a feeling you may need some moral support.'

She gave him a quick hug. 'Thanks.'

He opened the passenger door for her then hurried round to the driver's side.

Johannes flicked the windscreen wipers to fast wipe as spray from the truck he was overtaking momentarily obscured his vision. He released his nervous grip on the steering wheel when they were safely past, and shot a quick sideways glance at Marti. She hadn't spoken a word since they had got on to the autoroute. He cursed under his breath as an enormous Dutch – registered truck and trailer suddenly lurched out from the inside lane then began signalling that it was overtaking. 'Did you see that, Marti?'

'What?'

'Driver of that truck. Pulls out in front of me with no warning, *then* starts indicating he's pulling out.'

'Mmm. Dutch are all alike.'

He snorted in disgust. 'You can say that again.'

She turned her attention back to the whorls of raindrops on the window. They hovered for a second, before being brushed away by the continuous rush of air.

Marti's stomach gave a sickening lurch as the car swung into the familiar street. She lowered her head and looked up out of the window at the apartment block. 'You don't mind coming in, Johannes?'

'No. I said I would.' He reached out and squeezed her hand. 'Don't worry. Your father will understand.'

'I wish I had your confidence.'

'Look, Marti, it was his decision to hand over the business to Hendrik that forced you into leaving.'

'He didn't have much choice, did he?'

'And neither have you been given much choice. That's what he has got to understand.'

The housekeeper took Marti's travel bag from her and placed it by the side of the hall table. 'Nice to meet you, Miss Van den Fleet.' She nodded to Johannes. 'Dreadful weather, isn't it, Mr Witt?'

'Could be better.'

She gave a cheery laugh. 'You know, Miss Van den Fleet, I wouldn't have guessed you and Mr Hendrik were brother and sister. You don't look a bit alike, do you?' The expression on her face changed. 'Oh, I'm sorry. I hope you don't think I was being rude.'

Marti shook her head. 'How is my father?'

'Much brighter.' The housekeeper adopted a confiding tone of voice. 'He was rather depressed when he first came home, but I think he is getting used to us now.'

'Us?'

'The night nurse and myself. I don't think old people like too many strangers around them, do they? Well, let me take your coat. I'm sure you would like a cup of coffee or tea.'

Marti rubbed at the side of her forehead, trying to block out the sound of the housekeeper's idle chatter. 'Where is my father?'

'In the sitting room, Miss Van den Fleet.' The housekeeper hurried in front of Marti and led the way.

Erasmus gave a little cry of surprise at Marti's sudden appearance. He held out both his hands to her. 'Marti, nobody told me you were coming back today.'

The housekeeper gave a mock frown. 'Ooh, Mr Van den Fleet, you know that's not true. I told you yesterday.' She whispered a quick aside to Marti. 'We're getting a bit absent-minded, you know.'

Marti went up to her father's chair and bent down to hug him. He gripped at her hand. 'It's good to have you back, Marti. Bring that chair over here and tell me all about Hong Kong.' He turned his head and noticed Johannes standing in the doorway. 'Come on in, Johannes.' He tugged at Marti's hand. 'He's missed you a lot, you know, but then we all have, haven't we, Johannes?'

Marti laughed. 'Father, I've only been away three days.'

He tugged at her hand again. 'Long enough.'　　　　　　·

The coffee and cake provided by the housekeeper lay untouched on the tray. Marti and Johannes each stared down intently at the carpet. Erasmus had his head turned away from them, facing the window. He gripped his hands together tightly, his eyes brimming with tears. Marti was insisting on going away. He felt as if a giant hand was pressing against his chest. He noisily swallowed back his unshed tears then sighed heavily to himself. 'What do you think about Marti going away like this, Johannes?'

Johannes clasped his hands in front of him. 'I want whatever is best for Marti. She deserves it.'

Erasmus sighed again. Johannes looked down at his hands. 'I know it's hard, Mr Van den Fleet, but I think Marti should go to Hong Kong.'

'But why?'

Johannes glanced briefly up at the ceiling. They had been through this particular argument three times. 'Because Marti no longer has a job as a dealer at Van den Fleet's. Because there is a job as a dealer for her in Hong Kong.'

Erasmus turned to face the window again and lapsed into silence. He caught the movement of Johannes squeezing Marti's hand, out of the corner of his eye. 'Don't know why you don't marry her and settle down, then she wouldn't need to go to Hong Kong.'

'Father, please.' Marti raised her head and stared at him. 'You're embarrassing Johannes.'

Erasmus sniffed. 'Well, a girl of your age should be married.'

The housekeeper tapped on the door then bustled into the room. 'Oh, dear, none of you have had any coffee? Is there something the matter?' She looked from one face to the other then realised that there was. 'Shall I reheat the coffee?'

Marti got up. 'If you wouldn't mind. Thank you.' She picked up the tray, glad of the excuse to free herself from imprisonment on the sofa. She walked to the door with the housekeeper and opened it for her then half turned to face the room. 'I won't be a minute, Father. I just need to get something from my bag.'

Marti followed the housekeeper into the kitchen. 'Do you have any aspirin? I've got a terrible headache.'

'Yes, just a minute and I'll get one for you.' The house-keeper looked at her sympathetically. 'Poor you. You do look very pale. It must be the flight. I always get a headache when I fly. Don't know why, but I do.'

Marti nodded. She just wished the woman would stop talking so much. It was driving her mad.

Johannes stood up and walked to the window. He pushed his hands into his pockets. 'Hendrik didn't give Marti much option, Mr Van den Fleet. You can say that it is not really any of my business, but Marti has almost crucified herself in making up her mind what to do. She really cares about you, you know. I shouldn't say this, I know, but it was your decision to let Marti take all the responsibility of running the company until you retired. It was your decision to hand the business over to Hendrik, completely over Marti's head. Don't you think it's about time someone started to make decisions that are in Marti's interest for a change?'

Erasmus shut his eyes. Johannes didn't have the right to speak to him like that, but he didn't have the energy to tell him so. He leaned his head back against the chair. The boy's words were disrespectful but true. They had been his decisions and he had had to make them. A tremor shot through his hand. His fingers twitched nervously on the arm of the chair. Now he had the most painful decision to make of all.

Marti came back to the sitting room. She looked anxiously at Johannes. He tried to give an encouraging smile. Erasmus looked round and held out his hand. 'Come here, Marti.'

She went to the side of his chair and knelt down. Erasmus rested his hand on her head. 'I don't want you to go, Marti, but if it's what you want, well –' He left the sentence unfinished.

She got to her feet and hugged him. 'I'll be able to come

home once a month, you know. You can get some really cheap flights from Hong Kong.'

Erasmus nodded, his mouth trembling with emotion. Marti looked over the top of her father's head at Johannes. Her eyes asked if she had done the right thing. His eyes said she had.

Christian Debilius stared in irritation at his breakfast tray and at the food rapidly growing cold. He shifted the telephone to his other ear. 'Hendrik, I don't think I have made myself completely clear. It is quite out of the question for me to influence James Wu one way or the other. The IDE does not interfere in the internal affairs of its members.'

'But you do agree, that it does give Wu an unfair advantage over Van den Fleet's, if Marti works for him?'

'My dear man, if you think that, why on earth did you let her go in the first place?'

'Because I had to. I can't afford to pay top-dealer salaries to two people.'

Christian took a quick sip of coffee and cursed, as he managed to spill some on his tie.

'Sorry, I didn't catch that, Christian.'

'Nothing, nothing.' Christian pulled out his handkerchief and dabbed at the stain. 'I understand your predicament, but really this is something that you must sort out between yourselves. I am sure there is no doubting Marti's integrity. I have the utmost respect for her. However, if you genuinely fear that she is going to use her knowledge of Van den Fleet's pricing policy to James Wu's advantage then change your prices.'

'That is not, with respect Christian, the point.'

'Then what is the point?'

Hendrik gave a heavy sigh. 'I thought I had explained.'

'You want my personal opinion?'

'Yes.'

'I think you are probably blowing this up out of all

proportion. Look, give me one good reason why Marti should even wish to do anything that would hurt you or indeed her father?'

'It's just that Wu may winkle information out of her without her even realising what he's doing. You know what these oriental bastards are like.'

'I don't think Marti would fall for that one. Hendrik. She is a pretty shrewd girl when it comes to business. However, may I make a suggestion? Give it time. If you find that clients are staying away in droves after Marti has gone, let me know. Give me names and numbers and I will have Wu's books audited. If I find that they have gone over to Wu then we can do something about it. The IDE welcomes competition, but not unfair competition.'

'Thanks, Christian.'

'Not at all. Now I really must go. You will be attending the next option-bearer's day, won't you?'

'Definitely.'

'Good. Come and have lunch with me and let me know how things are working out.'

'Thanks, Christian.'

'Not at all. Goodbye.' Christian put the telephone down. He cursed again as he pulled off his tie. Hendrik Van den Fleet was becoming neurotic about his sister. He got up and went to the door. 'Rosie.' A young Hispanic girl rushed out of the kitchen at the bellowing voice.

'Yes, sir.'

'Get me some more breakfast, will you, Rosie? The muffins are cold.' He tossed the tie to her. 'Be a good girl and lose this for me and get the navy blue with the red dots out for me.'

'Yes, sir.' Her eyes darted quickly to the kitchen then to the bedroom door as she worked out which task to accomplish first.

Marti squeezed the last of the water from her hair and flipped a towel around her head. She turned at the sound of a light knock on the bathroom door. If it was the house-keeper fussing again, she would scream. She was prepared to admit that taking a shower and washing her hair before dinner had made her feel better, but she was not going to be bullied like a dim-witted schoolgirl.

'Marti, it's Hendrik. Can I come in?'

'Yes.'

He opened the door and slipped in quickly. 'Do you mind if we talk here for a minute?'

'No, go ahead.'

He perched himself on the edge of the bath. 'Look, Marti, we've got to discuss this client business. Get it sorted out?'

She bent her head and rubbed at her hair. 'What is there to sort out?'

'Well, it would be very damaging if you took clients away with you.'

'I have told you. I won't be taking any Van den Fleet clients away. It is up to the clients to decide who they want to deal with.'

'I appreciate that, but do you really know why Wu is employing you?

'What do you mean?'

'Your intimate knowledge of Van den Fleet's pricing could be, would be, extremely valuable to him.'

She pushed the towel up from her eyes. 'Do you really think I would give him or anyone else that kind of information?'

'I am not saying that you would, but you might accidentally.'

'Not a chance, Hendrik. If I start making mistakes like that, I'll take up market gardening.'

He pulled out his cigarettes and lit one. 'Father seems to have taken your news very well.'

'Astonishingly well. I had been dreading the whole thing.'

Hendrik drew on his cigarette and toyed with the idea of

raising the subject of Beni Yasim, but decided against it. He had to keep her in a good mood. If she got into one of her rages she could rip Van den Fleet's apart. Christian Debilius didn't know the half of it. He could think of at least two good reasons why she would want to hurt him. Marti straightened up and removed the towel from her head. 'Is that it?'

'What?'

'Is that the end of the discussion?'

'Suppose so.'

She ran her fingers through her hair and pushed it into shape. 'You don't sound very happy.'

He stood up. 'Do you expect me to be?'

'Look, Hendrik, I may be leaving the company, but I have no intention of sabotaging it, accidentally or otherwise. I don't know how to prove that to you, except to say that a Van den Fleet's word has been their bond for centuries.'

'You really are a bitch. You enjoyed saying that didn't you?'

'Hendrik, please, I didn't mean it that way.' She looked up desperately at the ceiling. That had been completely the wrong thing to say. 'Look, Hendrik, I meant that we have both been brought up to stand by what we say, as Father was, as his father was. I really wasn't trying to hurt or insult you.'

He stared at her in silence for a moment then stretched across to the washbasin and flicked the ash from his cigarette into it. 'You would be wasting your time anyway.' He turned on his heel and went out.

Marti placed her hands on the edge of the washbasin and stared into the mirror. Why, why, why, do you always say the wrong thing to him? She turned away and dropped the towel into the linen basket. There was no answer to that.

*　　*　　*

The Golden Gate Mansions were a series of old and crumbling apartment buildings, linked together by a labyrinth of alleyways. They were scheduled for demolition like many other old buildings in Tsimshatsui, but still carried on the trade of travellers' cut-rate accommodation; offering nothing more than a bed for the night and cheap heroin. Busy stopped by the food stall in front of the Mansions and lit a cigarette. He glanced up and down the street then turned to the man stirring a steaming cauldron of noodles. 'Looking for Four-ears Fu. Seen him?'

The man shot him a nervous glance then looked down into the cauldron and stirred the contents vigorously. 'Think he's collecting rent. Usually does on Mondays.'

'Thanks.' Busy leaned forward and let an accumulation of phlegm dribble from his mouth and fall into the gutter, before ducking into the alleyway leading to the adjoining street.

Four-ears Fu stuffed a wad of banknotes inside his shirt and tucked them into the moneybelt he wore around his midriff. He owned four of the lodging houses at the Golden Gate Mansions, four snooker clubs in Tsimshatsui, and three bars catering for tourists with paedophiliac inclinations. He was called Four-ears Fu, because there was little that went on in the area that he didn't get to hear about. He picked up a greasy brown paper bag and stared fiercely at the four little girls huddled together on an old leather chaise longue. 'You been good girls for the *mama-san*?'

The girls nodded silently. The Pakistani woman who controlled the girls pushed at the head of the one nearest to her, knocking her head against the girl sitting next to her. 'Answer Mr Fu, when he ask you question.'

The girl with a dusting of sequins glued on to her cheekbones smiled up at Fu. 'We all been good, Mr Fu.' She swung her legs nervously back and forth. 'Thank you very much.' She gave a darting glance at the woman, seeking her approval. The woman gave a brief nod.

Fu pushed a hand into the brown paper bag and distributed one Big Mac hamburger to each of the girls. 'You remember to be good girls.' He crumpled the bag into a ball and tossed it on the floor.

Busy caught sight of Fu dodging into an alleyway off the street of tailors. He hurried after him, flinging aside a pair of jeans, hung up to advertise the shopkeeper's talents, as he rounded the corner. Fu turned into another smaller alley and disappeared up a flight of steps. Busy swore as he stepped into a pool of liquid excrement formed by effluence from a broken drain. A rat, scuttling along the gutter, paused for a moment and held its front paw up, as if alarmed by the violent oaths. It gave a shrill squeak and disappeared into a large crack in the brickwork around the drain.

Fu turned round quickly at the sound of someone calling out his name. He narrowed his eyes and stared at the approaching figure of Busy. Busy slowed his pace and let his hands hang loosely at his sides in a gesture of non-violence. 'My boss, Frankie Heung, needs some information. Will see it as a favour to him.'

Fu nodded. Busy pulled out the photograph of Fang Ka-Shing and showed it to him. 'Ever seen him before?'

Fu took a quick glance then shook his head.

'Need to find him. He owes us. His name is Mui Shenlu. Carries loose diamonds around. Got a necklace made up here recently. Any idea who might have done the work for him?'

Fu rubbed slowly at his chin.

'If you don't know, say so. Someone else can earn Mr Heung's favour.'

Fu glared at him ferociously. Over his ancestors' shrine, they would. If Four-ears Fu didn't know, no one else did. He cleared his throat and spat into the gutter. 'Man with a limp, who works in the jewellery factory near the China Products store, been seen a lot in the bars lately.'

A slow smile crept over Busy's face. 'What's his name?'

'Zau, and remember it's a favour.'

'No worries.'

Busy leaned against the building on the street corner and pushed a cigarette in his mouth. He slipped his hand in his pocket to search for his lighter, then stopped as a man with a limp came out of a side-door of the jewellery factory and crossed to the food stall. Busy took the cigarette from his mouth as he watched Zau return to the factory clutching a steaming bowl of food to his chest. Busy sprinted across the road and caught up with him just before he reached the side door. He pushed Zau into an alleyway, spun him round to face him, and pushed the blade of his flick knife into the side of his neck. 'Don't spill the food on my shoes. They're new.'

Zau whimpered an unintelligible reply.

'The Thousand Clouds Society wants to know something.'

Zau's eyes rolled in their sockets. Busy pushed the photograph of Fang in front of Zau's face. 'You get a reward for information, and you get a reward for no information.' He jabbed the point of the knife into Zau's neck until blood trickled down to his collar. 'You made up a pendant-style necklace with a twist-effect gold chain. This the man?'

Zau's mouth moved in an effort to shape a reply, but no sound emerged.

Busy lessened the pressure of the knife against Zau's neck. 'Is it?'

Zau gave a rasping sob. 'Yes, yes.'

'What's his name?'

'Didn't tell me.'

'You want to collect both rewards?'

Zau cried out in terror and clutched the bowl of food to his chest so hard it tipped up, spilling bean curd and vegetables down his front. 'He didn't say. I needed the money, so I didn't ask.'

Busy released his grip on Zau. 'You are known to me

now. Remember that.' He stepped back and kicked at his lame leg.

Zau groaned in agony and slumped to the ground. Busy aimed another kick at him then straightened his jacket and walked swiftly back to the main street. The man at the food stall averted his eyes.

Marti drained her cup and set it down in its saucer. 'Thanks for breakfast, Johannes. I'd better be on my way. Taxi should be here soon.'

Johannes wiped his mouth with his napkin. 'I wish you would let me drive you to the airport. It's no trouble.'

'You've done enough for me. Besides, you spent most of yesterday away from your work.' She pushed her chair back from the table and stood up. 'I'll be back from Geneva tomorrow evening and, Johannes, I am going to take you out on the town.'

He sagged back in his chair as if overcome by her words. She came round to his side of the table and punched at his shoulder. 'It's your last chance, remember.'

'I know and I intend to make the most of it, if you are truly paying.' He too got up from his chair. 'Are you sure there isn't anything you want me to do while you are away?'

'No. Father's all-singing, all-dancing housekeeper has packed up every last stitch I own. Nothing for me to do. She has promised to have it freighted out to Hong Kong. All I have to do is complete my last deal for Van den Fleet's. Present Hendrik with a going-away present of a fat commission courtesy of Mr Yasim. And then goodbye, Marti.' She smiled brightly and rested her hand on his shoulder. 'Don't look so worried, Johannes.'

'I am worried, Marti, because you don't fool me. Other people perhaps, but not me.'

'O K. I confess. I am feeling –' She paused for a moment. 'I'm not sure how I feel. Something like stepping off a cliff,

I suppose.' She smiled again. 'Should have learned to hang-glide, shouldn't I?'

He laughed despite himself. 'You could always get some lessons from Beni Yasim. He's something of a high-flyer, isn't he?'

'Now, now, Johannes, let us not be bitchy.' She went to the window and peered out. 'A taxi has just pulled up. It's probably mine. I'd better, dare I say, fly.'

He laughed again. 'I'm coming to see you off.'

'Thanks. I could do with the company.'

'I'm glad to hear it!'

Beni Yasim finished dictating the last letter to one of the girls from the hotel's secretarial service then checked his watch. 'Please see that those papers are faxed to Paris and would you bring Miss Van den Fleet in please.' He placed a bundle of documents into his briefcase and snapped it shut. He crossed to the mirror overhanging the fireplace and carefully adjusted his tie.

The secretary walked swiftly across the ante-room of the hotel suite to where Marti sat. 'Miss Van den Fleet, Mr Yasim will see you now.'

Marti picked up her briefcase and followed the secretary back into the sitting room.

The ritual of doing business with Beni never varied. Based purely on mutual trust, when he required to purchase industrial diamonds, the price would be agreed over the telephone, and the stones escorted by courier to the vaults of Bank Christian Oertli in Geneva. The transaction would be carried out on the basis that the diamonds would be of agreed quality and payment would be made at the end of the month. Marti would then dutifully present herself at his hotel suite to conclude the documentation. The actual meeting would take less than ten minutes to conclude, but if Beni had the time, it was followed by a leisurely lunch.

Beni held out his arms towards Marti. 'Marti, at last we meet again. It's been too long.'

'Hello, Beni. You look very well, as usual.'

He shook hands with her and guided her to one of the two large sofas by the fireplace. She sat down and rested her briefcase on her knees. 'The diamonds are to your satisfaction?'

He laughed. 'Yes, and do you know how many years we have been having this same conversation?'

'Must be a few now.'

'Five to be precise. I think this calls for a rather special celebration, don't you?'

'Oh, absolutely.' She took the documents from her case and flicked through them.

Beni was adept at keeping up a constant flow of small-talk, but she knew from experience that he expected business to be conducted with the minimum of fuss and the greatest haste.

'If you would just sign both copies please, Beni. I have already signed for Van den Fleet's.'

He pulled a gold fountain pen from his breast pocket and quickly signed both sheets. She picked up the invoice and separated the two sheets. 'One for you and one for me.'

'Thank you.' He unlocked his own briefcase and slipped the sheet inside. 'Now a celebratory drink, Marti. We cannot allow five years of friendship to go untoasted.' He went to the fireplace and pressed the bellpush.

Marti hesitated for a moment, then abandoned her carefully rehearsed speech. The celebratory drink could celebrate her news as well. She smoothed her skirt over her knees. 'Beni, if we are celebrating, I might as well tell you my news now and kill two birds with one stone, so to speak. I am leaving Van den Fleet's today. I am going to work for a diamond dealer in Hong Kong.'

Beni's eyes quickly focused on her and, just as quickly, his startled expression was smoothed away from his face. 'Is this a joke?'

'No.'

He came and sat down beside her on the sofa. 'I think, Marti, I need to know a little more about all of this.' He glanced up as there was a gentle tap on the double doors of the suite. 'Just one moment, please.' He raised his voice. 'Come.'

A waiter opened one of the doors and pushed in a small trolley bearing a champagne bucket.

Beni occupied himself in the ensuing silence by lighting up a small cheroot. He leaned back on the sofa and crossed one leg over the other at the knee. The waiter poured out the champagne and presented two glasses to Beni and Marti. Beni gestured to him to leave them. When the waiter had gone, Beni half turned and chinked his glass against Marti's. 'First a toast to our friendship, then you must tell me why you are leaving your company.'

Marti raised her glass then took a small sip. 'Time to spread my wings. My father is retiring. My brother has returned home from Zaire to run the company. It leaves me free to pursue a more independent career.'

He gave a gentle smile. 'We have known each other for a long time, Marti. Perhaps you would like to start again. This time with the truth.'

She gave a small laugh of protest. 'It is the truth. Well, the bare bones of it. I don't want to bore you with the details.'

'Bore me.'

She took another sip of the champagne. 'It is simply a question of my not being an option bearer with the IDE. Hendrik is, and he also needs to groom someone in the company to become eligible. In fact, he has promoted our office manager, Justus. I admit that I have only been keeping the company ticking over the last year or so. We haven't been buying at the IDE, because Father has been too ill to travel to New York. Hendrik has plans to expand the business, but cannot afford to pay top-dealer salaries to two people. It really is time for me to move on. It gives Hendrik room to manoeuvre and it also gives me the opportunity to gain more international experience.'

His eyes roved over her face for several seconds. 'Thank you for telling me, Marti.' He picked up his glass and took a mouthful. 'I can see the problem that Van den Fleet's face with regard to option bearers, but does that really necessitate you leaving your family company?'

'I am a dealer, Beni, not an administrator.' She glanced around the flower-filled room. She seemed to have been saying this until she was blue in the face over the last couple of weeks.

'Of course, and a much-respected dealer, as well.' He rested his cheroot in the ashtray by his elbow then picked up his glass. 'To you, Marti. I know you will be very successful.'

'Thank you.'

'Who are you going to work for?'

'James Wu.'

'The name rings faint bells.'

'If we suit each other, I'm going into partnership with him.'

'Excellent.' He got up and removed the bottle from the champagne bucket. Christian Debilius had misread the situation completely. She was not a girl to be pushed into obscurity. She was ambitious. He tucked the napkin firmly around the bottle, and brought it back to the sofa. 'When do you start your new job?'

'I'm going back to Hong Kong in a couple of days.'

He replenished their glasses. 'Do you have a number in Hong Kong where I can reach you? A member of the Sheik's family has a birthday coming up. I will need something very special for that occasion.'

She looked down at her glass. His intended transition of business from Van den Fleet's to James Wu was too casual to be true. 'You don't wish to continue doing business with Van den Fleet's?'

'I prefer to do business with people I know. I don't know your brother.'

'Oh, really, I can assure you . . .'

'Don't.' He picked up his cheroot. 'I presume you still wish to do business with me?'

She shifted uncomfortably. There was an edge to his voice that indicated the question should not need to be asked. 'But, of course. I value your business very much, Beni, you know that.'

He gave her an appraising look, before nodding slowly to himself to indicate satisfaction with her response. She glanced around the room. She had almost and unintentionally risked offending him. It was a risk no one could afford to take with Beni. She twirled the glass between her fingers. He was arrogant, but then he could afford to be.

Beni rested his hand on hers. 'What is the matter?'

She looked at him in surprise. 'Matter?'

'Yes. You only fidget with a glass when you are nervous. So. What is the matter?'

'Ah – I had wanted to make it clear that I would understand perfectly if you wished to continue dealing with Van den Fleet's, but instead I have a feeling that I have unwittingly caused offence.'

He gave a very quiet laugh. 'You know as well as I do, Marti, that if you had caused offence you would not still be sitting where you are.' He brushed his fingers against hers. 'But, causing offence is something you would find very difficult to do.'

She let her breath out slowly, comforted by the mitigating compliment. If she had caused offence her feet wouldn't have touched the ground.

He glanced at his watch. 'Lunch, Marti. The chef has promised something special for us.'

Her lips twitched into an involuntary smile. She couldn't imagine the chef promising anything less.

The head waiter led Marti and Beni to a table set in an alcove of the hotel dining room. It gave an all-round view of the room, but two statues shaped like ships' figure-heads shielded its sitters from curious eyes. Beni despatched the waiters to their tasks of food and wine, then rested his elbows on the table and propped his chin on his hands. 'So. What made you choose Hong Kong and James Wu?'

'Necessity. His was the only offer of work I received, except from Christian Debilius, but that was only a job at the IDE.'

He raised his eyebrows in mock surprise. 'Only!'

'It was in admin. I am a dealer, Beni, remember.'

'I do, and I am glad you turned down Christian's offer.'

'Why?'

'Because I couldn't bear the thought of him seducing you.'

She laughed. 'I couldn't, either.' She leaned back in her chair. Flirting was as natural to Beni as breathing. As long as one never, ever, took him seriously there was no harm in relaxing and letting the lunch take its – or, more precisely, Beni's – course.

'Christian has a terrible reputation with women, Marti. Be warned.'

'So have you.'

'That is most definitely not true. I have a very good reputation with women. They all say so, in fact.'

She laughed again. She turned her head and noticed a posse of waiters approaching the table.

The service at the table was remarkable for its solicitousness. Genevans treated anyone who was not markedly one of them with cold, impenetrable reserve. Beni Yasim was accorded the honour of apparent warmth and friendliness, because he was a generous man, extremely wealthy in his own right, and his employer was wealthy beyond common imagination; a combination that Genevans found irresistible. Beni waited until the last of the waiters had left before resuming conversation. 'Is James Wu a client of yours, or do you know him personally?'

'Actually, I hardly know him at all. He asked us to authenticate some diamonds for him. In the course of conversation, he mentioned he was desperate to increase his management.'

'Ah, I see. I do know of him, but I was curious. I believe he deals mostly with dealers in England. London.'

'Mmm. I thought that too, but he talks a lot about 1997, when the British pull out.'

He laughed gently. 'When they are pushed out, you mean?'

'Correction. When they are pushed out. James, wisely I think, wants to broaden his marketing base in Europe.'

'Sensible.' He picked up his wine glass and washed down a morsel of food with a mouthful of wine. 'Does Christian know you are leaving your company?'

'Yes, both James and I spoke to him.'

'What did he say?'

'Apparently he agreed with James's plans to expand.'

'And you?'

'Not much. He seemed rather disappointed I hadn't eagerly snapped up the offer of a job with the IDE.'

'I would expect him to be. It's not every day Christian gets turned down.'

She stabbed at the remaining piece of fish on her plate. 'Well, he did this time. The trouble with Christian Debilius is that he expects everybody to behave like a performing seal.'

His eyes glimmered with amusement. 'You told him that, of course.'

She pursed her lips. 'I have to earn my living, Beni.'

'Quite.' He rested his elbows on the table again. 'So, what do you think of Hong Kong?'

'Didn't have much time to explore, really. I went up on the old tram to the top of Victoria Peak. The view is quite something.'

'Where are you going to live?'

'Don't know yet. Someone suggested I should find accommodation on one of the smaller islands. Forgotten the name of it. I think it's called Lamma.'

'Who is the someone?'

'Man I met at the Paulinsons'. Erwin Klein. Do you know him?'

A slow smile spread across his face. 'In a manner of speaking. By the way did the Paulinsons look after you properly?'

Marti smoothed the tablecloth with her fingers. 'They were very kind. They invited me to a luncheon party.'

He stared at her. 'That wasn't what I asked.'

'Sorry. Yes, they looked after me very properly.'

'You're lying, Marti. Don't do it. You are hopeless at it.'

She gave a surprised laugh. 'What a terrible thing to say.'

'But true. So. Why didn't you like the Paulinsons?'

'I think it was the other way around, if you want the absolute truth.'

'What made you think that?'

'Marietta.' She glanced around the room, undecided whether to be as truthful as he demanded. 'Beni, can I ask you a favour for the future?'

'Of course.'

'Please don't foist me on to one of your mistresses again. It can make for embarrassment all round.'

He picked up his glass and took a mouthful of wine then placed it back down on the table. 'I didn't and I wouldn't. What is all this about?'

She sighed. 'I am sorry we started this. Marietta seemed to think I was encroaching on her territory. I explained that you and I were business colleagues.' She looked at him desperately. 'Do you understand what I am trying to say?'

'Yes I do, and I am also trying to understand Marietta. She is not my mistress.'

She waved her hand in the air. 'Well, past, ex-mistress then.'

'No. She isn't that either. She is an attractive woman in her own way and I feel sorry for her, but I have never slept with her.'

She looked at him disbelievingly.

'It is true. I have certain business dealings with her husband. I would never dream of sleeping with the wife of a man with whom I was doing business.'

'Why?'

'Because, Marti, I never allow pleasure to interfere with business. You should know me well enough to know that that is true.' A frown settled on his brow. 'Perhaps I should have mentioned to you that Marietta can act rather strangely at times.'

She gave an abrupt laugh. 'Perhaps you should have.'

'I am sorry you have been embarrassed. Truly. I will speak to her. She will apologise to you.'

'No. Beni, please. Just forget it. It wasn't important.'

He signalled to the waiter. 'I will tell you something about Marietta in a minute.'

The waiter hurried forward to remove the plates from the table and was followed by a second waiter who replenished their wine glasses. Marti watched Beni. It was very rare to see him look disconcerted. He gave a brief smile. When they were alone again, he leaned forward across the table. 'Marietta had some kind of nervous breakdown a couple of years ago. It was very difficult for Piers. She developed certain obsessions.'

She picked up her wine glass and stared into it. And one of her certain obsessions was you. 'I must say I thought she seemed very tense.'

'She can be more than that at times. I feel sorry for her, but I must confess my real sympathies lie with Piers. I, frankly, wouldn't put up with it.'

'I'm surprised they are not divorced then.'

He gave a quick shrug of his shoulders. 'God help him, but he sees something in her that he needs. Why else does a man stay with a woman?'

'Love?'

'Love is another word for need, Marti.'

'Mmm.'

He tapped her wrist with his finger. 'We are drifting into a philosophical mood. This is not what I had in mind.'

Her mind snapped out of the wine-induced reverie. 'Actually, Beni, I have to get back to Antwerp as soon as possible and –'

'Stop flapping your wings, Marti. I am not about to suggest anything that I thought you would not agree to.' He turned slightly and gave a brief nod to the waiter to indicate that they had finished. A surge of irritation swept through her. One minute he was making up to her, the next minute he was patronising; treating her like a gauche schoolgirl. She clasped her hands in front of her. 'I am not flapping my wings, Beni, and may I ask what you had in mind?'

'No. The time is not, I think, right. Come.' He pushed his chair back and stood up.

A courtesy limousine pulled up in front of the hotel steps. The doorman stepped forward and opened the rear passenger door. Marti shivered as she got in. The fresh air felt icy after the excessively warm atmosphere of the dining room. Beni bent down to the window and held out his hand. 'The driver will collect your luggage from your hotel and take you to the airport.'

'Thank you.' Marti raised her hand to shake his.

He pressed his mouth to the back of her hand. 'I will be coming to Hong Kong soon. I will let you know when.' He squeezed her fingers. 'You won't forget to look out something special for the Sheik, will you?'

'No, I won't. I don't know what James has in stock, but if there is nothing suitable I will get him to come up with something.'

'Good. See you soon.' He stepped back and signalled to the chauffeur.

Marti waved through the back window to him as the limousine swung out into the street, then turned round to face the front. Her visit to Geneva had been more successful than she had anticipated. She settled back into the seat. She now had a client to take with her to James Wu. A client who would considerably increase her standing with him. She pulled her briefcase closer to her. Hendrik would probably make a fuss, but she wasn't behaving improperly. Beni had always been her personal client. Even when her father was still active, Beni had always insisted upon doing business with her. She idly stared out of the side-window. If James didn't have anything in stock to meet Beni's requirements, she would have to persuade him to apply to the IDE for a permit to buy from their stocks. The IDE occasionally granted permits to buy outside the monthly option days, if the transaction was made on behalf of a strictly bona fide client of quantifiable distinction. Beni met both requirements.

Candy adjusted the diamond pendant of her necklace. Having insisted on wearing her fur coat in the cocktail bar, then changing her mind, she sat and happily watched the boy, whom Fang had had summoned, walk through the crowded lounge to the cloakroom, with the coat reverently draped over his arms, and with the inside label uppermost. She gave a faint smile at those who had turned around to see from where the coat had appeared. Fang Ka-Shing lit up a cigarette. 'I told you to leave your coat at the cloakroom. Now you have made us both look foolish.' She thrust her breasts out and tilted her head back, as she had seen Marilyn Monroe do in countless re-runs of an old movie. He turned his attention back to the giant television screen, which listed every conceivable detail of the jockeys and horses entered in the next race. His brow furrowed. Every horse he betted on which had a name that reminded him of Candy had always won. Tonight there were two horses.

Sugarfly and Honeybun. Their form was not spectacular and neither were rated anywhere near the favourites, but . . . He scratched at the side of his face. But, who was Fang Ka-Shing to ignore the dictates of good fortune? He would bet on them both. The decision made, he flicked a finger at a waiter. 'Brandy, and a champagne cocktail for my companion.'

The waiter nodded and hurried away.

Candy froze in her chair as she saw Frankie Heung enter the lounge. He was accompanied by a slightly taller man with large, round eyes. She hastily turned her back on them. She smiled brightly at Fang. 'Which horse have you chosen, Ka-Shing?'

'Two. I am betting on two.' She saw, out of the corner of her eye, that Frankie was approaching. She gave Fang her full attention. 'Two horses. What are their names? Are they the favourites?' She held her breath as Frankie seemed for a moment to have paused a few feet away from her.

The waiter returned with the brandy and champagne cocktail. When she took another sideways glance, Frankie had moved on nearer the bar. Fang picked up his glass, took a large mouthful of brandy, then set it down again. His face creased into a knowing smile. 'I am betting on Sugarfly and Honeybun.'

She giggled. 'What would you do without me, Ka-Shing?'

He burst into laughter. 'I would be losing a lot of money.' He picked up his glass and finished off the remains of the brandy.

Frankie Heung leaned against the bar and surveyed the crowded lounge. He gestured to the man at his side. 'I appreciate you inviting me to the Jockey Club like this, Mr dos Santos.'

The swarthily complexioned man gave a slight smile. 'I think it is time to place our bets, don't you?'

'What's the name of your horse again?'

'The Navigator. It's the favourite.'

Frankie gave a gurgling laugh. 'It had better be. I don't like losing money.'

Santos smiled again. 'Neither do I. I've spent a lot on that horse, but I have faith in my trainer.' He picked up his glass and drained it. 'I am a man of faith, Frankie, until proved wrong.'

'Sure.' Frankie's gaze settled on Fang Ka-Shing and Candy. 'Regarding the other matter, your faith is not misplaced in that either. Your client will get the tender for the computerised container terminal. You have no worries on that score.'

'Let us hope not, Frankie.' Frankie finished his drink and followed Santos out of the lounge. He gave a casual glance in Candy's direction, as if admiring a particularly pretty girl, but taking in the diamond necklace and the man sitting with her. He shouldered his way through the crowds. Busy had done a good job. Mr Fang Shenlu, whatever he wanted to call himself, would become a more viable investment to Heung & Co.

The name of the winner flashed up on the television screen with prominent brightness. Fang gripped at Candy's hand. 'Look, look. Sugarfly first. Honeybun second. The Navigator third.' His face shone with a thin film of perspiration. 'We've won on both. On both.'

Candy laughed happily. She fingered the pendant at her throat. Good fortune had protected her yet again. Fang stared hard at the screen, as the names of the entrants for the next race were slowly scrolled. He scratched at the side of his face. Spice 'n' Rice? He shook his head to himself. Cocoboy. No. There was nothing in the next race for him. Perhaps the next. He gestured to the waiter to bring them more drinks.

Frankie tore up his betting slip. Doing business with Santos was becoming expensive. He had just lost five hundred bucks on the goddam favourite. He glanced at Santos.

The man seemed unperturbed that his horse had only come in third. Santos caught his eye and smiled. 'Better luck next time, eh?'

'I'd be happy with luck, period.'

Santos gave a quiet laugh. 'Let's go back to the bar and drown our sorrows.' He turned away from the corner of the balcony, then paused to allow a man and a woman to pass in front of him. 'You will have the German figures for me soon, Frankie?'

'No problem. Friday by the latest.'

'Good. It is important that my client wins this contract.' Santos nodded to someone passing through the glass doors. 'Most important, Frankie.'

'You've got it, Mr dos Santos.'

Astrid popped her head around the door of Hendrik's office. 'Mr Witt to see you.'

'Wheel him in.' Hendrik tucked his pen into his pocket and stood up. Johannes came in and dropped his raincoat on to a chair. 'Marti caught her plane.'

'Oh, good.' Hendrik rubbed his hands together. 'Thanks for doing the family duty.' He gestured at the heap of files on his desk. 'I just couldn't get away. OK, was she?'

'Er, yes, I think so. The flight was delayed for twenty minutes, which didn't help. Waiting gives you too much time to think, doesn't it? Still worrying about your father, I suspect.'

Hendrik looked about him. 'I should offer you some lunch, Johannes, but I'm really tied up here.'

'I couldn't manage lunch anyway. I've promised to take my two assistants out to celebrate.'

'They're not glad Marti has gone as well, are they?'

Johannes gave a half-embarrassed laugh. 'Good job Marti isn't here to hear you say that. No, actually, I heard from Christian Debilius, unofficially of course, that I've won the Diamond Cutter of the Year award.'

Hendrik immediately shot out his hand. 'Congratulations, Johannes. Can't think of a more deserving person. How many does this make it?'

'Well, this is the third time I've won. I expect they will want me to retire next year. It's getting rather monotonous.'

Hendrik slapped him on the shoulder. 'Not for business, Johannes, not for business.' He looked around him again. 'Well, I'd better get back to that lot on my desk. Thanks again for taking Marti to the airport.'

'Don't mention it. If you're not going home for lunch, do you want me to stop off at the apartment? See your father for a few minutes?'

'If you've got the time, I won't refuse the offer.' Hendrik rubbed the side of his jaw. 'To be honest with you, I try not to go home at lunch-time, unless something has cropped up. I find a midday conversation leaves nothing to talk to him about in the evening.'

'I'll sit with him for a few minutes then. See you later, Hendrik.'

'Ciao.' Hendrik returned to his desk and puffed out his cheeks. He regrouped the files he had deliberately spread out on his desk in order to appear busy, into a neat bundle, then searched in his pockets for his cigarettes. He had avoided last-minute farewells at the airport with Marti and had avoided being seen lunching with that little faggot, Witt. He pulled open the bottom drawer of his desk and removed a glass and a bottle of whisky. Time for a little celebratory drink. He pushed them back into the drawer at the ringing of the telephone.

Hendrik got to his feet at the sound of Beni Yasim's voice. 'Thank you for returning my call, Mr Yasim.' He cleared his throat. 'I just wanted to have the opportunity of introducing myself to you, and to assure you of Van den Fleet's continuing service to you.'

There was a slight pause on the line. 'Is there something you want, Mr Van den Fleet?'

'No, no, as I say I just wanted to assure you of our –'

Beni cut in abruptly. 'That won't be necessary, Mr Van den Fleet.'

'What do you mean?'

'I have Miss Van den Fleet's assurance of continuing service. I do not require further assurances.'

Hendrik gave a quick laugh. 'Ah, I think we are talking at cross-purposes. I thought she had told you. She has left the company.'

'I know, and we are not talking at cross-purposes, Mr Van den Fleet. Now if you will excuse me. Goodbye.'

Hendrik stared down at the telephone as it purred softly to itself. His breathing quickened. Bastard. He slammed the telephone down. Bastard wog had hung up on him. He picked up the telephone again. 'Astrid, get me Christian Debilius straight away.'

Hendrik drew on his cigarette as he listened impatiently to Christian's softly drawling voice. He stubbed out the cigarette and immediately lit up another one. 'I must have something done about this, Christian.'

'Then do it, Hendrik.'

Hendrik clenched his fist into a ball. 'I mean I must have something done about it by the IDE.'

'Why the IDE?'

'Because, Christian, Marti insists that Yasim is her personal client and he as much as told me to fuck off.'

'I cannot see what the IDE can do to assist in this matter, Hendrik. I think it was very much on the cards that Beni Yasim would continue doing business with Marti. I thought I had made that clear in an earlier conversation. The man is interested in her. I have known Beni for a long time, Hendrik; if he has a choice between doing exactly the same profitable business with a pretty woman and someone else, he will choose the pretty woman.'

'But Marti promised me. We have an agreement that she

would not attempt to take clients away from Van den Fleet's. She has broken that promise.'

'Is that really the case? It would be most unlike Marti to do so. We appear to be covering old ground, Hendrik. I thought I had made it clear. The IDE cannot become the pig-in-the-middle between brother and sister. Unless you have evidence that your sister is using her knowledge to undermine Van den Fleet's position in the market, there is little that the IDE can do.'

'Isn't Yasim sufficient evidence?'

'No. I think you have to accept the inevitable, Hendrik. You do not tell the Yasims of this world who they will or will not do business with. I wished you had discussed this matter with me before speaking to Yasim. I could have saved you the cost of telephoning him. Once he has made his mind up, neither you nor anyone else has a hope in hell of changing it for him. He is a powerful man, Hendrik. He runs the Arab Trustee Corporation. He always denies it, but he does; at least, behind the scenes he does.'

Hendrik ran his fingers through his hair. 'Well, surely something can be done about this. If he buys diamonds on a regular basis, why isn't he treated like any other dealer by the IDE, even if he only trades on an agency basis?'

'I am afraid, Hendrik, that I cannot discuss Yasim's status with the IDE. That is not within my authority. That would require permission from the governing committee. A permission, I have no doubt, they would refuse to grant.'

'All right, Christian. Sorry I bothered you.'

'Not at all, Hendrik.'

Hendrik put the telephone down and gave a disgusted laugh. Not within his authority. Christian *was* the governing committee. They did what he told them to do. He stubbed out the cigarette lying in the ashtray. Bitch. He opened the drawer and took out the bottle of whisky. She wasn't going to get away with it. No way was she going to bleed him dry.

*   *   *

Marti brushed the hair away from the back of her neck. Kai Tak airport was even more crowded and hot than on her last visit. She pushed her way forward to where she thought she could see someone who looked very like James Wu, waving a placard above his head. She brushed her hand across the moist skin of her neck again.

James stood on tiptoe and waved. 'Marti, over here.'

Marti pushed her travel bag in front of her to clear a path to James. 'Hello, James. How are you?'

'Very well, thank you. Let me take your bag.'

'How's Anna?'

'She is well, too. She apologises for her absence, but her assistant is ill. She has had to look after the boutique herself today.'

'No apologies needed, James.'

'Hold on to my jacket and I will lead the way out.'

She grabbed hold of his sleeve and hung on grimly as he struggled his way through the mass of people.

The hotel bedroom was identical to the one Marti had stayed in previously at the Continental, except it was one storey higher. She tapped the tips of her fingers together. James had said he had found an apartment for her. It was only on six-months' lease, while the occupants were in the USA, but they were good friends of James and they were happy for her to stay in it. She walked over to the window and lifted the curtain and looked down on the narrow street below. She had mentioned that Erwin Klein had said he would help her find accommodation and had recommended Lamma island. She let the curtain fall back into place. James had muttered that it was of course, popular with Westerners working in Hong Kong. She tapped her fingers together again. She had clearly offended him, but if Erwin Klein could find her an apartment, living with other Westerners would ease her entry into Hong Kong life. The thought of being continually surrounded by babbling, incomprehensible Chinese was not a happy one.

She hurried to the telephone by the bedside when it rang. 'I have Mr Klein for you now.'

'Thank you. Hello, Mr Klein? Marti Van den Fleet here. We met briefly at the Paulinsons' last week.'

A gentle laugh floated into her ear. 'No need for explanations. I know of only one Marti here.'

'I'm sorry to bother you, but –'

'You are not bothering me at all.'

'You did say something about helping me to find accommodation. I wondered if you knew of anything suitable.'

'As a matter of fact I do. A colleague of mine is returning home. Health reasons, I'm afraid to say. He asked me to find someone to take his place over for him and I had you immediately in mind. Would you be interested?'

'Yes. Where is it?'

'Cheung Chau.'

'I thought you mentioned something about a place called Lamma?'

'Yes, but nothing is available for rent there at the moment. Cheung Chau is a nice place. Very peaceful. It is about ten kilometres from Hong Kong. There is an excellent ferry service to and from Hong Kong. The apartment is frankly small, but quite comfortable. Do you speak any German, by any chance?'

'A little.'

'Excellent. There are two or three German couples living in the apartment block, I think. You should have no trouble in making friends. Would you like to go and see it this afternoon?'

'If it's not too much trouble.'

'No trouble. I have to visit Cheung Chau anyway. Shall we say two o'clock at your hotel?'

'Thank you very much, Mr Klein.'

'No, no, no. Not Mr Klein. Erwin.'

She laughed. 'I shall try to remember that, and thanks again. See you at two.' She put the telephone down and stared at it thoughtfully. She was not overly fond of Germans. On the whole, they tended to be loud and arrogant. She went to the wardrobe and took out a lightweight suit. Perhaps she would be lucky and they would be as amiable as Erwin Klein.

Heavy rain began to fall as Marti and Erwin made their way to the Outlying Districts Pier. He took her arm and hurried her to the waiting ferry. When they were safely aboard, she pulled out a handkerchief and mopped at her face. 'Does it always rain as heavily as this?'

'Not usually so in late September. The rains tend to die off at this time of the year. It is very wet in the height of summer.' He took her arm again and guided her to the front of the ferry.

They sat down and she stared out of the window as the ferry moved away from the pier. The rent for the apartment was HK$6,000 per month. If the place was in any way habitable she would take it. The apartment James had found in the Mid-Levels was more than that per *week*. She turned to Erwin. 'How long does the ferry take to Cheung Chau?'

'About an hour. That is the drawback, I'm afraid, although many people think it a little price to pay to escape the frenetic life of Hong Kong island.'

'I think, at the moment, I'm more worried about the language. I was told that most Hong Kong Chinese speak good English, but I haven't found it to be the case.'

He laughed. 'You will find their English improves considerably when they are trying to sell you something.'

'You speak fluent Cantonese, Erwin, have you been out here long?'

'Fifteen, sixteen years. I try to return home once a year,

if I can. It breaks the monotony. I have never totally
succumbed to the delights of Hong Kong.'

'Where is home?'

'Vienna.'

She looked at him in surprise, then realised that it would
account for his less-than-Germanic manner.

'Vienna has changed. It always does. That is how it goes
on existing. However, I still hold it dear to my heart. My
family is there. My daughter and grandchild.'

She wanted to ask about his wife, but that seemed impolite.

'My wife died many years ago, so only my daughter and
her child are left. They are very important to me.'

'Vienna is a place I have always wanted to visit, but never
got around to it.'

He smiled. She noticed it was something he did often, but
with little humour, or genuine warmth. He patted her arm.
'Then we must arrange such a visit for you. You will not be
disappointed.' He leaned across her and pointed to the window. 'We are approaching Cheung Chau now.'

She peered out through the rain-spattered window, but
couldn't see much through the mist of rain.

By the time the ferry had berthed, the rain had eased to a
light shower. Erwin took her arm again. 'The apartment
block is only a short walk away. If you look to your right
towards the western waterfront, you will see all the seafood
restaurants. There are those who say that they are infinitely
superior to the ones in Hong Kong and Kowloon.'

She wrinkled her nose. 'I am not always sure what the
Chinese mean by seafood.'

'Never ask, that is my best advice. There is also a restaurant at the rear of the beach that serves Western-style food.
It is very popular with the *gweilos*.'

'Who are the *gweilos*?'

'You and me. That is what the Chinese call us. It is
supposed to mean 'foreign devils', although that is not
an entirely accurate translation.' He touched her elbow.

'Up that street there. That's the apartment block.'

She stared up at the modest two-storey building. It was marginally less drab than the exterior of her hotel.

As they neared the building, she noticed baskets of flowers hanging over one or two of the balconies. A mongrel dog with a shaggy tail got up from the front step of the building, stretched back and forth, then came up to greet them. Erwin bent down to scratch at its head. 'Hello, Heinz, and how are you today?'

Marti broke out into laughter. 'Let me guess. He is owned by one of the German families.'

'No, no, you are wrong. He is actually owned by a French photographer who lives on the ground floor. She called him Heinz, because when she found him, he was licking at the inside of an empty can of Heinz tomato soup.'

'Oh, I see.' She bent down and stroked the dog's back. 'What is the owner's name?'

'Christina. I don't know whether she will be here or not. She works freelance. Travels around a lot.'

The apartment was on the second floor. Erwin bent down and felt beneath the doormat for the front-door key. 'Ah, here it is.' He straightened up and opened the door. 'Please.' He gestured to Marti to enter first.

She stepped into a minuscule hallway.

'The living room is straight ahead. The door on the left is the bedroom. The door on the right the bathroom.'

She nodded and opened each door in turn. She pursed her lips. Erwin hadn't exaggerated the smallness of the place. It could easily fit into the sitting room of her father's apartment in Antwerp.

A voice called out. 'Mr Klein, is that you?' Marti turned quickly and stared at the woman standing by the door. Erwin took hold of Marti's arm. 'Ah, Mrs Bachmann, let me introduce Miss Van den Fleet. She is interested in taking the apartment.'

Mrs Bachmann stepped inside the doorway. She cautiously held out her hand to Marti. Marti smiled and shook her hand. 'How do you do, Mrs Bachmann.'

'Very well, thank you.' Mrs Bachmann's gaze swept over Marti from top to toe. 'The residents here are very quiet. They don't like noise of any kind.'

Marti smiled again. 'Glad to hear it.'

Mrs Bachmann gazed into Marti's face. 'You are Dutch?'

'No. I come from Belgium.'

'Ah.'

Marti suppressed a sudden grin. For some mysterious reason her reply seemed to have impressed Mrs Bachmann.

'Well, when you have finished looking around, you are welcome to come for a cup of coffee in my apartment.'

'Thank you very much.' Marti smiled politely again. She must have earned Mrs Bachmann's seal of approval.

The view from the sitting-room window would, on a clear day, give a glimpse of the beach. Marti turned away from the window and looked around the room again. Erwin lit up a cigar. 'What do you think, Marti?'

'I'll take it, if the owner is agreeable.'

'Leave that to me. He wants to get rid of it as quickly as possible. I will arrange everything for you.'

'When is the earliest I can move in?'

'Tomorrow suit?'

'Yes. It would suit me very well. I want to get settled in before I start my new job.'

'Then there is nothing further to do, except to invite you out to dinner.' He checked his watch. 'We shall be back in Hong Kong by five-thirty. I will pick you up at seven, yes?'

She hesitated for a moment, toying with the idea of refusing, but then decided that Erwin Klein was a useful man to know. 'I can't promise I shan't fall asleep.'

He gave a gentle laugh. 'Do not worry. I am told I have a very comfortable shoulder.'

'There are two conditions.'

For a moment his eyes held hers. She found his gaze slightly uncomfortable. 'I must be back at my hotel by ten o'clock and I expect you to fill me in on what goes on in Hong Kong.'

He smiled in genuine amusement. 'Miss Marti Van den Fleet, the first condition is easy to meet. You will be back at your hotel by eight, if you so wish. The Chinese eat early by Western standards. The second condition is not so easy. It would take all night and the next day to tell you everything I know about Hong Kong.'

She laughed. 'I believe you.'

'Then we shall be on our way. The ferry leaves in fifteen minutes.'

'What about Mrs Bachmann? She did invite us for coffee, or was that just being polite?'

'No, she doesn't issue invitations unless she means them, but I suggest we give it a miss. She makes terrible coffee.'

Marti followed him out through the tiny hall, wondering how to get out of an earlier invitation given by James, to dine with him and Anna. She slung her bag over her shoulder. She would plead jet lag. They were very hospitable, but perhaps it was better if she distanced herself just a little from them, until she got to know them better. Friendship in business was better left to develop at its own pace.

Frankie flipped quickly through a computer printout of the previous month's accounts. 'Give yourself a drink, Busy. I'll be through in a couple of minutes.'

'No hurry, Mr Heung.' Busy walked to the filing cabinet and perused the bottles of drink. He picked out the brandy bottle and poured some into a glass. He glanced back at Frankie and swallowed the measure of brandy, then refilled the glass again.

Frankie made a small notation at the side of one sheet. 'I was speaking in the singular, Busy. Just one drink.'

'Sure, Mr Heung.'

Frankie scooped up the printout and dumped it into a filing tray. 'OK. I want you to put a tail on this guy Fang. Correction. Tails. You can triple it. In fact, use as much back-up as you need. I want to know which clubs he goes to. Candy says he won a lot of money last night on the horses. I want to know how he spends it, apart from on her.'

Busy nodded. 'No problem, Mr Heung.'

'You've been doing good work for me lately, Busy. I appreciate that. I want this job doing real fast, right?'

'Right, Mr Heung.'

Frankie pushed his chair away from the desk and stretched out. 'I'll have a whisky. No soda. No ice.'

Busy hastily put his glass down and reached for the whisky bottle.

Frankie clasped his hands behind his head. 'I believe in keeping staff informed. It's the basis of good management. I want this information on Fang *rapido*. You know what *rapido* means?'

'Like yesterday, Mr Heung?' Frankie gave a rare smile. 'You got it. Look, I want Candy off the payroll by the end of the week. The money I pay her, I could employ three runners in Wanchai. I can't afford people who are not cost-effective and she most certainly ain't.'

Busy brought a glass of whisky to the desk. 'What are you planning to do with her, Mr Heung?'

'Nothing. She will not be my problem by the end of the week, will she, Busy?'

Busy's eyes flicked back and forth, as he rapidly translated the meaning behind Frankie's words. 'No problem, Mr Heung. I get the information on Fang to you straight away.'

Frankie picked up the whisky glass and held it up to the light. 'Tell you something else, Busy. I am considering promoting you. I believe in rewarding good work.'

Busy's face broke out into a proud smile. 'You can always rely on me, Mr Heung.'

'That's what I like to hear. OK, Busy, finish your drink.'

Busy picked up his glass and quickly swallowed the contents. It was time to leave.

James paced up and down the sitting room, the telephone clamped to one ear. He glanced at the silent figures on the television for a moment. He had listened patiently to Marti's apologies for not having dinner with him and to her reasons for having taken an apartment in Cheung Chau. He felt strangely dispirited. When she had first arrived in Hong Kong she seemed fragile, dependent. He had found it very attractive. Now, she was none of those things. He hitched the belt of his trousers up, as if trying to prevent the empty, falling-away feeling in the pit of his stomach. 'Maybe the apartment in Mid-Levels is expensive, but it would be very convenient for you. You should have said if money was a problem, Marti. The company could have made you a loan.'

'Money isn't a problem, James, but it is a finite source as far as I am concerned. I simply don't want to commit myself to too much expenditure at this early stage. I suppose when I have lived here for a few months, I will have a better idea of how far my financial resources will stretch. Am I being difficult?'

'No, no. I understand perfectly.'

'Fine. Well, I will see you tomorrow morning at the office. I am looking forward to my first day at work.'

'Yes, yes, so am I. See you tomorrow.' James put the telephone down and stared at the television screen. There was a side to Martina Van den Fleet that he didn't know. A bright, hard, determined side that didn't allow for compromise once she had reached a decision.

Anna came into the sitting room. 'What do you think, James?' She hung her arms out to display the outfit she was wearing. 'Will this be suitable?'

He gave her a quick glance. 'We're not going out.'

'What is the matter?'

'Marti rang to say she couldn't make dinner. She needs a good night's sleep to shake off the jet lag.'

'That is a wise thing to do. Sleep is the best cure.'

He inspected one of his hands and flicked at a fingernail. 'She's not taking the apartment I found her. Someone she knows has offered her an apartment elsewhere.'

She clasped her hands in front of her. James always rushed at things and was always made disappointed by them. 'Where is Marti going to live?'

'Cheung Chau.'

'Ah.' Anna glanced down at her hands. Many *gweilos* lived there. She looked up quickly at James, then cast her eyes downwards. He should have realised that she would wish to live among her own people.

James picked up the remote-control pad and switched the sound up on the television. He flung himself down on the sofa and sprawled out.

'Do you wish me to cook something here, James?'

He shook his head. 'I'll get something at the club. I'm going out when I've seen this programme.'

She nodded and went out, quietly closing the door behind her. She went to the kitchen and opened the door of the refrigerator. Western women held a strong and lasting fascination for James. She removed a plastic tub of bean curd and shut the door. His fascination for them could be numbered in days.

Erwin Klein had changed into a formal navy-blue suit. Marti appraised his back as he led the way to his car. His physique was too comfortably proportioned to allow much elegance. She suppressed a smile. Ageing Care Bear. That was what he looked like. He opened the passenger door for her and ensured that she was properly ensconced, then moved swiftly round to the driver's door. He eased himself behind the steering wheel and started up the engine. 'As you do not care for Chinese food, would you like to try some Hungarian food?'

'Ooh, yes.' She turned to look at him. 'I didn't know you could get Hungarian food here.'

'Hong Kong caters for all types. Actually, where we are going, the food is very good. I know the woman who runs the place. She –' He stamped on the brakes and cursed under his breath, as a small, heavily laden van narrowly overtook him as he pulled away from the kerb. He swung the car into the street and accelerated rapidly, overtaking the offending van before they reached the T-junction. 'Ah, as I was saying, she was married to a Portuguese. They lived in Macao. He owned a big fireworks factory. She used to run a little restaurant. They got divorced. The time I speak of was in 1966. When the Red Guards invaded Macao, she escaped with only the clothes on her back to Hong Kong. She's done very well for herself since. Her restaurant is very popular with Europeans.'

'Fascinating story.'

'Fascinating lady.'

She shot him a sideways glance. 'Aha, do I detect a special interest here?'

He laughed. 'You women, you are all alike. You will weave romance from an abandoned shopping list. I am an old man. I gave up romancing a long time ago. Besides, I do not believe in wasting time. Irene has many admirers.'

'Is that her name?'

He nodded.

She smiled to herself. 'Erwin, claiming to be an old man is not the same as not wishing to waste time. I suspect the latter is your real reason.'

He lifted a hand off the steering wheel and gesticulated. 'I am old. I am sixty. I am a grandfather.'

'How old is Irene?'

'Difficult to say. Hungarian women never look their age. Perhaps she is in her early fifties.' He turned to look at her.

'That must seem geriatric to you. You are very, very young.'

'I'm not. I am twenty-seven.'

He laughed again. 'Oh yes, that is very, very ancient.' He lapsed into silence as he jostled for position in the approaches to the cross-harbour tunnel.

Marti glanced out of the side-window. Grandfather he may be, but he carved up other drivers as ruthlessly as Hendrik.

The Magyar was brightly lit with fairy-lights strung beneath the scalloped wooden fascia of the restaurant. Erwin got out of the car and swiftly came round to Marti's side and opened the door for her. She quietly raised an eyebrow. There were not many young men of her acquaintance who displayed such impeccable manners.

'Good name for a Hungarian restaurant, yes?'

She smiled. 'Can't think of any better.'

Irene looked up from the appointments book in front of her. 'Erwin, how are you?'

Marti stared in silence at her. Erwin had forgotten to add that Irene was also very attractive. Irene turned to look at Marti and bathed her in a radiant smile of welcome. Erwin placed his arm around Marti's shoulders. 'I want you to meet Miss Martina Van den Fleet, Irene, she has just arrived on the island. She is a diamond dealer from Antwerp.'

Irene's smiling eyes, that were ready to charm anything in their path, narrowed slightly as dawning respect tinged their brilliance. Her voice dropped to a low note. 'I am very pleased to meet you, Miss Van den Fleet. Welcome to the Magyar. I am always glad to meet Erwin's colleagues.'

Erwin looked around the restaurant. 'You have kept a quiet table for two, as I asked?'

'Yes, of course, Erwin. Would you like a drink at the bar, or would you prefer to go straight to your table?'

He glanced at Marti. 'The bar looks crowded, shall we have a drink at the table?'

'Yes, that's fine.'

'What would you like to drink?'

Marti turned round to look at the rows of bottles behind the bar. 'Vermouth, if they have any.'

'Sweet or dry?'

'Dry, please.'

Irene led them personally to a table in the corner and offered the menu to Marti and the wine list to Erwin. He flicked through it quickly. 'Do you like wine, Marti?'

'Yes.'

'And may I recommend something from the menu for you?'

Marti nodded and passed the menu across to him.

'What about baked mushrooms paprika to begin, followed by the Stephanie roast? It is Irene's speciality.'

'What's Stephanie roast? Sounds interesting.'

Irene moved quickly to Marti's side. 'I think you will like it very much, Miss Van den Fleet. It is thinly sliced beef stuffed with egg and herbs and sautéed in a brandy and cream sauce.'

Marti rolled her eyes. 'Not only sounds interesting, but fattening as well.'

Erwin handed back the wine list to Irene. 'And a bottle of your Portuguese red, please, Irene.'

Irene collected up the menu and the wine list. 'Ah, here are your drinks. May I wish you both very enjoyable eating.' She gave a slight bow of her head and bustled away.

Erwin picked up his glass. 'To good health and to good money.'

Marti picked up her glass and raised it to his. 'Is that what they say here?'

'It is what I say.'

She smiled wryly. 'To good health and good money, Erwin.'

The plates used for the main course had been removed from the table and the remains of the bottle of wine shared equally between the two glasses still remaining. Marti had declined to sample Irene's famed desserts. Everything on the trolley, ceremoniously wheeled to the table, had been smothered in an assortment of chocolate, nuts and yet more cream. Erwin leaned back in his chair and spoke to the waiter who had tried so persuasively to tempt Marti into having a dessert. 'Just two coffees and two cognacs, please.'

'Yes, sir.'

Erwin took out a cigar and lit it. 'You look very relaxed, Marti. Almost a different person to the one I first met.'

She glanced around the restaurant. 'This is a very relaxing place.'

'Not like the Paulinsons'. You were not very happy there, I think.'

'Not very, but I didn't know at the time that Marietta Paulinson had been ill. Knowing has helped to explain certain things, in retrospect.'

He nodded. 'Knowledge is an essential asset anywhere, but none more so than in Hong Kong.'

'Come on, Erwin, you promised to spill the beans. What should I know?'

'Do you intend doing much business with the Paulinsons?'

'I doubt it. My brief is to expand James Wu's European market.'

'Ah, I suspected that he was buying-in European expertise. Interesting. As regards the Paulinsons, you need know nothing more about them than that Paulinson Pacific are quietly selling off all their assets. The Americans have a saying "cash poor". As a trading company Paulinson Pacific have done badly in recent years, but they do own large and very important tracts of land, which they are selling to the People's Republic of China at great profit. Presumably that is why your colleague Mr Yasim bought his way into Paulinson Pacific a year ago.'

'Asset stripping.'

He gave a slight shrug of his shoulders. 'It is not a criminal offence.'

'Is doing business in Hong Kong difficult? I didn't have time to do much homework before I came, but I imagine the island is in a state of transition. Is China exerting greater influence?'

'To answer your first question, doing business is not difficult, it is just a case of following the local rules. Corruption is a way of life here. Every contract negotiated requires an unofficial premium.'

'Premium?'

'Yes, no one does anything in Hong Kong unless they can personally benefit, so tenders, in fact any business transactions, require money to pass into the appropriate hands. Plus the cost of insurance that every business has to pay out to the Triads, that too has to be added on. The Triads have a hand in practically everything on the island. Construction, garment manufacture, electrical goods, right down to the humble steam laundry and street food stall.'

'The Triads are supposed to be very secret, like the Italian Mafia, aren't they?'

'But a thousand times more efficient.' He flicked the ash from his cigar. 'To answer your second question, when you do business with the PRC, there is only one simple rule to remember. Never expect the person you are dealing with to take a decision.'

'Why is that?'

'Acting without prior permission can mean demotion, even worse if you make the wrong decision. Chinese authority is like a pyramid.'

'Oh, I see, so it's just a question of getting to the man at the top?'

He smiled. 'If you know who he is. There are so many separate ministries in Beijing, each supposedly responsible for dealing with one particular industry, but in practice they often overlap. Too frequently, one finds oneself at the mercy of a power-struggle going on between two ministries, and that means getting a decision out of them can take months or years. My dealings are usually with MOSAC, that's the Ministry of Science and Communication. It's headed up by a man called Pa Jiaming. He is one of the forward thinkers and good to do business with. Quite Westernised in his way. MOSAC is responsible for a series of enterprises mainly involving anything high-tech, but it's when you get down to grass-root administrators in the various industrial sectors that corruption begins to rear its ugly head again.' He picked up his brandy glass and warmed it in his hand. 'Above all, the best advice I can give anyone is to be sure who is in power and who is not. It can change suddenly.'

'How do you recognise who is powerful?'

He gave a quiet laugh. 'By the cut of his clothes. They are very like the Russians in that sense. A smart suit and a chauffeur says a lot about you.'

She propped her chin on her hand. 'You are a fascinating man, Erwin.'

He looked away from her, his gaze becoming abstract, like a man who has been deeply flattered. She turned her head as Irene hovered into view. Irene lightly rested a hand on Erwin's arm. 'Another cognac, Erwin, this time on the house.'

'I wouldn't dream of drinking away your profits.'

'Nonsense.'

'Well, thank you and will you join us for a few minutes?'

Irene gestured to the waiter clearing the next table. 'Tony, bring a bottle of our finest cognac over and another glass.'

'Yes, madame.' He pulled a chair away from the table

he was clearing and set it down between Erwin and Marti.

'Thank you, Tony.' Irene turned to Erwin and Marti. 'I hope you both enjoyed your meal. I did not come over sooner, as you were both so engrossed in conversation; I did not want to disturb you.'

Erwin dropped his cigar butt into the ashtray. 'Just talking business and yes, the meal was excellent. I think Marti's faith in human nature has just been restored.'

Marti burst out laughing. Irene looked questioningly from one to the other.

'I am sorry, Irene, that was a private joke. Poor Marti doesn't like Chinese food very much.'

Irene turned to look at Marti with open curiosity. 'Erwin said you were a diamond dealer. That sounds so glamorous. I would love to work with diamonds all day.'

Marti laughed again. 'If you did, you wouldn't think it glamorous.'

'I would, I would. All those beautiful sparkling gems.' Irene squeezed her shoulders together in a tremor of excitement. 'I should want them all for myself.'

'I'm afraid I usually deal in industrial diamonds.'

'What are industrial diamonds?'

'Uncut diamonds of varying grades used in manufacturing industries. The tips of mining drills, surgical instruments. They are used a lot in optical engineering.'

Irene nodded as if she found the subject now slightly boring. A waiter appeared at Irene's side and bent his head to her ear and whispered. She nodded and drew her chair back from the table. 'Erwin, Miss Van den Fleet, you must excuse me. I have to take a telephone call.'

Erwin hunched his shoulders over the table again. 'You know, Marti, I think you must be the only woman I have ever met who does not enthuse about diamonds.'

'I suppose I have never seen the point of hanging bits of compressed carbon around my neck. That is all diamonds are, you know.'

He laughed. 'What an unromantic girl you are.'

'Maybe, but just remember the next time you buy someone diamonds, Erwin, you are simply reacting to a very powerful marketing concept.'

'It is something I rarely do, if ever. I confess to not being a wealthy man.' His eyes glinted. 'But, I should like to know more secrets of the trade.'

'Not all that secret. The Intercontinental Diamond Exchange rigorously controls the supply of uncut diamonds to ensure their continuing exclusivity and price. In actual fact there are sufficient supplies of diamonds to hang a necklace on the neck of every woman in the world, but that would be spoiling things, wouldn't it?'

He shook his head in amusement. 'You are a very pragmatic and shrewd young lady. I like you.'

She picked up her brandy glass and took a sip. He too was as shrewd as a fox and quite likeable in his way. She set her glass down again. And perhaps just a little lonely for female company. She felt a yawn coming on and discreetly stifled it.

'Marti, I'm afraid I have broken your first condition. It is almost eleven o'clock.'

She looked at her watch in surprise. Time had flown. Erwin gestured to a waiter to bring the bill. She gathered up her shoulder bag. 'Erwin, thank you very much for dinner. You must let me return the compliment. When I am installed in my apartment you must come to dinner.'

He raised his eyebrows. 'You cook as well?'

'Basic but competent is a fair description, I think. I used to cook for my father when I lived at home. I can promise not to give you indigestion, Erwin.'

He glanced at her. It would never occur to her to be concerned about the state of a young man's digestion. He bent his head to search inside his jacket for his wallet. He was a foolish old man. He had been neatly categorised and neatly slotted into place. He found his wallet and removed a

wad of notes. But, no doubt all men were accurately slotted
into place by Miss Marti Van den Fleet.

James sat at his desk and stared at the calendar. It was time
to sell the diamonds for Chan Chunling. He rolled his pen
between his fingers. There were four parcels. One he could
sell in Hong Kong within hours, together with a useful
commission for Anna to make one of her unique pieces of
jewellery. The second, he would negotiate with Chaim
Eichler. He slotted the pen back into its stand. The third
parcel he would offer to Marti. It would be a test of her
abilities. If she could produce the promised buyer, all well
and good. He got up from his desk and stepped across to the
window. That left the fourth parcel. If Marti passed the
first test, he would give her a further, more difficult task.
Negotiating a sale to Tony Bergman in New York. He leaned
against the window and peered down on to the busy street
below. If she failed either test, he could always fall back on
Mark Singh of Bombay.

Marti waited in the outer office of James Wu & Co., while
the receptionist buzzed through to James's office. Within
seconds James had come out of his office with outstretched
hand. 'Marti, come through. Like some coffee, tea?'

'Coffee will be fine, thank you.' She followed him back
to his office.

James shut the door behind him and gestured to her to sit
down. 'Did you sleep off the jet lag?'

She hesitated for a moment. It was wise to stay with the
truth, at least part of it. 'Not exactly. Someone who knows
a colleague of mine rang and insisted we met. I even pleaded
insanity, but –'

He gave a loud laugh. 'I'm not surprised that didn't
work. One has to be a little insane to work in Hong Kong.
Actually, I did ring your hotel in the evening to ask if you
were all right. They said you had gone out for the evening.'

She took time to sling her bag over the back of her chair.

That was a close call, Martina. 'You shouldn't have bothered, James, but it was a kind thought all the same. I appreciate it.'

He gave a wide smile and went to sit down at his desk. He had been stupid. She did like him. She had simply been very tired yesterday evening.

Marti picked up her coffee and gave it a quick stir. 'Right, James, just point me in the direction of work.'

'I am going to do just that, actually, but I thought you might like to see the IDE newsletter. It arrived this morning. Not bad likenesses are they?' He got up again and handed her the newsletter. 'See the back page.'

She flipped the newsletter over and ran her eyes down the page. Halfway down was an item marked 'special addendum'. The article, entitled 'East and West Join Forces', included two small photographs of James and herself and conveyed the IDE's pleasure in announcing that Martina Van den Fleet, only daughter of Erasmus Van den Fleet of Antwerp, was joining the highly successful Hong Kong diamond dealers, James Wu & Co. She quickly scanned the short paragraph beneath. It described her as a respected dealer in Europe and James as one of the up-and-coming, dynamic young option bearers with the IDE. The article ended by warning the world to watch out for this newly combined explosive force of talent. She raised her eyebrows. The copywriters had gone over the top. They made her and James sound like Batman and Robin.

'Did you see what they say about me?'

She glanced up at James's beaming face. 'All true, James, all true.' His grin grew even wider. She puzzled for a moment that there was no mention of Hendrik, then flipped back through the pages of the newsletter. Under 'retirements' it was noted with great sadness that the most respected dealer in Europe, Erasmus Van den Fleet, had retired, regrettably through ill health. There was a footnote. Tribute by Christian Debilius. See page two. Under

the heading 'new appointments' there was a large photograph of Hendrik announcing his appointment as head of
Van den Fleet's of Antwerp. The item briefly listed his work
in Zaire and described him as the sixth-generation Van den
Fleet to take up office, and a notable option bearer with the
IDE. It ended by wishing him every success in the future.
She quickly found page two. Her eyes filled with tears for a
moment. The entire page was devoted to fulsome praise of
her father and his work as chairman of the European Diamond Merchants' Association. Ostensibly written by
Christian Debilius himself, the tribute ended by wishing
Erasmus every happiness and much improved health in the
future. She blinked away the tears of affection. She must
telephone Father as soon as she could. He would be very
proud of Christian's words. She automatically turned to
the front page which carried details of the Diamond Cutter
of the Year award. It showed a photograph of Johannes's
design for a necklace of heart-shaped diamonds, with the
caption 'the enduring image of love'. She smiled to herself.
Next year every man in the street would be demanding
heart-shaped diamonds, if the IDE had anything to do with
it, which it always did. She folded the newsletter. Johannes
deserved his award. He really was a brilliant cutter.

Marti handed the newsletter back to James. 'Fame at
last, James.'

'What do you think of my photograph? Do you think it is
a good likeness of me?'

She bit her lip to stop herself from laughing. His vanity
was almost childlike. 'Er – I have to say, James, no. You
look much younger in the flesh.'

He stared down at his photograph. 'Perhaps you are
right, but wisdom accompanies age and people respect
that.'

'Indeed. Did Anna enter for the Diamond Cutter of the
Year award?'

'Er – no, she doesn't bother.'

'She should. It's about time a woman won the award.' She glanced at James and saw that he looked uncomfortable. She decided to let the matter drop. Perhaps Anna wasn't registered with the IDE.

James clapped his hands together. 'Let's have some more coffee, then we can get down to business.'

She reached for the coffee pot. 'I'll do it.'

There was a gentle knock on the office door and a young girl shyly put her head around. 'Excuse me, James, but there is a package from Miss Wu. Apparently you left it behind at home this morning.'

He clapped his hand to his brow. 'Did I?'

The young girl just smiled.

'Leave it on the desk, will you, and no further interruptions for half an hour.'

'Yes, James.' The girl carefully placed the large envelope on the corner of the desk and smiled politely at Marti.

James puffed out his cheeks. 'Sorry about that, Marti. Anna wanted you to see her designs, but you know what she is like. She was too shy to show you them herself, so I said I would bring them into the office and –' He clapped his hand to his brow again.

Marti laughed. 'And you forgot.'

'Anyway, if you have a moment in the day, perhaps you could take a look at them. I know Anna will very much respect your opinions.' He returned to his desk and sat down. 'Now, down to business. I have been instructed to sell a valuable collection of cut diamonds.' He plucked the pen from the pen holder and rolled it between his fingers. 'Discretion is absolutely essential on this one, Marti, I cannot stress that too strongly. One whiff of publicity and I can say goodbye to my nameless client.'

'He's acting through agents?'

'Yes. Let me show the diamonds to you. See what you think about them.' He turned around in his chair and opened a small safe behind his desk. He withdrew a box and pushed it across the desk to her. She opened the lid of the box and carefully removed the diamonds. She half turned and searched in her bag for her eyeglass.

James closed the door of the safe then swivelled around to face his desk again. He folded his arms against his chest and waited for Marti to finish her examination of the diamonds. She removed her eyeglass and stared down at the diamonds. 'I might be suffering from a bad attack of *déjà vu*, but didn't I authenticate these diamonds?'

His face broke out into a smile. She had barely hesitated in scoring a direct hit. 'Look in the box.'

She removed the envelope from the box and didn't even bother to examine the contents. The Van den Fleet crest on the flap of the envelope was enough.

'You said you had a buyer for them, Marti. Does that still hold good?'

'Very much so. Actually, when I met my client last week he was pressing me to come up with something special.'

'Mr Yasim?'

'He acts as an agent.'

'For whom?'

'Like your client, he demands absolute anonymity. What I can tell you is that he is wealthy beyond most people's dreams, but that is in strict confidence, James.'

'The Middle East?'

She gave a brief smile. 'I won't answer that question, James.'

'I understand.'

She looked across at him. 'I didn't press you for information when I authenticated these diamonds, but my client will need to know something about them, James.'

'I wish I could oblige.' He leaned his elbows on the desk. 'I can give something of a calculated guess. I think they are Russian.'

She picked up her eyeglass again and re-examined one of the diamonds. 'What makes you think that?'

'It happens occasionally that someone in the Politburo needs some hard currency.'

She laughed. 'As good an explanation as any.' She placed the diamond back on the desk. 'I can sell these within seventy-two hours for you, James, perhaps earlier, if I can get hold of Beni Yasim. What's the price?'

'$1 million.'

'No problem. What about commission?'

He gestured with both hands. 'He is your client. Shall we say, two per cent to cover the company's costs. Anything above that you take for yourself.'

'Agreed, James.'

'Fine.' He raised a hand to his mouth and gently cleared his throat. 'I have a second parcel of diamonds to dispose of, from the same source I may add. I have a dealer in New York who is interested. He has authenticated them himself. Would you be prepared to negotiate for me?'

She glanced at him sharply. He was testing her. She leaned back in her chair. If the roles were reversed she would do exactly the same thing. 'Who is the dealer?'

'Tony Bergman. You know him?'

'No problem there, James, I know him very well.' She tucked her tongue into the fold of her cheek. That statement was not entirely true. She consoled herself with the thought that if she had ever taken up Tony's invitations whenever she saw him, she would by now know him extremely well.

James clapped his hands together. 'That is what I call a good start to the business of the day.'

Marti laughed. 'Let me get my meetings fixed up first, before you say that.' She removed her bag from the back of the chair and searched for her filofax. 'Can I use your telephone, James, or should I use the one in the outer office?'

'No, no, always use this one. It has a direct outside line.' He gathered up a file from his desk. 'I'll leave you then.'

She glanced up at him. 'No need.'

'That's all right, I've got some letters to give to my secretary.'

Marti drew a ring around Tony Bergman's name. It had taken less than ten minutes to contact him and agree to see him in New York at the end of the week. She tapped her pen on the page. She now just needed Beni to call back. His office had said he was travelling, but they had instructions to pass on any communication from her. They would try and raise him. She picked up the envelope containing Anna's designs and looked through them.

The telephone rang out and Marti instantly picked it up. 'James Wu and Company, good morning.'

She was greeted by a familiar laugh. 'Marti, hello. I thought for a moment I had been given the wrong number. I was half expecting you to say Van den Fleet's.'

'Ah, Beni, thank you for returning my call so quickly. How are you?'

'Much the better for speaking to you. How are you?'

'Fine. Could you speak up just a little? The line is rather faint. Where are you, if I may ask?'

'Somewhere over the Mediterranean. About thirty-five thousand feet, I think.'

'Oh, you're in your jet, I hadn't realised. Beni, you asked me to look out for something special for the Sheik. I have it. It is a parcel of loose diamonds of impeccable quality. I think you will approve.'

'If you say so. Just a moment and I will consult my diary.'

She cradled the handset against her shoulder.

'Sorry to keep you, Marti. I had buried it under a mass of papers. I will be in Hong Kong next week, but that will be too late for me. Can you be in Paris the day after tomorrow?'

'Yes, no problem at all. What time at your office?'

'Er, not the office. I won't be arriving myself until very late in the afternoon. Make it my apartment at six, all right?'

'Fine, see you then.'

'Will you be bringing the diamonds with you?'

'Yes. There isn't time to arrange for a courier.' A sudden thought struck her. 'Beni, as you are pressed for time, would you be interested in looking at some designs as well?'

'Are they Johannes Witt's? I wouldn't be interested in hearts. Too passé, now.'

'Oh, you've heard about his award?'

'Yes, but what have you got for me, Marti?'

'There is a young designer out here. Her work has a strong oriental theme. It certainly is different. I think you will be impressed.'

'I hope so. Marti, I must go now. See you at six in Paris.'

'Yes, 'bye, Beni.' She replaced the handset and turned her attention back to Anna's designs. Incorporating diamonds into a design, already cut and polished, could be difficult. Johannes always preferred to work from scratch and let the cleave of the uncut stone influence the final shape of the design. She pushed the drawings back into the envelope. She was no expert, but one of Anna's designs might be suitably adapted.

James stared at Marti with growing excitement. The *sing pui* were never wrong. She had arranged everything with the speed of a thunderbolt. Marti slipped her filofax back into her bag. 'James, I've had a thought. Is Anna very busy?'

He shrugged. 'She is always busy, but what is your thought?'

'Beni's client likes anything different, unusual, in the way of design. I might be able to come up with a commission for her, if she is interested.'

His eyes flicked open in anticipation. 'Anna is always interested in obtaining commissions.'

'There is one problem. The client requires everything to

be in multiples. I have it on very good authority that he has a much adored wife and two daughters. Can't give one without the other.'

'Ah, yes, I understand. Just a moment and I will ring Anna now.'

Marti finished the remains of her now cold coffee while James dialled Anna's number. He picked up a packet of cigarettes and shook one out as he talked to his sister. 'Yes, Anna, he is extremely wealthy. Extremely. OK, I will tell her.' He put the telephone down and reached for a cigarette. 'Anna says she has a half-finished sketch of a design. Would you like to come and have dinner with us? She will have it finished by this evening.'

'Thank you very much. Er, James, can someone arrange a courier case for me and documentation? I will need to take the diamonds to Paris myself.'

'Sure. I'll arrange for everything to be ready by tonight.'

The housekeeper switched off the television at the end of the evening news then returned to sit by Erasmus's side. She smiled brightly. 'I wonder if Mr Hendrik has seen the newsletter, Mr Van den Fleet.'

'Suppose so.'

'Would you like me to read it to you again?'

Erasmus nodded casually, as if it was totally unimportant. 'If you want to.'

She picked up the newsletter and cleared her throat. ' "The International Diamond Exchange most regretfully informs its members of the retirement of Mr Erasmus Van den Fleet of Antwerp. As one of its most senior members, Mr Van den Fleet's untiring and incomparable support of the highest ideals –" '

'Read the bit about the war.' He bent over and pointed a finger at the lower half of the page.

'Oh, yes, here we are. "Erasmus Van den Fleet is not only a man of integrity, but a man of courage. In the Second

World War when the Belgian peoples were living under the tyranny of Nazi occupation, he was sentenced to death, by hanging, for refusing to collaborate with the Nazi regime. After making a daring and dangerous daylight escape from custody, he stayed only long enough to bid his heart-broken parents farewell, before joining the small, but supremely gallant band of resistance fighters. He –'' '

'Didn't hear that last bit.'

'Sorry, Mr Van den Fleet.' The housekeeper adjusted her glasses. ' "After making a daring and dangerous escape –'' ' She looked up suddenly at the sound of the front door slamming shut. 'I think that must be Mr Hendrik. Just a moment and I will go and see.'

Erasmus reached out and picked up the newsletter and continued reading it to himself.

Hendrik pulled off his raincoat and pushed it into the arms of the housekeeper. 'How's my father?'

'He's very well today, Mr Hendrik. We have just been reading the newsletter from the IDE. Have you seen it? It's got almost a whole page about Mr Erasmus.'

'Yes, I have seen it.' Hendrik ran his fingers through his hair as he turned and went into the sitting room.

Erasmus peered over the top of his glasses at Hendrik. 'Had a good day?'

'Not bad.' Hendrik went to the sideboard and poured himself a drink.

'Don't suppose you've had time to see the IDE newsletter. It's got an article about me in it.'

'I did see it, Father. Excellent article.'

'Marti rang up as soon as she saw it. I've got two special international telegrams from Hong Kong. One from James Wu and Company, and one from the Hong Kong Diamond Merchants' Association. Come and read them.'

'Actually, I've brought home a stack of telexes for you from the office.' Hendrik downed his drink and went out to fetch his briefcase.

The housekeeper knelt by Erasmus's side and helped to sort out the telexes into a neat pile. 'Ooh, look, Mr Van den Fleet, here's one which says it is from the desk of Christian Debilius. Isn't he the head of the IDE?'

Erasmus snatched the paper from her hand. 'Of course, he is, you silly woman. I told you.' He adjusted his glasses before reading the missive. His hands shook slightly as he carefully reread the words of greeting and tribute.

The housekeeper got to her feet at the sound of the doorbell. She pushed her glasses into her pocket and hurried out. Minutes later she returned, bearing a large bouquet of flowers in front of her. 'Look what's arrived for you, Mr Van den Fleet.'

Erasmus turned and peered over his shoulder.

'Shall I read out the card, Mr Van den Fleet?'

He nodded. The housekeeper took the card from the envelope stapled to the cellophane wrapping. 'Oh, look, isn't that sweet?' She held up the card for Erasmus to see. The front of the card depicted six kittens in gingham dresses, each waving a tiny paw. She opened the card and slowly read it out loud. ' "Our very best wishes to Mr Van den Fleet on his retirement." ' She held the card closer to her face to read the writing. 'It's from Astrid, Christina, Martha, Marie-Christine, Lilly, and another Christina.'

Erasmus reached out for the card. 'It's from the office. Silly girls, wasting their money on flowers. They're obviously being paid too much. Hendrik?' He turned around in his chair. 'Where's Hendrik?'

The housekeeper vaguely looked around her, as if knowing Hendrik had to be somewhere in the room. 'Er, I don't know, Mr Van den Fleet. Perhaps he has gone to wash his hands. I'll go and see.'

Erasmus settled back into his chair and looked at the card. He pushed a knuckle into the corner of his eye and wiped it. Silly girls. He leaned over and carefully placed the card on the table by the side of the chair.

Hendrik propped his arms behind his head and stretched out on the bed. He stared up at the ceiling. He was beginning to wonder what he had possibly done to offend Christian. He swung his legs off the bed and sat up. He picked up his cigarettes from the bedside table and lit one. The article about Marti had run to twelve lines and was a load of bullshit. The article about himself just managed to make four lines. He drew on the cigarette. Sixth generation Van den Fleet. He rubbed a hand across the back of his neck. They had managed to make him sound fucking fossilised. If he didn't know Christian better, he would dismiss the idea that Christian was playing one off against the other. He lay back on the bed again. Christian didn't give a shit about anything except the IDE's profit and loss account. All he was concerned about was who made the most money for his organisation. Wu. Van den Fleet. The names were immaterial. He stretched an arm out and picked up the ashtray, and rested it on his chest. Van den Fleet's had had one of its quietest days in months. He tapped the ash from his cigarette. If Marti had anything to do with it, he would kill her.

Anna laid out the sketches on the coffee table in front of the sofa. 'I hope you will approve of these.' She knelt down by Marti's side. 'I have slightly adapted the design to the shape of the diamonds and to meet the client's requirements. You will see that the necklace can be divided into three. The centre piece can be separated into a pair of matching brooches, and the lower section can be unclipped and worn as a pendant.'

Marti looked intently at the drawings. 'That's very clever, Anna. In fact, it is brilliant.'

Anna's face flushed. 'I am so glad you approve. I have called the design the Third Waterfall of the Heavenly Gate.'

Marti suppressed a smile. The title was a little whimsical, but the design did look a little like cascading droplets of water.

James bent down and looked over Anna's shoulder. Marti glanced up at him. 'What do you think, James? It is a beautiful design, isn't it?'

He placed his hands on Anna's shoulders. 'I have a very clever sister.'

'You do indeed, James.'

Anna's blush deepened.

'Can I take these to Paris with me, Anna?'

'Oh yes, I would wish you to.'

'I promise only Beni will see them. I wouldn't want anyone to steal your ideas. I usually get a fast answer from Beni. If it is in the affirmative, how long would it take you to make up the necklace?'

'A week?'

Marti pursed her lips. James shook Anna's shoulder. 'You can do it quicker than that.'

Anna looked at James doubtfully. He shook her shoulder again. 'You know you can.'

'Yes, I can. If I work all night, I can have it finished in three days.'

Marti shuffled the sheets of paper together. 'Are you sure, Anna? Beni doesn't make any allowances for someone who sets a deadline then fails to meet it. He's a charming man, but very tough.'

'I won't fail him, Marti, I promise.' Anna flushed again. 'I have never had an international commission before. I would be very honoured if my design was accepted.'

Marti crossed her fingers. 'I'll do my best for you.'

James straightened up. 'Let's all have another drink.'

Anna looked at her watch. 'We must not be late at the restaurant, James.'

'We won't. Same again, Marti?'

'Er, yes. Thank you. By the way, where are we eating?'

'Thought you might like to try the Indonesian restaurant near Central.'

Anna folded her hands in her lap. 'James says the Dutch

eat Indonesian food, so we thought that you would like it, too.'

Marti nodded slowly. For the moment, she couldn't quite get her mind around that piece of logic.

'Belgium is next to Dutchland, isn't it?'

'Ah, yes, that is correct. Although in Europe it is referred to as Holland.'

Anna nodded politely.

An elderly woman pushed her way through the door and brought a papier mâché tray to the desk. She placed a small bamboo basket in front of Frankie and a pot of tea. 'Steamed shredded chicken and a pot of keemun, Mr Heung.'

Frankie pushed his hand into his trouser pocket and pulled out a few coins. 'That's for your trouble.'

She took the money and tucked it into a cloth bag tied around her waist.

'You tell the guy outside to come in here, OK?'

She tucked the tray under her arm. 'Yes, Mr Heung, I go tell him now.'

Frankie picked up the pot of tea and poured some into his tea bowl. He looked up as Busy came into the office. 'What've you got for me, Busy?'

'Fang.'

Frankie placed the pot down on the desk. 'That's good work, Busy. Sit down. Want some tea?'

'No thanks, Mr Heung. Just had some.' Busy pulled the chair away from the side of the desk and slumped into it. 'He doesn't frequent any of the clubs on either Hong Kong side or Kowloon.'

Frankie bit into a dim sum. 'I don't want to know what he doesn't do, Busy.'

'Sure, Mr Heung. He goes to Macao.'

Frankie raised his head.

'He favours two places. The Kam Pek Casino and the Macao Palace.'

Frankie laughed to himself. 'Should have figured that out myself. Where else would a guy with a respectable reputation to upkeep go.'

'Apparently he's a big spender, Mr Heung.'

'Apparently?'

'Had to go a little easy in Macao, Mr Heung. Golden Cockerel Gang don't like strangers asking too many questions.'

'That isn't going to be a problem in the future. They have returned our fraternal greetings.' Frankie pushed the remains of the dim sum into his mouth. He pushed his chair back and went to stand in front of the window. He wiped his hand across his mouth. The Golden Cockerel Gang would be a problem. Sending fraternal greetings was one thing, doing business was another. He turned away from the window. 'They using Fang?'

'Not that I know of, Mr Heung. I passed the photograph around. Couple of people weren't sure about the likeness, but a Fang Ka-Shing definitely was a frequent visitor. Said he wasn't a problem. Pays his debts. Doesn't seem to get involved in any heavy business.'

Frankie nodded. He sucked at his front teeth with his tongue. 'OK, Busy, pick Fang up. No, wait a minute, pick him up when he's with Candy Lai. Bring them both in.'

'Sure, Mr Heung.'

'And make sure he's in a very receptive frame of mind before I see him.'

Busy smiled. 'No problem, Mr Heung.'

'And keep Candy on ice. She usually entertains him on Wednesdays, but check it out.'

Busy got to his feet. 'I'll have them both for you by tonight, Mr Heung.'

'Make sure she wears that necklace he gave her.' Frankie took another dim sum from the basket and pushed it into his mouth.

*   *   *

Fang woke up with a scream, as his head was wrenched up from the pillow by his hair and a knife was jabbed into his neck. 'Candy, what are you doing, Candy?'

Busy jabbed the point of the knife deeper into Fang's neck. 'She's waiting for you downstairs.'

Fang rolled his eyes sideways and stared in fright at the empty space beside him.

'Get dressed.'

Busy kept a grip on Fang's arm as he pushed him down the stairs. Fang's stomach turned over at the sight of a man standing in the hall, pointing a gun at the head of the maid. Candy stood quietly by the side of a second man. She looked deathly pale. When Fang reached the foot of the stairs, he noticed the gun pushed up against the small of her back. Busy shoved the knife in front of Fang's face. 'Someone wants to meet you, but no tricks,' he pushed Fang forward in the direction of Candy, 'or your good fortune dies here and now.'

Fang swallowed. 'No tricks, no tricks.'

Busy nodded to the man standing behind Candy. 'Take her out.'

Candy cried out. 'Ka-Shing, save me, save me. They will –' The man swung his fist up and caught her on the side of the head. She let out a wail and staggered forward. Busy pushed Fang in front of him.

As he passed the maid he shot out a hand and twisted her face upwards. 'You're still asleep in bed, OK?'

She shut her eyes. 'I haven't seen anything. Not a thing.'

Busy nodded to the man. 'Don't let her give you any trouble.' He pushed Fang forward again to the front door.

Frankie lit up a cigar then scooped up Candy's necklace with one finger. He dangled it so that the diamonds sparkled in the electric light. 'Nice piece.' He dropped it on the desk again. 'OK, Busy, let's see the real merchandise.'

Busy went to the door and called down the stairs.

Fang was bundled in through the door and flung forwards. He screamed as his body hit the floor. Frankie
pulled his chair away from the desk and sat down. Fang
slowly drew himself up, clutching at his crotch with one
hand. He braced his other hand on the floor to steady himself. Frankie stared at him then beckoned to Busy with his
finger. Busy bent down to Frankie. 'What is it, Mr Heung?'

Frankie took the cigar out of his mouth. 'Guy doesn't
photograph well, does he?'

Busy shrugged.

'Are you sure Seven-toed Wing has got it right?'

'Ronnie Lee says Seven-toed Wing is reliable, Mr Heung.'

'He'd better be. Let me see that photograph again.'

Busy searched in his inside pocket. 'Here it is, Mr
Heung.'

Frankie took the photograph and studied it for a few
moments. 'With these snap-shot booth photographs even
your own mother would have difficulty recognising you.'
He looked across at Fang and stared at him.

'Don't worry, Mr Heung. He's just not looking his best
at the moment.' Busy bent down again to point at the
photograph. 'The gold tooth's the same.'

Frankie shot a finger at the man standing behind Fang.
'Show me his teeth.'

The man knelt down and pulled Fang's head up and
dragged his upper lip back. Frankie nodded. 'OK, I guess
Seven-toed Wing is right.'

Fang tried to blink to clear his vision. Both his eyes were
swollen and heavily bruised. He pleaded to know what was
going on, but it sounded like a faint croak to his own ears.
He cowered on the floor as Frankie got up and walked
round to the front of the desk.

'Mr Fang, or can I count you as one of my friends and
call you Mr Mui.' Frankie gestured to the two men standing
by the door. 'Get him on his feet.'

Fang cried out again as he was hauled to his feet. Frankie

drew on his cigar. 'You want to know what's going on? That's good. We share a common interest.'

Fang blacked out as Frankie came to stand in front of him. Frankie shook his head. 'Busy, I do not like wasting time, you know that. How can I have a conversation when the guy's in that condition?'

'Sorry, Mr Heung.'

'OK, OK, but do something about it.' Frankie turned away in disgust and went to stand at the window.

Busy pulled a chair away from the desk and the two men pushed Fang into it. Busy opened a bottle of mineral water and poured it over Fang's head.

Fang lolled back in the chair. He shut his eyes to shield them from the ceiling light, but still it burned into his eyeballs like fire. The pain was real, but what the man with the cigar was saying was only a dream. Fang licked his lips. He wasn't Mui Shenlu. The diamonds were just for Candy. No one else. He had not intended to steal from Jiaming. He had not profited from what little he had taken. A tear ran down the side of his cheek. His good fortune had vanished; to be replaced by dragons threatening destruction. He wasn't Mui Shenlu. He wasn't. He dropped his head on to his chest. Fear gnawed like rats at his stomach.

Frankie lit up another cigar and perched himself on the corner of the desk. 'OK. Let's be clear about this. You call yourself Mui Shenlu.'

Fang raised his head to look at the bright outline of the man in front of him. He tried to blink away the jumping, blurred image. In the back of his head a tinny, persistent voice ticked like a metronome. No one must know the diamonds are artificial. No one must know. Bright Mountain must remain a secret. His hands jerked convulsively at the imagined sound of a firing squad. He would be shot like a common thief. Pa Jiaming would not save him. He had stolen from him.

Busy went to strike Fang as punishment for his silence,

but Frankie snapped his fingers at him and shook his head. Fang looked up at Frankie and nodded slowly. He shut his eyes. He had to pretend to be Mui, he had no choice. It was the only way to protect the secret of Bright Mountain. Frankie blew a smoke ring into the air. 'You paid your debts to the Bear's Paw Gang with loose diamonds.'

Fang swallowed and nodded.

'The necklace was made up by a man called Zau in Tsimshatsui.'

Fang nodded again. His eyes brimmed with tears. That was the only truth. He raised a hand to his head to ease the pounding pain. The only truth.

'OK. What's the figure for the German bid for the container terminal at Lo Wu?'

Fang's mouth moved in an attempt to shape the words. Frankie picked up a notepad and pen off the desk and handed it to Fang. 'Write it down.'

Fang clumsily balanced the pen between his broken thumb and his forefinger. He looked up at Frankie when he had finished writing. Frankie removed the pen and blood-stained pad from Fang's grasp and put them back on the desk. 'I am going to say this once, OK?'

Fang nodded.

'This piece of paper is going with the diamond necklace into that safe over there. See it?'

Fang managed to turn his head to look at the safe.

'When I want information, you give it to me, right?'

Fang moved his lips again.

'When I want diamonds, you get them, right?'

Fang nodded.

Frankie dropped his cigar into the ashtray. 'OK. These monthly visits you make to Shanghai. You give the information to a guy with no name. He pays you in loose diamonds.' Frankie sucked at his front teeth with his tongue. 'You don't ask questions. You figure the guy has a reason for wanting to know what goes on in Hong Kong, but that's not your problem. The guy just wants a piece of the action, right?' Fang dutifully nodded his head again.

Frankie leaned against the corner of the desk and folded his arms. 'I have to tell you that not many people would believe your story, but being a businessman myself, I do. You're lucky. I understand these things. There is no profit without growth, without expansion.' He nodded slowly to himself. 'I think maybe your friend in Shanghai knows that also.' He studied the slumped figure in the chair. 'Ordinarily, I would deal directly with your source, but I will do you a favour. You obviously have a good deal going for you. I won't spoil that.' He spun round on his heel and bent over Fang. 'Just as long as you keep that information coming, right?'

Fang stared up at him. He cried out when Frankie rested a hand on his shoulder.

'OK, OK. Relax. We have a deal.' Frankie gestured to Busy. 'Get Mr Fang a drink.' He waited until half a glass of brandy had been poured down Fang's throat and Fang had stopped spluttering. 'Give Mr Fang a cigarette.'

A lighted cigarette was pushed into Fang's mouth. He raised his uninjured hand and held on to the cigarette, as if holding on to a lifeline.

Frankie folded his arms again. 'The German tender. Is there anything you wish to tell me about it, that at a later date you may regret not bringing to my attention now?'

Fang drew heavily on the cigarette. He looked up at Frankie as if he was staring into the face of death. 'The HK$1.4 billion includes a five-year service agreement on the software.'

'Thank you, Mr Fang. Good communication is important in business.' Frankie smiled. 'But I guess you know that already.'

Fang shivered as Frankie walked behind his chair. Frankie shot a finger towards the corner of the room. Busy followed him. Frankie spoke in low tones. 'Clean him out and leave him somewhere where he can be found.'

'Sure, Mr Heung.'

'Is that whore still downstairs?'

'Yes, Mr Heung.'

'I don't want to see her again, OK?'

A smile crossed over Busy's face. 'OK, Mr Heung.'

A policeman shone a torch into Fang's face. Fang stirred and gave a low moan. The policeman pulled out his walkie-talkie. 'Mugging at Star Ferry Terminal. Victim requires medical assistance. Will stand by. Thank you. Over.' He switched off his radio and bent down to take a closer look at Fang.

Fang dimly realised that the man looming over him was a policeman. He closed his eyes as he heard the distant sound of an ambulance. He shivered violently in the damp night air. The truth would kill him. Good fortune had deserted him and now he had aroused the dragon. He broke out into a sudden burning sweat as he felt its breath upon him.

As light streaked the sky, a woman stepped out of a doorway of a derelict apartment block and into the dank alleyway. She dropped her water bucket as she tripped over the legs of a body propped up against the wall. She cursed to herself and peered around in the gloom for the bucket. She jumped back as the body of Candy Lai slumped sideways and fell into the gutter. She caught her breath then slowly reached out and felt on the ground for the handle of the bucket. The body was naked and covered in blood. The woman looked away. It wasn't any of her business. She picked up the bucket and hurried down the alley to the fresh-water standpipe.

By eight o'clock, a passing motorcycle policeman had noticed the body sprawled in the alleyway. After a brief investigation he had returned to his motorcycle and radioed a message to headquarters informing them of a homicide in the Mong Kok district. He straddled his motorcycle, arms folded, until fifteen minutes later a police car pulled up alongside him. The driver stuck his head out of the window. 'Where is it?'

The policeman swivelled around and gestured with his arm. 'Halfway up the alley. Female. Strangulation. Multiple stab wounds. One of her clients must have cut up rough.'

The driver nodded and wearily pushed open the car door.

The private-hire water taxi sped through the harbour and out towards Macao. Frankie rested a hand on the rail and leaned against the stern of the boat. 'I appreciate this meeting, Mr dos Santos. Ordinarily, these matters would be finalised by our principals, but as this is the first time we are doing business together –' Frankie gestured with his hand and left the sentence unfinished.

Santos nodded. 'I was very sorry to hear about your father. Very sorry. We knew each other very well.'

'Thank you for your sentiments, Mr dos Santos. They are truly appreciated. But, like me, you are a very busy man, so I will get down to business with you. The Germans have placed a bid of HK$1.4 billion.'

A smile of satisfaction crossed Santos's face.

Frankie turned his head and looked back at the harbour. 'You know, Mr dos Santos, San Francisco is a great place, but there's nothing to beat this view.'

Santos pulled a bulging envelope from his pocket and passed it to Frankie. Frankie stared down at the envelope as if taken by surprise. 'Well, thank you, Mr dos Santos.' He plucked at the front of his jacket and slipped the envelope into his inside pocket then turned back to inspect the harbour view again. 'I have a further piece of information for you, Mr dos Santos.'

'What is it?'

Frankie puckered the corners of his mouth. 'We only

negotiated for the value of the bid, Mr dos Santos.'

Santos pulled out a packet of cigarettes and lit one. 'The information is important?'

'I would say that it is very material.'

'I hope so, Frankie. I am working on a tight budget.'

'Sure, who doesn't. Shall we say HK$150,000?'

'Maybe. I would need to evaluate the information.'

'The price is not negotiable, Mr dos Santos. I can think of two other people who would buy at that price.'

'OK, let's hear it.'

'The tender includes a five-year service agreement on the software.'

Santos turned to look at him. 'You sure?'

'I'm always sure about my facts, Mr dos Santos. I'm a businessman like yourself.'

Santos flung the end of his cigarette into the water. 'I'll see you get paid tomorrow.'

'Thank you, Mr dos Santos. I appreciate that.'

Santos stepped up to the front of the boat and told the skipper to turn it around.

PART 4

Marti rang the old-fashioned brass bell outside Beni Yasim's apartment, on the Right bank of the Seine. After several moments, a woman with elegantly coiffed hair opened the door. Marti smiled. 'I have an appointment with Mr Yasim at six. My name is Martina Van den Fleet.'

The woman stared at her blankly. Marti pursed her lips. Parisians always took pleasure in not understanding what they considered to be the thick, provincial accent of the Belgians. She searched in her bag and handed the woman a business card. 'I have an appointment at six with Mr Yasim.' She spoke slowly, carefully enunciating each word.

The woman took the card and examined it. She looked up at Marti. 'You are from Belgium?'

The blatantly patronising manner made Marti grind her teeth. 'That is correct.'

'Ah.' The woman's eyes swept scornfully over her, as if Marti's reply somehow explained the unpleasant sight confronting her.

'And presumably you are Mr Yasim's housekeeper?'

'Of course.' She spoke haughtily. 'I am Madame Rochas.' She reluctantly opened the door a little wider, enabling Marti to enter.

Marti was told to sit on an uncomfortable carved chair in the hall. Mr Yasim had not yet arrived home. As a gesture of goodwill, Madame Rochas invited her to lay her briefcase on the table next to her. Marti declined. Madame Rochas raised one eyebrow and walked away down the hall

to a door at the end. Marti carefully placed her briefcase on
her knees. She pushed the cuff of her sleeve back and
checked her watch. The time-lock on the metal-lined briefcase would de-activate in five minutes. She wrapped her
fingers more comfortably around the handle. The diamonds were protected by two devices: the time-lock, and
the electronic wristband on Marti's arm. The electronic
wristband measured her body heat and transmitted it to a
micro-sensor in the handle of the briefcase. As soon as
contact between her fingers and the handle was broken,
both she and the briefcase would erupt into a series of
ear-piercing alarms that could not be silenced until contact
was re-established.

As Beni put his key into the lock, Madame Rochas
appeared again, as if by magic, and swept past Marti.
She held the door open wide for him. 'Welcome home,
Monsieur Yasim.' She smilingly took his briefcase and a
small duty-free plastic bag from his grasp. 'I trust you had
an excellent journey.'

'Seem to be flying backwards half of the time. Very
strong headwinds over the Atlantic.' He gestured to the
plastic bag. 'Little gift for you. I hope it gives you pleasure.'

She raised a hand to her bosom. 'For me? You are too
kind, Monsieur Yasim. Too kind.'

Marti rolled her eyes. Fawning bitch.

As Madame Rochas closed the door behind Beni, he suddenly noticed Marti sitting in the hall. 'Marti, I am so sorry
to keep you waiting. My flight was very delayed. But what
are you doing in the hall, like this?' He turned to Madame
Rochas. 'Why was Miss Van den Fleet not taken into the
sitting room?'

Madame Rochas looked at him in surprise. 'I beg your
pardon, Monsieur Yasim. Should she have been? I had no
idea. I thought she was some kind of salesperson.'

Marti curled her fingers around the handle of the briefcase. Of course. She looked a dead ringer for a carpet sales-

man and no mistake. Beni nodded in a resigned fashion.
Madame Rochas was the most efficient and discreet housekeeper he had ever employed. He ran his hand down the
back of his head. Her irrefutable logic was a small price to
pay. 'Very well, but please see that in future she is treated as
a most honoured guest.'

'As you wish, Monsieur Yasim.'

Marti stared up at the ceiling. She wished Beni and his
housekeeper would not discuss her presence as if she was
some unclaimed baggage left in the hall. Beni hurried to
where Marti sat and held out his hands. 'Thank you for
coming to Paris, Marti. The week seems to be rapidly
overtaking me. Come into the sitting room.' Marti got up
from the chair and followed him into the lofty-ceilinged
room.

Beni shut his eyes and pressed a thumb and forefinger to
either side of his nose for a moment, to relieve the pressure
of an incipient headache. 'Do sit down, Marti. Will you
give me ten minutes to shower and shave? Madame Rochas
will serve you with a drink.'

'Yes, of course. Take your time.'

He glanced at her. 'I don't know how you do it, Marti!
You have travelled from Hong Kong and yet look as fresh
as a rose.'

'I suspect my schedule hasn't been as tight as yours.'

'Maybe. Ten minutes. Then we can get down to
business.'

Marti adjusted the start mechanism on her wristband and
then on the base of the briefcase. She released her grip on
the handle and flexed her fingers. Madame Rochas
appeared and enquired what Marti wished to drink. She
nodded when Marti requested dry vermouth with ice and
lemon, and silently crossed to the sideboard. Marti sat back
on the sofa and watched her hip-swinging, oddly gliding
walk with some fascination. She decided she must have
little wheels attached to the soles of her feet, or, more likely,

she was actually a humanoid. Marti glanced up as Beni swept back into the room. He had changed into casual trousers and an open-necked shirt and cashmere cardigan.

'Ah, good. I see you have a drink, Marti.' He glanced at the housekeeper and she immediately handed him a glass of whisky and soda. 'Thank you.' He gave a quick smile and she walked to the door. Marti glanced after her. Definitely humanoid. Beni must operate the controls by eye-movement.

Beni brought his drink to the sofa and sat down next to Marti. 'You look lost in thought, Marti. What are you thinking?'

'Forgive my curiosity, but that's not the same housekeeper you had the last time I came.'

'Ah, don't remind me. You're thinking of the one with the little dog.'

'Yes, that's right.'

He sprawled out in the corner of the sofa. 'A dear woman in many ways. She pleaded to have her dog with her and I agreed, but it went insane in its old age and started biting everyone. In the end I said she would have to choose between me or the dog.' He took a mouthful of whisky. 'She chose the dog.'

She laughed. 'Can't win 'em all, Beni.'

'Indeed not. Now, important matters first. Will you forgive me if I don't invite you out to dinner? I am expecting a couple of important calls sometime during the evening, but you will stay and have supper with me?'

'Thank you, but I won't stay.'

He touched her arm. 'You must. I shall be offended if you don't.'

She picked up her briefcase and balanced it on her knees. She stared at the lock for a moment. 'I suggest you stick your fingers in your ears. If I've got this wrong, all hell will break loose.' She carefully eased the catches sideways and let out a quick sigh of relief at the sound of a faint click. 'So far so good.'

He leaned across to take a closer look at the briefcase. 'Is this one of the new ones with a nuclear detonator?'

She laughed. 'Mercifully, the Japanese haven't got around to that one yet, but given time they probably will.' She removed the box containing the diamonds and passed them across to him.

Beni slowly examined each diamond in turn. Marti settled back into the sofa and watched him. When he was tired, he looked closer to his middle forties. Usually, he could pass for a very energetic and youthful late thirties. She clasped her hands in her lap. And he looked on edge about something. That was unusual. He placed the last diamond back into its slot and got up from the sofa. 'What's their background?'

'Don't know. Anonymous client. James Wu thinks they could be Russian.'

He bent down and flicked open the envelope containing the authentication certificate. 'I see you authenticated these?'

'Yes.'

'Allow me to replenish your drink.'

'This is fine, thanks.'

He picked his own glass up and went to the sideboard. 'What is your price?'

'$2 million.'

He gave a gentle laugh. 'Marti, we are here to do business, not play games. That comes later. $1 million.'

Marti picked up her glass and took a sip of vermouth. The housekeeper had got it right. The exact amount of ice to vermouth. She edged the glass around between her fingers. With luck she would get it right also. She had pitched the starting price at $2 million to include James's two per cent commission, her own commission, and Beni's need to beat the price down a little; purely as a face-saving exercise. She could afford to go down to $1½ million, but no further.

Beni returned to the sofa. 'Can we wrap this up fairly quickly, Marti. I like the diamonds. I am prepared to buy them. $1 million.'

'You have been given first refusal, Beni. If these went to auction, your figure would quickly look ridiculous.'

He thought for a moment. '$1¼ million.'

'$1¾.'

'My client is a wealthy man, Marti, but not a foolish one.'

'I believe he is also a wise one, too. These are not stones that you are going to extract blood from.'

He gave a quick laugh.

Marti took another sip of vermouth. If she was not mistaken he looked ready to settle. At the beginning he hadn't even cast a glance at the diamonds. Now, his glance strayed to them more and more. She gathered up the box and closed the lid.

'$1½ million, Marti. My final offer.'

She twitched her lips. When Beni made a final offer, it was final.

'$1½ million it is, then.'

He held out his hand. 'Done.'

She shook hands with him. She unwound one foot from the other and winced as the blood rushed back to her leg. The deal had been swiftly and smoothly concluded, but not without some tension.

He took the box from her and and placed it back on the table. 'Pay at the end of the month?'

'Beni!'

'Tomorrow suit you?'

'Fine.'

He rubbed his hands together. 'How about another drink to seal the bargain?'

'Thank you.'

'You said you had some designs for me, Marti.'

'Yes, I have. I'll get them out for you.'

'If you will excuse me one moment, I will just tell the housekeeper there are two for dinner. I should have done it before.'

'Not for me, thanks, Beni.'

He turned round to look at her. 'What is the matter?'

'Nothing.'

'Then why won't you dine with me?'

'Because you are being your usual polite self. You are tired and I suspect you have a busy evening's work ahead of you. I really don't expect to be wined and dined every time we meet, you know.'

'I know, but I happen to enjoy your company and I refuse to be deprived of it. So, please stay.' He brought her glass back to the sofa. 'Now let's see these designs.'

Marti turned round in surprise as Madame Rochas appeared in the doorway. She hadn't noticed Beni pressing any bells to summon her.

'Yes, Monsieur Yasim?'

'Miss Van den Fleet is staying for dinner.'

'Very good, Monsieur.' She smiled sweetly and went out again.

Marti removed an envelope from her bag and laid out Anna's sketch on the table. 'This has been done by James's sister, Anna. I think she is very good. The design allows for the necklace to be divided into three separate pieces.'

Beni laughed. 'Your assumptions are usually correct but not, I'm afraid, on this occasion. The diamonds are destined for just one very special lady, I believe.'

'Really?'

He nodded. He picked up the sketch and studied it.

'It's called the Third Waterfall of the Heavenly Gate. Looks a bit like a cascade, doesn't it?'

'I don't know about that, but the title certainly conjures up images of the exotic and the erotic.' He cast a lascivious glance in her direction. 'Doesn't it?'

'Mmm.' She picked up her glass. Bargaining did things

for Beni's libido. She took a sip of the vermouth. Not that it needed all that much doing to it.

He picked up the sketch and held it up. 'You know, this would really look magnificent made up in aquamarines rather than diamonds.'

She stared at the sketch. 'Clever you. Yes, it would look absolutely beautiful.'

'Can I take this sketch to show to the Sheik?'

'Please do.'

'I'll get in touch with the details of the commission, probably next week.'

'Actually, I've got one of Anna's business cards with me, somewhere.' She picked up her bag and searched through it. 'Here we are.'

'Thanks.' He slipped the sketch and the business card into the envelope. 'The maddening thing is, you know, I saw some aquamarines a couple of weeks ago. They would have done perfectly for this.' He pulled out his diary and flicked through it. 'I could manage to get to Hong Kong next week. I would like to see Anna's work for myself. When are you going back to Hong Kong?'

'Not sure at the moment. Possibly by the weekend.'

'What are you doing in between times, or shouldn't I ask?'

'I'm going to New York. Tomorrow, actually.'

He raised his head. 'So am I.' His eyes flickered with surprise and sudden anticipation. 'What a coincidence. Will you travel with me?'

'Won't say no to a free lift in your jet, Beni.'

'Good.' He groaned as the telephone rang out. 'Excuse me, Marti. I didn't really expect it to stay quiet for long.'

She thought quickly, wondering how best to leave him in privacy. 'Er, may I wash my hands?'

'Of course.' He stretched out and picked up the telephone. 'Turn left as you go out. Second door on the left.'

Marti washed her hands and patted them dry on the linen guest towel. She glanced at a second door leading off to somewhere. Curiosity overcame her and she opened it quietly. The bedroom was dominated by a king-size bed swathed in dark blue brocade. She caught sight of a photograph on the bedside table. She bit her lip. Prying was not a very nice thing to do. She tiptoed to the bed and looked at the photograph. A boy and a girl stared back at her with merry eyes. She glanced around. Odd. No photograph of a wife anywhere. She tiptoed back to the door and eased it shut.

Chan Chunling followed the flow of tourists around the Jade Buddha Temple and into the antique store. He looked with respectful interest at the miniature gongs and drums on display. He glanced around before flicking his cuff back to look at his watch. He had visited the gold Buddhas twice, but the 'faceless one' had not arrived at either of the appointed times. In half an hour, at five o'clock, the temple would close. He edged his way out of the store. He could only risk one more visit to the Buddhas, then the next rendezvous would be the Yuyuan Bazaar.

When Chan returned to the gold Buddha, a group of students were clustered around it, listening earnestly to their tutor. He turned on his heel and headed for the entrance. The 'faceless one' would not appear with so many people around. Chan checked his watch again and hurried out. He hesitated at the sight of a vacant taxi, but decided against it. He would be safer travelling along with other sightseers on the No. 16 bus.

Yuyuan Bazaar was sited around the Wuxinting Teahouse. Chan crossed over the network of small bridges and looked in on the Teahouse. As on most days, it was crowded with tourists. He entered, and managed to get a seat near one of the windows. He took off his raincoat and folded it neatly in his lap. If all went well, someone would approach and suggest that he visited the fan shop.

Chan placed the lid firmly on the teapot, to indicate that he did not wish it refilled. He glanced around him. No one had approached and he could stay no longer. It would arouse suspicion. He stood up and slung his raincoat over his arm. His seat was immediately taken by a youth and a girl, who both managed to squeeze themselves on to the chair, with much giggling.

The small shops in the Bazaar sold mostly tourist junk. Chan edged his way through the crowds to the corner of a small alley. On the opposite corner stood the fan shop. He stopped to light up a cigarette. He slipped his lighter back into his pocket and looked up at the rain clouds merging into one dark mass. He felt a sense of great foreboding. The fail-safe list of rendezvous had only been used once before. Then, the explanation had been that the 'faceless one' had been delayed. Chan glanced at the strings of gaudily coloured fans hung up outside the doorway of the shop. He would make one last attempt. He dropped his cigarette in the gutter and ground it out with the heel of his shoe before crossing the alley.

An old man raised his head from his newspaper as Chan entered the shop. Chan nodded to him and went to inspect the hundreds of fans lining the walls. The old man stared at him sullenly when he realised that Chan had no intention of buying, then turned his attention back to the newspaper. Chan pushed his hands in his pockets and looked up at the fans hanging from the ceiling. He couldn't wait any longer. He removed his hands from his pockets and strode out of the shop. Now it would be up to the 'faceless one' to make contact. He would take no more risks.

Fang drove slowly up the twisting road of the Peak. He steered with one hand, resting the hand with the broken thumb in his lap. When he reached the driveway of the mansion, he swung the car round and groaned as his ribs reminded him that two of them were cracked.

The kitchen was empty apart from the remains of the meal Fang had shared with Candy two nights previously.

Fang rested a hand on the table and leaned against it. He stared around him as if dazed. The maid's bedroom in the attic had looked as if it had been hastily vacated. He fumbled in his pocket for his cigarettes. He had harboured a faint hope that it had all been a dream, but the empty house crushed such a thought. He lit the cigarette and slipped the packet back into his pocket. He jumped at the sound of the telephone ringing. He went out into the small lobby adjoining the kitchen to answer it.

'Mr Fang?'

'Yes, speaking.'

'Miss Lai won't be back.'

Fang's hand trembled. They must be watching him. Somehow they had followed him, although he had carefully checked his rear-view mirror all the way up the Peak road. He cleared his throat. 'Where is she? I must speak to her.'

'I'm afraid she cannot talk to anyone, Mr Fang. She met with an unfortunate accident.'

Hysteria swept over Fang. 'You've killed her. You've –'

The line went dead. Fang shut his eyes and sagged against the wall.

The flowers Fang had presented to Candy on his previous visit had wilted, although the vase was still brimful with water. He crossed the sitting room and bent down to pick up one of the petals that had fallen on the floor. He held it in his hand. It was a sign. He straightened up and went to stand by the window, overlooking the terrace. He looked up at the sky and wondered what he must do to recover his good fortune, if ever. For the moment he had to go on pretending he was Mui Shenlu to the men who had beaten him up. He must somehow ensure a regular supply of artificial diamonds from Chan, without arousing suspicion. He must go on deceiving Pa Jiaming. The cousin who had so generously invited him to share in his money-making scheme. He hung his head in shame. Perhaps he should end his life; end the torment. He looked down at the petal in his hand. But what would happen to his wife and children? He closed his fingers around the petal. They would suffer, not prosper, from his death. He flung the petal away from him and stumbled out of the room.

Chan Chunling went to the door of his office and checked that there was no one within earshot. He went back to his desk and picked up the telephone. 'Yes, esteemed Comrade. I visited the Temple as arranged, but you were not there.' He pressed the telephone closer to his ear. Fang's voice sounded faint and strangely shaky. 'Yes, esteemed comrade, I had a call from James Wu. Everything is going according to plan. Three parcels of diamonds have been sold. I expect confirmation of the fourth by tomorrow.' He closed his eyes. 'With respect, esteemed Comrade, it is difficult for me to make another visit to the Temple so soon. I cannot afford to arouse suspicions.' His eyes flicked open at the suggestion that a lot worse could happen to him if he didn't. 'Yes, esteemed Comrade, I shall most certainly do as you say, but it will take a little time. If you wish me to bring a parcel of diamonds I shall need to make a visit to Anshan.' Chan shifted the telephone to his other ear. 'Yes, esteemed Comrade, I shall attend at the temple with the diamonds on Monday.' Chan put the telephone down. He stared down at it. The same sense of foreboding swept over him as before. He shook his head quickly, as if trying to rid himself of it. He picked up the telephone again and dialled Professor Li's number in Anshan.

Marti stretched her legs out beneath the table. She looked around the cabin of the private jet. Travelling with Beni had certain advantages over Business Class. Space being one of them. She glanced across at him. He sat with head bent, studying a report that looked as if it spanned at least twenty pages. She too bent her head and returned her attention to her letter writing.

A brief telephone call to James Wu the previous night, to tell him that the first parcel of diamonds had been sold, had drawn generous praise from him. A second telephone call, before she had flown out from Paris, confirming that a banker's draft for the proceeds of the sale had been safely deposited, drew a good luck response from him for her meeting with Tony Bergman.

She looked up again from the letter she was writing to her father, and stared out of the small window at her side. She needed more than good luck with Tony Bergman. He was reputed to be a real tough cookie. She chewed on the end of her pen. Keep your head. Don't get anxious. Just think of it as another boring deal on another boring day at Van den Fleet's. She stopped chewing for a moment, surprised that, quite without thinking, she had used the word 'boring'. She took the pen from her mouth. But it was true.

Beni flung his pen down and stretched his arms in front of him. 'I need a break. Would you like something to drink, Marti?'

'Yes, thank you.'

He got up from his chair. 'Excuse me for a moment.' He walked the few feet to the cabin door and slid it open, calling out to the steward as he closed it behind him.

Marti shifted in her seat. She needed to visit the lavatory too, but wasn't quite sure what the etiquette was on a private jet. It didn't seem quite the right thing to queue.

She arched her back from the seat and stretched. Beni was a strange man. She had learned more about him in two hours than she had in the five years she had known him. He was a nomad. The Lebanon, the home of his forebears, no longer existed. He was a doubting Christian. It was difficult to believe in a god who allowed mankind to indulge in wanton destruction. He was divorced. The marriage hadn't been arranged as such, more something he and his wife had both felt had been expected of them at the time, but goodwill and affection had proved insufficient for both of them.

He had two children. They lived with their mother and stepfather. His lifestyle was too erratic to make him anything other than a bad father, but he compensated by indulging their every whim. She swung her legs out from beneath the table and rotated each ankle back and forth in turn. Perhaps enforced time together had encouraged self-revelation. She frowned to herself. Martina. Beni never said anything to anyone without excellent reason.

Beni returned with the steward in tow. 'Marti, what would you like to drink?'

'Something non-alcoholic, please.'

'Very wise. I am having some iced tea. Would you like some?'

'Yes, that sounds lovely.' She picked up her bag and looked vaguely towards the cabin door.

The steward responded to the gesture immediately. 'If madame wishes to freshen up, perhaps she will follow me.'

Marti stood up with relief. 'Thank you.'

The co-pilot came into the cabin to announce that they had been slotted into a holding stack, but expected ETA to be no more than twenty minutes. Beni thanked him and began filling his briefcase with papers. 'No excuses, Marti, I insist that you dine with me this evening.'

'Thank you.'

'Would you also do me a favour?'

'What's that?'

'Come with me to a cocktail party. Just for ten minutes, for form's sake, then we can escape.'

'OK. Who do you want to escape from?'

'The madding crowd. I shan't be in the mood for one of Christian Debilius's parties.'

Her eyes flicked open in alarm. 'Ah, Beni, I don't think I should really attend without a specific invitation.'

'You have a specific invitation. Christian insisted I bring a friend.'

She looked at him doubtfully. 'I am not strictly speaking a member of the IDE.'

'It is a private party. Nothing at all to do with the IDE.' He shot her a teasing glance. 'You're not by any chance a teeny-weeny bit afraid of him, are you?'

'Of course not.'

'Good.' He snapped his briefcase shut. That was exactly the reply he had expected. 'So there is no problem. I will pick you up at your hotel at five-thirty.' He rolled the cuffs of his shirt down and fastened them. 'Perhaps I should mention that it is the fashion for ladies in New York to be very glamorous in the evenings. I think it must be a revolt against their usual daytime power-dressing.'

'I can take a hint, Beni.'

He smiled to himself. That wasn't always the case.

Fang reached out for the telephone, then drew his hand back quickly. He refilled his glass with another large measure of brandy and downed it in one mouthful. He reached out for the telephone again. This time he would do it. His hand shook as he dialled the number. Relief shot through him as he listened to the engaged signal. Reprieve for a brief moment from the shaming task. He cleared the line and redialled. 'Ah, Jiaming. It is Ka-Shing here.' He reached out and poured another measure of brandy into the glass. 'No, no, there is nothing wrong. I just have a slight cold.' He cleared his throat. 'Everything is going according to plan. There is nothing to worry about. I just thought you would like to know, Jiaming, that the *gweilos* have seen the treasures of Bright Mountain and have succumbed.' He gave a shrill laugh. 'Yes, yes, three of the parcels of diamonds have been bought. I am awaiting confirmation of the fourth.' Colour suffused his face. 'Jiaming, your compliments embarrass me. I have done nothing more than you have asked. Nothing more, I can assure you. Yes, I shall keep you informed. No, no, Chan Chunling has done exactly what has been asked of him. The proceeds are being transferred, as I speak. You need have no fears, Jiaming. I will call you again as soon as I have further news.' Fang put the telephone down and mopped his brow with his handkerchief. He tossed back the brandy and refilled the glass. He walked unsteadily back to his chair and slumped into it. He gave a quick start as he thought he heard a noise outside. He held his breath for a few moments then let it out shakily. The silence pounded in his ears. He clutched the glass to his chest. A thousand tortures could be no worse than his present predicament.

Tony Bergman took a sip of coffee, then grimaced. 'Roz, is this that god-awful skimmed milk again?'

''Fraid so, Tony.'

'Make me a cup of black will you? I really can't stand the taste of that stuff. Have you got Yoshino for me yet, and when's Marti Van den Fleet due?'

Roz gave a cheerful smile. 'Black coffee coming up. Mr Yoshino's line is engaged. Marti Van den Fleet is due in half an hour.'

'Get Yoshino for me, before I see Marti. Tell Max to be on hand. I may need him.'

'Will do.' Roz picked up the telephone and redialled the Tokyo number. 'Ringing out.'

'Put it through to my office, will you?'

'Line three, Tony.'

'OK. Listen, if the Japanese snap at the bait, I'll take you out to dinner.'

'You've got a deal.'

Tony flung himself into his chair and picked up the telephone. 'Mr Yoshino? Tony Bergman, New York, here. I'm just fine. How are you? Glad to hear it. Look, I have been offered a parcel of diamonds I authenticated myself a couple of weeks ago. You know Van den Fleet's of Antwerp? Yeah, well the diamonds are being sold by Martina Van den

Fleet. The lady never deals in garbage. Interested?' Tony's face creased into a smile. 'OK, Mr Yoshino, I'll do my best for you. Usual terms. I'll get back to you pronto.' He put the telephone down and got up from his chair. He hitched his trousers up and went back into the outer office.

Roz put her hand over the telephone. 'Marti Van den Fleet's on her way up. She's a little early.'

'Take care of her for me, and you can book a table for two at your favourite restaurant, and think about what you would like to do after dinner. I'm willing to take on anything except a disco.'

She laughed. 'Night at the disco would help to get the weight down, Tony.'

'I prefer to take my exercise on my back. Listen, get me Don Reynolds before I see Marti.'

'Sure.'

Tony hitched his trousers up again and ambled back to his office. He whistled a tune to himself. Fixing for his wife to be elected chairperson of the Artists' Guild Foundation Luncheon Club should safely cover his night on the town with Roz.

Roz was already on her feet and walking towards Marti, with hand outstretched, when Marti pushed open the swing doors. 'Miss Van den Fleet? Hi, I'm Roz, Tony's assistant.'

Marti briefly took Roz's hand.

'Tony's just taking a call at the moment, but he won't be long. How was the flight from Antwerp?'

'I travelled from Paris, actually.'

'Oh, I see.' Roz smiled cheerfully. 'Can I get you coffee?'

'Not for the moment, thank you.'

'Would you excuse me? Tony has just cleared his line. I'll tell him you're here. Please take a seat.'

Marti glanced behind her then sat down on the edge of the sofa. She placed her briefcase by her side. At least she didn't have the added tension of coping with one of James's state-of-the-art briefcases. There had been time to send the diamonds on to New York by professional courier. She reached out for her briefcase again as Tony swept the door of his office open. Her stomach knotted. He was a good-humoured man, but he could take you down to your socks.

'Marti, you look terrific. Good to see you.' Tony strode up to the sofa and held out his hand. He lightly held Marti's fingers for a moment, then released them. 'Sorry to keep you waiting. Come right along. How is Erasmus? His retirement is a great blow to the organisation.' He took her elbow and guided her to his office. 'Would you like coffee? How was your flight? Hear you are doing great things in Hong Kong these days.' He pushed open the door of his office and stood to one side. 'Did you say you'd like coffee?'

She suppressed a smile. She hadn't managed a single word so far. 'Black with no sugar, will be fine.'

'By the way, notice anything different about me these days?'

She glanced up at him in alarm. He looked exactly the same to her, but politeness required some difference to be noticed. She took a quick look at Roz. Roz grinned and tapped at her stomach with her finger. Marti let her breath out. Thank you Roz. 'Er, actually, Tony, would you think me rude if I said I thought you've lost weight.'

'No, I would not think you rude at all. You really think I have?'

'Oh yes. Noticed it straight away.'

He smiled in happy satisfaction. 'Funny you should say that. Everyone keeps saying that to me, but I can't see it myself.' He gave a slight shrug of his shoulders. 'Must be the exercise. I work out every day, you know, Marti.'

She glanced back at Roz again, in time to see Roz rolling her eyes in utter disbelief.

Marti made herself comfortable in her chair while Tony went through the ritual of buzzing through to Roz and telling her he didn't want any interruptions while he was in conference with Miss Van den Fleet. He leaned back in his chair and smiled. 'OK, Marti, let's talk dirty.'

She blinked then realised he meant talk money. '$2 million.'

'Love your sense of humour, Marti. $500,000.'

She gave him a long look. She didn't like his at all. 'I am here to do business, Tony, not play games.'

'OK, time is money. $750,000.'

'I have my instructions, Tony.'

He shrugged. 'Who doesn't?'

'You authenticated the diamonds at $1 million.'

'So?'

'So let's take it from there.'

'Like hell we do. No offence, sweetheart, but you are selling and I am buying. That's where we take it from. $750,000.'

'You're buying goods with your name on them, Tony. You're not exactly Bloomingdale's, but you come close. $2 million.'

He leaned back in his chair. 'You know, my basic problem is that I have never gotten around to understanding female logic. You are telling me, because I have authenticated these diamonds I have to pay twice the price for them.'

'I will read that as $1½ million.'

'You will do no such thing, young lady. That was just a figure of speech. $750,000. Final.'

'You don't buy rarity at $750,000.'

'Come on, I can get diamonds like that on the street any time.'

'I stopped believing in fairy stories when I was six, Tony. Nothing has come on the market like this for possibly ten years and you know it.'

He clasped his hands behind his head. 'You're lucky. You've caught me on a good day. Make it $1 million.'

'I can close at $1¾ million.'

He shook his head. 'Looks like you have had a wasted journey, sweetheart.'

'Not entirely, I am simply keeping James Wu's promise to give you first option on buying. It's immaterial to me who in New York buys them.'

He stared at her. 'Let's keep this polite, Marti.'

'And let's keep it sensible. $1¾ million. They are perfectly matched diamonds.'

'OK. Let me tell you what I'm prepared to close at. $1¼.'

'$1¾ or no deal.'

He shrugged. 'So break my heart.'

She clasped her fingers together. She was going to be lucky to get $1½ million out of him. Very lucky. She could probably sell the diamonds to Beni, but in James's eyes it wouldn't have the same kudos as having successfully done business with Tony Bergman.

Tony opened the drawer of his desk and took out a cigar. She openly checked her watch, to indicate passage of time. He slowly rolled the cigar between his fingers. She could wait. She wasn't going anywhere until she sold the diamonds. Marti got up from her chair and held out her hand. 'I'm sorry we couldn't do business on this occasion, Tony, but perhaps some other time.'

He smiled to himself. Nice one, Marti, but I don't fall for that line either. He got up from his chair and slowly walked around to the front of his desk. 'Me too, Marti, but nice to see you again.'

'Can we consider your option to buy closed? I promised my other client not to keep him in suspense.'

'You want to call him?'

She tensed her stomach muscles as her stomach gave a warning growl. 'Er –'

He gestured to the telephone. 'Feel free.'

She pursed her lips. Damn him. He was calling her bluff. 'Thanks, just let me find his number.' She picked up her bag and made a slow search for her filofax.

Tony hitched his bottom on to the corner of the desk. She

deserved an Oscar nomination for her performance, but there was no other client. He would be prepared to bet on it. 'Can I help you at all?'

'He's staying at the Regency. I've got the number here somewhere.' She didn't look up at him, but sensed that the information had made some impact.

Tony lit up his cigar. 'Must be a wealthy guy.'

'Mmm. Ah, found it.' She gave a bright smile. 'Sure you don't mind my using your telephone?'

'Not at all.'

She took a deep breath and prayed that Beni would not be in his suite. She dialled the number. 'Ah, Mr Yasim's suite, please. Martina Van den Fleet calling. He is expecting me.'

Tony grabbed at her arm. 'Hey, not so fast. I think you and I should have a little talk, sweetheart, before you rush off to your Mr Yasim.' He snatched the telephone from her and slammed it down. 'Sit, young lady.' His eyes flashed angrily. 'You're too goddam cute for words. I have an option to buy and it ain't closed yet. I don't know what your father taught you, but you sure as hell don't do it in New York and not to me.'

'I'm sorry, I don't understand.'

'Then let me spell it out for you, Marti.' He held his hand up to her face and rubbed his fingers together. 'Commission. You make a private deal with your Mr Yasim, but first you have to knock me out of the running. You pitch the price so goddam high that I don't take up the option. Leaving you with a profit-margin as wide as the Hudson River.' He gave a short laugh. 'I've been in this business thirty years, Marti. I know all of the tricks.' He ground his cigar into the ashtray. '$1½ million.'

She stared at him not quite believing what he had just said. She slowly sat down in the chair. She had done it. She had got the great Tony Bergman on the run. She clasped her hands together. 'You have a deal.'

'OK. We have a deal.'

'Plus my retainer.'

'Let's talk about it.' The temper that had flared so quickly, vanished and was replaced by a quick smile. He sat on the corner of the desk again. 'Keep the numbers simple. I'm a poor man.'

She laughed more from relief than amusement. It had been a very close call. She could just as easily be making her way to the elevator.

'$50,000, Tony.'

'$25,000.'

'Tony, are you trying to put me out of business?'

'Split the difference?'

'Agreed.'

Tony turned and looked at the ashtray in dismay. 'Did I do that?'

She looked at the shredded cigar. 'Think so.'

'See what you do to me, Marti? Got me ruining a perfectly good cigar.' He shook his head to himself. 'Hey, what I said before, no offence taken, OK?'

She slung her bag over her shoulder. 'Glad we could do business together.'

'Me too, me too. Listen, I've got an idea. Why don't you come and have dinner with me and Mrs Bergman tonight?'

'That is very kind of you, but I can't.'

'You're still sore with me, because I gave you a bad time.'

'No, I take the rough with the rough, but I have two engagements I really have to keep tonight.'

'Some other time then, and that's a date.'

'Look forward to it.'

Tony walked to the door with her and opened it. 'Shall we conclude business tomorrow morning?'

'I would be grateful. I have to get back to Hong Kong.'

'OK, Marti.' He took her hand and shook it warmly. 'Hey, listen, I've got an idea. Let's have breakfast together.

Lila's. Just tell the cab driver to take you to Lila's. Even the goddam Hispanics know where Lila's is. Eight o'clock, all right?'

'Thanks, Tony.'

'My pleasure.'

James Wu gave an excited yelp of laughter and crooked the telephone on his shoulder as he quickly scribbled a note on the pad in front of him. 'Marti, I don't believe this. How did you do it?'

'How did I do what?'

'Get a retainer fee out of Tony Bergman? It's unheard of.'

'Personality, James, personality.'

He shook his head to himself. 'I really am impressed. Tony has a reputation for chewing people up and spitting them out before breakfast.'

'I think he probably feels he has to rein in a lot when he is dealing with a woman. Either that, or he has a client who doesn't care how much money he spends.'

James laughed again. 'I'll accept both explanations. When are you coming back?'

'Day after tomorrow. No, wait a minute. You're twelve hours ahead of me, so it will be tomorrow your time. Sorry, I don't think I've got that quite right.'

'Don't worry. Have you booked your flight yet?'

'I'm going to.'

'Look, give me a call when you have and then I will know when to collect you at the airport.'

'Thanks, James. See you soon.'

''Bye.' He put the telephone down and rubbed his hands together. Marti was bringing him much fortune. He made a rapid calculation on the notepad. His commission from Chan, plus two per cent on the deal with Marti's client, plus a fifty-fifty split on the retainer from Tony Bergman. He stared down at the figures on the pad and smiled to himself.

Much fortune. He picked up the telephone and dialled
Chan Chunling's number.

The drawing room of Christian Debilius's apartment
housed the overspill from the party going on in the sitting
room. Marti held on to Beni's sleeve and edged her way past
various groups of people. She turned as she felt a hand on
her shoulder.

'It is Martina, isn't it?' Christian looked at her with
bright and curious eyes.

'Yes, it is.' She tugged at Beni's sleeve. 'I've found our
host.'

Beni turned around. 'Christian, good to see you. You've
got quite a crowd here tonight.'

Christian kept his eyes firmly on Marti. 'I am delighted to
see you, Martina.'

'I'm something of a gate-crasher. Beni invited me. I hope
you don't mind?'

'On the contrary. Why didn't you let me know you were
in New York?'

'Just a flying visit.' She glanced around and saw with
alarm that Beni had drifted away and was talking to a
blonde-haired woman. Christian took her arm in his.
'Come with me and I'll find you a drink. Unless, of course,
you want to keep a strict watch on Beni.'

She glanced at him with a puzzled look. 'Why should I
want to do that?'

He smiled. 'No reason.' He signalled to one of the waiters. 'Tell me, Martina, what brings you to New York?'

'Business.'

He took two glasses of champagne from the tray proffered
by the waiter. 'How are you getting along with James Wu?'

'Very well so far.'

'Good.' He handed a glass to her. 'He's an up-and-
coming young man. We expect great things from him.' He
turned to face her squarely, blocking off an approach from

a fair-haired man. He took hold of her arm again. 'May we have a word in private?'

'Mmm.'

Christian shepherded Marti to a corner by the windows. He accidentally moved her too close to a potted palm. Its leaves brushed her shoulder. She glanced round at it. 'Is there really room for two behind this?'

He laughed and took a step back to allow her more space. 'Forgive me for spiriting you away like this, but your brother, Hendrik, seems rather concerned about things.'

She grimaced. 'Things in general or things in particular.'

'Things in particular, I'm afraid. He seems to think you have a cunning plan to steal all of Van den Fleet's clients. I must say I find it rather difficult to believe.'

'Hendrik is being rather stupid. We have discussed this and I have made it perfectly clear that I have absolutely no intention of using information about the company, which would threaten its trading position. Unfortunately, the word of a Van den Fleet appears no longer to be acceptable.'

'I am sorry to hear you say that. I cannot conceive a situation where that should be so.'

'Thank you. Although, I suppose what I say is irrelevant to some extent. It is for the clients to decide who they will buy from.'

He glanced over his shoulder. 'I see one already has.'

'Ah, you mean Beni?'

'I am not surprised. Forgive me for being chauvinistic, but Hendrik isn't as pretty as you.'

She gave a wry smile. 'He isn't as bright, either. He is blowing this whole thing up out of all proportion. You know, if I was going to do anything underhand it would show up immediately when the IDE did a diamond audit of James's books.'

'Quite. Well, I am glad we have been able to have this little conversation, Martina.' He took a mouthful of champagne. 'How is business going with Beni?'

'Beni?'

'Presumably that is why you are in New York.'

'No, I'm not in New York to do business with Beni. I just hitched a lift from him, that's all.'

He looked at her quizzically. She caught a glimpse of Tony Bergman pushing his way towards them. There was no point in holding back now. 'Actually, I came to see Tony Bergman.'

His eyes fastened on hers. 'I don't know what Hendrik is worrying about then. You obviously don't need Van den Fleet's clients or anyone else's.'

She shot him a warning glance. 'Tony is right behind you.'

He turned around just as Tony was about to clap a hand on his shoulder.

'Hey, what is all this? You stood me up just to be at this guy's party?' Tony leaned across and planted a kiss on Marti's cheek.

Christian smiled. 'Martina is a woman of taste, Tony.'

'I know, I know, that's why she does business with me, but I tell you, Christian, you want to watch her. She is lethal.'

Marti glanced at Tony warily. His face was flushed with alcohol.

Christian nodded slowly. 'I'll bear it in mind, Tony, but I take it you survived?'

Tony raised a warning finger. 'Just, pal, just.' He turned and slung an arm around Marti's shoulders. 'But we got ourselves a good deal, didn't we kiddo?'

She eased herself gently away from beneath his arm. '*You* did a good deal, Tony.'

'Now come on, you can't hold that against me. It's just my job, it isn't personal or anything.' He swayed slightly towards her. 'I respect you. I do.'

She peered over Tony's shoulder and was relieved to see

Beni waving at her and tapping at his watch. 'If you will excuse me, my dinner-date is signalling.' She held out her hand to Christian. 'Sorry for gate-crashing your party.'

'Not at all, but you must promise to let me know when you are next in New York. We must dine together.'

'Thank you.' She edged her way past Tony. 'Nice to see you again, Tony.'

'You too, kiddo.' Tony took a gulp of champagne and watched her thread her way to Beni's side. 'Who's the guy she's got in tow?'

'His name is Beni Yasim.'

Tony's eyes widened suddenly. 'You know him?'

'Quite well.'

Tony took another mouthful of champagne. 'Good-looking guy.'

'You could say that.'

Tony looked at his watch. 'I mustn't keep my dinner-date waiting, either.' He set his glass down on the window-ledge. 'Fantastic party, Christian, best yet.'

'Glad you enjoyed it.' Christian followed Tony back to the centre of the room.

Christian stood for a moment, surveying his guests like a battle commander. Hendrik had been very stupid. He had left the door of the cage open and the little bird hadn't hesitated to fly away. He quickly made his way to the hall in time to catch up with Marti and Beni. 'Beni, so sorry we didn't have time to chat. Can I persuade you to stay a little longer?'

'We're due at your restaurant, Christian, in ten minutes.'

'Well, *bon appetit* and don't forget to mention you are a very dear friend of mine.'

Beni smiled. 'I already did. How do you think I managed to get a table?' He glanced around in irritation at Tony Bergman as he brushed past him.

'Oh, excuse me.' Tony stopped and winked at him. 'No hard feelings, OK? At least you got the girl.' He gave a brief wave of his hand as he headed for the door. 'Don't forget, sweetheart. We have a date. Eight at Lila's.'

Beni raised both eyebrows. 'Can anyone tell me what all that was about?'

'I'm afraid I can't.' Christian's eyes gleamed wickedly. 'Perhaps Martina can.'

Marti took a deep breath, promising herself to kill Christian Debilius one day. She slipped her arm through Beni's. 'He was my business appointment. I had to decline his dinner invitation this evening. We are having breakfast at eight tomorrow.'

'Ah, I see. Well, shall we go?' Beni gave a brief nod in Christian's direction.

'Enjoy yourselves and good-night.' Christian smiled to himself as he watched them leave. There were beautiful women and there were clever women, and Martina Van den Fleet belonged to the latter category.

The limousine pulled up outside the Regency Hotel. Beni removed his arm from the back seat. 'Let's have a night-cap, Marti.'

She looked about her. They had been laughing and talking so much, she hadn't realised they had been driving in the direction of his hotel. She drew her bag to her, suddenly feeling deflated. It was time for the evening to end. He didn't mix business with pleasure and neither did she. 'I don't think I want a night-cap, Beni. We have wined and dined rather too well, but it has been a lovely evening. I am very impressed with Christian's restaurant.'

He picked up her hand and brushed her fingers against his mouth. 'Forget about Christian. I want you to be impressed with me, not him.'

She stared at him in surprise. His touch had spread through her arm, leaving it tingling with expectancy. She couldn't remember the last time any part of her had felt like that. He turned her face to his. 'We have known each other a long time, Marti.' He put his arms around her and kissed her. His mouth eased its way down to her neck. 'Stay with me.'

She pulled away from him. 'That is not a good idea, Beni.'

He hugged her to him. 'Yes it is.'

She rested her hands on his chest, putting a little space between Beni and herself. She needed to get out quickly before she succumbed to an ever-increasing temptation. 'You said you never allow pleasure to interfere with business.'

'That is true, but our business is finished, at least for the time being. Now it is time for pleasure.'

'Beni, I like you very much, but –'

He placed a finger on her mouth. 'You are free from the shadow of your family. Don't live in the past.'

She brushed his finger away from her mouth. 'What do you mean, free from my family?'

'Your father, your brother. You have, I think, always been dominated by them. Now you are free.'

She stared at him, quite shocked by his words. 'Is that what you really think?'

'Yes.'

She turned her head and looked out of the window at the discreet but welcoming lights of the hotel. 'You make me sound very boring.'

'No. Dutiful, not boring, Marti.'

She pressed her lips together. That sounded even duller. The lights of the hotel twinkled and beckoned her. Why not? She needed more than just a brief reminder of what it felt like to feel alive. She reached out and touched his hand. He raised her fingers to his mouth and kissed them, then reached in front of her and opened the passenger door.

The suite was elaborately furnished with French reproduction furniture with large bowls of flowers on every available table top. Beni poured out two glasses of cognac.

He had, for one daunting moment in the limousine, thought he had made a mistake; that for once, his instinctive feeling for time and place had let him down. He looped his fingers beneath the bowl of each glass. But something had changed her mind. He was very glad it had. She had been on the point of refusing him. He took the glasses to the sofa and handed one to Marti. 'You're very quiet. You haven't changed your mind, have you?' She shook her head. She had no intention of changing her mind. She had served her father's purposes. She had served Hendrik's purposes. In a way she had served Johannes's purposes, too. She had been his token girlfriend. He was a dear man in many ways, but could only want women in theory, not in practice. She took a mouthful of brandy. Her body felt like a non-existent mass again. She hastily swallowed the brandy, glad of the fiery warmth burning a downward path in her chest.

Beni sat down beside her and put his arm around her shoulders. 'Tell me what you are thinking.'

She twirled the glass between her fingers. She couldn't tell him that. 'I was thinking how strange it is. I know you and yet I don't. Does that sound stupid?'

He laughed. 'Yes.' He ruffled her hair. 'I was only teasing. It happens when a man and a woman have stayed friends for too long, before becoming lovers.'

She gave a wry smile. 'That sounds a very well-rehearsed line.'

'Perhaps, but it happens to be true. I am not exactly inexperienced in these matters, Marti.' He brushed his mouth against her cheek. 'But perhaps it is time for you to judge for yourself.' He set his brandy glass down and got to his feet. 'Shut your eyes for three minutes.' He tapped her nose. 'And don't even think of moving.'

Marti dutifully kept her eyes shut, but turned her head to one side as she heard sounds of hurried ablutions coming from the direction of the bathroom. She jumped as hands

were gently rested on her shoulders. She opened her eyes
and looked at Beni kneeling in front of her. She had vaguely
expected him to surprise her by suddenly appearing completely naked, but he had only removed his jacket and tie.
He leaned forward and kissed her. She tasted the minty
smell of toothpaste on his breath. She pulled away from
him. 'I need to freshen up.'

He held on to her hands. 'No, don't. You smell of
woman. Don't destroy it.' He drew her to her feet.

The bed was overhung by brocade drapes surmounted by
a coronet. It reminded Marti of the illicit peep at his bed in
Paris. Beni turned her around to face him and slid his arms
around her waist. He felt beneath the folds of chiffon and
deftly unhooked the back fastening of her dress. He pushed
the dress away from her shoulders, his fingers caressing the
length of her arms, as he slid the dress down until it fell to
the floor of its own accord. She slipped a foot out of one
shoe and tottered slightly, as she took a step backwards to
shake her other foot free. He placed his hands on her hips to
steady her then knelt down and brushed his mouth against
the front of her briefs, before removing them. He stood up
again and looked at her. For a moment she felt embarrassed
by the sweeping gaze that appeared to be taking in every
blemish, every imperfection.

'You are beautiful.' He rested his hands on her shoulders. 'You have very beautiful breasts.'

She relaxed at the clichéd but reassuring words and slid
the palms of her hands up his chest and clasped them
around his neck.

'And very erotic eyes.' He brushed his mouth against her
eyelids. 'They tilt up at the corners. It was the first thing I
noticed about you.'

She felt for the hand at her breast and tugged gently at his
fingers as she turned to the bed.

The canopy over the bed was lined with blue damask,
fancifully mimicking a night sky. Marti stared up at it and

ran her fingers experimentally over Beni's firm, tense flesh. She closed her eyes and responded with deep pleasure to his vigorous caresses. Johannes's body had felt soft, oddly passive, from what she could remember. She opened her eyes and stared up again. A body without an urgent and desiring need. She clutched at Beni's shoulders as he positioned himself over her. It had left her own body devitalised. A feeling she had avoided having to experience ever again. She lay still as Beni eased himself into her. Breathy words filled her left ear. 'I feel enveloped in silk.'

Hendrik pulled himself upright in the chair at the sound of the telephone ringing. He had dropped off to sleep without realising it. He reached over the arm of the chair and searched for the channel-changer, then switched the television off and got up to answer the telephone. 'Oh, hello, Christian. How are you?'

'Fine. Hope I'm not disturbing you?'

'No, no. I was just finishing off some work from the office.' Hendrik rubbed the back of his neck and stretched.

'I thought I might call you up for a chat. I had the pleasure of your sister's company this evening.'

Hendrik straightened up, his body tensing at the word sister. 'Really?'

'Yes, she dropped in for a few minutes at my party. She looked exceedingly well.'

Hendrik looked around desperately for his cigarettes. Christian was trying to tell him something. 'What was she doing in New York?'

'Oh, didn't you know? Business, I understand.'

'I hope she hasn't been causing any trouble.'

'I doubt it. Tony Bergman and she seem to get on like the proverbial house on fire, I think.'

Hendrik tilted his head back and stared up at the ceiling. Stop playing cat and mouse, Christian. Out with it.

'Martina and I managed to have a quiet little chat. It was

very enjoyable. You know, we really don't see enough of her in New York.'

'What about?'

'Sorry?'

'May I ask what you were chatting about?'

'Oh, you know, this and that. Actually, the thought occurred to me afterwards that you really don't need to worry about Martina. She seems to be doing very well for herself.'

Hendrik spotted his cigarettes and lighter on the coffee table. 'Er, Christian could you just excuse me a second?' He dropped the telephone, rushed to the table, grabbed his cigarettes and lighter, and rushed back to the telephone again. 'Sorry about that, Christian. You were saying?'

'Martina seems to be doing very well for herself. Obviously very happy in her new job, but then she always has been a very sensible, astute girl. Takes everything in her stride, so to speak. She made it quite clear that she understands perfectly your anxieties about Van den Fleet's, so I really don't think you have any worries there, Hendrik.'

'I'm sorry if Marti has been bothering you. This is something between her and me. She had no right to raise the matter with you.' Hendrik spoke stiffly.

'She didn't. It just came up in our conversation. Oh, by the way, Tony Bergman sends his regards. Wishes you well in the future.'

Hendrik's eyes blinked rapidly. That was the second hint. 'What was Marti seeing Tony Bergman about?'

'Business. I didn't quite catch all of the conversation. I think they are concluding a deal tomorrow. Tony seems very taken with her.'

Hendrik's mouth tightened.

'Well, Hendrik, I shan't keep you from burning the midnight oil. Nice to have chatted. I'll see you next week, shall I?'

'Yes, I thought I would come to New York the day before option day.'

'Good. Look forward to seeing you.'

Hendrik put the telephone down and scowled at it. Christian was slithering in and out of the rocks again. He lit up a cigarette and inhaled deeply. Christian hadn't rung up just to have a little cosy chat about nothing. He walked back to the chair and flung himself down in it. He chewed at his thumbnail. James Wu must really be wheeling and dealing. Tony Bergman never touched the small stuff.

Marti woke up to the sounds of Mozart. She craned her neck and stared at the clock radio. She raised her arm to her face and looked at her watch. The realisation of the time suddenly penetrated her mind. She gasped and leapt out of bed. She had thirty minutes to get to Lila's, wherever it was. She hastily gathered up her clothes from the floor and dashed into the bathroom.

Beni turned his head on the pillow, then he too leapt up. He slipped his watch over his hand. 'Marti, where are you?'

'Bathroom.'

He went to the bathroom and pushed the door open. 'My precious darling, I wish we could stay here all day, but I have a meeting at eight-thirty.' He came to her and wrapped his arms around her.

'Beni, please, I must go. I have a breakfast meeting.' She looked at her watch again. 'Oh no, in twenty-seven minutes.' She wriggled away from him and ran into the bedroom.

He followed after her and pulled her to him, burying his mouth into her shoulder. Her eyes scanned the floor. Shoe. She could only see one shoe. 'Beni, please, I mustn't be late. Dealers must exchange on time. It is an unbreakable rule.'

'There is no such thing as an unbreakable rule.'

She struggled from his grasp.

'My darling, what is the matter? Didn't I please you last night?'

She crouched down on the floor. 'You did. It was marvellous. Thank you.' She raised the valance on the bed. 'Oh, thank God for that.' She grabbed at the heel of the missing shoe and dragged herself up again.

He reached out to hold her again. 'That is not true. I can see it in your eyes.'

She stepped into her shoes, struggling into her dress at the same time. 'Beni, the only thing you can see in my eyes is panic at the moment.'

'But you cannot leave just like this?'

She glanced down at herself; at the chiffon dress, the evening shoes. She had no choice. She smoothed her hair with her hands. 'Will I be able to get a cab outside?'

'I'll get one of the hotel cars for you.'

'Oh, Beni, thanks.' She looked at him for a moment. He looked disappointed. 'Beni, I'm not very good at expressing myself, but this morning I feel like the princess who woke up after a hundred years of sleep.'

A smile crossed his face. He held out his arms to her, but she side-stepped him. 'Beni, I really have to go.' She blew a kiss as she ran out of the bedroom.

Marti came to a full stop in the middle of the sitting room. Bag. She hadn't got her bag. She stared frantically around the room. Sofa. She rushed to the sofa and pulled her bag from beneath a cushion. Beni had already reached the door of the suite. 'There is a car waiting for you downstairs. Now a kiss before you go. It is my right.'

She submitted to one quick kiss then pulled away and grabbed at the door-knob.

'Marti, when are we going to meet?'

'Call me when you can.'

'Will you be in Hong Kong?'

'Yes.'

He held on to her arm.

'Beni, I must go. I hate going like this, but I have to. Please understand.'

'I will come to Hong Kong as soon as I can.'

'Thank you, Beni. It's been marvellous and I'm going to

miss you until you do.' She blew a kiss and flung herself out of the door. Beni shut the door behind her and leaned against it. He stared up at the ceiling. He had never been left by a woman before. He walked slowly back to the bedroom. It was a very unsettling experience.

By the time the doors of the elevator slid open to reveal an already busy lobby, Marti's coat was firmly buttoned to her chin and her breathing had steadied. She straightened her back and stepped out of the elevator, feeling reasonably confident that she didn't look as if she had just leapt out of someone's bed.

The driver slowed the hotel car to a crawl then stopped. Marti peered anxiously over his shoulder at the solid mass of traffic in front. She gnawed at her knuckles. Please God, get me to Lila's on time and I will never do this again. The car moved forward a few feet then halted again. She tapped the driver on the shoulder. 'How far away are we from Lila's?'

''Bout five blocks.'

'How long would it take to walk?'

He glanced round at her. 'Maybe eight to ten minutes. Depends if the lights are kind to you.'

She opened her bag. 'I'll get out here and walk. I really am in a terrible hurry. How much do I owe you?'

'Nothing.'

'Oh well, have this for your trouble.'

'Thank you ma'am.'

She swung the rear door open and leapt out.

Marti took a last look at her watch. Four minutes past eight. She pushed the door of Lila's open, scanned the crowded tables and went up to the counter. 'Excuse me.'

The young man raised a hand. 'Be right with you.' He cupped his hand to his mouth. 'Number forty-nine. Juice. Scrambled egg.'

A waitress rushed to the counter and picked up the tray.

The young man came back to Marti. 'Want to see the menu?'

'I am meeting a Mr Tony Bergman here. My name is Van den Fleet.'

The young man rested his hands on the counter and stood on tiptoe. 'Can't see him. He's usually here by now.'

A waitress returned with an empty tray.

'Hey, you seen Mr Bergman?'

She shook her head. 'Try the message board.'

The young man turned round to look at the blackboard behind him. 'There's a message for a Miss Vanefleet. Mr Bergman delayed twenty minutes. APGs.'

Marti almost sobbed with relief. 'It's me, it's me. When did you get the message?'

'I'll check.' He shouted across to the woman at the cash desk. 'Know when Mr Bergman called?'

'Five minutes ago.'

He grinned at Marti. 'There's your answer.'

'Thank you. I'll come back in about fifteen minutes.'

Marti stood for a moment on the pavement outside Lila's. She had passed a clothes shop advertising a pre-autumn sale, half a block away. She hurried up the street and breathed a sigh of relief when she reached the shop and saw an 'open' sign on the door. The girl in the shop glanced up as Marti came in, then turned her attention to sorting out a heap of coathangers. Marti flicked through the first rail of garments. They all claimed to be designed by Giorgio Bonatello. She pulled out a skirt and searched the next rack until she found the plainest blouse she could see. She turned round to the assistant. 'Could I try these on, please?'

'Sure.' The girl shot a finger towards a small cubicle at the back of the shop.

Marti pushed her way through the curtain and hurriedly removed her coat and dress. She hastily put on the blouse and skirt and smoothed her hair. She took a step back and looked at herself in the mirror. She looked terrible. She bent down and hastily picked up her dress and coat.

The shop assistant looked up. 'More over there, if you want to browse.'

'No, I'll take the skirt and the blouse, thank you, and I'll - er - wear them. Could I have a bag, please?'

'Sure.' The girl bent down for a moment, then flicked a plastic carrier bag on to the counter.

Marti grabbed the bag and pushed her dress into it.

'Always better to get the guy to stay with you. Less hassle.'

Marti stared at the girl. 'What?'

'Better if the guy stays at your place. Isn't so much hassle the next morning.'

Marti flushed and bent her head to search in her bag for her credit card.

Tony Bergman was just removing his overcoat when Marti returned to Lila's. 'Marti, what can I say, except I'm sorry. It was just a complete gridlock on Fifth. Did you get my message? No way could I get here unless I had a pair of wings.'

'Tony, I have a confession. I was late myself. I had to abandon the cab and practically run here.'

'Aw hell, you shouldn't have done that. I would have waited. If I had been on time myself, that is. OK, let's cut the APGs and get something to eat. They do the best croissants in New York here.'

After two cups of freshly brewed coffee and a croissant stuffed with scrambled egg and smoked salmon, Marti felt the world was spinning at a more comfortable rate. Tony wiped his mouth with his napkin and leaned back in his chair. 'Have a good time last night?'

'Yes. We went to Christian's restaurant. Impressive.'

'Yeah.' Tony leaned forward in his chair. 'What time do you want to go to the repository?'

'Whenever it's convenient to you.'

'Like now?'

'Fine.'

'Sorry to rush you, but my client is eager to see what he's bought.'

She laughed. 'You don't waste time, Tony.'

'Come on, diamonds lying in a vault don't pay the overheads. I sold them three minutes after you left yesterday.'

'Good for you.'

'Good for me while it lasts.'

'What do you mean?'

He leaned closer to her. 'I do a lot of trade with the Japanese.'

'Ah, I see.'

'You know, the first six months of this year, fifty per cent of my trade was with Japan?'

'They seem to have an obsession for diamonds.'

'Not so sure about the obsession. I have a strong feeling the Japanese are quietly stockpiling. They deny it, but that's what I figure.'

'And when they stop?'

He raised his arm and dive-bombed the table with two fingers. 'Collapse of Japanese market, sweetheart. I've taken up wood-carving lessons.'

She laughed.

'Say, would you like some more coffee?'

'If you're going to have some.'

'Why not?' He reached out and touched the apron ties on the back of a passing waitress. 'Coffee, please.'

Marti propped her chin on her hands. He had previously said he wanted to be on his way, but she was content to dawdle. Conversation with Tony was getting close to the heart of the IDE. 'You don't rely on the Japanese market that much, do you, Tony?'

'Be a fool if I did. I just take my profits while I can, like everyone else. Although not for too much longer.' He beckoned to her to lean closer and dropped his voice almost to a whisper. 'I hear on the street that a lot of people are going to be disappointed at the next option-bearers' day.'

She raised her eyebrows.

'My sources tell me Debilius is going to hold back on IF roughs to cool the market down. If the Japanese do try to pull the rug from beneath our feet, all we have to do is sit tight and sweat it out.'

She stared at him thoughtfully. Perhaps she should have held out yesterday for the full $2 million. 'If the Japanese stockpiles are sufficient, prices could drop like a stone when they stop buying.'

'That's panic talk, Marti. It won't happen if everyone keeps their heads and isn't pushed into selling at any price. Like I said, you just have to sit tight and sweat it out. Come on, your father kept practically the whole of Europe from collapsing in the eighties, by preaching that sermon.' He grinned. 'Well, maybe with a little help from Debilius.'

'Well, if anyone can stop the rot, so to speak, it is Christian.'

'Hope so.'

The waitress returned to the table with a fresh pot of coffee. Tony flashed a quick smile at her. 'You're an angel, thanks.'

'You're welcome, Mr Bergman.'

Marti picked up the pot and refilled their cups. 'You said "hope", Tony. Hope doesn't sound a very strong sentiment.'

'Well, you know, Debilius has the diamond-mine owners like that.' He held up a clenched fist. 'People think that we dealers brown our –' He gave a quick laugh. 'I should paraphrase. Dealers are a little harder to pin down. There are still a lot of stones gathering no moss in the market-place, if you will forgive the mixed metaphor. If there wasn't, you and I would not be sitting here doing business, would we?'

'True.'

'So when Debilius snaps his fingers at us, we don't run.'

'What do we do?'

'We walk.'

She laughed.

'Seriously, Marti. We dealers have to stay together. Have

to agree on a uniform policy. No one can do it for us. I respect Debilius, but only for as long as he keeps doing a good job. Know what I mean?' He looked down at his watch. 'Jesus, we really should get moving.' She picked up her cup and gulped at the steaming, hot coffee.

Tony searched in his pocket for loose change to leave for the waitress. 'You know, we must do this again, Marti. It's been very pleasant. I get sick of the continual crap, if you will pardon the word, I hear from guys. Everyone has just done the greatest deal. Like they really should get someone to pay in at the bank for them, they're developing hernias. It's not often I get the chance to listen to some intelligent conversation.'

Marti suppressed a grin. She had hardly managed more than a handful of words.

Pa Jiaming paused to light up a cigarette as he crossed the deserted square in Zhongnanhai. As he drew on the cigarette he glanced up at the sky. He stared at the shooting star curving down and away to the west. In ancient times it heralded the death of an emperor, the end of a dynasty. He sighed to himself. It was an omen of some kind meant for him. He would not have been summoned to a late-night meeting otherwise.

Chen Chih was a remarkably small man. He drew himself up to his full height and stared stony faced at Pa. Pa clasped his hands in front of him. The shooting star had been an omen. He had assumed that the demand for him to attend the office of the leader of the Leading Group for High Technology had come from Ma Yun. The man staring at him was not Ma. In fact he had never set eyes on him before. Chen picked up a document from the desk and handed it to Pa. 'I have been appointed leader of the Leading Group for High Technology by directive of the Central Committee.'

Pa quickly glanced through the document. It said all that

needed to be said. There was no mention of Ma Yun. Pa reread the brief statement of Chen's appointment. The conservatives must have won another battle. That meant that radical progress on any front would immediately be halted, if not reversed. He handed the document back to Chen. 'As Vice-leader of the Group may I welcome you, Leader Chen. May I also enquire what has happened to Leader Ma Yun?'

Chen stared at him, as if looking at a fool. 'Ma Yun is no longer leader. Did you not read the document?'

'I meant –'

'May I remind you, Vice-leader Pa, that to ask questions is merely a privilege bestowed.'

Pa bent his head and stared at the floor. His instincts had been correct. The man was a conservative with a dislike of even the slightest whiff of liberalism. He flexed his fingers together. The man had not tried to hide his dislike of him. Perhaps he was bound to follow the unknown path of Ma Yun. He watched Chen, out of the corner of his eye, as Chen sat down at the desk and stretched out his forearms.

'I require, Vice-leader Pa, a detailed report on the activities with which the Group has concerned itself, on my desk at midday tomorrow.'

'Yes, Leader Chen.'

'You may go.'

Pa bent his head in acknowledgement and quietly left the room.

The bright moonlight reflected on the surface of the lake. On any other night, Pa would have stopped to admire its perfect, shimmering beauty. Instead he craned his neck back and stared up at the sky. His breath quickened as he saw a second shooting star travelling close to the horizon. He turned on his heel and hurried back to his car. The first shooting star had been a portent of Ma's doom. The second must surely be his. Perhaps there was time for Bright Mountain to be of one final service to him, before Chen got rid of him.

*   *   *

Professor Li nervously plucked at a loose thread on the cuff of his white coat. He shot a sideways glance at Pa Jiaming. Pa's visit had been unannounced and at first Li had feared the worst of reasons, but Pa looked on edge and strangely subdued.

Pa lit up a cigarette and leaned back in his chair, although he was feeling far from relaxed. 'Out of respect, Professor Li, I thought I should inform you myself that there has been a change of leader in the Group.'

Li stopped fussing at the loose thread.

'His name is Chen Chih.'

Li jerked his head up. 'A very small man?'

Pa nodded. He leaned forward to flick ash into the ash-tray on the side of the desk. 'It is possible that I too will be taking on duties other than Vice-leader in the future.'

Li swallowed nervously. It could mean only one thing. A purge.

'I have one, probably final, task for you, Professor Li. I want you to make me the largest diamond you can within two days.'

Li fiddled at the loose thread. 'You say "probably final". What does that mean?'

'You will not be called upon to face such a task again and you will never speak of Bright Mountain to anyone.'

Li got up from his chair and paced up and down the small office. His mind dwelled on each of Pa's words in turn, as he tried to carefully examine the reasons and implications of Pa's demand, while the fear rising up from his stomach threatened to choke him. Chen Chih. It was a disaster. He would be humiliated. He would lose everything. He paused in his pacing and stared down at the floor. He must save himself, if he could. 'I cannot do what you ask, Vice-leader Pa. It is impossible.'

'You are lying.'

Li jumped at the harshly spoken accusation. 'You do not understand, Vice-leader Pa.' Li looked around him as if in desperation. 'If Chen finds out what has been going on –'

'You will be punished severely, Professor Li.'

Li looked up at Pa. 'And so will you.'

Pa shook his head. 'No, Professor Li. I will be rewarded for discovering the treachery of you and Chan Chunling against the State.'

Li's breathing quickened. Disaster. He always knew it would all end in disaster. He returned to his desk and sat down. He bent his head. 'If I do this, I need a favour in return. I plead for a favour in return.' He shut his eyes. 'I beg for a favour in return.'

Pa drew on his cigarette. Plead. Beg. They were the words of a very frightened man. 'You will make the diamond?'

Li nodded.

'Then tell me the reason for this favour you require and I will consider it.'

Li leaned over his desk and buried his head in his hands. 'I must be transferred to another institute. Anywhere. I don't care what work I am asked to do.'

'Why?'

Li gave a long shuddering sigh.

'You must tell me, Professor Li.'

Li drew his hands down his face. 'Chen. It was a long time ago, but he will not have forgotten. I have not forgotten and neither will he.'

Pa stubbed out his cigarette and immediately withdrew another one from the packet.

'I was forced to denounce him in the Cultural Revolution.'

'Why?'

'I had to. I had to protect myself, my work, everything that is my existence.'

Pa shrugged. 'That happened to many, but it was a long time ago.'

Li shook his head from side to side. 'You don't understand. He was going to denounce my work. I was to be accused of being a revisionist capitalist. A bourgeois academic.'

Pa lit up his cigarette. 'And?'

'I had friends who valued my work. They warned me that I had to do something, otherwise I would be sent to the country. I would die. My work would die.' Li raised a shaking hand to his mouth. 'I told a falsehood. I said he had plagiarised the work of others for his own academic advancement. I accused him of corruption in obtaining funds for non-existent research. A friend helped me to forge the documents to prove his guilt.' He licked his lips. 'It was Chen, not I, who was sent to the country.'

Pa slowly rolled his eyes. He had wasted unnecessary energy. The fear of Chen was more than sufficient to get Li down on all fours, whining like a dog. 'Make the diamond, Professor Li, and I will see what I can do.'

Li shook his head back and forth again. 'I live only for my work. Nothing else.' He suddenly raised his head and stared at Pa. 'I will kill myself. Better that, than to wait for Chen to do it.'

Pa drew on his cigarette nervously. The man was in such a state he would probably do it. 'Calm yourself, Professor Li. I think I can probably arrange something. The head of the Lhasa Institute is retiring. I will see that you replace him.'

Li looked at him, his mouth working with emotion. He pushed his chair away from his desk and stood up. 'Excuse me, Vice-leader Pa, but I need to compose myself. Excuse me.' He rushed past Pa's chair and out of the office.

Pa paced up and down the office almost in as much agitation as Li had done. Li had been gone almost five minutes. He checked his watch, half expecting to hear the sound of a single gun-shot. He spun around as Li quietly opened the door and came into the room. Li nodded to him as if to indicate that everything was now all right. As he passed by Pa's side, Pa caught a whiff of vomit on Li's breath and turned his face away. Li sat down at his desk and clasped his hands in front of him. 'You say that the head of Lhasa Institute is retiring?'

'Yes. You will replace him within the week.'

'Chen may not agree.'

'For some reason, and I don't know why, Chen has left as quickly as he arrived. He has called a meeting of the Group for next week. I will see that your appointment receives approval in his absence.'

'I will be safe there?'

'You should be. You are probably aware that the institute is concerned with research for the testing site at Qinghai. Your work on ultrasonic sound levitation is not incompatible with their research into nuclear fusion. You will, of course, come under the direct command of the Central Military Commission for Scientific Advancement.'

Li gave a slow nod of his head. 'Of which you are the head.'

'And over which Chen Chih has no authority.'

'He may in the future.'

'Let us take things one step at a time, Professor Li.'

Li nodded again.

'Make the diamond. Pack your bags and be ready to travel as soon as the diamond is ready.'

Li raised his head and stared up at Pa, as if in homage to an awesome deity. 'I will make the most beautiful diamond in the world, in return for this great favour you bestow.'

Pa smiled.

Marti knelt down and felt under the doormat of the apartment in Cheung Chau for the key to the front door. She gave a quick sigh of irritation when she picked up the mat and discovered that the key had been removed.

'Miss Van den Fleet?'

Marti turned and stood up quickly at the sight of Mrs Bachmann. 'Oh, hello.'

Mrs Bachmann held up the key to the front door. 'Your belongings arrived yesterday. I told the man to put them in the apartment for you. I did not think it wise to leave the key out.'

'Oh, thank you, Mrs Bachmann. That was very thoughtful.'

Mrs Bachmann stared at her with open curiosity. 'A bouquet of roses arrived also. I took them in and put them in water. I did not think you would like them to wilt before you arrived.'

Marti smiled apologetically. 'I am making a nuisance of myself before I settle in. Thank you for dealing with things for me.'

'Flowers are expensive. It is a waste to let them die.' Mrs Bachmann held the key out to Marti. 'I have baked for my husband this morning. Come and have coffee and cake when you are ready. You can collect the flowers, too.'

Marti smiled again. 'Thank you. Was there any message with the flowers?'

'I have it here.' Mrs Bachmann pulled a small envelope from the pocket of her apron. 'I thought you would want to see it now.'

'Thank you.' Marti slipped the envelope in her pocket. 'If I come round in half an hour, will that be convenient?'

'Yes, any time.'

Marti slotted the key into the keyhole and opened the front door. As she closed the door she caught sight of Mrs Bachmann still standing in the small corridor, watching her intently. Marti raised an eyebrow. Strange woman.

The light on the answering machine glowed intermittently, indicating that it had been activated. Marti pressed the playback key and pulled the envelope out from her pocket. The card inside had a neatly copied message. 'See you very soon. B.' She slid the card back into the envelope. Making love with Beni had made her feel erotic.

It wasn't until she was on the plane and flying back to Hong Kong that she had the time to luxuriate in the discovery. She replayed the telephone messages again and made a quick note on the pad by the answering machine. Erwin Klein was abroad for three days, but if Marti had any concerns she should speak to Mrs Bachmann. She listened to Beni's slightly husky voice and smiled to herself at the images it conjured up. She wrote down the Kuwaiti telephone number, as he explained that a message would eventually reach him via that number, wherever he was, but he would appreciate it if she only used it in an emergency, and would she please erase it from the tape when she had made a note of it.

Marti picked up the book of international telephone codes and flicked through it. She made a note of the dialling code for Belgium on the note pad and stared at it thoughtfully, undecided whether she should call Hendrik or not. As soon as she had had a chance to have a quiet word with James when he had collected her at the airport, she had mentioned Tony Bergman's suspicions that the Japanese were stockpiling. James had nodded and said he had heard the rumour also. People could get their fingers burnt if they weren't very careful. She glanced at her watch. It would be almost time for dinner in Antwerp. She picked up the telephone and dialled her father's number. It rang out for such a long time that she felt a sudden panic, believing that something must have happened to her father. She let her breath out when she heard the housekeeper's voice. 'Hello, yes I am well, thank you. Can I speak to my father, please, or if not, Hendrik if he is home?' She frowned to herself as she heard faint whispering then the sound of Hendrik's voice on the line. 'Hello, Hendrik? How's Father?'

'Much the same. The housekeeper says he's just fallen asleep in front of the television.'

'Oh, well, don't disturb him. Hendrik, I actually wanted to have a word with you.'

'Oh yeah.'

She grimaced as his voice became taut, guarded. 'Look, I had to go to New York this week and –'

'I know. A little bird told me.'

She blinked in surprise. 'Who told you?'

'Christian.'

She raised one eyebrow. Christian didn't waste time. 'Hendrik, I simply don't know whether you have heard or not, but I was speaking to Tony Bergman while I was in New York and he says he is pretty sure the Japanese are stockpiling.'

'So?'

She took a deep breath. Why she was bothering at all was a mystery. 'So, it could be that when they stop buying and hold back, it will force the market price right down. There will be a terrific glut with no outlet.'

'Not necessarily so. Anyway, it's only rumour.'

'Yes, but the Japanese have been gearing up to a fight with the IDE for some time, I think. Their market is strong enough to rock the boat quite a bit.'

'Well, I'm glad to hear going to New York has suddenly turned you into an expert on the Japanese.'

She sighed again. 'Hendrik, I only mentioned it because you said you were expanding into the Japanese market and I just wondered if you had heard this news or not.'

Hendrik gave a snort of laughter. 'Well, thank you very much for your concern, Marti. I really don't know how I could manage to run Van den Fleet's without these terribly important little morsels of information from you, I'm sure.'

'Look, just forget I spoke, Hendrik. Give my love to Father.'

'OK.'

She stared at the telephone as the line went dead and shook her head to herself. She was a fool. A complete fool. She should have known trying to do Hendrik a favour was a waste of time. She checked her watch again. There was time to unpack a few items and try to make the apartment feel a little like home. She tapped a finger on her forehead when she remembered Beni's flowers and the invitation to cake and coffee at Mrs Bachmann's. Perhaps she should get that over with first.

Chan Chunling stared out of the window of the taxi as it honked its way through the crowds of cyclists wearily making their way home from the factories in Anshan. He drew on his cigarette. Professor Li had seemed strangely excited about something when he had spoken to him on the telephone. When questioned he had refused to say anything except that the diamond would be ready the day after tomorrow. It wasn't until Chan had put the telephone down that he realised that Li had spoken in the singular. He stubbed out his cigarette as the taxi swung into the street leading up to the Sound and Vibration Institute. Perhaps it was just a slip of the tongue, but then Li was always very precise in his speech. He was also not given to displays of anything, least of all excitement. Chan gave an unconscious shrug of his shoulders. Perhaps he had met with success with one of his more obscure experiments.

Professor Li darted about the office, offering Chan a chair, wiping an ashtray clean with his handkerchief, hastily dismissing the young technician who had brought in a tray of tea with dire threats if he and Director Chan were disturbed. Chan sat down and lit up a cigarette, wondering when Li's manic activity would finally come to a halt. Li went to the door, opened it, looked outside to the left and to the right then closed it again. He rushed back to his desk and removed a small lumpy parcel from the pocket of his coat. He removed the wrappings and set the diamond on the desk in front of Chan.

Chan stared open-mouthed at the diamond. He looked up at Li then back to the diamond. A horrible suspicion was forming in his mind. Li looked at him, his eyes strangely bright. 'What do you think of it?'

'It is beautiful.'

'Yes, it is, isn't it?' Li picked the diamond up and placed it back into its wrappings. 'It weighs 200 carats. Uncut, it actually weighed 375 carats.'

Chan leaned forward and stubbed his cigarette out, although he had smoked only half of it. 'Why have you made such a large stone?'

'I was instructed to, and you are instructed to sell it.'

Chan stared at him in stunned silence.

Li ran a finger around the pear-shaped diamond. He gave a strange shrill laugh. 'You know, I didn't believe I could produce such a thing of great beauty, but I have, haven't I?'

Chan continued staring at him. 'You are mad. That can never be sold without all of us ending up in front of a firing squad. Our esteemed comrade is mad, too.'

'So we are mad. What does it matter? Your instructions are to sell it to the highest bidder. The starting price is to be $1 million.'

Chan felt cold sweat breaking out in the middle of his back. 'You don't know what you are saying. You cannot present a stone of that size for sale. It is lunacy. Questions will be asked. Important questions that will have to be answered. What is its origin? Why is it up for sale?'

Li shrugged. 'Those are your problems, not mine.'

Chan pulled another cigarette from the packet. 'May I remind you that they are *our* problems, Professor Li, and I am telling you that it cannot be done.'

'It must be done. Listen, Director Chan, I will let you into a secret. It will be the last sale.' Li gave a shrill little laugh again. 'Bright Mountain will no longer exist.'

'What do you mean?' Chan stared suspiciously at him. Li had definitely been drinking.

Li got up and came to stand in front of Chan. 'This is going to be the very last time that you and I will meet. Pa Jiaming is releasing us from our task when the diamond is sold.'

Chan's eyes flickered for a moment. He paused to light the cigarette. So that was the name of the 'faceless one'. Pa Jiaming. 'Why doesn't he want any more diamonds sold?'

'I think because of the new premier of the Leading Group for High Technology. Things are changing, Director Chan. I am leaving here to take up another position.'

'What is going to happen to me?'

Li shrugged. 'As far as I know, nothing. Unless you are foolish enough to do something very stupid. Like refuse to sell the diamond.'

Chan glanced around the room. He wanted to believe what Li was saying, but it was too good to be true. Li reached out and shook his arm. 'Listen to me, Director Chan. I am authorised to tell you that this will be the last sale. Bright Mountain will no longer exist. If we both carry out our tasks efficiently, we will no longer be required, both of us will be free. Don't you understand what that means?'

Chan slowly nodded his head. 'And if we fail, Professor Li. What if we fail?'

'I am also authorised to tell you that we will both be shot. So we do what we are told. I have completed my task. You must now complete yours.'

Chan stared blankly at the far wall, his mind frantically trying to scrape together some skeletal plan of action that could possibly meet this latest and suicidal demand. He drew on his cigarette, scattering down his front the length of ash that had formed. He quickly brushed it away. 'You do realise that a stone of this weight and quality will have to be sold through the Intercontinental Diamond Exchange?'

'No, no. You must only use your existing channels of business. It will be safer for all of us that way.'

Chan raised his eyebrows until they almost reached his hairline. He doubted that very much. Li tugged at his sleeve again. 'You have no choice. You must sell the diamond. You have no choice, if you wish to be free.'

Chan dropped his head back and shut his eyes. 'Can we really believe the word of Pa?'

'Yes, yes. I have told you, if we complete this last task, we shall never be troubled again. Ever.'

Chan lowered his head. 'Very well, but I do not know how I am going to explain the existence of the diamond.'

Li made a hissing sound through his teeth. 'Be logical, Director Chan. You sold the other diamonds. What did you say about them?'

'I told James Wu that they were Cambodian, but that it was to be kept strictly confidential.'

'Well, use the same story.'

'How can I? Now it is you who is not being logical. How can I suddenly arrive in Hong Kong with what could possibly be one of the world's largest diamonds and simply say it is from Cambodia?'

Li clasped his arms across his chest. He did not truthfully know the answer to that question.

Chan rubbed at his brow, dragging his fingers across one eye. Freedom from this torture, this fear of discovery, was worth the greatest risk of all. There would be no more hated visits to the Temple. No more nights lying shivering in bed, imagining the terrible things that could easily happen to him, his wife, his children. He got up from his chair, 'I will do my best. The gods will either protect us or not.'

Li looked at him in disgust. 'What is this talk of gods? It is man's endeavours that achieve.'

Chan nodded. 'I need to get back to Shanghai as soon as I can. I'll take the usual parcel of diamonds with me and get those out of the way first.'

Li looked at him in puzzlement. 'What are you talking about?'

'The diamonds. Our esteemed comrade called me up and told me to collect another parcel.'

'I have had no instructions. I was only told to make this single diamond. Nothing more.'

Chan scratched at his head. 'And I was instructed to collect a parcel of diamonds without delay. I was told what would happen to me if I didn't.'

'Wait one moment. You must have made a mistake. I will call Pa Jiaming. He will confirm or deny what you say.'

Chan glanced at him almost enviously. 'You have a number where you can reach him?'

'Of course. How else could I call him, if I didn't have one?' Li shook his head to himself, as if wearying of Chan's stupidity.

Li put the telephone down and looked across at Chan. 'The matter is settled. I have spoken to Pa Jiaming. Forget about the parcel of diamonds. I was correct. He authorised only one diamond.'

'But –'

'But nothing, Director Chan. You are to ignore any instructions you may have previously received.' Li's voice took on an imperious note. 'You will only take instructions from me and no one else, until the diamond has been sold. Those are Pa's own words.'

'Very well.' Chan reached out and picked up the diamond. A feeling of nausea swept over him as he placed it in his briefcase. May the gods protect him.

James snapped his briefcase shut and smiled. 'I leave James Wu and Company in your safe hands, Marti.'

'Don't worry, James. I promise not to do anything you wouldn't do.'

'Er, until we hear from the Great One.'

'The who?'

James grinned. 'That is what I call Christian Debilius. The Great One.'

'Apt title. Sorry, I interrupted you. You were saying?'

'Keep any Japanese enquiries on hold. I should be back from New York by tomorrow night. I don't know what Debilius intends doing about the Japanese, until his address at option-bearers' day, but the Japanese have tended to concentrate on buying up the larger roughs, so if Debilius runs to form, he will increase the price of large roughs again on option day. He may also hold a lot back in reserve, then flood the market as soon as the Japanese try to manipulate it.'

'Which will teach the Japanese not to speculate.'

'True, but I want to avoid suffering along with them. Debilius doesn't allow anyone to get the better of him, but his actions take time to have any effect on the market. Anyway, as soon as I know what we have in our box, I'll call you and let you know. If it's large roughs, I think we should hang on to our supply of small roughs. The scarcity of small roughs in the pipeline is bound to raise the price. If we get an abundance of small roughs, then I want to hold back our stock of best large roughs, until the market has stabilised. I had a call from Tony Bergman. We are of like mind on this. He has asked everyone to attend a private meeting with him.'

'What's it about?'

He shrugged. 'He didn't say too much. Whatever Debilius does, I think Tony's looking for stronger, organised action amongst the dealers.' James checked his watch. 'Well, I must be off. Thanks for looking after Anna for me.'

Marti laughed. 'I honestly don't think Anna needs looking after, James. She is a grown woman.'

'You know what I mean. She is very excited about this commission from Beni Yasim, but she does find meeting strangers for the first time rather intimidating.'

'Don't worry about a thing. I am going to the boutique with Beni, so introductions will be properly conducted. Anna will not be made to feel any embarrassment.'

He smiled wryly. Marti read people like others read books. It was what made her an exceptionally talented dealer.

Pa Jiaming frowned in irritation. He got up from his chair and went to his son's bedroom and banged on the door.

'Turn that music down.' He went back into the living room and resumed his casual study of the newspaper. He glanced at the door. The sound from the other room had been marginally reduced. He sighed to himself. Why his son should have such an appetite for Western music was beyond him. He flung the newspaper on the floor and got up to switch the television on. At least it would drown the cacophony coming from next door.

Having turned the television on, Pa folded his arms and went to the window. He looked down on to the courtyard below at the three uppermost branches of the cherry tree. Of the three men, only one could be trying to cheat him. He sighed heavily. If it had been Li and Chan, or either of them, they would have kept it a secret from him. They were also too fearful to do anything, other than what they were told.

Pa's wife came into the room. 'Jiaming, when do you wish to eat? I would like to visit my sister when we have eaten.' He didn't reply and she came to his side. 'Jiaming, is there something wrong?'

'Yes, but do not let it worry you.'

'Then let us eat, Jiaming.'

'I will come in a moment.'

She shot him an anxious glance, but refrained from questioning him further and returned to the kitchen.

Pa turned back to the window. Ka-Shing. He was the only one of the three men who was cheating him. Li had been insistent that Chan had been ordered to produce a further parcel of diamonds. An order that had not come from himself. He turned away from the window and went to switch off the television. Ka-Shing had deceived him and had tried to steal from him. His cousin had brought shame upon himself and his family. He pressed his fingers to his eyelids. No more would Ka-Shing share in his secrets, and nor would he profit from them.

* * *

Marti waited at the ferry pier. She shielded her eyes and could just make out the Hong Kong ferry approaching. She had arrived at the pier ridiculously early, but could not have stayed in the apartment any longer. She had been plagued by an attack of nerves. The sudden telephone call from Beni that he would be in Hong Kong to visit Anna had sent Marti scurrying around the apartment re-arranging everything. Despite her efforts, the apartment still looked cramped and drab. It was not the ideal venue for someone who was used to luxurious surroundings.

Beni stepped off the ferry and quickly looked around. He caught sight of Marti waving and adroitly weaved his way through the crowd of people in front of him. When he reached her side, he brushed her cheek with his mouth and took her arm. 'I can't tell you how much I have longed for this moment. I don't think I will ever forgive you for rushing away from me like that.'

'I'm sorry. Thank you for the beautiful roses.'

'Ah, you received them. Good.' He glanced around as they walked up the street. 'What time is the last ferry back to Hong Kong?'

She felt a stab of disappointment. 'I think about eleven-thirty.' She glanced up at him. He had already set the pattern for their time together. She looked away from him. She had told herself not to become addicted. Unfortunately, Beni was very addictive.

The little dog sitting at the front door of the apartment block stood up and wagged its tail when it saw Marti. Beni glanced apprehensively at it. 'I do not like dogs very much, particularly Chinese dogs and, more particularly, those who bite.'

Marti laughed. 'Don't worry, Heinz is very careful to cultivate anyone's friendship.'

Beni reached down and gave the dog a quick pat on the head. The dog's body swung from side to side in rhythm with his wagging tail. 'Why is he so friendly?'

'His owner is sometimes away, so everybody in the apartment block feeds him, believing no one else has. Mrs Bachmann thinks he must get through about ten meals a day.'

'Who is Mrs Bachmann?'

'My next-door neighbour. She is German. Rather a strange woman, but not too bad when you get to know her.'

Beni stood in the middle of the sitting room and looked around him. Marti bit her lip. He didn't like being here. Beni held out his arms to her. 'I think the word is bijou, yes?'

She laughed despite herself. 'I believe it is.'

'Come here and let me hold you.' He kissed her, then sank his face into her hair. 'Now I feel much better.'

'Would you like a drink?'

'I would love one.'

She moved away from him and went to the rattan chest of drawers that served as a sideboard. The embrace had been less than rapturous. Not like New York. She poured a glass of whisky and handed it to him. 'Please sit down, Beni.'

'Thank you.'

She watched him sit in a chair by the window. She poured herself a glass of vermouth and sat down on the sofa. She gave an awkward smile then took a hasty sip of her drink. He was holding back, distancing himself. Perhaps it had been the sudden appearance of Mrs Bachmann as they walked past her door. She had stared suspiciously at Beni and then at Marti, as if she was convinced she had a whore for a next-door neighbour.

'Is it convenient to visit Anna Wu tomorrow morning?'

She raised her head. 'Yes, everything is organised.' She smiled again, glad for a safe topic of conversation. 'She is looking forward to your visit very much.'

Beni turned to look out of the window. 'You have quite an attractive view from here.'

'Mmm.' She twirled the glass between her fingers again.

'Would you like to go and see the waterfront sometime? It is quite interesting.'

'What a charming idea. I would love to.' He drained his glass and stood up.

'I'll just fetch my coat.' She got up from the sofa and hurried out. She went into the bedroom and stood in front of the mirror. It had been a mistake to invite him. She frowned at herself in irritation. Stop it. He will either stay, or he will go. She opened the door of the wardrobe and took out a coat.

The proprietor of one of the seafood restaurants smiled cheerily at Marti and Beni as he chalked up the evening menu on a blackboard by the entrance.

'Do you like Chinese food, Beni?'

'Like is not a word I would want to use. I admire the freshness of their ingredients, but not always the ingredients themselves.' He tucked her arm through his. 'Shall we walk along the coast? I think maybe it will be a little quieter.'

'Yes, if you want to.'

'Marti, thank you for inviting me here, but I must get back to Hong Kong.'

'Yes, of course. I think there is a ferry back in half an hour.'

'Come back with me, Marti.' He stopped and turned to face her. 'I want to make love to you again, but not here.'

'You don't like the apartment do you?'

'It is fine, but it is not the right place for you and I to make love.'

'And your hotel is.'

'I think so, and don't be offended. I think your apartment is very charming.' His eyes appealed to her to understand. He covered her hand with his. 'Please do not be offended.'

She nodded and they turned to retrace their steps back to the apartment. She tucked her arm more firmly through his. She wanted to make love, too, but couldn't face the

German watchdog again. Mrs Bachmann would no doubt think of some excuse to be at her door when they returned to the apartment.

Fang hurried across the underground private car park to his car. As he unlocked the door and opened it, he found himself slammed up against the side. He moaned as the top of the door bit into his shoulder. His head was pulled back and he stared up helplessly at the strip-lighting in the ceiling.

'Mr Heung wants to see you with the merchandise. Day after tomorrow.' Busy glanced around the car park as he spoke.

'I have to go to Shanghai first. I won't be back in time.'

'Mr Heung likes everyone to be punctual. He is a busy man.'

Fang tried to turn his head as he heard a vehicle approaching very fast, its tyres squealing. He gasped as an unseen force bore down on him, making him sag at the knees. Busy pushed him face forwards onto the car then sprang into the back seat of the waiting vehicle. Fang gripped the door handle and struggled to his feet in time to see a blaze of red light as the vehicle carrying Busy braked heavily and swung around a concrete pillar. Fang got back into his car and struggled, with shaking fingers, to insert the key into the ignition.

Chan Chunling snapped off the light on his desk and pushed his chair back. He walked across to the window and stared out on to the broad avenue below. He lit a cigarette and leaned against the wall. *Gweilo* greed. That was the only thing he could rely upon to sell the diamond. They could never resist the craving to possess. The idea had come to him in the early hours of yet another sleepless night. He turned quickly as the telephone rang out.

Chan quietly pulled his chair up to his desk as he recognised the voice of the 'faceless one'. He reached across to the ashtray and stubbed out his cigarette as he listened to Fang's almost breathless voice demanding that Chan meet him at the Buddha Temple without fail the next day. Failure to attend or to bring the diamonds would result in punishment. Severe punishment. Chan hesitated for a moment, then hung up. He maintained his grip on the telephone as he pondered whether he had not just made a terrible mistake. He picked up the telephone and hastily dialled Professor Li's number.

Fang swallowed a shot of brandy and refilled the glass. His body shook alternately with rage and a sickening fear. He downed the second brandy then picked up the telephone and tried Chan Chunling's number again. He breathed in deeply when he heard Chan's voice. 'Chan, listen to me.'

'No. You listen to me. I don't know who you are, but I no longer take orders from you.'

Fang gripped the telephone and hissed into it. 'Just be careful what you say, Chan, if you do not wish to suffer the torture of the rats.'

'Tell that to Pa Jiaming.'

Fang's eyes widened in fear as Chan hung up on him. He clutched the telephone to his chest as Chan's words hurtled around his brain. Pa Jiaming. Pa Jiaming. He reached out for the bottle of brandy and slopped some into the glass. If Chan knew Pa's name then he must know his as well. He picked up the glass and drained it in one mouthful. One of the links in the chain had broken, leaving him dangerously vulnerable. He poured another measure of brandy into the glass, spilling some on to the table. He pulled out his handkerchief and mopped at the brandy. Be careful. Be very careful.

Fang clutched at the table with his free hand to steady himself. 'Good evening, Jiaming. I hope I find you and your family well.'

'Yes thank you. I hope I find you the same.' Fang

gripped at the telephone. Jiaming sounded cold and distant, as if conversing with a stranger.

'Yes, I am pleased to say that we are very well. Er – Jiaming, when do you require the next consignment to be authorised? I can be in Shanghai tomorrow.'

'There won't be a consignment.'

Fang shut his eyes.

'There have been changes, important changes. Bright Mountain will need to be shut down.'

Fang leaned against the table for support. 'But why is that, Jiaming?'

'Professor Li is being transferred from Anshan.'

'Can't you prevent it?'

'No.'

'But, but what are we going to do, Jiaming?'

'Do nothing, Ka-Shing. Do nothing more than you have already done.'

Fang clutched a hand to his head. Jiaming was warning him he knew what he had done. He swallowed noisily. 'What about Li and Chan? Can they be trusted?'

Pa gave a sharp laugh. 'Have no fears, Ka-Shing. You will find that they will remain silent about Bright Mountain.'

'Yes, Jiaming.'

'Goodnight.'

'Goodnight.' Fang dropped the telephone and sank to the floor. He drew his knees up to his chest and rocked back and forth. Diamonds. He must have diamonds. Unimaginable pain awaited him if he did not.

The one photograph of Candy that Fang possessed was kept in a padded envelope at the back of the safe. Fang reached inside and pulled the envelope to him. He removed the photograph and looked longingly at it. 'My beloved Candy and my good fortune, gone away. Gone away.' He whimpered to himself as he clutched the photograph to his chest. 'I cannot bear this any longer, Candy.' He staggered and clutched at the door of the safe. 'I have had too much to drink, Candy.' He giggled softly. 'You do not want me when I am drunk, do you?' He reached into the safe and dragged out a small automatic. He closed his fingers over the butt of the gun. He raised the photograph to his face and kissed it, as he pressed the gun to his head and pulled the trigger.

Anna stepped back from the side of the window as a limousine pulled up outside the boutique and Marti stepped out, followed by Beni. Her cheeks flushed. He was very handsome, in the Western manner. She raised a hand to smooth her hair back and straightened the front of her dress with the other.

Marti swept through the door. 'Sorry we are a bit late, Anna.' She half turned to Beni. 'Let me introduce you both. Beni Yasim. Anna Wu.'

Anna held out her hand. 'How do you do, Mr Yasim. I am very pleased to meet you.'

Beni smiled politely. 'How do you do.'

'Would you like some coffee or tea or fruit juice?'

'Coffee will be fine. What about you, Marti?'

'Yes. Would you like me to make it, Anna, then you and Mr Yasim can have a chat?'

Anna looked at Marti anxiously, not wishing to chat alone with Beni so soon after being introduced.

'I am most interested to see some of your work, Miss Wu.' Beni glanced at his watch. 'Unfortunately, I do not have too much time available.'

Anna smiled politely. 'Yes, of course. I understand. Would you like to come through to my workshop?'

'Thank you.'

Marti pushed her way through the workshop door with the tray of coffee. Beni had perched himself on one end of the workbench, arms folded, while Anna described each piece of jewellery she had laid out. Marti smiled to herself. When Anna talked about her work, she forgot about herself and stopped acting like a wilted flower. Marti handed Beni a cup of coffee. His fingers brushed hers as he took hold of the saucer. 'You've done it again, you clever girl. I am very impressed with Miss Wu's work. Very impressed.'

Anna's face flushed. Marti passed her a cup of coffee. 'Have you explained how you use the concept of nature, the things around you, Anna?'

Anna bowed her head slightly, as if embarrassed by Marti's revelation. Beni shot an amused smile in Marti's direction. Anna delicately cleared her throat. 'I try to create a sense of harmony in my designs. In China we call it *da tung*, the great harmony, which we must all strive to achieve. The –'

'Anna, sorry to interrupt.' Marti slung her bag over her shoulder. 'I must get to the office. With James away, I really need to be there. Can I leave you both to continue your conversation?' She smiled encouragingly at Anna. 'See you later?'

Anna nodded. She turned away and looked down at one of the pieces of jewellery, so as not to be seen observing her guests. She rearranged the bracelet slightly. They were doing it again. Talking with their eyes. Like lovers. He was not interested in her jewellery. He was only interested in Marti. She raised her head as Marti left. Beni picked up his cup of coffee. 'You were saying, Miss Wu, that you use nature to achieve harmony in your designs. Isn't that rather difficult? Nature is the least harmonious state I can imagine.'

A puzzled frown appeared on Anna's forehead. 'Forgive me, but I do not think I understand what you mean?'

'Think of a desert. When the khamsin blows it leaves nothing unchanged in its path.'

'Ah yes, I understand.' She nodded politely. She picked up her cup of coffee and took a small sip. Sometimes, foreigners could be very stupid. *Da tung* was achieved by understanding, not by change.

Frankie pulled the cigar from his mouth as he stared at the front page of the newspaper. He reached across to the intercom. 'Find Busy. Now.' He put the newspaper on the desk in front of him and smoothed it flat.

Busy politely knocked on the door and waited until Frankie called out to enter. 'Good morning, Mr Heung. You wanted to see me?'

'Come over here.' Frankie stabbed a finger at the newspaper. 'Would you mind explaining what the hell has been going on?'

Busy leaned over Frankie's shoulder. His lips moved cautiously as he read outloud. ' "Premier Fang Ka-Shing of the Chinese People's Association for International Trade found dead with bullet –" '

Frankie snatched the paper up. 'I said explain it, not fucking read it.'

Busy gave a slight shake of his head. 'Not sure that I can, Mr Heung.'

Frankie pushed his chair back and stood up. 'I can. You just screwed up. What in the name of God did you do to him?'

'Nothing, Mr Heung.'

Frankie stuck his hands on his hips. 'You must have done something, Busy? A guy doesn't blow his brains out without good reason.'

'Maybe it was an accident, Mr Heung?'

Frankie looked up at the ceiling. 'Sure. He was playing Russian roulette with himself. OK. OK. Let's take it a step at a time. The guy had an appointment with me tonight, right?'

'Right.'

'You went along to tell him when the appointment was for, right?'

'Right.'

'So what happened?'

'Nothing, Mr Heung.'

Frankie gave a loud sigh. 'What did you say to him?'

'What you told me to, Mr Heung. To bring the merchandise with him. He said he couldn't get back from Shanghai in time to keep the appointment. I informed him that you expected people to be punctual.'

'And?'

'That's all, Mr Heung.'

'Well, was the guy hysterical or something?'

Busy stared thoughtfully at his shoes for a moment. 'I would say he was surprised by my appearance at that moment in time.' He unconsciously mimicked Frankie's style of speech.

Frankie nodded. ' What happened then?'

'The transportation arrived and I left.'

Frankie sat down in his chair and rested his hands on his thighs. 'Maybe I was a little hasty in removing Candy Lai from the payroll.'

'Oh no, Mr Heung, I wouldn't say that. You had Fang set up. No problem.'

Frankie stared up at Busy. 'There is now. He's dead.' He rubbed a hand across his brow. 'Jesus, how many times do I have to tell you, Busy? A little fear is a good thing. It makes for respect.' He sucked at his front teeth with his tongue. 'But not so much it makes a guy so shit scared he blows his brains out. Do you read me, Busy?'

'Oh yes, Mr Heung.'

'Well, read this as well. I see Fang's demise as sloppy and inefficient management of human resources. If it happens again, you should consider blowing your own brains out, too. Right?'

'But I didn't do anything to the guy. Honest, Mr Heung.'

'OK. Maybe, the guy had other problems. See what you can find out about who's taking over from Fang. I can't keep clients hanging around for ever waiting for information. One other thing. If you come across Ronnie Lee, tell him to call me. I'd like another personal meeting with him before we set the agenda for the full meeting of the fraternity.'

'Get on to it now, Mr Heung.'

Frankie picked up the newspaper and laid it out flat on the desk again. He tugged at his lower lip as he stared at the photograph of Fang. You've just created one hell of a problem for me, Mr Fang.

Marti checked her watch. The office was quiet and now was a good time to call home and check up on her father, but it was still rather early in Antwerp. She glanced up as James's secretary tapped on the door and pushed her head round. 'Miss Van den Fleet, there is a Mr Chan Chunling outside.'

'Has he got an appointment? James didn't mention he had one.'

'No, Miss Van den Fleet, he hasn't. I told him James was away in New York, but he asked if he could see you.'

'OK.' Marti got up and walked around the desk.

Chan held out his hand to Marti. She shook it and noticed it was damp and sweaty. 'I'm afraid James isn't here, Mr Chan. Option-bearers' day tomorrow at the IDE.'

'Ah yes.' Chan glanced around him.

'But please sit down. Can I be of assistance to you?'

'Yes, I think you can.' He sat on the edge of the chair. 'I have been instructed to arrange a sale of a diamond.'

She nodded.

'It is a very special diamond.' He drew his briefcase on to his lap. 'Perhaps you would like to examine it.' He removed a leather pouch from the briefcase and passed it across to her.

She clasped it carefully in both hands. She shot a glance at him. Unless it was some kind of joke, he was talking very, very big. The diamond must weigh more than a hundred grams. She removed the diamond from the bag and set it in front of her. She held her breath for a moment. If it wasn't a fake, then she was looking at one of the largest diamonds since the discovery of the Richmond diamond in the seventies.

Chan clutched at the handle of his briefcase. The gamble had paid off. He could almost smell the *gweilo* greed from where he sat. Marti took out her eyeglass. 'You will excuse me, Mr Chan.' She walked over to the viewing table and snapped on the light. 'You have authentication documents for this?'

'No.'

She turned around to look at him. 'It is extremely unusual for a stone of this kind not to have any.'

He nodded. She turned back to the table and adjusted her eyeglass.

Marti spent five minutes examining the diamond, until her eyes watered so much with the strain, she had to give up. She straightened up and rubbed at her eyes. 'D' grade. Flawless. Clever fake. She placed the stone on the scales and weighed it. 200 carats. And if it wasn't a fake, James wouldn't have to worry about selling another diamond for some time. She returned to the desk and placed the diamond back into the pouch. 'You wish to instruct Wu and Company to sell on your behalf?'

'Yes.'

'I do not have the authority to accept the commission in James's absence, but he should be back the day after tomorrow.'

'How will he sell it?'

'Probably by auction, but I think I should explain, Mr Chan, that this diamond will need at least two separate authentications by respected Western dealers that it is genuine, before we even think of arranging any kind of sale. Its background, history, must be investigated.'

'My client wishes to remain totally anonymous.'

She gave a wry smile. 'Understandable, but without some

background information, he will have very little chance of selling it.'

He stared at her. 'What do you mean? If it is authenticated, what should its history matter?'

'If there is no record anywhere of its existence, then, forgive me, but one has to consider that it is just a very clever fake, or it has been acquired by criminal means.'

'I can assure you that it is neither.'

'With respect, Mr Chan, your assurances will not suffice. Neither would mine, nor James's for that matter.'

Chan reached across the desk and plucked up the pouch. 'Perhaps I should have waited to see Mr Wu.'

'By all means, Mr Chan, I can make an appointment for you now, but may I say that he will only tell you exactly what I have told you.'

He searched in his pockets for his cigarettes and lighter. 'I can only tell what I know about the diamond.' He lit up a cigarette and inhaled deeply. 'It was acquired many, many years ago by a person visiting Thailand. The diamond is believed to have come originally from Cambodia. From a private collection. It is very old. My client was told that the diamond was early nineteenth century.'

She nodded thoughtfully. 'When did it come into your client's hands?'

'I understand recently. It was a deathbed gift. I do not know for why. My client tells me that it must remain a secret.'

'You were told it was early nineteenth century from Cambodia?'

'That is correct.'

She rested her chin on her fingertips. 'Further tests would have to be carried out to establish that the diamond is genuine, but if it is, I would be inclined to date it early twentieth century and from the Russian school.'

He glanced at her sharply. 'Russian?'

'Mmm. The faceting reminds me of the Gorchakov style.

He was a – or rather, the – diamond cutter to the Russian Imperial Court in the very early part of the century. He perfected the cutting style known as inner-fire faceting. It is extremely difficult to do by hand. I suppose that is why he had few imitators. Even Gorchakov was reputed to take up to a year to perfect one stone. His style does, however, create the optimum refraction of light.'

He put the pouch back into his briefcase. The diamond had been fashioned by laser within ten minutes. 'What would be an expected figure if the diamond was put on sale?'

'I couldn't tell you, Mr Chan. Apart from the basic value, you would be dealing with the unknown factor of buyers' interest. Get two or more buyers bidding against each other and the sky can be the limit.'

'A rough guess?'

She pursed her lips. 'With sound authentication, we are possibly talking about $1 million. With some evidence of its history, that could be doubled. I am only guessing, you understand.'

'Who do you think would be interested in such a sale?'

'Japan and the Middle East for certain. You could possibly attract a lot of American interest, as well.'

'I see.' He looked down at the briefcase and lapsed into silence.

'I am so sorry, Mr Chan, I didn't offer coffee. Would you like some?'

'Yes, thank you. I would like some very much.'

She buzzed through to the outer office. 'Coffee please, for Mr Chan.'

Chan lit up another cigarette. 'You seem convinced that the diamond is a fake.'

She smiled. 'I am not convinced, Mr Chan, but neither would I commit myself to its authenticity at this stage. In any event, I think this is properly a matter for James to handle. I am only here in a consultancy capacity.'

James's secretary brought in a tray and placed it on the corner of the desk. She placed a cup of coffee in front of Chan and passed the other to Marti. Chan waited until she had left the office before speaking again. 'Supposing the sale went ahead, my client would wish as little publicity as possible, you understand.'

She gave an amused laugh. 'The buyer would demand it, Mr Chan. The people who would be interested in the diamond would be phobic about the idea of publicity.'

'That is good.' He picked up his cup and took a sip. That piece of information was very good.

Beni opened the door of the hotel suite himself. He grabbed Marti and pulled her inside. 'Thank God, you have arrived.'

She looked at him in alarm. 'Why, what's the matter?'

He kissed her then hugged her to him. 'You have just saved my sanity. After half an hour of your Miss Wu's Confucian theories on life, I needed saving badly.' He kissed her again then led her by the hand to the sofa. 'I adore her designs, Marti, but not her.'

'Why? I don't understand.'

'I just cannot tolerate this superior arrogance the Chinese possess. This belief of theirs that their understanding of life and the universe, and only theirs, is of significance, is worthy of merit.'

'I can't believe you are talking about Anna. She is usually very quiet and the least arrogant person, but I am sorry if she annoyed you.'

'She didn't annoy me, Marti, she simply bored me.'

'Did you give her a commission for the necklace?'

'Yes. I told her to get in touch with you when it is ready. Do you mind?'

'Not at all.'

'Good. Let us have a drink before lunch and concentrate on far more important matters than Miss Wu.'

'What are they?'

'You and I.' He raised her hand to his mouth and kissed it. 'I am afraid it is now my turn to abandon you. I cannot stay overnight. Something has cropped up which requires my attention. I need to leave for Paris this afternoon.'

'Apart from looking very disappointed, I shan't say a word.'

'Thank you. I am sorry, truly sorry, I cannot stay longer. So. Would you like to make love before lunch, or after?'

'Beni, I can't stay longer than an hour. I have to get back to the office. James is away.'

'Then what is it to be? Lunch or love?'

She pursed her lips. 'Difficult decision, Beni.'

He stood up and pulled her to her feet. 'Then I shall make it for you.'

She reached down and snatched up her bag from the sofa. She could always buy a bowl of vegetables with crispy noodles from one of the food stalls in Central, on her way back to the office.

Chan cradled the telephone on his shoulder and raised the bowl to his lips to take a mouthful of chicken soup. He hastily put the bowl down when Professor Li came on the line. 'Ah, Professor Li, I thought I should tell you. I will need to stay in Hong Kong for a couple more days. James Wu is away in New York. I spoke to his consultant, Martina Van den Fleet.'

'Was that wise? Who is she?'

'She is a dealer from Europe. She authenticated one of the previous batches of merchandise. I think she was very impressed with this particular merchandise, but insisted on knowing something of its history.'

'What did you tell her?'

'I made up a story about it being Cambodian. I needn't have bothered. She seemed to have convinced herself it was Russian.'

'Then be very careful, Director Chan.'

'Why?'

'Perhaps I have been too clever, if I am to admit my mistakes. I didn't know what design our esteemed comrade required, so I chose one myself. I have a very old collection of French stereoscopic glass slides. They depict anything from the Eiffel Tower to the British crown jewels. Anything that showed the three-dimensional system to advantage. They were very popular at the turn of the century. Did she say why she thought it was Russian?'

'She talked on about a diamond cutter to the Imperial Court of Russia by the name of Gorchakov.'

'Ah, she is a clever woman. I did wonder if anyone was clever enough to notice. It is a Gorchakov design.'

Chan pushed his bowl of soup away from him. 'I wished you had informed me of that sooner, Professor Li. I now look very stupid, having invented a story about Cambodia. You have made my position extremely difficult.'

'Why so? Now you have two stories. The *gweilos* can choose which one they want to believe.'

'It is not a question of choice. I have to convince them.'

'You will do that, Director Chan, I have no doubt.'

'Thank you, Professor Li, but before any more mistakes are made, how accurate is the design?'

'Extremely accurate. I separated the stereoscopic glass slides and scanned each image separately with a digital scanner. The information was fed into our cad/cam computer to obtain a three-dimensional representation, then the coordinates were fed into the computer that operates the laser.'

'I see.' He didn't see at all, but nothing further would be achieved by admitting that. 'Very well, if you will pass my information on to our esteemed comrade.'

'I will do so. Goodbye Director Chan.'

Chan put the telephone down and stared at the food on the tray. He no longer felt like eating anything. It was a popular pastime to blame the Russians for everything, but passing off a diamond as a Gorchakov gem was another matter.

The man behind the food stall beamed happily at Marti. 'You see, you buy?'

She peered into the various steaming pots. 'Er – you have *fan*?'

'*Fan*, yes, yes.' He immediately flung a handful of noodles into a pot of boiling oil and stirred them.

'And, er –' She looked around the stall, wishing she could remember the name for vegetables.

'Yes, yes?'

'Vegetable?'

'Yes, yes, have vegetable.'

'Thank you.'

He removed the lid from a steamer and deftly scooped delicately shredded slices of vegetables into a bowl then topped them with the fried noodles. She handed over a HK$10 note. He pushed his hand into his apron pocket and gave back HK$2. She put the change into her purse. He was honest, if nothing else. He handed the bowl to her. 'Eat soon, yes.'

'Yes, thank you.' She stepped off the pavement and threaded her way through the crowded street. She hitched her bag higher on her shoulder. If anyone had told her a month ago that she would be buying lunch from a Hong Kong food stall, after making love with Beni Yasim at the Mandarin, she would have thought them completely and utterly mad.

James's secretary handed the telephone to Marti. 'The number is ringing out, Miss Van den Fleet.'

Marti swallowed the last of the steamed vegetables and brushed her hand across her mouth. 'Hello, Marti Van den Fleet here, could I speak to my father, please?' She rolled her eyes upwards as the housekeeper launched into one of her monologues.

'Glad to hear that. Yes. Can I speak to my father now, please? This call is going to cost me an arm and a leg.'

'Ooh, sorry, Miss Van den Fleet. I'll take the telephone to him straight away.'

Marti brushed her hand across her mouth again. 'Hello, Father, how are you?' She pressed a hand to her ear. 'Sorry, can't quite hear you.'

'I said I am all right. How are you?'

'OK. I thought I would call to see how you were, because Hendrik said he was going to New York.'

'Don't worry about me. I'm fine.'

'You won't be lonely?'

'No, no. Johannes is coming round to dinner to keep me company. We are going to have a game of chess afterwards. I beat him last time.'

She laughed. 'Well, you certainly seem in good spirits.'

'I am going out tomorrow afternoon. We are going to drive into the countryside for a breath of good fresh air.'

She widened her eyes in alarm at the thought of the housekeeper attempting to drive and talk at the same time. 'Well, tell the housekeeper to drive very carefully.'

'No, no. She's not driving. Johannes is taking us.'

'Oh, I see. Well, I hope you have a lovely time. I have to go now, Father. Hope to see you very soon.'

'Don't rush home for me. I am feeling very well.'

'OK. Give Johannes my regards. 'Bye.' Marti handed back the telephone to James's secretary. 'Could you make a note of the cost of that call for me?'

'Yes, certainly, Miss Van den Fleet.'

Marti turned away from the window and returned to the desk. She sat back in James's chair and folded her arms. The diamond Chan Chunling had produced, like a rabbit out of a hat, was extraordinary. She felt a surge of excitement. To sell that would be to make the sale of the century.

She leaned forward and pulled a file from the tray by her side. The diamond was probably fake. Some luckless traveller in Thailand had been persuaded into parting with a lot of money for very little. She rested her chin on her hands. She had seen enough fake diamonds in her time to be able to spot one at five miles, but she couldn't find fault with this one. She opened the file. There is always the first time, Martina.

The offices of the Intercontinental Diamond Exchange were discreetly situated in the basements of a Renaissance-style building, in midtown New York. Most passers-by, if they could afford the luxury of pausing for a moment, would have only noticed the large name plaque of Florenz, Stevens, deMagio, Houston Assocs., advertising agents.

Bill Stevens was the senior partner of Florenz, Stevens, deMagio, Houston Assocs., and personally handled the IDE account. He sat with arms folded, while Christian took a telephone call.

'Sorry about that, Bill.' Christian put the telephone down and rested his forearms on the desk in front of him. 'I appreciate that you haven't been given much time on this campaign, but I need to push it through *rapido*.'

'Sure.' Bill got up from his chair and walked across to a row of concept boards lined up on the sofa. 'We have taken maximum utilisation of small diamonds as critical in the campaign, in line with your brief. The concept of the campaign is fantasy. Fantasy is really very strong right now, Christian.'

Christian nodded.

'We have also concentrated on an oriental theme. For one, we feel this does need a separate identity from the hearts campaign we are running later in the year. For two, I thought you might appreciate the irony of an oriental theme.'

Christian gave a low laugh. 'I appreciate your sense of humour, Bill.'

'OK.' Bill folded his arms. 'The concept. It is based on the very old legend of the thousand lotus flowers.' Bill paused, waiting for Christian to ask what the legend was.

'What is this fascinating legend about, Bill?' Christian spoke with a hint of resignation in his voice.

Bill grinned. 'See. You're interested already. The legend of the thousand lotus flowers tells the story of a handsome young prince, expelled from his rightful kingdom by his cruel stepmother. He roams the land far and wide, until one day he is set upon by bandits and robbed of his few miserable possessions, then left to die. A beautiful young peasant girl finds him lying near a cave. The prince manages to raise his hand and cry out for water. She immediately falls in love with him and hurries up the steep hill to a mountain spring and collects fresh water in a large leaf, then carefully carries it down to the dying prince. She cradles his head in her arms and he takes a few sips of water. He dies in her arms and she weeps bitter tears for the handsome prince. As she does so, a thousand lotus spring into bloom on the hillside. A lotus blossom for every tear the beautiful young peasant girl sheds. Forever after, whenever tears of love fall to the ground a lotus blooms eternally.' Bill stepped across to the desk and poured himself a glass of water. 'As you will see from the first and second concept boards, the television commercial will begin with two young lovers quarrelling. The girl rushes away in tears and the angry young man turns away.'

'Ah, Bill, I don't want diamonds associated with such negative emotions.'

Bill held his hand up. 'I know, I know. Just bear with me. Going on to the third and fourth boards. The next shot is the girl alone, reading a book of oriental poetry by the fire. She stares into the fire and imagines the images of the handsome prince and the beautiful peasant girl in the flames. This, Christian, will be done in very, very soft focus. You will like it. The young man rings the doorbell and when the young girl answers it –'

'How young is young, Bill? Seventy-five per cent of the audience must be able to identify with the role models.'

Bill gestured with his hand. 'Indeterminate. Twentyish, thirtyish. OK. So the girl opens the door and he looks contrite and presents her with a gift. She opens it and sees a lotus blossom diamond piece of jewellery. At this point, Christian, we have not decided on exactly what. Discussion is needed on this.'

'A ring, perhaps?'

'That is an excellent idea, Christian.' Bill pointed to the final board. 'The girl throws her arms around the neck of the young man. The final shot is of the smiling, happy face of the girl, with a single tear formed on her cheek. I repeat, Christian, *happy* face of the girl. She is crying tears of happiness not of sadness.' Bill paused for a moment. 'Christian, you have just given me a terrific idea.'

'I thought I paid you to come up with the ideas.'

Bill grinned. 'How about this? Make the piece of jewellery a ring. Definite. Commercial ends with a close-up shot of her hand around the guy's neck and the ring, then track in the voice-over. Love blooms eternally with a lotus blossom diamond.'

Christian nodded his head slowly.

'This concept is very strong, Christian. The diamonds can be marketed as single lotus blossoms or as clusters of lotus flowers. The make-up potential is enormous. One teardrop or many. A guy can buy a whole waterfall of tears if he wants to. What do you think?' Bill raised his eyebrows at Christian, as if appealing for him to agree.

Christian got up from his desk and came to stand in front of the concept boards. He swept the jacket of his suit back and rested his hands on his hips. 'The girl's tears must be strongly identified with happiness, not sadness.'

'You got it.'

Christian pushed his hands into his pockets. 'What's the motivation here? Guilt?'

Bill nodded. 'Got it in one. You've been a bad guy. Diamonds make you both feel better.'

Christian bent down and examined that final concept board. 'I like this very much, Bill.'

Bill relaxed his shoulders. Because the IDE account was the cornerstone of the agency's output, he and two assistants had brainstormed through half the night to come up with the concept. 'I've got everyone lined up. We can start shooting tomorrow, Christian.'

'What's wrong with today?'

'We could certainly make a start.'

'I need a demo video as soon as possible, Bill. My dealers have to know that they are going to be able to shift small roughs with no problems.'

'Understood. I'll get it to you as soon as I can, together with billboard and magazine support material.'

'I am obliged to you, Bill. I'm having a meeting with the heads of the various merchants' associations before box opening. Can you repeat this presentation to them? Nine o'clock?'

'Sure, no problem.'

'OK, let's grab some breakfast.'

'Could I possibly use your telephone for a moment, Christian?'

'Go ahead.'

'I think I can get some blow-ups ready of the actress we've got lined up for the role of the girl. She's really something. You'll like her, Christian.'

'I don't want anyone too sexy. We're selling love. Not a quick fuck.'

'No, no, she's not sexy-sexy. She's just got something about her. I fell for it as soon as I saw her, and I don't fall easy. Assured, but a hint of vulnerability.'

'Will the older woman identify with her?'

'The older guy certainly will. Look, Christian, we need to discuss this in depth, but we would like to do separate material for the mature woman. Targeting is more accurate that way.'

'What did you have in mind?'

'With this tears of happiness concept, the sky's the limit, Christian. Birth. Silver wedding. First grandchild. The potential is limitless.'

Christian smiled for the first time.

Tony Bergman slung one arm over the back of his chair as Bill Stevens wound up the presentation for the visiting heads of merchant associations. Bill stepped into the centre of the room. 'We are convinced, gentlemen, that the tears of happiness concept provides enormous potential for the marketing of diamonds within the small to very small range. As you will see from the use of concept boards, we have responded to the immediacy of this campaign. We hope to have a demonstration video very, very shortly. In the meantime, I can show you a blow-up of the actress who will be playing the role of the girl.' Bill pulled a cloth from a large photograph propped up against Christian's desk. 'I think you will agree, gentlemen, that she has a face to remember.'

Tony leaned forward to take a closer look. 'I'd certainly like to remember her telephone number.'

A ripple of laughter carried around the office. Christian straightened up from leaning against the far wall. 'What do you think, Tony?'

Tony put his head on one side. 'She kind of draws you to her, doesn't she?'

Bill smiled in quiet satisfaction.

Tony raised his hands to his head and leaned back in his chair. 'I like the concept. It's really strong. What kind of sales forecast are we looking at, Christian?'

'We're still running figures through the computer, but we should be looking at $1.56 billion.'

Tony nodded. He stood up and walked over to take a

closer look at the blow-up. 'I don't know what the other guys think but, you know, I think I really prefer this to the hearts campaign.'

There was a general murmur of agreement.

Christian returned to his desk and perched on the corner, 'OK, Tony, perhaps we should have an in-depth discussion on this sometime, if you feel strongly about it. Bill, there's no reason why this campaign couldn't be extended is there?'

'None at all, Christian. We are still in the ideas stage at this moment in time, but we do propose to present material closely targeting the mature woman. The milestones in her life, of birth, silver wedding, grandchild, etcetera.'

Tony nodded. 'That's really strong. You know, we should be really going for the older, more affluent purchaser. There's a lot of them out there.'

Christian nodded his head vigorously. 'We shall be devising a very tight customer profile on this, Tony.' He glanced at his watch. 'Well, gentlemen, before we make our way to the viewing hall, I will reiterate my earlier words briefly. Although there is no firm evidence that the Japanese are stockpiling large roughs, I do most seriously take into account your anxieties. I have therefore only allowed small to very small roughs in the boxes this month. If the Japanese do hold back from the market, I think we have clearly demonstrated that the IDE intends to offer full support not only to its producers, but also to its dealers. The tears of happiness campaign will stimulate the market for small roughs, I think you will all agree.' Christian gave a brief nod of his head to indicate that he had finished.

Tony stood up and straightened his jacket. 'And those goddam Japanese are going to be left sitting on a heap of roughs that nobody wants.'

'Quite.'

'Nice work, Christian.'

Christian allowed himself a small smile. Tony grinned. 'Don't forget my commission, Christian. I'm the guy who feeds you your best lines.' Christian's smile managed to remain in place.

The attendants in the viewing hall placed a box in front of each dealer. The silence was broken only by the occasional clearing of a throat, the rustle of someone shifting position in their chair. The attendants stood back and a bell rang out. Each option bearer quickly reached out for his individual box. Christian stood at the far end of the hall, arms folded. His gaze swept over the bent heads of the dealers. The silence was swiftly broken by the sound of voices. Hands were raised in the air, as dealers signalled their acceptance of their boxes. Some pulled personal telephones from their pockets and began talking into them urgently. Others sprinted to the main doors leading to the reception area and the banks of telephones available for their personal use.

Hendrik stared at the box in front of him, as if not quite believing what he was seeing. He clenched his fists as burning anger surged through him. Debilius had promised he would upgrade the Van den Fleet box. Bastard. There wasn't one large rough in it. He looked up as an invisible voice announced over the PAS that the option period would end in one minute. Hendrik reluctantly raised his arm to indicate acceptance of the box. An attendant moved forward and quickly sealed the box. 'The IDE thanks you for your custom, Mr Van den Fleet.' He moved along to the man on Hendrik's right and also sealed the box in front of him. 'The IDE thanks you for your custom, Señor Domingo.'

Hendrik dragged his chair back and strode over to where Christian stood.

Christian glanced out of the corner of his eye and saw Hendrik approaching. He turned his back and engaged the senior security guard in conversation. Hendrik stood to one side, but in Christian's vision, and waited impatiently. Christian finished speaking to the guard then turned to look at Hendrik, as if he had only just realised he was there. 'Hendrik, good to see you. Sorry we couldn't dine last night. My time frame was just impossible.'

'Could I have a word in private, please, Christian?'

'Yes, of course. Come this way.' Christian led the way out into the reception area and to a small office.

Hendrik declined Christian's invitation to sit down. 'I think there must have been some mistake, Christian, with Van den Fleet's box.'

'I trust not, Hendrik. That would be unthinkable.'

'Well, you promised to upgrade our box this month and there isn't a single large rough in it.'

'Yes, that is quite correct.'

'But you said you would upgrade our box. It is vital to me to have a supply of large roughs.'

A small frown appeared on Christian's face. 'Ah, you did receive a copy of the circular, didn't you, when you came in?'

'Yes.'

'Well, I think it made it quite clear that there would be no large roughs available. The IDE has been asked to respond strongly to the threat of the Japanese stockpiling.'

Hendrik rubbed a hand across his brow. 'Yes, I know that, Christian, but we agreed that I would get a higher percentage of large roughs this month. I need them urgently to upgrade Van den Fleet's sales.'

'But that was before the Japanese problem cropped up.'

'I need to get into the Japanese market now. I need to make a profit now. Van den Fleet's has lagged behind other dealers, because of the quality of its boxes.'

Christian stared at him coldly. 'That is quite untrue, Hendrik. Van den Fleet's problems have been caused by not taking up its options.'

Hendrik took in an unsteady breath. 'I had believed you understood the problems that I have inherited at Van den Fleet's, Christian.'

'Indeed I do.'

'Then you must understand that I need a supply of large roughs.'

Christian turned towards the door. 'I think you will find the contents of your box more than adequate, Hendrik. The tears of happiness campaign will boost considerably the sale of small roughs. You will not lose out. I can assure you that the IDE has and is taking every precaution to protect the interests of its members.'

'I know that, Christian, but I am talking about a very different situation. I am not talking about losing out. I am talking about having lost out. I need to recoup those lost profits.'

Christian placed his hand on the door knob. 'I am sure you will, Hendrik.'

'But I need a supply of large roughs to do that. I must get into the Japanese market before it collapses.'

'I would not advise that, Hendrik.'

'Why not? It may not even happen.'

'Do you always wait until it rains before carrying an umbrella?'

'Come on, Christian, it's only a rumour at the moment.'

'There is circumstantial evidence. The Japanese have specifically bought large roughs only.'

'I'm willing to take the risk. I have no choice. Can't you make an exception under the circumstances? Van den Fleet's circumstances.'

'An exception.' Christian spoke in deliberately shocked tones. 'I couldn't do that, Hendrik. All members must be treated equally and fairly. I am sure you would be most upset to discover that the IDE had given another member preference, purely because of his circumstances.' He turned the knob and opened the door. 'The IDE does not function in that manner. It looks after all members' interests, Hendrik. All. Now, if you will excuse me, I have a meeting to attend.'

Hendrik turned round and smashed his fist against the wall. He turned and leaned against the wall, and pulled out a packet of cigarettes. The advertising campaign would take six months to show effect. He had to be effective now. He lit up a cigarette. God damn Father for leaving things so late.

Marti rushed into the sitting room and picked up the telephone.

'James, I thought it might be you.'

'Marti, we've got small roughs. Hold back on the medium and large roughs, will you?'

'Will do.'

'Debilius has been forced to take the Japanese threat seriously. He's launching a new advertising campaign. It is very exciting. Lots of potential.'

'Good. Boosting sales means business for everybody.'

'True. Saw your brother, Hendrik. He didn't give me a chance to speak to him, I'm afraid.'

She rolled her eyes. 'He wasn't rude to you, was he?'

'No. Don't worry about it. How are things?'

'I've been fending off the Japanese most of the day. I think there is definitely something going on, James. You were right.'

'Of course.' He laughed. 'I am always right.'

'James, Mr Chan turned up at the office yesterday. He has a single piece of merchandise his client wishes to sell. I haven't committed you to anything and I reserve my judgement on its genuineness, but if it is for real, we are talking double telephone numbers.'

'Marti, I'm rather busy right now. Let me call you when I get back to the hotel. We can discuss this properly.'

She sensed a hidden meaning in his words. 'OK, James.'

'Get back to you in half an hour.'

''Bye.' She checked her watch and decided to postpone washing her hair until James had called back.

Marti switched off the television and picked up the telephone when it rang again. 'Hello, James.'

'Sorry about that, Marti. I don't trust the telephones at the IDE.'

'Why?'

'I think they tape all the conversations. I think they offer free use of the telephones as an incentive. So. What's this about Chan?'

'He has produced a polished diamond "D" grade flawless, weighing 200 carats, in perfect condition.'

'Will you repeat that?'

'Grade "D" flawless. 200 carats.'

He gave a faint laugh. 'That was what I thought you said.'

'I think it's genuine, but I am a bit suspicious. There is no authentication. Chan is very non-communicative about its history.'

'Chan usually is.'

'He says it is believed to be early nineteenth century and Cambodian. I would not date it earlier than the beginning of this century, possibly late 1800s at the most. From the faceting, I think it's from the Russian school. A Gorchakov or a very clever likeness.'

'I see.' James' voice suddenly sounded faint. 'What have you arranged with him?'

'He's coming back when you return. I have been doing some checking up. There are ten Gorchakov gems catalogued, as far as I can make out, but there are estimated to be a further two or possibly three in private hands. Apparently Gorchakov's own records of his work were partially destroyed during the Russian revolution, so it's difficult to be accurate.'

'Fascinating.'

'You'll be even more fascinated when you see it, James. I haven't seen anything like it since the Richmond diamond. If it is genuine, it is a remarkable piece of work. The stone is sort of egg-shaped and the faceting on both sides is, to my eye anyway, absolutely identical. One cannot imagine how even the most experienced cutter could be so accurate.'

'OK, Marti, I'll come back right away. I was going to a meeting with Tony Bergman, but I'll skip that. I'll try and get the soonest flight to Hong Kong.'

'I think you should, James.'

'Er, did you look after Mr Chan?'

She laughed. 'I didn't frighten him away, if that's what you mean. Seriously, I just said that in my capacity as a consultant I couldn't really advise him. It was definitely a matter that must be dealt with by you.'

'Thanks, Marti. See you as soon as I can.'

Marti put the telephone down and switched on the television again. She watched the figures on the screen with half an eye. The Sheik would kill for that stone. She got up and went to the kitchen to make a hot drink. But Beni would have a fight on his hands with the Japanese, if it went to auction.

Hendrik slid his arm along the back seat of the cab. 'It's really good to see you again, Melanie.'

'It was just great going over old times. I enjoyed it.'

He leaned over and kissed her. She turned her head away from the aggressively searching mouth. 'Hey, take it easy, Hendrik.'

He forced his hand into the front of her blouse. 'You didn't object the last time we saw each other.'

She grabbed at his hand. 'That was two years ago.'

He leaned back in the seat and stared out of the window. He was too old to play will-she-won't-she games. She had been the sixth girl he had rung when he had arrived in New York and the only one still at the same address. He stroked her thigh. 'You used to tell me I was very good in bed in those days.'

She laughed and patted his hand. 'Weren't we all?'

The cab pulled up outside the apartment block where

Melanie lived. She lightly kissed Hendrik on the cheek. 'It's really been a great evening, Hendrik. Goodnight.'

Before he could open his mouth to speak, she had stepped out of the cab and shut the door on him. He struggled out of the cab and hurried after her up the steps to the front door. 'Melanie, what are you doing?'

She turned back to him. 'I am saying goodnight, Hendrik.'

'Melanie, come on, stop fooling around. You don't have to lead me on.'

'I'm not leading anyone on, Hendrik.'

'Give me your key.'

'I can't do that.'

'Melanie, let's not play games. I want you, you want me. Things didn't used to be so complicated between us.'

She sighed. 'Hendrik, you are just not listening to me. That was a long time ago. You have this – ah – certain animalistic energy, which is a terrific turn-on for a girl, believe me, but I promised myself to remain celibate until the New Year.'

'Is this some kind of joke?'

She shook her head. 'No, and I know you will respect my feelings, because you are a nice guy.'

His face flushed in sudden anger. 'Feelings? You let me buy you dinner, expensive wine, get you a cab, then you tell me to go and screw myself?'

'Take it easy, Hendrik. You've been in Zaire a long time. Things have changed a lot in New York since you were here. It's nothing personal, you understand. Our time together has been wonderful. I have enjoyed your company. I hope you have enjoyed mine. Thank you.'

The driver stuck his head out of the window of the cab. 'Hey, fella, remember you're paying for my time back here.'

Hendrik turned and waved to him to wait. Melanie quickly opened the door and slipped inside the hall.

Hendrik turned back to the door and found it shut in his face. He pounded on it with his fist. He waited for a few seconds then turned on his heel and ran down the steps to the cab. He flung himself into the back seat. 'Know anywhere where a guy can get some fun?'

'Sure. What's your preference? Male? Female? Black? White?'

Hendrik pulled out a packet of cigarettes. 'Female. The colour doesn't bother me.'

'OK, pal.' The driver glanced backwards, then pulled away from the kerb.

Hendrik removed his tie and unbuttoned the collar of his shirt. He sat on the edge of the bed and stared at the telephone, willing it to ring out. He reached for the bottle of whisky on the bedside table and unscrewed the top. He had contacted twenty dealers and not one would part with one single large rough. He poured a measure of whisky into the glass. Bastards. They were all hanging on because they could afford to. He swallowed a mouthful of whisky. So would he, if he was in such a fortunate position. He set the glass down on the table when the telephone rang.

'Your call to Zaire, Mr Van den Fleet.'

'Thanks. Gerry, that you?'

'Hi. Nice to hear from you. How's the big wide world?'

'OK. Look Gerry, I need a favour doing.'

'Shoot.'

'I need a quantity of large roughs urgently. Can do?'

'Ah, do I take it this would be a private transaction? Not through the IDE?'

'You could take it that way.'

'Sorry, Hendrik. No can do. If the IDE found out, I would be blown away, before I could draw breath.'

'Come on, who's going to find out?'

'Sorry, Hendrik, I can't take the risk.'

'You've done it before.'

'In the old days, maybe, but with everything computerised things are different.'

'Forget I asked.'

'Wait a minute, Hendrik, don't get annoyed. Look, let me ask around. I'll call you back.'

'Owe you one, if you do.'

'OK.'

Hendrik put the telephone down and picked up the whisky glass. Debilius had everyone in an arm-lock. He rubbed at the side of his jaw as weariness crept over him. If Father hadn't been so stubborn, he wouldn't be in this position. He kicked off his shoes and swung his legs up on the bed. He had to make a fast profit. Whatever Debilius advised. Rules or no rules. He rubbed at his eyes. No profit, no wherewithal to buy diamonds. No diamonds, no profit. He balanced the glass of whisky on his chest and shut his eyes. Even Marti had understood that basic premise.

Hendrik opened his eyes and blinked, then realised that the sound in his dream of the sports' teacher ringing a bell at the start of the cross-country race, was the telephone by the bed ringing out. He rolled over and picked it up.

'A Mr Gerry Walden calling from Zaire, Mr Van den Fleet.'

'Oh yeah, thanks.' Hendrik yawned. 'Gerry?'

'Hendrik, I've got something for you. You set me a real problem, I don't mind telling you. You can get anything here but large roughs at the moment, but I've found a dealer in Kinshasa who can accommodate your requirements.'

'God bless him.'

'I don't know if he would or not. The guy is not exactly squeaky clean.'

'You mean the merchandise is hot?'

'No, but I should be very, very careful. The grapevine has it that his finances are shaky. Possibly why he isn't holding back on large roughs. His name is Duiss with two s's.'

'Wait a minute, Gerry, let me write this down. Actually, I think I know him, or know of him.' Hendrik searched in his jacket pocket for his filofax then hastily wrote down the dealer's name and telephone number. 'Gerry, I'll remember this. Thanks.'

'No problem. How is your father getting on?'

'He's fine, I only wish I could say the same for myself. Thanks again.' Hendrik put the telephone down. He yawned again and rubbed at his face with his hands. He got up and went to the bathroom, removing his shirt as he went. He stifled another yawn. No point in trying to sleep now. He had a flight to catch in four hours.

James removed his eyeglass and rubbed at his eye. He bent his head again and scrutinised the diamond. Chan looked across at Marti. She gave him an encouraging smile. 'Would you like some more coffee, Mr Chan?'

'Thank you, yes.'

Marti got up and walked as quietly as she could to the desk and picked up the coffee pot. James's secretary eased the door of the office open and beckoned to Marti. Marti nodded and the secretary closed the door again. Marti refilled Chan's cup. 'Excuse me for a moment, Mr Chan, I am needed in the outer office.'

He nodded.

James's secretary held out the telephone to her. 'It's a Mr Daniel Schmidt. He said he would hold while I found you.'

Marti picked up the telephone. 'Daniel, how are you? Nice to hear a voice from the recent past.'

'I'm fine and you?'

'Never better.'

'Marti, I would give an arm and a leg for any, absolutely any, small roughs you've got.'

'Daniel, this is very difficult for me. My brother and I agreed that I would not trade in Hong Kong with Van den Fleet's clients. You really should get in touch with him.'

'Marti, I have tried. He's not there. Look, I understand your problem, but look at it from where I am sitting. I need supplies. I cannot wait around until a dealer condescends to do business with me. If he's not available then I have to go to another dealer. I am really desperate, Marti. I need to do business with someone I know, I trust. Who else is there, but you?'

She laughed. 'Flatterer.'

'Please, I mean it.'

'I'll consult James and I'll call you as soon as I can.'

'Thanks a million, Marti.'

She handed the telephone back to James's secretary. 'No more calls, please, until Mr Chan has left.'

'Yes, Miss Van den Fleet.'

Marti returned to the main office. She prayed Hendrik would get back to Antwerp soon. Daniel Schmidt had placed her in an awkward position.

James removed his eyeglass and switched off the viewing lamp. Chan gripped the handle of the briefcase resting on his knee. 'If you will excuse me for a few moments, Mr Chan, I would like to consult with Miss Van den Fleet.'

'Yes, of course.'

James reached the door just as Marti opened it. 'Quick word outside?'

'Mmm.' She stepped back into the outer office.

James moved to the other side of the room. 'I have done all my tests. It is genuine.'

Her stomach fluttered in excitement. 'What are you going to arrange? An auction?'

'Almost certainly, but my findings need verification, of course.'

'Who are you going to ask?'

'Difficult, that. I rule you out, Marti, because I suspect you will want to act for Mr Yasim, if he's interested. It has to be someone unlikely to have a client with any serious intent. We are talking very big money here, Marti.'

'I know.'

'I need someone with a very solid reputation.'

'I would suggest Tony Bergman, but he will surely want to bid.'

James scratched his ear. 'The only two names that spring to mind are Chaim Eichler and Mark Singh.'

'Of the two, James, I would think Singh has the stronger reputation.'

'I agree, and Eichler might just surprise us and have a client. I'll get in touch with Singh right away. Get him to come over here.'

'Assuming he's interested.'

James laughed. 'I know Singh. He couldn't let an opportunity slip to display his superior knowledge.' James rubbed his hands together. 'Right then, let's inform Mr Chan of the good news.'

Chan sat upright in his chair, convinced that every drop of blood in his body had rushed to his head. The first obstacle had been overcome. James formed his fingers into a steeple. 'As I have mentioned, both Miss Van den Fleet and I are in agreement as to the quality of the diamond and I am willing to issue an authentication document. However, it is prudent to have a second dealer of excellent reputation to issue an independent authentication.'

Chan cast a suspicious glance at James. 'Is not the word of Miss Van den Fleet sufficient for the purpose?'

James smiled. 'Very much so, Mr Chan, but there are other matters to be considered. I believe Miss Van den Fleet has already spoken to you about the need to auction the diamond to get the best possible price. It is because she has a client who would wish her to act as his agent in such an auction, that she has asked to be excluded from any authentication procedure.'

Chan relaxed his shoulders. 'Ah, now I understand.'

'In fact, this is our major problem, Mr Chan. Finding a reputable dealer who is unlikely to receive instructions to bid for the diamond.'

Marti leaned forward in her chair. 'If I may rudely interrupt, James, perhaps we should explain that to avoid publicity and, frankly, time-wasters, we would intend only to invite a select number of dealers to the auction. Dealers who we know have clients with the financial resources to purchase the diamond.'

Chan smiled in dawning recognition. 'Ah, yes, I now clearly see the situation.'

James picked up his pen and rolled it between his fingers. 'So. We have finally decided to call upon Mark Singh of Bombay and invite him to authenticate the diamond. Of course, it may well be that he will decline, but we doubt it. Singh, we believe, does not have a suitable client. He is a most respected dealer. In fact, he acts as a consultant to the IDE.'

'Very good.' Chan pulled a cigarette out from the packet on the desk. 'I will leave these matters to you, Mr Wu.'

'Thank you. As a matter of courtesy, we shall also be inviting a bid from the IDE itself.'

Chan tensed his body. 'Is such courtesy necessary?'

'I think so. It will add something of an edge, if they do decide to bid. The IDE's resources are unknown, but considered to be vast. That element could push the price up even further. Now, are there any other questions you wish to ask, Mr Chan?'

'No, I am more than satisfied with the information you have provided. I shall leave this entire matter to you.' Chan removed the briefcase from his lap and stood up. 'You will keep me informed?'

'Every step of the way, Mr Chan.'

Marti accompanied James and Chan as far as the door, then shut it behind them. She walked across to the window, in growing elation. She looked down at the usual stream of traffic and people passing by. This was what it was all about. There was little that could match the buzz of launching the sale of the century. She turned away from the window as James came back into the office.

'I've put a call through to Mark Singh.'

Marti held up her fingers and crossed them. 'Good luck, James.' He gave a half smile. 'I think I have good luck.' He snatched up the telephone as it rang out. 'Ah, Mr Singh, glad I caught you. I wonder if you would be interested in authenticating a diamond that I have been asked to sell?'

Marti turned back to the window, one ear listening out for James's conversation. A heavy burst of rain curtained off the scene in the street below. She drummed her fingers on the window-ledge. Mark Singh would feel at home in Hong Kong, at least as far as the weather was concerned. She looked around at James as he put the telephone down.

'He'll be here tomorrow.' A smile of triumph crossed James's face. 'You didn't need to cross your fingers after all. Er – I have offered all expenses paid, naturally. Could you help entertain him?'

'Yes, of course.'

'Have you met Singh?'

'Not personally.'

'He is very English in his manner.'

She laughed. 'I understand, James. He couldn't be any worse than the Paulinson people I met.'

Hendrik smoothed his tie flat then returned to staring at the toe of his shoe. Why the bank manager was having difficulty reaching a decision was probably nothing more than the usual posturing to be expected from them. He flexed the toe of his shoe. Perhaps he should have become a banker instead of a dealer. There was something to be said for making a living out of using other people's money. It had to be better than being at everyone's beck and call. He folded his arms against his chest. At least Marti had had the decency to let the office know Daniel Schmidt had called her, if too late in the day for them to strike a deal with him. His business had gone to London instead.

The bank manager cleared his throat. 'I believe the bank would be prepared to make a short-term loan of $200,000. There is of course, the question of collateral.'

'Mr Miekle, your bank has been dealing with my family for two hundred years. You know the collateral is there. What is there to question?'

Miekle looked up at him. Hendrik was a most abrasive young man. Not like his father at all. He picked up the copy of Van den Fleet's accounts that Hendrik had provided. 'Interest on the $200,000, would of course need to be met in full, in one single payment, on the date due.'

Hendrik shifted in his chair. 'I have a buyer waiting for the diamonds, Mr Miekle. The loan and interest will be paid back to you within seven days. Probably less.'

Miekle nodded. 'I may keep these accounts?'

'Yes.'

'Very well, Mr Van den Fleet. I will advise the bank to accept your application.'

Hendrik got to his feet. 'Thank you, Mr Miekle. I will need a banker's draft by this afternoon.'

Miekle raised an eyebrow. 'I will see what can be done, Mr Van den Fleet. Good day to you.'

Hendrik walked briskly along the street. When the repository in Kinshasa confirmed that Duiss had lodged the diamonds, he would get his money. The deal with Yoshino could be completed within forty-eight hours. That bastard Miekle would earn his bank less interest than he had calculated. And Father need never know about it. He was an old man, completely out of touch with the reality of today's world. Incapable of understanding that risks had to be taken to survive.

The members of the governing committee of the IDE stirred as the curtains at the windows were drawn back and began talking amongst themselves. Christian got to his feet. 'Gentlemen, shall we adjourn for coffee? I am sure you will welcome the opportunity of off-the-record discussion about the tears of happiness campaign.' He turned as his PA came to his side. 'Yes, Margaret?'

'If I may have a word when convenient, Mr Debilius?'

He looked at her quickly. Convenient was a code word for urgent.

'Yes of course, Margaret. Gentlemen, if you will excuse me for two minutes.' Christian turned and followed Margaret to a door at the rear of the room.

Christian ushered Margaret through the door to his office then closed it firmly. 'Problem?'

'I think so, Mr Debilius. Finance has received a complaint against Duiss and Company of Zaire. Infringement of dealing rules. A payment is overdue. Finance say this is a second complaint. The first was lodged three months ago. When Finance contacted Duiss, payment was made immediately, but this time, his office say he is on vacation. They can't raise him. I called Zaire myself, but got the same answer. I have instructed Finance to investigate Duiss immediately.'

'Good girl, Margaret.' Christian's expression turned forbidding. 'Close him down. Fax all members to cease trading with Duiss and Company forthwith.'

'Yes, Mr Debilius.'

Christian turned on his heel and went out.

Christian waited until the members of the governing committee had quietly settled. 'Before we discuss the matter of the Japanese, there is one item I would like to bring to the notice of the committee. I am informed that Duiss and Company of Zaire are involved in infringement of dealing rules for the second time. Action has already been taken to investigate the matter and trading with them will cease as from now.' Several of the men nodded and murmured approval.

'Now, gentlemen, the matter of the Japanese. Since option-bearers' day and notification of the new IDE advertising campaign, I consider that the Japanese have had sufficient time to consider the implications. It would appear that they have chosen to ignore such implications and I propose that all members are informed that it is the express advice of the IDE that all sales to the Japanese should be discontinued immediately. I consider this action appropriate, gentlemen. Let us hope for the sake of the Japanese that they take heed of this further warning that the IDE will not tolerate the undermining of its trading structure.'

'Why not a total ban?' A man at the far end of the table spoke up.

'I consider that to be unnecessary at this moment in time. Advice to members will, I think, be sufficient. However, we shall not hesitate to impose a ban should it become necessary. Now, gentlemen, shall we discuss the tears of happiness campaign?'

There was a general murmur of agreement and the committee turned its attention to the infinitely more important matter of making money.

Mark Singh accepted a cup of coffee. He half turned and surreptitiously wiped the rim of the cup with his handkerchief. Marti twitched her lips. Hygiene in Hong Kong was no worse than in Bombay. He cautiously took a sip then set the cup down in its saucer. 'That is an exceptional diamond, Mr Wu.'

James beamed. 'We are instructed to offer it at auction. May I enquire if you will wish details to be forwarded to you?'

'I should be most interested to receive details, but it is unlikely that I would be instructed to bid.'

James shot Marti a quick glance. She picked up her cup of coffee and stirred it. James was right yet again. Clever James.

Mark opened his briefcase and pulled out a blank authentication document. 'I always carry a few spare documents with me. It is more efficient.'

'Indeed, Mr Singh. I do the same myself.' James smiled again.

Mark glanced at him as though he thought it inconceivable that James was that efficient.

'Perhaps you will join Miss Van den Fleet and me for dinner tonight, Mr Singh?'

'Thank you, no. I intend to return to Bombay this afternoon. Your invitation is most kind, but I must return as soon as possible. My wife is expecting our fourth child the day after tomorrow. I must be there.'

'Congratulations, Mr Singh.' Marti smiled politely. 'What are you hoping for? A boy or a girl?'

Mark turned to look at her as if her congratulations were inappropriate and somehow vulgar. 'Mrs Singh and I will be content with either one or the other.'

Marti's smile faded. She clasped her hands behind her back. James was right. He was a cold fish. She quietly observed Mark. His acquired – from God knows where – posturing looked faintly ridiculous: trying so hard to maintain indifference about a diamond that he would, if given the chance and the capability, want to sell himself. She turned away, suddenly feeling rather bored with him.

When James returned to the office, after having seen Mark Singh off the premises with more than a degree of relief, he looked serious, almost downcast. Marti stared at him. 'Something wrong, James?'

'Mmm. Just had two faxes from the IDE. All trading with Duiss and Company is to cease forthwith.'

'Do they owe you anything?'

'No, no. I don't think I have ever done any business with them.'

'Then what's the problem? You look worried about something.'

'My belief in my good fortune was ill founded. The sale of the diamond is off.'

'What?'

'Read this. It came in with the fax about Duiss. The IDE is advising all members to cease sales to the Japanese.'

Marti took the sheet of paper from him and scanned it quickly. 'Well, I suppose you could exclude the Japanese.'

'How could I ensure that?'

She pursed her lips. 'If someone acted on behalf of the Japanese without your knowledge, you couldn't be blamed.'

'I could. The IDE would see it as collusion and I wouldn't be able to prove otherwise.'

'But this is only advice, James. It is not an instruction.'

He looked down at his shoes glumly. 'By the time of the auction, it might just be that. Besides, only the foolish or the desperate ignore the advice of the IDE. Advice to members is tantamount to instruction.'

She placed the sheet of paper on the desk.

James looked at his watch. He picked up the authentication document and placed it in an envelope. 'Let's go and have some lunch, then try and do some real business. So far all we have done is waste time and money on this whole thing.'

She picked up the sheet from the desk again and reread it. Poor James. This would have to happen now. The diamond was genuine. It had the best of authentications. Only the IDE barred the way to huge commissions for both of them. She stared down at the signature of Christian Debilius, her breath quickening. 'James.'

'What is it?'

'We have overlooked something. I am not an option bearer.'

He stared at her blankly.

'I am not a member of the IDE, James.'

She looked at him excitedly. Slowly, his eyes filled with burning recognition. 'You could sell the diamond.'

'With your agreement.'

'Yes. No, wait a minute. That wouldn't work. You work for me. James Wu would be held responsible.' He raised his hand. 'One moment. There is an answer to that. You don't work for me, you are my consultant.' He shook his head. 'No. That wouldn't work either. The IDE would still consider the company responsible for your actions, as agent for the company.'

Marti thought for a moment. 'Listen, James, I think I've got it. I haven't received any fees from you yet. We could consider our agreement null and void. James Wu and Company, as far as the IDE is concerned, would not be involved.'

James stared at her. 'I hear what you say and I cannot find fault with it.' He shook his head in bemusement. 'How devious is the female mind.'

'Not devious, James, clever.'

He scratched his ear. 'I see a future problem. If the diamond went to the Japanese, you might face covert retaliation by the IDE. They might make it known to all members that you are not a fit person to employ or to engage as a consultant.'

'They wouldn't dare.'

'You don't know Christian Debilius. If he can't achieve something one way, he will do it another.'

She gave a loud sigh of irritation. 'I am getting fed up, James, with the way everyone behaves as if Christian is God. He is not. Let me tell you something, James. Christian has no power over me. He has consistently refused to make me, or indeed any other woman, an option bearer. He cannot have it both ways. I will sell the diamond, if you wish, and please do not worry about the consequences, because I am not. If I conclude the sale I can't think how I could truthfully be described as being unfit as a dealer. Unless, of course, it was used to discriminate against me. If that was the case, then I would have no hesitation in filing a law suit against the IDE and Christian himself.'

'Would you really do that?'

'Without hesitation, James. Of course, it would be unlikely to come to court. I doubt if the IDE are interested in that kind of publicity.'

He shook his head again. 'You know, I think I believe you. You would do it.'

'A Van den Fleet's word is their bond, James.'

'Indeed.' He held out his hand. 'And so is mine. Let's go and have some lunch and discuss our plans. No, forgive me, your plans.'

She shook his hand. 'If it comes to it that I do sell the diamond, you will of course accept a commission for personal and private advice etcetera.'

He grinned. 'Whatever made you think I wouldn't?'

'Fifty, fifty?'

He shook her hand again. 'You are very fair in your dealings, Marti.'

'Chan is your client.'

He laughed. 'As of now, he's yours.'

Hendrik glared at Astrid as she tiptoed into the office. 'I said no interruptions.'

'I think you should see these two faxes from the IDE, Hendrik. One is marked for immediate attention, the other is extremely urgent.'

He stretched out a hand. 'Give them to me and, Astrid, no more interruptions. I am expecting a very important call. Understand?'

'Yes, Hendrik.' She hesitated for a moment. 'What if your father –'

'Even he will have to wait.'

'Very well.'

Hendrik glanced at the fax marked extremely urgent and let his breath out slowly. He had just clinched the deal in time. Duiss & Co. had gone under. The repository in

Kinshasa had notified him barely an hour ago that the diamonds had been deposited. He lit up a cigarette. It would be interesting to know where the $200,000 was now. He drew on his cigarette. Where it wouldn't be, was in Duiss & Co.'s account. He glanced quickly through the other fax then tossed it into the filing tray. He couldn't afford to take Debilius's advice not to sell to the Japanese.

Pa Jiaming shuffled his papers together and placed them in the file. He glanced across at Chen Chih. The man was more of a fool than he looked. He had tried to find fault with the workings of the Leading Group for High Technology and failed. He had tried to find fault with the work of Pa Jiaming and failed. Pa smiled to himself. Chen was too eager to seek out corruption to worry about seeking out individual private enterprise.

Chen straightened up in his chair. 'This visit to Geneva, Vice-leader Pa. I consider it unnecessary for you to stay longer than two days.'

Pa looked across at him. 'Forgive me, Leader Chen, but I had only intended to stay for one.' He caught the eye of the man sitting opposite him and saw him stifle a smirk.

Chen shifted in his chair. 'It is good to see you setting standards to others, Vice-leader Pa.'

Pa bowed his head in acknowledgement.

Chen pushed his chair back and looked at each of the men around the table in turn. 'The meeting is at an end. Remember, we must all recognise that without restraint there cannot be efficient progress. Without restraint, progress is nothing more than the capitalistic exploitation of the State's resources.' He turned on his heel and strutted out of the room.

Pa gathered up his file and returned to his office. He stopped by the young girl sitting at a desk outside the door. 'I require you to work late.'

She smiled. 'Of course, Vice-leader Pa.'

'Later than usual. I am concerned that you will not have your evening meal at the correct time.' He rested his hand on the desk close to her arm. 'The food at the Beijing New Duck is very recommended.'

She cast her eyes downwards. 'You are very kind, Vice-leader Pa.'

He smiled and went to his office.

Pa sat down at his desk and placed the file in front of him. He lit up a cigarette. One day spent in Geneva would allow him to spend two days in Austria. He blew a smoke ring into the air. He wondered if Chen knew that Austria could be particularly foggy at this time of year; playing havoc with airline schedules. He opened the file and began to make swift notes in the margin. An hour's work then a meal at the Beijing New Duck, followed, if he was not mistaken, by a little pleasure. He stopped writing for a moment and raised his head. The news from Professor Li that the diamond had been twice authenticated was welcome. He smiled to himself and bent his head again. The news that the proceeds of the sale were safely deposited in his bank account would be particularly welcome.

Christian Debilius's contented post-luncheon mood dissipated as he entered his suite of offices and caught Margaret's warning look. He sighed. 'Margaret, I trust you are not going to spoil my afternoon?'

'No, Mr Debilius, but I think you might well spoil the afternoon for others.'

He laughed.

Margaret stood by Christian's side as he flicked through the computer printout. 'Our Middle Eastern representative called while you were at lunch to say that he had received complaints that the Israelis were selling to the Japanese.'

Christian groaned. 'Not the Kuwaitis again.'

'Afraid so, and complaints have been received from the Israelis that the Kuwaitis are still dealing with the Japanese.'

He ran his hand down the back of his head. 'I really do not need this, Margaret. I really do not. Whatever the IDE does to protect both sides, they see it as an excuse to beat the shit, if you will forgive the phrase, Margaret, out of each other.'

'As you weren't available, I got Mr Evans to sign an enforcement computer check.' She leaned in front of him and pointed to the end page of the printout. 'The Kuwaitis appear to be clean, but there's the evidence on the Israelis. They definitely have continued trading.'

He shook his head to himself. 'You know, perhaps I should become a restaurateur.'

She suppressed a smile.

'Dealers are the first, Margaret, to accuse producers of stepping out of line. Yet they feel free to operate as they choose.' He handed back the printout. 'Inform all members of total ban on all, and I mean all, sales to the Japanese as of now. Quote relevant section of riot act.'

'Right away, Mr Debilius.'

'And circulate the governing committee of the action.'

'Will do. By the way, Mr Yasim called and wanted to have a word with you.'

'Isn't life full of little surprises, Margaret?'

She laughed. 'I'll get him for you now.'

Christian spun his chair away from the desk and crossed one leg over the other. 'Beni, delighted to hear from you. Ah, if I may, Beni, interrupt you. I have a piece of information that you may find interesting. You may be aware that we advised members to suspend sales to the Japanese. We did random checks and have discovered some covert trading. We have now issued a complete ban.'

'Actually, Christian, that was precisely what I wanted to speak to you about. I had been asked to speak to you unofficially.'

Christian laughed. 'We appear to have saved you the job. Seriously, Beni, your principals can be assured that anyone,

I repeat anyone, because that goes for them too, found to have transgressed the IDE ruling will face expulsion.'

'I am very glad to hear that.'

'When are you next in New York?'

'Possibly at the end of the month. I'm not sure at the moment.'

'We must have dinner together.'

'Thank you. I must go now. I have a plane to catch. Goodbye.'

Christian put the telephone down and went into Margaret's office.

Margaret turned around as Christian came to sit on the edge of her desk. 'Here's the memorandum for the governing committee, Mr Debilius, and the mailing department have just confirmed all members have been faxed.'

'Good girl, Margaret.' He removed his pen from his inside pocket. 'Thank you for getting Mr Yasim so quickly for me.' He bent down and quickly signed the memo. 'You know, Margaret, instead of becoming a restaurateur, I think perhaps I am more suited to election as Secretary-general of the United Nations.'

'Oh absolutely, Mr Debilius.'

James's secretary got up from her desk as Marti came in through the main door. 'Miss Van den Fleet, James is taking a call. Will you deal with this, please. It is a very urgent communication from the IDE.'

'I'll see he gets it.' Marti took the sheet of paper from her as she passed the desk, then stood still as her eyes flicked over the contents. She raised both eyebrows and went into James's office.

James put the telephone down and picked up the fax sheet Marti had placed in front of him. He looked up at her. 'You are definitely on your own now, Marti. With a total ban on sales to the Japanese, we must handle the transaction very carefully. I know you will understand when I say that I must not compromise my own position.'

'Actually, James, I have been thinking about this while I was waiting for you to finish on the telephone. What do you say to my leaving Hong Kong altogether? It would put a lot of air between you and I. Somewhere like Geneva, perhaps.'

He thought for a moment. 'It's an idea that has its attractions for me, I must admit. Why do you suggest Geneva?'

'The security is the best in the world there, James. We have enough to contend with without worrying about someone stealing the diamond.'

'That is very true. OK. Geneva it is.' He scratched at his ear. 'What about finance? I can't be seen to be involved.'

'Don't worry. I have sufficient funds to cover intermediate costs. The final costs can come out of the proceeds of sale.'

He reached out for the telephone. 'I'll call Chan now and tell him the good and the bad news.'

'Actually, before you do that, James, another idea came to me. I think we should send out preliminary details and a video of the diamond, to whet the appetite, so to speak, inviting sealed bids. The five highest bidders to be invited to a preview to examine the stone themselves. After which, if they are still interested – and they will be – the auction can begin. What do you think?'

'Excellent. Look, I'll call Chan and get his agreement.'

'Would you like some coffee?'

'I think I am going to need some. That ban on sales to the Japanese is going to hurt.'

'You can stand the pain, James, I'm sure.'

He laughed.

When Marti returned with cups of coffee, James covered the telephone with his hand. 'He agrees, but he wants to speak to you. He says he has been instructed that the sale must be conducted as soon as possible.' He uncovered the telephone. 'Mr Chan, Miss Van den Fleet is here to talk to you.'

Marti grasped the telephone. 'Hello, Mr Chan. I understand that you have agreed to our suggestions?'

'Yes and thank you, Miss Van den Fleet, for taking over the sale. Mr Wu has been explaining to me about the IDE ban. There is one thing I do not quite understand. If there is a ban, won't other dealers be prevented from attending the auction?'

'No, Mr Chan, we are reading the IDE instructions literally. The ban is on sales to the Japanese, not purchases. It is a technicality, but correct. I am the seller. The people attending the auction are buyers.'

'Ah, I see now what you are saying. You are not affected by the ban?'

'No, Mr Chan. I am a woman and women are not allowed to be members of the IDE. I am therefore not within the IDE's jurisdiction.'

Chan gave a chuckle. 'Perhaps you will not remain so for long, Miss Van den Fleet.'

'We shall see.'

'One important matter I must make clear to you. My client requires that there should be no delay in selling the diamond. Will selling it in Geneva cause delays?'

'No, on the contrary. If you can bring the diamond to the office we can have it videoed and taken to Geneva by courier to Bank Christian Oertli. I can recommend the bank highly. I have often used their repository services in the past. Their vaults are as secure as the IDE's.'

'You will not be taking it yourself?'

'No, Mr Chan, it will travel far more securely with diamond couriers. Please don't worry. Vast quantities of diamonds traverse the globe every day in perfect safety. Now, I will see you get copies of all documentation. Would you like me to make hotel arrangements for you in Geneva, or would you prefer to make your own?'

Chan made a small gasping noise. 'I have to go to Geneva?'

'You don't have to, Mr Chan, but I imagined that you would wish to.'

'I see. I do not know at the moment. I must consult with my client.'

'Very well, Mr Chan, let me know what you decide. Can you bring the diamond to the office? The sooner we get started, the less time we waste.'

'I shall be there in twenty minutes.'

'Thank you, Mr Chan.' Marti put the telephone down and smiled at James. 'We are on our way, James.'

Hendrik bent down and pulled out the bottom drawer of his desk and took out a bottle of whisky. He unscrewed the cap and drank straight from the bottle. He replaced the cap and put the bottle back in the drawer. He picked up the fax sheet and reread it. If Yoshino had called him back when he said he would, he could have made the deal before the ban was imposed. The IDE didn't exactly execute people for ignoring advice. He pushed his chair back and paced up and down the office. He had spent the last four hours trying to move the diamonds. Every answer was the same. Dealers had enough problems keeping back their own, without buying more. His winced at the sharp, hollow pain in his gut. He stopped by the desk and lit up another cigarette. He had to sell the diamonds. He had to repay the loan to the bank in five days. He rubbed at his midriff. Otherwise, Van den Fleet's would be bankrupt. They couldn't afford to make the interest payments even if the bank extended the loan period.

Astrid knocked on the door and popped her head round.

'Get out.'

'Hendrik.'

'I said get out.'

'Mr Yoshino.'

'What?'

'I think there must be a fault on the extension. Mr

Yoshino is on the line, but I can't get an answer from your office.'

Hendrik almost knocked her over as he barged his way past her and out of the office.

Hendrik snatched up the telephone on Astrid's desk. 'Mr Yoshino? Yes, Hendrik Van den Fleet here. My apologies for keeping you waiting. Problem with my telephone. Yes, I can still deal.' He wrapped the flex around his hand. 'Mr Yoshino, I haven't wasted your time, please don't waste mine. The price to you is $800,000.' He clenched his fist around the flex. 'That is the price, Mr Yoshino, if you can get quality diamonds elsewhere, please do so. Although we both know that you can't. Yes, agreed. You have a deal, Mr Yoshino. Settlement the day after tomorrow? Agreed. Nice to do business with you, Mr Yoshino.' Hendrik put the telephone down, feeling suddenly lightheaded.

Astrid looked at him anxiously. 'Are you feeling all right, Hendrik?'

He gave a faint smile. 'Never better.' He massaged his stomach as it rumbled. 'Could you get me a sandwich, cake or something? I haven't had time to eat all day.'

'Yes, of course.'

Hendrik walked slowly back to his office and quietly closed the door behind him. He went and sat down at his desk and buried his face into his hands. It suddenly felt like the longest day in his entire life. He straightened up and leaned back in his chair. He had done it. All he could hope for was that it was in Duiss's interests to keep quiet about the transaction. Yoshino would keep his mouth shut. He closed his eyes. He was safe, if he didn't put the transaction through the books.

Marti tasted the fish stew provided by Mrs Bachmann. She rubbed at one eye. She felt almost too tired to eat. The afternoon had been hectic if not hysterical. Arrangements had been made to despatch the diamond to Geneva. The manager of Bank Christian Oertli had been his usual efficient, courteous self. She had eagerly taken up his suggestion that Bank Christian Oertli would be a suitable venue for the auction. They could provide and make arrangements for all the necessary security. The making of the video had introduced the note of hysteria. The video crew had worked fast and efficiently, but the girl doing the voice-over was a disaster. She spoke very good English, but there was no disguising the slightly sing-song Chinese accent. James had panicked and said he would be compromised. The IDE would immediately assume the video had been made in Hong Kong. Marti had eventually done the voice-over herself, after five takes. She rubbed at her eye again. She had never realised how incoherently she spoke. She groaned aloud as the telephone rang out, and spoke more sharply than she had intended.

'Oh, sorry, Marti. Am I calling at an inconvenient time? It's Erwin here.'

'Erwin, hello. Nice to hear from you and no, it's not inconvenient.'

'I wondered if you would like to come out to dinner tomorrow night, or whenever you're free?'

'Thank you, Erwin, but I am going away tomorrow for a few days.'

'May I ask where?'

'Geneva.'

'Ah, I see. I envy you.'

She grimaced. He sounded so disappointed. She thought of Mrs Bachmann's stew. 'Er, are you doing anything this evening?'

'No, nothing.'

'Would you like to come over here?'

'Thank you. Am I to sample this cooking of yours?'

'No, you will be relieved to hear. Actually, I wondered if you would like to share one of Mrs Bachmann's stews with me. She saves some of whatever she cooks for herself and her husband for me when I come home. Relieves me of the chore of preparing something myself, but the portions are always very large. So there is more than enough for two.'

'I shall be delighted to come over, Marti. Say, an hour and a half?'

'You don't mind toing and froing on the ferry?'

'Not at all. I enjoy the journey. I find it very relaxing.'

'Fine. See you soon.' She put the telephone down and tapped her fingers on the table. She needed more Italian noodles, if Mrs Bachmann would oblige.

Erwin swished the noodles around in the saucepan. 'Must always have lots of boiling water, Marti. Lots. Can't cook noodles properly otherwise.'

'Yes, Erwin.' Marti leaned against the kitchen wall with a glass of vermouth in her hand.

Within minutes of arriving Erwin had followed her into the kitchen and taken control of the cooking: adding more salt to the stew; crying out in horror at the small amount of water she was heating up.

Marti took a sip of vermouth and smiled quietly to herself. Erwin might be a widower, but he was still very domesticated. He seemed quite at home in the kitchen, with a tea towel tucked into the belt of his trousers as an apron.

'You seem to have got on very good terms with Mrs Bachmann, Marti. She doesn't cook for just anyone.'

She twirled the glass between her fingers. 'We have reached a sort of an agreement. I let her be the guardian of my morals in return for cooking for me.'

He laughed. 'Did you have much choice?'

'Not really.'

He wiped his hands on the tea towel. 'I should have asked. Am I here with or without official approval?'

'Oh, very much with, Erwin, I have a strong suspicion that Mrs Bachmann is extremely enamoured of you.'

He chuckled. 'I have a devastating way with women.'

'Indeed you do. When I went to borrow some noodles, as soon as Mrs Bachmann knew I was entertaining you, she produced that huge chocolate cake. I assume it was meant actually for Mr Bachmann.'

He shrugged. 'So we save him a slice. Now, these noodles are ready. Always remember never to overcook them, otherwise they go slimy.'

The remains of the fish stew was dutifully eaten up by Erwin, because he said to waste good food was criminal. Marti toyed with a few strands of noodles to keep him company. 'So, Erwin, what's the latest gossip in Hong Kong?'

He looked up from his plate. 'I would be more interested in hearing yours.'

'Haven't got any.'

'Oh yes you have. I overheard an acquaintance of mine at the club saying that the International Diamond Exchange was waging war against the Japanese. Is it true? You should know, if anyone does.'

'War is not a word I would use.'

'What word would you use?'

'Genocide?'

He burst out laughing.

'No, seriously, it's not as bad as that. The IDE is just standing on its hind legs and growling very fiercely.'

'What have the Japanese done?'

'It's what they plan to do that is the real problem.'

Erwin pushed his plate away from him. 'Do you mind if I smoke?'

'Not at all.' Marti got up from the table. 'Let me get you an ashtray.'

'So what are the Japanese up to?'

'They have been buying up enormous quantities of large rough diamonds. Too many to be considered as normal trading requirements. The conclusion has to be that they are trying to make the tail wag the dog. The dog being the IDE.'

'Will the Japanese succeed?'

'I doubt it very much. Dealers, sometimes producers, in concert have tried to break the cartel in the past. They never have. Resentment occasionally builds up against the trading regulations of the IDE, but no one group is ever strong enough to cope with a prolonged stand-off situation.' She brought an ashtray to the table and placed it by Erwin's side.

'The way to break a cartel is to leave it.'

'If you can. You see, the IDE is very crafty. It operates with a tight grip on the throat, but it also protects its members when the going gets, if you will forgive the pun, rough.'

He winced.

'Sorry about that. When – if – there is a glut, prices fall, the IDE still buys from producers. It has the financial resources to stockpile until things right themselves and the market recovers its equilibrium.'

'Surely, if the IDE was doing its job properly there wouldn't be any instability.'

'In theory, no. In practice, not so easy. The IDE controls a very large amount of the output from the world's diamond mines, but not all. Economic factors play their part. World recessions are the real enemy. If you've lost your job, or have to face living on a reduced income, buying diamonds is not your first priority, is it?'

'True.'

'Someone once described the IDE as a brilliant high-wire act.'

He gave a quiet laugh.

'It's not a bad description, actually. Christian Debilius certainly knows how to balance on a tightrope.'

He pulled out a cigar and lit it up. 'Do I detect a hint of disdain in your voice?'

'Sour grapes, Erwin. Christian is the archetypal male chauvinist.'

'Why is that?'

'Just by coincidence, of course, there happens to be

not one woman amongst the members of the IDE.'

'Dare I ask if that is so very, very important.'

'Extremely. If you are not elected as an option bearer, you simply cannot trade.'

'What is an option bearer?'

'Someone who is authorised by the IDE to buy from them. The word option is something of a misnomer. Members have to buy what the IDE offers them each month.'

Erwin gave a puzzled frown. 'I don't quite follow. You are a diamond dealer, but not an option bearer. How can you be one without the other, from what you say?'

'Ah, that is how the IDE keep women in their place, Erwin. Taking me as an example, I am a diamond dealer and function as such, because I either work in a company that has an option bearer registered with the IDE, or I work as a consultant to a company with similar option status. Theoretically, I could start up my own dealing business tomorrow, but I wouldn't last until the end of the week, without being able to buy from the IDE. Solely buying-in from other dealers would make your prices uncompetitive. So, if you cannot buy from the IDE, you cannot stay in business. On the other hand, unless you can show operating profits that satisfy the requirements of the IDE, you cannot buy from them. Neat?'

'A very cleverly run cartel.'

She stood up and cleared their dinner plates from the table. 'Anyway, enough about the IDE. It's boring.' She wagged a finger at him. 'You have cleverly avoided telling me all the gossip. What's this story I read in the newspaper about the head of the Chinese Trade Association shooting himself?'

'Corruption.'

She laughed. 'That's your favourite word, isn't it? It's a bit drastic though, shooting yourself in the head.'

He leaned back in his chair. 'The rumour is that he shot himself before someone else did.'

'That bad was he?'

'I would have shot him myself, if I could have got away with it.'

'What for?'

'My favourite word again, corruption. It is a difficult thing to fight. You file specifications on behalf of your company for a tender, knowing full well that Fang will give your competitors every detail they wish to know, so that they can undercut you on price. All this is, of course, for a certain consideration.'

'Which goes into Fang's piggy bank.'

'How else do the Fangs of this world own mansions on the Peak, drive around in Rolls Royces, become elected to the Royal Jockey Club?'

She studied his face for a moment. 'And you have to be part of the system to make it work.'

He nodded. 'You most definitely do.'

'I thought you said the way to break a cartel is to walk away from it.'

'In theory, Marti, only in theory.'

'Do you know who is taking Fang's place?'

'Yes, we heard very quickly. A man called Bai Hao is taking over. He arrived from Beijing a few days ago.'

'Have you met him yet?'

He shook his head. 'I don't deal with the Association unless it is about something specifically in Hong Kong.'

'Well, if Bai is from Beijing, perhaps he won't be as corrupt as Fang.'

He gave a wry smile. 'Don't you believe it. Fang was a PRC man, too.'

'Would you like some coffee?' She groaned as the doorbell rang and a faint voice echoed down the hall through the letter box.

'Miss Van den Fleet, Mrs Bachmann here.'

Marti grabbed Erwin's jacket from the back of the sofa. 'Quick, Erwin, put this on, and straighten your tie. Otherwise, she will think I have been indecently assaulting you.'

He struggled to put on his jacket, his shoulders heaving with laughter.

Frankie Heung pushed his chair back from the table and stood up. 'Hey, Ronnie, I was beginning to think I smelt or something.'

Ronnie Lee shook hands with him and sat down. 'I haven't been avoiding you, Frankie. I got your message, but you're a busy man, I didn't want to arrange a meeting unless I had something to give you.'

'You're a good man, Ronnie. What's the score?'

Ronnie propped his elbows on the table and leaned forward. 'The relatives have finally agreed to your terms.'

Frankie nodded his head. 'Good, good.'

'I had quite a tough time getting them all to see sense, but we made it in the end.'

'Let's drink to it.' Frankie beckoned to the waiter.

'Er, there is just one thing, Frankie.'

Frankie stared at him. 'Oh yeah.'

'It's not really your problem, or even mine, but I seem to have fixed myself up with the job of nursemaid. One of the young girls has been behaving a bit strong since Mr Song's demise. Her mother doesn't like it. Apparently the daughter has been seeing a guy working for the Third Moon Gang.'

'So?'

Ronnie gave a nervous smile. 'So, as you are in negotiations with the Third Moon, I thought maybe you could have a word with a certain person. Get the guy to stop seeing her.'

Frankie picked up his glass and drained it. He set it down again and stared at it for a moment. 'OK, Ronnie, you can tell Mrs Song that the guy stops being a problem from tomorrow night.'

'Thanks, Frankie, that's going to be really appreciated.'

Frankie nodded his head. 'Good, good. OK, I need a favour doing, too.'

'Sure Frankie.'

'Had time to read the newspaper recently?'

'Yes.'

'Then you know the new chairman of the Chinese People's Association for Foreign Trade is a guy called Bai Hao?'

'Read something about it.'

'I hear he's turning into a real enthusiast for Hong Kong.'

Ronnie looked at him for a moment then grinned.

'I haven't see Four-ears Fu around, Ronnie.'

'Been ill.'

'Send him my regards if you see him. Tell him I'd like a word sometime.'

'Can I say what about?'

'Tell him I have a friend who's just arrived from Beijing. Likes schoolgirls. I'd like to fix him up with something.'

'Bai?'

'Did I say that?'

Ronnie grinned again. 'I'll pass the message on.'

Chan Chunling sat on the edge of the bed in his hotel room. He crooked the telephone on his shoulder and lit a cigarette. He quickly took the cigarette out of his mouth at the sound of the voice on the other end of the line.

'We are unable to locate Professor Li.'

Chan cursed. 'He must be in the building somewhere. I am expecting a call from him.'

There was a pause. 'If you are expecting a call from him, why are you ringing?'

Chan's mouth tightened. 'That is none of your business. Go and find Professor Li.' He pressed the telephone to his ear as he thought he heard another voice in the background.

'Professor Li has just returned to his office.'

'Thank you.'

'Director Chan, is that you?'

'Yes, Professor Li. I have been expecting a call from you. Why haven't you rung?'

'I am very busy. I have to organise things here before I leave.'

'Have you heard from Pa Jiaming?'

'Yes, yes, I was going to call you later. He says you must not go to Geneva with Miss Van den Fleet. He will make arrangements himself.'

'Oh, I see.' Chan looked glumly at his cigarette. He had been looking forward to a foreign trip.

'Have you given Miss Van den Fleet the telephone number in Geneva?'

'Yes.'

'Then Pa has instructed that you return to Shanghai immediately.'

'Very well.'

'I shall be leaving for Lhasa tomorrow. Have you memorised the number you must call when you have information?'

'Yes, Professor Li.'

'Then there is nothing more to be discussed.'

Chan put the telephone down as the line went dead. He drew on his cigarette. He had at least hoped to remain in Hong Kong and renew his acquaintance with Anna Wu.

Marti gave her name to the receptionist at Bank Christian Oertli. 'I have an appointment with Monsieur Henri Chillon.'

'Yes, Miss Van den Fleet, he is expecting you.' The receptionist turned and signalled to a uniformed attendant. 'Please take Miss Van den Fleet to see Monsieur Chillon.'

Marti followed the attendant into the elevator. Hopefully, by now certain people were watching the video and reaching for their telephones. The doors slid open and the attendant moved to one side. She stepped out of the elevator and followed him along the corridor to a door at the far end. He knocked once then opened it. 'Miss Van den Fleet, Monsieur Chillon.'

Henri Chillon got up from his desk and came to greet Marti. 'And how does Geneva find you, Miss Van den Fleet?'

'Well, thank you.'

'May I offer coffee?'

'Yes, that would be most welcome.'

'Good, but naturally you will wish first to inspect the diamond.'

'Thank you.'

Henri turned to the attendant. 'Inform security that Miss Van den Fleet and I wish to inspect the Cambodian diamond.'

She looked at Henri in surprise. 'Is that what you call it?'

He smiled. 'I thought the name was a little more esoteric than its given serial number.'

'Of course.'

'Here is your identity pass, Miss Van den Fleet.'

'Thank you.' She pinned the plastic card on to the lapel of her jacket.

'And your vault personal identification card.'

She turned the plastic card over. 'Have you changed the system? This card looks different to the one I had last time.'

'Not changed, just operating a different system. All of our systems are secure, you understand, but the protection of the Cambodian diamond requires a different one to that which we usually use.'

'Ah, I see.'

Four armed guards were stationed at the entrance to the corridor leading to the vault. Henri bent his head and whispered to her. 'On the day, the security won't look quite so obvious, but will be just as effective.'

'I understand.'

'Now if you will insert your voice-print identification card into that little slot there and say your name clearly.'

She slotted the card into the panel in the wall. 'Martina Van den Fleet.'

The card was sucked in, as if by an invisible hand. The red light flickered intermittently.

'It is comparing your voice pattern with that on the card.'

She nodded. The card slid out again and a green light winked.

'If you will take your card, Miss Van den Fleet, and go through the door when it opens. I shall follow in a few moments. Only one person can pass through the door at any one time.'

She collected the card and watched as the door slid back. She quickly stepped forward across the threshold. At the end of the small corridor a further two armed guards were in attendance.

Henri gave a quick smile as he came to join her in the corridor. She followed him to where the guards stood and went through the same voice identification procedure to gain admittance to the vault itself.

Henri raised a hand to the panel on the wall. 'Here we are, at last, Miss Van den Fleet.'

She looked around the room which was empty apart from a small table. 'Where is the diamond?'

'You will see it in a moment.'

She thought she detected a sudden shadow out of the corner of her eye, then blinked as she saw a small steel box on the table. She gave a gasp of astonishment. 'That wasn't there a moment ago.'

He smiled. 'It has been there all the time. We use certain scientific trickery to make it disappear.'

She raised an eyebrow. 'Very clever. I remember once

seeing a film about diamond thieves. They got into the vault by walking on the ceiling.'

He gave a quiet laugh. 'Not on this ceiling, they wouldn't.'

She looked up. 'What have you done to it?'

'I cannot say, Miss Van den Fleet, but I would feel genuinely sorry for any fly who attempted to cross over it.'

After coffee and biscuits in Henri's office, Marti was taken to inspect the boardroom, which was to be used for the auction. She glanced around the room and the windows. As if guessing her thoughts, Henri gestured to them. 'They are special armour-plated glass.'

She nodded and looked around the room again. 'I think this will be ideal, Monsieur Chillon. Thank you for your preparations. I am very impressed.'

'At Bank Christian Oertli, Miss Van den Fleet, we give of our very best at all times.'

'Indeed.' She glanced at her watch. Every moment of his time was costed and itemised. 'I am expecting a number of sealed bids. Would you be kind enough to witness my opening them when they arrive?'

'With pleasure.'

'Well, I must be on my way. I'll be in touch.'

Henri gave a small nod of his head by way of a bow and ushered her out into the corridor again, and back to the reception desk.

Christian stared at the heading on the sheet of paper. He blinked. For a moment the words 'Martina Van den Fleet, Geneva' seemed to jump up from the paper. He leaned across to the intercom and buzzed through to Margaret. 'Come in right away, please.' He returned his attention to the formally worded invitation to the IDE inviting it to make a bid for a diamond of exceptional quality. He dropped the paper on to the desk. The impertinent little bitch.

Margaret hurried into the office. 'Yes, Mr Debilius?'

'Put this video on for me will you?'

Margaret picked up the cassette. She looked at it curiously, then went to the video recorder and slotted it in.

'Thank you, Margaret.' Christian leaned back in his chair. He shot to his feet at the first sight of the diamond and stared as if transfixed by the image on the screen.

Margaret glanced at him quickly then turned her attention back to the video. She held her breath as she watched the diamond turning slowly, showing off its faceted perfection. When the video ended she managed to drag her eyes away from the screen and look at Christian again. He remained perfectly still for several moments, then slowly walked across the room and removed the cassette. 'Get me James Wu of Hong Kong, Margaret, *rapido*.'

She hurried out and back to her own office.

Christian put the telephone down and picked up the letter from Marti. She was more than an impertinent little bitch. He leaned back in his chair and folded his arms. His conversation with James Wu had been pleasant and brief. Martina Van den Fleet was no longer connected with his company. Yes, he had authenticated the diamond, but at her request. So had Mark Singh of Bombay. Apart from that James Wu & Co. had no connection with the sale.

Margaret came into the office again. 'Mr Debilius, I'm afraid Mr Bergman is away from the office.'

'When will he be back?'

'They're not sure.'

'What do they mean, not sure? Where is he?'

'Apparently he's on a visit to Geneva.'

Christian's mouth tightened into a thin line. 'Get me Max Bergman.'

Christian paced up and down in front of his desk with a heavy tread. 'Max, I personally don't give a shit what Martina said to your uncle. If he bids for this diamond, I will have both of you expelled from the IDE.'

'I don't believe that you can do that, Mr Debilius, and neither do you.'

'Do not, Max, adopt that tone with me. When you next speak to your uncle, and I suggest you see that it is very soon, you will remind him that there is a ban on sales to the Japanese.'

'So?'

A muscle flicked in Christian's cheek. 'So, if I find that your uncle is bidding on behalf of the Japanese for this diamond, I will considered that a grave transgression.'

'I am sure you will, Mr Debilius, but who said we were? If we choose to buy a diamond, any diamond, that is our business. Who we sell it to might conceivably become your business.'

'Max –'

'And please do not threaten me, Mr Debilius. Bergman's are not doing anything wrong and have no intention of doing anything wrong. Another thing, Mr Debilius, I have my uncle's permission to tell you to get off our backs.'

Christian slammed the telephone down. The muscles worked in his face as he struggled to gain control of his temper. Martina Van den Fleet was trying to be very, very clever and she was going to have to be taught a short, sharp lesson. Christian strode to the door and flung it open. 'Margaret, I want George Forrester in my office in five minutes.' He turned on his heel and slammed the door shut again.

George Forrester sat quietly in his chair, as if oblivious to Christian's simmering rage. He reread the letter from Marti then looked through the instructions that had been faxed to the IDE members. 'It is quite clear, Christian, from these faxes that the ban only covers sales to the Japanese. Unless you can prove prima facie intent to sell to the Japanese, you cannot prevent anyone bidding for this diamond.'

'What are you trying to say, George?'

'Presumably, at some time in the future the ban on the Japanese will be lifted. Dealers will recommence selling. So, unless you can prove intent, you cannot prevent a dealer buying this diamond and waiting until the ban is lifted and then selling it on to the Japanese.'

'Why not?'

'Because, Christian, you would have to apply that criteria to all diamonds, not just one. How could you prove that one diamond had been bought with the intention of selling on to the Japanese, and another had not? Many of our dealers are holding back stocks until the ban is lifted, right?'

'Right.'

'When that time comes are you going to prevent them from selling those same diamonds to the Japanese, because they have been holding them back until the ban was lifted? I am sorry, Christian, but the idea is preposterous. You would cause chaos.'

'Not as much chaos as I am going to cause Martina Van den Fleet. She has the impertinence to invite the IDE to bid for this diamond, when she knows perfectly well that members are expected to consult the IDE on a sale of such –' Christian waved his hand in the air – 'such magnitude.'

George crossed one leg over the other. 'I am sure she does know, but she doesn't strictly speaking, have to consult the IDE.'

Christian sighed. 'I sometimes doubt whose side you are on, George.'

'I am just pointing out the facts from a legal viewpoint, Christian. Martina Van den Fleet is not bound by the rules of the IDE. She is not a member.'

Christian folded his arms. 'She is doing this deliberately, you know, because we turned down her application to become an option bearer.'

'I should be careful then, Christian, she might set up in opposition to you.'

Christian glared at him. 'George, you are paid to give legal advice not to make third-rate, unfunny jokes.' Christian walked to his desk and sat down. 'Well, let her play her little games and when she is finished, she will never work for any member of the IDE ever again.'

George looked at him in alarm. 'Be very careful, Christian. Don't let her wind you up. If she could prove that as your intention, that would constitute personal discrimination. We could find ourselves paying damages to her. If she could prove it was sexual discrimination we would be paying punitive damages. We must be one of the few remaining organisations that lacks women executive members.'

'OK, George, thank you for your time.'

George got up from his chair. 'Coming for lunch?'

'No. I have some calls to make.'

Hendrik felt a sinking feeling in his stomach as he picked up the telephone. Christian Debilius did not call without good reason and he thought he knew what that reason was. Duiss. He ran his fingers through his hair. 'Hello, Christian, how are you?'

'Not as good as I would wish to feel.'

'Sorry to hear that. What's the matter?'

'Your sister, Martina, that is what is the matter. Presumably you have received a copy of the video. Everyone else seems to.'

Hendrik frowned to himself. He was half relieved that it was Marti and not Duiss that Christian was bothered about. 'Er, what video?'

'The video of the Cambodian diamond.' Christian spoke patiently as if to a backward child.

'Sorry, Christian, I don't follow.'

'I beg your pardon, we appear to be talking at cross-purposes. Am I to assume you have not been invited to bid for the Cambodian diamond in Geneva?'

'You assume correctly, but what's this about a Cambodian diamond?'

'The one your sister is auctioning in Geneva, Hendrik. *That* Cambodian diamond.'

Hendrik ran his fingers through his hair again. Oh my God, what was the stupid bitch up to now? 'I know nothing at all about any diamond, Christian.'

'You will, Hendrik, you will. I have done you favours in the past, have I not?'

Hendrik picked up his cigarette. Not in the recent past, he hadn't. 'What can I do for you, Christian?'

'I want you to represent the IDE in Geneva and bid for the Cambodian diamond. Your sister, Martina, has informed us that she is initially accepting sealed bids. It will save time, as you are already in Europe, if you will act on the IDE's behalf.'

Hendrik scratched at the front of his brow. 'I don't really think I can, Christian; she is my sister, people might think we were colluding.'

'I doubt if they will, Hendrik. Your sister is not handing out favours this week.'

'Have you spoken to her?'

'No.'

Hendrik raised an eyebrow. The answer had been short and very sharp. 'Well, if you really want me to handle this for you, of course, I'm happy to oblige.'

'Thank you, Hendrik. Get over to Geneva right away. I will fax our bid to you immediately.'

Hendrik grimaced at the telephone as the line went dead. He got up from his chair and went to stare out of the window. What was little sister up to now? And what the hell was the Cambodian diamond?

Pa Jiaming lit up another cigarette. He had been kept waiting for over twenty minutes in an outer office, although his appointment with Chen Chih was for ten o'clock. A moon-faced, youngish man came out of Chen's office and beckoned to Pa. 'Leader Chen will see you now.' Pa stubbed out his cigarette and got to his feet.

Chen remained seated, hands clasped in front of him, when Pa entered the room. Pa came and stood in front of Chen's desk and, when he was not invited to sit down, knew he was facing the worst. Chen cleared his throat. 'Vice-leader Pa, you are from this moment relieved of your duties as Vice-leader of the Leading Group for High Technology.'

Pa managed to summon up a look of complete astonishment. 'You are not satisfied with my work, Leader Chen?'

Chen tapped his fingers together. 'I consider that your future work for the Group may suffer, because of your other commitments. As head of the Central Military Commission for Scientific Advancement, many demands are made upon you. It is for that reason that you are relieved of your duties here.'

Pa stared at him. The reason for his being relieved was because Chen wanted to put one of his own men in.

'I can assure you –'

'Assurances are not enough. Progress is not built upon assurances.' Chen fidgeted with a file in front of him. 'As you are relieved of your duties, your visit to Geneva will not now be necessary.'

'With respect, Leader Chen, perhaps not for the Group, but my duties as head of the Central Military Commission demand that I attend the UNCTAD meeting.'

Chen nodded. 'See that your expenses are directed to the appropriate authority and not to the Leading Group.'

'Very good, Leader Chen.'

'You may leave. I am sure you have much work to attend to in your other capacity.'

'Thank you, Leader Chen.'

Pa walked swiftly down the pinky-beige marble corridor. At least Chen was correct about one thing. He did have much work to attend to. He hurried down the steps into the quadrangle and signalled to his chauffeur that he was ready to leave.

Hendrik caught the eye of the woman at the reception desk at Bank Christian Oertli. She stared coldly at him for having been so uncouth as to dare to do such a thing. Hendrik glanced away. Ugly old bat. He stared around the wood-panelled reception area. He felt like a whore waiting for an audience with the Pope. When he died he hoped it wouldn't be in Geneva. Genevans were as cold and ugly as their city.

The receptionist glanced up as Henri Chillon's assistant appeared in the corridor. She picked up her pen and pointed it at Hendrik. 'Mr Van den Fleet, Mr Bianchi.'

Bianchi nodded. 'Monsieur Chillon is in conference, Mr Van den Fleet, can we assist you?'

Hendrik's face settled into a mutinous expression. 'I think we just might. I have a sealed bid from the IDE for Miss Martina Van den Fleet. What I want from you is a little piece of paper acknowledging receipt of the bid.'

Bianchi looked him up and down. Hendrik pulled an envelope from his breast pocket and handed it to him. Bianchi took hold of it gingerly, as if wishing it had been fumigated first. 'One moment, Mr Van den Fleet, and we will attend to the matter.'

Hendrik turned away in disgust. Bianchi murmured something to the receptionist and she opened a drawer of her desk and removed a receipt pad. Bianchi wrote swiftly then tore the sheet from the pad. He handed it to Hendrik. 'Your receipt, Mr Van den Fleet.'

'Thank you. Er, have you got a telephone number where I can reach Miss Van den Fleet? I didn't have time to contact her before I left Antwerp.'

Bianchi looked at him suspiciously. 'We are not authorised to give Miss Van den Fleet's telephone number.'

Hendrik drew in a deep breath. 'I can appreciate that, but I do happen to be her brother.'

Bianchi seemed unimpressed by the claim. 'You have means of identification?'

Hendrik pulled his wallet from his inside pocket and opened it. 'Take your pick. Driving licence. Credit card.'

'May we see both, please.'

Hendrik pushed them into his hand.

'One moment please and we will consult Miss Van den Fleet.'

Hendrik looked at him in growing and murderous exasperation. He took back the driving licence and credit card and stuffed them into his wallet. He watched Bianchi retreat down the corridor. We were a pain in the arse.

When Bianchi returned, Hendrik got up from his chair, relieved to see Bianchi carrying a piece of paper. 'Miss Van den Fleet has authorised us to give you her telephone number.'

'Thank you.' Hendrik glanced at it then pushed it into his pocket.

'Good day, Mr Van den Fleet.'

'Good day to you.' Hendrik turned on his heel. When he reached the revolving doors he glanced back. Bianchi and the receptionist appeared in deep conversation, with heads bent. A conversation that the receptionist appeared to find amusing. Hendrik gave one of the doors a hefty push as he exited, leaving them spinning wildly.

Marti hurriedly paid off the driver of the taxi and climbed the steps of the bank. She had been politely summoned by Henri Chillon to deal with the sealed bids that had arrived, and the men who had descended upon the bank like a flock of hungry crows, demanding to see her and the dia-

mond. He had also received an urgent telephone call from
her brother, advising that he had been asked to represent the
Intercontinental Diamond Exchange and would be in
Geneva as soon as possible. Hendrik's call to the apartment
had been less polite. She slung her bag over her shoulder.
Within seconds they had ended up shouting at each other.

Henri Chillon's smile showed very little warmth.
'Thank you for coming so promptly, Miss Van den Fleet.
While we, at Bank Christian Oertli, do strive in our
endeavours to be of service, I have to say that I consider it
would have been more appropriate to allow more time in
which to make arrangements to hold the auction. I speak,
of course, not of ourselves, but of those attending the
auction, Miss Van den Fleet.'

'I agree absolutely, Mr Chillon.' She gave her sweetest
smile. 'Agree absolutely, but, unfortunately, I must abide
by my client's wishes.'

He gave a brief nod. 'Here are the bids we have received
so far, and here are the calling cards left by the gentlemen.'

She flicked through the envelopes, rapidly counting. All
the invitations had been accepted. A thrill of excitement
shot through her. The fish had swallowed the bait. She
sifted through the business cards and raised an eyebrow
when she saw Beni's. He didn't go anywhere unless everything was previously arranged for his sole convenience.

Henri cleared his throat. 'If you are ready to open the
envelopes, Miss Van den Fleet?'

'Yes. Thank you.'

He gestured to Bianchi who was standing by the windows. 'I have called upon my assistant to record what
takes place.'

She nodded and picked up the first envelope, carefully
removing the folded piece of paper from inside.

As Marti recorded each bid, she handed the sheet of
paper to Henri, who confirmed the bid out loud, then

passed it to Bianchi, who did the same. When the last bid
was read out and confirmed, Marti picked out the five top
highest bids. 'The names of the highest bidders are Mr
Yasim, Mr Bergman, Mr Bardy, Mr Emerson, Mr Van
den Fleet. Mr Yasim has the highest bid at $50 million,
therefore the bidding will open at $50 million.' She
glanced up at Henri.

His eyes glittered. 'I think, Miss Van den Fleet, this is
going to be a most interesting auction.'

She smiled. She bent her head again and looked down at
the bids. There was one more hurdle. Who and how many
would drop out at this stage of the proceedings. Beni's
Sheik was taking few chances in offering $50 million. She
gathered up the pieces of paper. That, as they say, would
sort out the men from the boys.

'May I offer you coffee, Miss Van den Fleet?'

'Thank you, that would be very welcome.'

'And please allow me to put my office at your disposal.'

She gave a wry smile. Henri's voice was positively
oozing with warmth. But then he was counting up the
bank's charges, and the prestige that went with being the
host bank for the auction.

'And perhaps you may wish to inspect the diamond
again?'

'Thank you.'

'I trust, Miss Van den Fleet, that you are completely
satisfied with our arrangements?'

'Very. You have been most helpful and, may I say,
reassuring. After my dream last night, I place great importance on reassurance.'

'Dream, Miss Van den Fleet?'

'Yes. I woke up in a cold sweat. I had been dreaming I
was in the vault. When I pressed the switch, the diamond
appeared, but when I went to touch it, I put my hand right
through it. That was when I woke up. When I realised it
was a hologram, and the diamond had been stolen.' She

placed the back of her hand to her brow in a mock gesture of anguish.

Henri laughed and even Bianchi managed a smile. Henri took her arm. 'In that case, perhaps we should inspect the diamond at once. We cannot have our clients suffering bad dreams.'

Pa Jiaming lit up a cigarette while he waited for his call to the People's Security Bureau in Anshan. He hastily picked up the telephone as it gave a first ring. 'Ah, yes. You will appreciate that I cannot say too much over the telephone? Good. You received the consignment of washing machines and refrigerators? Excellent. I hope they will prove to be of satisfaction to the recipients. Now, I am informed that Professor Li of the Sound & Vibration Institute will be travelling to Lhasa tomorrow. See that he is accompanied discreetly. Contact me when you have completed your mission. Thank you.' He cleared the line and reached out for a cigarette from the packet on the desk. There only remained a call to Cao at the People's Security Bureau in Shanghai.

Pa tapped the ash from his cigarette. 'Cao, you have received the merchandise you requested? Excellent. No, no, do nothing yet. I will contact you again.' He replaced the telephone and leaned back in his chair again. A smile crept over his face. Even if they had little enough clothes to fill a washing machine, or little enough food to stock a refrigerator, that did not diminish their avidity and their eagerness to do his bidding.

The four men chatted about matters totally unrelated to the reason they were sitting in a comfortable interviewing room at Bank Christian Oertli. When Warren Emerson reappeared they lapsed into silence. Tony Bergman stood up and hitched his trousers higher up around his waist. 'Worth the journey, Warren?'

Warren gave a brief nod. Bianchi came into the room
and glanced around. 'Mr Van den Fleet, if you would like
to come this way, please?'

Beni's eyes followed Hendrik as he went out with
Bianchi.

The five bidders had been allowed to examine the diamond individually, in strict alphabetical order. Beni
stretched his legs out in front of him and crossed them at
the ankles. Between them, the Sheik and Marti had dis-
rupted his work schedule for the entire month. The Sheik
he must forgive, but not Marti. He suspected that she
secretly enjoyed calling his tune. Pleasures of the boudoir
had been arbitrarily banned. As had any contact other
than the purely formal. He looked up as Hendrik returned
to the room. He adjusted the cuffs of his shirts. Now it
was his turn and not before time.

Marti positioned herself in front of the five men and
loosely clasped her hands in front of her. 'You have all
had the opportunity of examining the diamond, gentlemen. You are all satisfied as to its condition?'

They all nodded.

'Would you indicate by raising your hand if you wish to
be present at the auction?' She took in a quick breath as
each of the five raised their hands. 'Then gentlemen, I propose that we take a break for lunch. The auction will commence at two o'clock. A buffet lunch awaits you, which I
hope you will enjoy.' She gave a brief smile.

Hendrik stood up. 'We don't have to pay for the lunch
as well, do we?'

The other men gave a quick laugh.

'No. Lunch is on the house, Hendrik.'

Tony also got to his feet. 'Hey, I suddenly feel real
hungry. What about you, Warren?'

'Could eat a horse.'

Pierre Bardy and Beni stood up and followed the other
men to the door. Beni failed to manoeuvre himself next to

Marti and had to content himself with walking one man behind her to the room where lunch was being served. He gave a sigh of exasperation when she opened the door and invited them to go inside, then quickly walked away down the corridor.

James picked up the channel changer, reduced the volume of the television with one hand and reached out for the telephone with the other. 'James Wu.'

'Hello, James, Marti here.'

He hauled himself up from the depths of the sofa. 'How are things going?'

'We are starting the auction in half an hour.'

'Who's bidding?'

'Beni Yasim, Tony Bergman, Warren Emerson, Pierre Bardy and, would you believe, my brother, Hendrik, for the IDE.'

He laughed. 'That is a not untypical, crafty move by Debilius, isn't it?'

'Indeed. I'm a bit confused by Warren Emerson. Beni, I know, is bidding on behalf of the Kuwaitis. Tony has to be bidding for the Japanese. By the way, Tony was saying that Christian has been making threatening telephone calls about bidding for the diamond.'

'Doesn't seem to have bothered Tony.'

'I think because of his heavy involvement with the Japanese, he must have been expecting some reaction, because he left instructions with his nephew Max to tell Christian politely what he could do with himself.'

James chortled. 'Wish I could have been there to see it.'

'Anyway, Beni and Toni are here, as predicted. I think Pierre Bardy usually acts on behalf of the Saudis. It's Warren Emerson I can't quite figure out. What do you think, James?'

He scratched at his ear. 'Emerson only represents purely American interests. If Hendrik is bidding for the

IDE then Emerson must be for a private collector.'

'I think you're probably right. Look, I've got to go now. I'll call you as soon as I know the result.'

'I'll be waiting. Don't worry about the time. There's an old movie I want to stay up to see.'

'OK, James. I'll get back to you. 'Bye.'

He put the telephone down and turned up the sound on the television. He sat for a moment then got up and poured himself a drink. He would give his right arm and leg to be in Geneva, in Marti's place.

The boardroom at Bank Christian Oertli had been converted into an auction room. Marti glanced around the room. There were more security guards than there were bidders. She gave a brief nod to the four grey-suited men, standing two abreast, either side of the table upon which the diamond was displayed. As she turned to go out, one of the guards standing either side of the door opened it for her.

Marti stopped in the corridor to have a word with the senior security guard. 'I think we should be about ready to start.'

'I'll convey the message.' He raised his personal radio to his mouth and spoke a few words into it.

Marti returned to the auction room and sat down on one of the chairs at the back of the room. The door opened again and the bidders came into the room led by Beni. They chatted amongst themselves as they sat down. Tony and Hendrik suddenly laughed loudly. She twitched her lips. They had to be swapping dirty jokes. She glanced at the security guards around the table. They stood impassively, their hands loosely clasped in front of them, their steady gaze taking in every apparent sudden movement, every twitch of a muscle.

Marti got up and walked across the room to the table. She went to speak, but was forestalled by a telephone

ringing at the back of the room. One of the guards went to
answer it then just as quickly put it down and resumed his
position. He looked across the room at her and gave a
quick nod. She switched her gaze to the group of men
sitting in front of her. Each of them had his eyes trained
on her. 'Shall we commence, gentlemen?' She unconsciously took a step backwards, overwhelmed by the
suddenly charged atmosphere. The amiable chatter, the
laughter, had vanished. Each of them stared at her with
the aggression of an animal scenting the kill.

The auctioneer came into the room and made his way to
the rostrum. A small, rather bland-looking man, he smiled
and formally greeted the men sitting in front of him and
confirmed his agreement of their individual signals to him.
Marti took up a position to one side of the group and
leaned against the wall.

'Gentlemen, I propose to commence the bidding for the
Cambodian diamond at $50 million. I will accept bids in
multiples of $500,000.' The auctioneer managed to give
the impression of looking at everyone, without engaging
eye-contact with anyone. There was slight shuffling. Both
Bardy and Emerson shifted in their chairs, as if both suddenly found it more comfortable to sit with legs splayed
apart.

Within seconds, the bidding had reached $2 billion. The
occupants of the room remained deathly silent, apart from
the auctioneer calmly intoning each rapidly spiralling bid.
Marti slipped her hands behind her back and secretly
crossed her fingers for Beni, although the bidding was
beginning to make his initial offer appear paltry. She
glanced across at him. He maintained constant eye-contact
with the auctioneer, as if his life depended upon it.

When the bidding reached $4 billion, a whiff of acrid,
male sweat stung at Marti's nostril, overlaying the pungent
mixtures of aftershave. She discreetly wiped her damp
palms on the back of her skirt. Her hands were running

with perspiration, although she played no part in the intense and silent battle being conducted in front of her. The auctioneer remained silent for a few seconds then glanced enquiringly at each of the men in turn. 'At $4 billion, gentlemen.' She looked across at Hendrik. The collar of his shirt looked limp.

Pierre Bardy, followed by Warren Emerson, suddenly indicated they were dropping out. The auctioneer began again to intone the further bids offered by the remaining three men. At $5 billion, Hendrik also signalled defeat. Marti gripped her hands behind her back. As she had anticipated it was now a straight fight between Beni and Tony.

Beni lowered his gaze and looked away from the auctioneer at $6 billion. He breathed deeply. The Sheik would be disappointed. But. He moistened his lips. Desire knows no sense, and by his estimation, it had just sunk to the ridiculous. The auctioneer looked around the silent room. 'At $6 billion, gentlemen.' He paused for a few moments then tapped the rostrum with his gavel, as if realising that nothing more was to be gained by waiting. 'At $6 billion.' He tapped the rostrum again. 'At $6 billion, the Cambodian diamond to Mr Antony Bergman of New York. Thank you, gentlemen.'

Tony flung his head back for a moment and drew in a harsh breath. Beni was the first to get up from his chair and to offer his hand to Tony. Marti moved away from the wall and realised the muscles in her thighs were fluttering. Beni turned to her and gave a brief smile and inclined his head in a wry gesture, as if to indicate that you win some, you lose some. She glanced around the room. It was still strangely quiet, as if all of the occupants were shell-shocked by what had taken place. Tony loosened his tie, then jerked a thumb at the diamond. 'Don't bother to gift-wrap it.'

A harsh burst of laughter erupted, making Marti jump.

The sudden, sharp release of tension had sounded like a thunder clap. The security guards around the table allowed themselves a faint smile, but didn't relax their attention on the diamond.

Warren Emerson stood up and stretched his arms. He went up to Tony and slapped him on the back. 'Congratulations. That was a crazy price, Tony.'

Tony shrugged. 'I've got a crazy client, but a happy one as of now.'

Marti came to offer her hand to Tony. 'Congratulations, Tony.'

He shook her hand, then bent his head to hers. 'I got the diamond again, didn't I? Much prefer to have the girl.'

She laughed as much from relief as amusement. She turned away and took up a stance in front of the table. 'If you will be kind enough to remain where you are for a few moments, while the diamond is removed, gentlemen, champagne will be served in the dining room. Telephone and telex facilities are also available in the adjoining room.'

One of the security guards turned to the table and picked up the diamond. A second placed a steel box by his side. Tony stepped forward to take a closer look at what they were doing. 'Careful, pal, don't drop that thing.' He winked at the guard. The guard smiled again.

When the diamond had been removed, the security guards opened the double doors and stood back, like zoo keepers opening a cage. Marti led the way out, followed by Tony Bergman. As they walked along the corridor, she glanced back. The previous hostile tension had gone. Once again, they were indulging in amiable conversation as if, having determined the victor, the battle was no longer of any importance to any of them. Tony touched her arm. 'Marti, could I make a quick call?'

'Yes, of course. Telephones are in the next room along.'

'Great.'

Hendrik moved to Marti's side. He gently punched her shoulder. 'Nice one, little sister. You must be feeling very pleased with yourself.'

'Yes.'

'Wouldn't like to be in Tony's shoes when Christian hears about this.'

'Why? What can Christian do? He isn't God, although he likes to think so.'

'True. Actually, Emerson said there was a rumour that the Japanese arranged a European consortium to finance Tony on their behalf.'

'Really?'

'Understand so. Clever way of getting around the ban.' He stepped in front of her and opened the door.

'Good heavens, Hendrik, your manners have improved.'

'Just making a good impression. Lead me to the champagne. I am dying for a drink.'

Marti stared into her glass of champagne, watching the bubbles rising to the surface, in a pale imitation of the bubbles bursting inside her. She had done it. She had made the sale of the century. She looked up at a gentle touch on her elbow. Beni stood at her side. 'Am I permitted to speak to you now?'

She smiled. 'Yes, of course. Sorry, if I have been a bit distant.'

He raised his eyebrows. 'A bit? You have been behaving like the Ice Queen.'

'That's not fair. If I had been anything less than impartial, you would not have respected me, would you?'

He stared around the room. 'Dinner and some time alone together in celebration, yes?'

'But you didn't get the diamond.'

'We can always celebrate your successful sale.'

She took a sip of champagne. 'Now why didn't I think of that.'

He laughed.

Pa Jiaming sat at a window table in a café, across the street from Bank Christian Oertli. He lowered his newspaper as two men came out of the bank and got into a waiting taxi. He picked up his spoon and stirred his coffee, as a tall, fair-haired man appeared and set off down the street. Another taxi pulled up as a fourth man appeared through the revolving doors. He climbed into it and the taxi quickly sped away. Pa drank his coffee, still appearing to stare out of the window, as a person alone would do; grateful to witness the visual goings-on in the street as an antidote to boredom. He waited for a few moments then picked up his paper again.

Several minutes later a limousine with darkened glass pulled up outside the bank. Pa lowered his newspaper. The revolving doors of the bank spun. Pa thought he caught sight of a woman, but wasn't sure. The limousine was obscuring his view. He stood up and pushed his hand into his trouser pocket, as if searching for money. He stared intently at the woman leaving the bank and the dark-haired man at her side. He carefully folded his newspaper and picked up his raincoat. He watched the chauffeur open the rear door and the woman and the man get inside. So. That was Martina Van den Fleet.

Christian dropped the video cassette of the Cambodian diamond into the waste-paper bin. He had personally not liked it. Typically vulgar Russian. He sat down at his desk and clasped his hands together until the knuckles showed white. Martina Van den Fleet was an extremely disruptive force. A siren, luring the Tony Bergmans and the Warren Emersons of this world to believe that they could disregard the will of the IDE.

Margaret knocked on the door and hurried to his desk.
'The latest report by our investigator into the Duiss affair,
Mr Debilius.'

'I suppose it is naïve to ask if there is any sign of Duiss
himself?'

'He seems to have vanished into thin air. Our representative in Kinshasa offered Duiss's office manager complete immunity in return for information. Apparently,
Duiss did most of the accounting himself, but the manager
says that last week, he received a telephone call from Duiss
telling him to arrange for $200,000 of large roughs to be
sent to the repository, to the order of Van den Fleet's of
Antwerp.'

Christian stared up at her. 'And?'

'There is no trace of the transaction in the books in the
office.'

Christian let his breath out in a sigh. 'I don't know what
has come over these Van den Fleets. Advice seems to fall
on deaf ears. Only a complete fool would buy large roughs
at this moment in time. Least of all put themselves in debt
for it. No way could Van den Fleet's afford to buy that
quantity without taking out a loan, or doing a back-to-
back deal with someone. Get Finance to run an immediate
diamond audit on Van den Fleet's. Their accounts will
show where the payment to Duiss was actually sent.'

'Do you wish me to contact Mr Van den Fleet first, as a
courtesy?'

'No point. He is somewhere between Geneva and
Antwerp at the moment, but get that diamond audit done
immediately, Margaret. I want to nail Duiss and hang his
scalp above the doors of the IDE.'

'Right away, Mr Debilius.'

Marti glanced at the piece of paper as she dialled a local
Geneva number. Chan's client was taking anonymity to
cloak-and-dagger proportions. She pressed the telephone

closer to her ear. 'This is Martina Van den Fleet calling. Will the gentleman call me back, as arranged? Thank you.' She put the telephone down and sat down to wait. She picked at the chipped nail-varnish on her thumb. If her mysterious gentleman called back quickly, she would have time to wash her hair before meeting Beni. She rubbed at her nail. Plans to celebrate the sale had almost ended up in a blazing row. She wished he would understand that she was not going to trail after him from hotel to hotel. She was tired of hotel staff looking at her, as if she was some kind of high-class prostitute summoned to his suite. She bent down and searched in her bag for a nail file. If he was that interested, he could come and stay the night with her. If not . . . She unconsciously shrugged her shoulders. She smoothed the roughened nail with the file. She was probably only the flavour of the month, anyway. Where women were concerned, Beni's enthusiasms were undeniably intense, but probably inclined to be shortlived.

The sound of the telephone ringing interrupted her thoughts. She reached out and picked it up. 'Martina Van den Fleet.'

'You asked me to call you back, Miss Van den Fleet. It is cold for the time of year, isn't it?'

She smiled wryly. There was the secret code and not exactly in the same league as James Bond. 'You wish me to give you the details?'

'Yes, please.'

She pressed the telephone closer to her ear at the sound of English spoken with a very soft lisp. 'The sale produced $6 billion.' She paused at the harsh intake of breath on the line. 'More than was estimated, but that can't be a bad thing. The merchandise was sold to a Mr Tony Bergman of New York. I have this afternoon received a banker's draft from Mr Bergman for $6 billion. All agreed charges and fees have now been settled and the balance of the proceeds have been forwarded to your – the bank in Austria.'

'Thank you, Miss Van den Fleet. I hope we have the pleasure of doing business again in the future.'

'Thank you.' She heard a sudden click on the line and realised the caller had hung up. She raised her eyebrows and put the telephone down. Another happy client. She picked up her bag and went into the bedroom. When she had called James, he had been as excited as if he had sold the diamond himself. She stood in front of the dressing-table mirror and stared at herself. She suddenly didn't feel like celebrating anything. The tensions of the day had left her feeling emotionally drained.

Christian placed his hands in front of his chest, as if in prayer. Margaret leaned towards him to catch what he was saying. He spoke softly, almost to himself. 'If the evidence was not before me, I would not believe it.'

'Perhaps there is a simple explanation, Mr Debilius.'

'Is there such a thing, Margaret?'

He got up from his chair and pushed his hands into his pockets. He walked to the front of the desk and paced up and down. 'Of all companies, I would never have believed it of Van den Fleet's.'

'Would you like me to double-check the diamond audit again?'

'No thank you, Margaret, that isn't necessary. The facts are there to be seen. Van den Fleet's books show they received a loan from their bank for $200,000. The loan was paid back within four days, but they cannot account for the reason for the loan, nor how or why it was paid back. Duiss and Company claim that they deposited $200,000 worth of large roughs in the repository to the order of Van den Fleet's. There is no record of such stones being held by Van den Fleet's and no record of any trans-action between themselves and another buyer.' He turned and looked at Margaret.

She dutifully finished his statement for him. 'Except

that the manager at Duiss's claims that Van den Fleet's instructed them to send the diamonds to Japan.'

He returned to sit in his chair. 'After the IDE had issued a ban on sales to the Japanese.'

'You did allow transactions in the intermediate stage to be concluded after the ban was imposed, Mr Debilius.'

'This was not a transaction in the intermediate stage, Margaret. It is likely that there is a gap of at least twenty-four hours between the imposing of the ban and the transaction between Van den Fleet's and the Japanese. A covert transaction, Margaret. A clear intention to conceal the transaction. Would you issue the usual notification that a formal investigation will be conducted by the governing committee of the IDE? Arrange a meeting of the committee for, say, Friday. Get George Forrester to stop by my office this evening. No, on second thoughts, scrub that. I will call him myself.' His eyes moved restlessly over the objects on his desk, as if making sure everything was in its place. 'Do we have a number in Geneva for Martina Van den Fleet?'

'Only Bank Christian Oertli.'

'Call James Wu. He might have a personal number for her. Explain that we need to get in touch with Martina on a personal matter concerning Van den Fleet's. That might help him to be more forthcoming. Thank you, Margaret.'

Beni rolled over into a sitting position and clasped Marti's hands to her breasts. 'I much prefer you when you are not being a diamond dealer.'

'I much prefer you when you are not being your jet-setting wheeler dealer.'

'Touché, but that is my job, Marti.'

'And diamonds are mine.'

He bent forward and kissed her shoulder. 'No more words. Let us continue our celebration, while there is still some time left.' He muttered an oath as the telephone rang out.

Marti eased herself from beneath his body and reached out for the telephone. He grasped at her wrist. 'Don't answer it.'

'I think I should.' She felt with her fingers for the telephone. 'Hello, Martina Van den Fleet.' She stiffened at the sound of Christian Debilius's voice.

'Martina, I hope I am not calling at an inconvenient time for you?'

She stared up at the ceiling and rolled her eyes. Whatever gave him that idea? She was only lying naked in bed with a man who was doing everything possible to distract her attention. She struggled up on one elbow. 'Not inconvenient in the least, Christian.' She gave special emphasis to the name and turned to glare at Beni, punching him in the ribs with her free hand.

'Martina, may I offer the IDE's congratulations to you on what I understand was a most successful auction. Of course, we are sorry that our bid failed.'

She focused on the softly, drawling voice. The more tranquillising the tone, the more lethal the intention. She pulled herself up into a sitting position. 'Actually, someone remarked after the auction that desire knows no sense and it had just sunk to the ridiculous.'

Christian laughed. 'I don't know about desire being ridiculous, but it comes very expensive at $6 billion.'

'What did you want to speak to me about, Christian?'

He laughed again. 'Always straight to the point, Marti. We are doing an audit check at Van den Fleet's. Usual random yearly check. Can I take it that if there are any little queries, we can rely on your assistance?'

'Yes, of course. You realise that I no longer have any connection with the firm. Justus, the office manager, should be able to deal with any queries with last year's accounts, but if there is anything he can't deal with, tell them to get in touch with me right away. I shall be back in Hong Kong the day after tomorrow.'

'I knew I could rely upon you, Martina. I appreciate it. There is another matter I would like to raise with you. Could you possibly delay your return to Hong Kong?'

'Why?'

'If possible, could you arrange to come to New York? I would like to have an informal discussion with you about your status with the IDE.'

'I don't have one.'

'Quite. This is what I would like to discuss with you. The governing committee has received a report from our study group on the positive role women must play in the future growth of the IDE.'

She raised both eyebrows.

'We seem to have created a Catch-22 situation for ourselves, in that to protect our members we must demand that newcomers to the IDE have a strong financial base. It goes without saying that competent members should not bear the burden created by the incompetent. However, this does create a barrier to those women, like yourself, who are extremely capable, but are restricted by the traditional structure of the typical merchant's business.'

'I don't quite follow what you are trying to say, Christian.'

'If I may use you as an example. Your work at Van den Fleet's has been very much respected. Very much respected. However, as is family tradition, the business has been passed on to Hendrik, as eldest son. We are not unmindful at the IDE that this tradition, worthy as it is, creates enormous handicaps for women like yourself in realising their full potential.'

'Ah, I see what you mean.'

'Good. In response to the study group's report, it is the IDE's intention seriously to consider how best to ensure positive discrimination when considering the question of appointing women option bearers.'

'Glad to hear it, Christian.'

'I thought that might be your response. I speak in confidence, Martina, of course, but I wanted you to know that in taking this course of action, your name will be the first to be given positive consideration by the governing committee. In fact, I can, with confidence, say that the committee will be recommending that you become a full option bearer at the IDE.'

She glanced at Beni, who had become bored and was sitting on the edge of the bed. Thoughts rushed pell-mell into her mind. The governing committee's task had been made easy. They only had two names, as far as she knew, to choose from.

'Martina, are you still there?'

She swung her legs off the bed and sat up. 'Sorry, Christian, I just went into a dead faint.'

He laughed. 'My apologies. I would hate to be held responsible for the sudden demise of our first woman option bearer.'

'I think I can manage a complete recovery.'

'Splendid. Now, would it be possible to come to New York? Although official approval by the governing committee has yet to be given, I think it is important that you and I have an opportunity of discussing matters.'

'Yes, certainly. I can be in New York tomorrow. Late tomorrow, that is.'

'I will have someone meet you at the airport, Martina, and perhaps we can have a working dinner together.'

'Thank you.'

'Well, I will say goodbye until tomorrow.'

She put the telephone down. Option bearer. She wrapped her arms around herself. It was tempting to think that the auction of the Cambodian diamond had something to do with the sudden change of heart. She grinned unashamedly. Good girls go to heaven and bad girls go to the IDE.

She scrambled across the bed and put her arms around

Beni. 'You will never guess what that was about.'

'Then tell me.'

'I am probably going to be appointed an option bearer at the IDE. It just requires official approval by the governing committee.'

'Congratulations.'

She put her arms around his neck. 'Now we have even more to celebrate, don't we?'

He brushed his mouth against her cheek. She ignored the little warning voice at the back of her mind. She kissed him and slid a hand down to his groin. 'I bet you've never slept with an option bearer before.' She looked at him as he stopped her hand. 'What is the matter?'

'Nothing.' He stroked the fingers of her hand. 'If you are going to New York tomorrow, you need a good night's sleep. You are going to be very busy.'

She looked into his eyes then drew away from him. The desire had gone from him, like snuffing out a candle. She moved her hand away from his body. 'I suppose you're right.' She stood up and went to the other side of the bed and pulled on her bathrobe. She looked at his back, the curve of his shoulders. Damn you. Anger spread through her, smothering the discomforting feeling of rejection. She felt like beating his shoulders to pulp. She tugged at the bathrobe, pulling it closer around her. His curiosity had been satisfied. She was no longer of interest to him. She tied the belt of her bathrobe tightly. He had conveniently chosen to make her work come between them. She pushed her hair back from her face and turned on her heel. She supposed it was as good an excuse as any to send her drifting quietly out of his life.

Marti stepped out of the shower and wrapped a towel around her. She looked up to find Beni watching her. She held the towel tightly to her, as if finding herself in an embarrassing confrontation with a stranger. He was already dressed. 'Marti, I think I'd better be getting back to my hotel. I have to make an early start myself, tomorrow.'

'Yes, of course.'

'Er, I'll call you. I'm not sure when. I've got a very heavy schedule this coming week.'

'So have I, perhaps we will manage to catch up with each other sometime.'

'Yes. There will always be a time and place for us, Marti.' He came to her and kissed her cheek.

She watched him back away, give a smile as he reached the door, then heard the bedroom door close. She picked up the hand towel that had slipped from the rail and hung it up again. Beni hadn't exactly changed her life, but she was going to miss him.

George Forrester sat in one of the leather club chairs in Christian's apartment. Christian picked up a bottle of gin from the sideboard. 'The usual, George?'

'Thank you. That bronze over there. Is that new?'

'Yes. I don't mind admitting I paid too much for it, but I couldn't resist it.'

George smiled. Christian so loved to give himself the common, human touch. Christian handed him a glass of gin and tonic. 'I much appreciate your coming over at short notice, George.'

'Not at all. Have you reached any decision about Van den Fleet's?'

'It is what I think we should discuss, George. Rules must be obeyed. Examples must be set. I would suggest that the governing committee is recommended to impose a heavy fine and issue a public warning to Van den Fleet's.'

George inclined his head. 'Van den Fleet's have never been censured before. That is likely to kill off the old man.'

Christian sprawled out in the chair opposite. 'That is precisely what has been exercising my mind. I do not wish to see the IDE held responsible for anyone's death, George.'

'What do you propose to do?'

'Temper the bad news with the good?'

'Such as?'

'I am considering the wisdom of recommending that Martina Van den Fleet is made an option bearer, and I should like your opinion, George.'

George gave him a long look. He raised his glass to his mouth. Christian had already considered it, and didn't need his opinion. 'What has prompted that startling thought?'

Christian gave a faint smile. 'Not as startling as it seems. Two reasons. Firstly, I think it is unwise to leave her free to operate outside the IDE. She will gain a lot of kudos from that auction. Incidentally, I had a drink with Tony Bergman. He was very impressed with the way she handled things.'

'I thought the last time we spoke, you had in mind to tie his balls into a knot.'

Christian shrugged. 'We kissed and made up. Apparently the auction was run exactly by the rule-book. She kept everything and everyone on an extremely tight rein.' He leaned forward. 'Fascinating little piece of gossip, George. Apparently, Beni Yasim was not, repeat not, amused by the proceedings. I gathered from Tony that it took Beni a little time to realise that he wasn't in line for any preferential treatment from Martina.'

'I thought you said he was screwing her.'

'But not that hard to sway her judgement. I spoke to Warren Emerson as well. He, apparently, is seriously thinking of offering her a consultancy position. I think, George, it is time that the lamb was brought into the safety of the fold, don't you?'

George nodded thoughtfully. 'You said there were two reasons.'

'Ah, yes. Let me top that up for you, George.' Christian got up and took both their glasses to the sideboard. 'You know we have been having exploratory talks with the Chinese again?'

'Mmm.'

'This time, I think they have a serious intent to join the IDE. They took the initiative in reviving the talks.'

'Are we offering anything new?'

'Of course not.' Christian came back to where George sat and returned his glass to him. 'We will, as we promised in earlier discussions, provide the know-how, the backup, to assist them in the development of their mine. I detect a significant change of stance, George. A very significant change. I was obliquely advised that when Hong Kong reverts to PRC rule in 1997, they wish to be in a position to commence trading with the IDE, using Hong Kong as their base.'

'That should please the Hong Kong Diamond Merchants' Association.'

Christian smiled. 'Quite. However, George, there is one slight problem. All of the members are ethnic Chinese and, therefore, liable to persuasion by the PRC, if you get my meaning.'

'You want to get some of our people in?'

'Softly, softly catchee monkey, George. The Chinese are very sensitive to interference of any kind in their affairs. It would be more a question of utilising what European people we have in Hong Kong already.'

'Martina Van den Fleet.'

'The name did cross my mind.'

'We have our own representative out there.'

'But he is not an independent dealer. He is employed by the IDE. A situation that the Chinese would be the first to point out. Martina would make a suitable candidate, if you think about it, George. She was invited to Hong Kong by James Wu. By the time the Chinese are in a position to commence trading, she will have worked there for some appreciable time. The Chinese could not complain that she had been foisted upon them.'

George took another mouthful of gin. 'And if she was an option bearer in her own right, she could act on behalf of the IDE.'

'I asked you here for your advice, George, as you know how much I value it. What do you think?'

George rubbed at his jaw. 'If the Chinese joined the IDE, that would have a sobering effect upon some of our more insubordinate mine owners. Your idea is tempting, but whoever we placed in Hong Kong would have to speak some Cantonese, or Mandarin whatever.'

Christian shrugged. 'Martina is Belgian. She speaks at least three languages already. I'm sure she could manage another one.'

'You are overlooking one small thing, if I may say so.'

'What is that?'

'Martina may not accept option-bearer status. She may refuse just for the sheer hell of it.'

'I can assure you, George, that will not be a problem. She will be delighted.'

George gave him another long look. 'You have already spoken to her.'

'We have talked about having talks, yes. So, what do you think of the idea?'

George stretched his legs out in front of him. 'Brilliant, Christian. What more can one say?'

Christian smiled. 'Thank you, George. Am I to take it that you will second my proposal to the governing committee?'

'I will.'

'Now. Shall we eat? Rosie has prepared your favourite chilli con carne. By the way, the governing committee is meeting on Friday. You will make sure you have no other appointments, won't you, George?'

George nodded. He got up and followed Christian to the door. He shook his head to himself in amusement. Christian was never happier than when spinning one of his little webs of duplicity.

The men scraped back the chairs from the table and sat themselves down. Frankie Heung tapped the glass in front of him with his pen. 'I bring this meeting to order. First, I should like to welcome Mr Ronnie Lee as a new member of the Thousand Clouds Society. Mr Ronnie Lee, gentlemen.'

Ronnie half rose from his chair and gave a little bow in acknowledgement of the clapping of hands.

Frankie tapped at the glass again. 'Before we ask Turtle to read out the agenda for this meeting, I call upon Mr Ronnie Lee to join with me in the sharing of fire and blood, as proof of his allegiance to the Thousand Clouds Society until he shall die.'

Ronnie got to his feet. 'Mr Heung, I declare that it is my solemn wish to share fire and blood with you.'

Frankie nodded to Busy. 'Busy has been nominated as flame master.'

Busy pushed his chair back and went to the table by the door and lit the small bronze lamp.

The men gathered around Frankie and Ronnie, in respectful silence, as both men bared their forearms and held them over the flame. Busy held the knife in the air for a moment then quickly brought it down, first against Frankie's wrist, then against Ronnie's wrist. The flame flickered as drops of blood fell on it. It appeared to almost die, then sputtered and flared up again.

Busy carefully wiped the knife clean and placed it back into its sheath. Each of the men present filed past Ronnie and shook his hand. Frankie wrapped a handkerchief around his wrist. He moved close to Busy's side. He whispered in a low voice to him. 'It is a bad omen if blood does not mingle with the flame, right?'

'Right, Mr Heung.'

'It is the duty of the flame master to ensure that it does, right?'

'Right, Mr Heung.'

'It is not the duty of the flame master, Busy, to try and sever my fucking arm off, right?'

'Oh, sorry, Mr Heung. It's the first time I've been flame master. Didn't want any mistakes, Mr Heung.'

'OK. OK.'

Frankie took a mouthful of fruit juice and set the glass down on the table. 'Last item on the agenda, gentlemen, and please refer to Item One. Your chairman has to report that negotiations with the Third Moon Gang regarding the reclamation works at Causeway have broken down. I do not need to remind you that insurance premiums against uninterrupted work schedules would represent a significant contribution to our cash-flow forecast for the next year. Referring to Item One. Manpower resources. Now that the shortfall in personnel, courtesy of Mr Ronnie Lee and remaining members of the Brotherhood of the Bear's Paw, has been met, your chairman recommends that we take over the Third Moon Gang. We have the manpower, gentlemen. We have the resources.' Frankie looked around the table. There was a general murmur of approval and a small round of applause. Frankie nodded in satisfaction. 'I now declare this meeting closed.' He picked up the glass of fruit juice and took another mouthful. Busy took out his flick knife and ran his finger along the edge. He snapped it closed again. Mr Heung sure knew how to run things.

Hendrik stared out of the window. He cracked each of his knuckles in turn. Astrid quietly entered the office and came to his side. 'Would you like a cup of coffee, Hendrik?'

'No. Oh, all right, yes.' He jerked his head towards the door. 'Are they still in the accounts office?'

'Yes. Mr Dwyer said he should be through in about ten minutes. He said for you to remain in your office. He has some questions to ask.' Hendrik swallowed hard. He could have got away with it, if it hadn't have been for that arsehole Duiss running away. He drew in a shuddering breath.

Astrid bit her lip. Hendrik looked as white as a ghost. She had thought he was going to kill her, when she casually mentioned that the IDE had asked to do a routine diamond audit. She touched his arm. 'I really am sorry I didn't try to call you in Geneva, Hendrik. They said they needed to check up on the activities of another member. I just assumed it could wait until you got back.'

He shrugged. 'Wouldn't have made much difference if you had.' He searched in his jacket pocket for his cigarettes and pulled out a crumpled packet. 'Go and get me another packet of cigarettes, will you?'

'Mr Dwyer said no one was to leave the office.'

'Forget it. Just get the coffee.' Hendrik raised his hand to his face and rubbed at his eyes. This was going to kill his father. He rested his forehead on the windowpane. The only chance he had was to deny everything. He walked slowly back to his desk. If he could.

Dwyer tapped politely on the door of Hendrik's office. 'May I come in, Mr Van den Fleet?'

'You've been everywhere else. Why bother to ask?'

Dwyer quietly closed the door. 'I hope that this interview can be conducted in a civilised manner, Mr Van den Fleet. I am only doing my job.'

'Then I suggest you get on with it. You've brought this company to a standstill for almost a whole day.' Hendrik straightened his shoulders. 'Now what are all these allegations that we have been trading illegally?'

'On the eighteenth, the IDE issued a ban on sales to the

Japanese, at precisely twelve noon. We are informed by the office manager at Duiss's that on that same afternoon you purchased $200,000 of roughs and confirmed that they were to be held to your order in Kinshasa. Is that correct, Mr Van den Fleet?'

'I did not purchase the roughs on that day. I *confirmed* the purchase. I made the purchase with Duiss himself on the seventeenth.'

'Have you any proof of that?'

'No.'

'Is it not usual to back up telephone conversations with telex, fax?'

Hendrik gave a deliberately exasperated sigh. 'Have you ever worked in Zaire, Mr Dwyer?'

'No.'

'Then let me explain to you that things do not work the same out there, as they do here. Telexes, faxes, are useless, Mr Dwyer, unless the person at the other end bothers to collect them, or even knows how to operate the goddam machines.'

'Very well, Mr Van den Fleet. Just let me make a note of that.'

Hendrik lit up his last remaining cigarette. 'Could my secretary possibly be allowed to get me a packet of cigarettes?'

Dwyer nodded. Hendrik reached across the desk and angrily pressed the button on the intercom. 'Astrid, I have permission for you to go and get some cigarettes. Don't take longer than five minutes, otherwise I shall be held as a hostage or something.'

Dwyer pursed his lips. He waited until Hendrik had settled back in his chair before speaking. 'On the nineteenth, the day after the IDE imposed the ban, you instructed Duiss's to despatch the diamonds to Japan. Is that correct?'

'Yes.'

'Despite the ban imposed by the IDE?'

'I considered it to be an ongoing transaction and not subject to the ban.'

Dwyer nodded. 'If I may turn to another matter, Mr Van den Fleet. According to your records, your bank made a loan of $200,000 to this company on the sixteenth.'

'Yes.'

'What was the purpose of the loan?'

'To finance the purchase of the diamonds from Duiss.'

'The loan was repaid to the bank on the twentieth. Is that correct?'

'Correct.'

'You say that the diamonds were to be sold on to the Japanese. Why is there no record of this transaction in the Company accounts?'

'An oversight on my part, for which I take full responsibility.'

'How did that occur?'

'I had received an advisory fax from the IDE warning members not to do any further deals with Duiss. I was very alarmed and was more concerned about getting to Zaire as quickly as I could to see what the hell was going on.'

'Did you go to Zaire?'

'No. I received a telephone call from Japan to say that the diamonds had arrived.'

'Is there any record of this in the office?'

Hendrik gave a loud exaggerated sigh. 'There is a time-lag between Antwerp and Tokyo, Mr Dwyer. I took the call at home.'

'I see. Have you paid Duiss's for the diamonds?'

'Yes.'

'But the transaction has not been recorded in your accounts, Mr Van den Fleet.'

'As I say, an oversight on my part, for which I take full responsibility.'

'Who did you make the payment to?'

'Duiss himself.'

'Is that not a little strange, Mr Van den Fleet?'

'Not in Zaire, no.'

'Once you knew that the diamonds had been forwarded to Japan, why did you not take the opportunity to bring your accounts up to date?'

'Because, Mr Dwyer, Christian Debilius personally asked me to go to Geneva immediately and attend an auction on behalf of the IDE.' His eyes flashed with anger. 'And no, Mr Dwyer, I can't fucking prove that, either. Perhaps you should question Christian Debilius.'

Dwyer stared at him for a moment. 'I know that these interviews are very difficult, Mr Van den Fleet, but I think it will help if you try to remain calm. These investigations have to be carried out. It is in your interests that this matter is properly cleared up.'

Hendrik stubbed out his cigarette. 'I am sorry.' He thought he had detected a slight thaw in Dwyer's manner. 'Look, forgive me. I've been rushing around so much, I'm surprised I have been able to keep track of anything. My main concern was about Duiss. If he reneged on the deal, it would have made Van den Fleet's bankrupt. We couldn't have gone on supporting the bank loan, not under present trading conditions. I –'

'Please just let me make a note of this, Mr Van den Fleet.' Dwyer bent his head and wrote quickly. 'One final question, Mr Van den Fleet. What is the name of the Japanese buyer.'

'Yoshino.'

Dwyer nodded. He placed his notebook into his briefcase. 'Thank you for the time you have spent answering my questions.'

'Is that it, then?'

Dwyer gave a brief smile. 'Yes, that's it.'

'What happens now?'

'I shall make my report to the Finance Department of the IDE.'

'Can you give me any idea what that will be?'

'Mr Van den Fleet, you know I am not allowed to do that.'

'Off the record? This whole thing is very worrying. Very worrying indeed. I've got enough problems to contend with, without this hanging over my head.'

Dwyer thought for a moment. 'I can say that you will be penalised for keeping inaccurate accounts, but in view of the fact that you were acting for Christian Debilius at the time, Finance will take that into consideration.'

'What about the other?'

Dwyer pursed his lips. 'Off the record, Mr Van den Fleet, is there any reason why Mr Yoshino cannot corroborate what you have told me?'

'No reason whatsoever.'

'Then I should think you don't have too much to worry about. There will be disciplinary action for failure to maintain good trading practices.' Dwyer picked up his briefcase. 'You know, Mr Van den Fleet, it really is in your own interest to ensure that meticulous attention is made to the making and recording of telexes, faxes. You leave yourself in a difficult position if a transaction has to be audited, if you don't.'

Hendrik gave a short laugh. 'Don't I know it.'

Dwyer held out his hand. 'I'll say goodbye then.'

'Yes. Sorry about the way I behaved before. No hard feelings?'

Dwyer gave a tired smile. 'I am used to it.'

When Astrid returned to the office, she found Hendrik sitting with his head resting on his arms. 'Hendrik, are you feeling all right?'

He raised his head and stared at her blankly.

'Are you feeling all right, Hendrik?'

'Never better.' He straightened up. 'Go home now, Astrid. There is nothing more you can do here tonight.'

As she closed the door behind her, Hendrik picked up the telephone and dialled Yoshino's number in Tokyo. 'Hello, Mr Yoshino, it's Hendrik Van den Fleet here. Er – seems I've got a bit of a problem on my hands with the timing of our deal.'

'How is that?'

'I had it in mind that we agreed the deal on the seventeenth, but the IDE seem to think it was done on the eighteenth. The day the ban came into force against you. I have been looking at the transaction again, Mr Yoshino, and on reconsideration I could see my way to letting you have those roughs at basic trade price. That would be $300,000 not $800,000.'

'I should be very pleased if you could see your way to doing that, Mr Van den Fleet. Did you say the deal was on the seventeenth?'

'Yes.'

'Then I am sure you are correct, Mr Van den Fleet.'

'Er, it is possible that the IDE will be checking with you.'

'Then I shall tell them what I have told you, that Mr Van den Fleet is correct.'

'Thank you, Mr Yoshino. I will make the correct calculations and forward the balance owing first thing tomorrow morning.'

'Thank you, Mr Van den Fleet.'

Hendrik put the telephone down and pulled open the bottom drawer of his desk and took out the bottle of whisky. He rested the bottle against the side of his face. His fingers shook as he unscrewed the cap and raised the bottle to his lips. He replaced the cap and wiped his mouth with the back of his hand. There was no reason for Yoshino to let him down. He was getting a $500,000 bonus. Van den Fleet's would show a small profit. He put the bottle back in the drawer. If the IDE found Duiss, it would simply be Duiss's word against his.

Marti quietly watched Christian giving the waiter his instructions. He showed elaborate courtesy to everyone. She picked up her glass. Until they stepped out of line. She glanced around the restaurant. The last time she had been here, Beni had been sitting opposite her. She twirled the glass between her fingers. That had been very nice, while it had lasted, which hadn't been very long. She focused her attention back to Christian. His usual predatory charm had been replaced by something more avuncular; even to the extent of using her nickname.

'Marti, another aperitif?'

'Thank you.'

'Now, where were we? Ah, yes, what do you think of my idea of arranging a little celebration in Antwerp for Erasmus? Nothing too strenuous, of course. Maybe a luncheon at the Association's headquarters? I should visit Europe more often, anyway.'

'I think it is a lovely idea. My father will feel very honoured, I know.'

'Good. Now, we can talk about your future, Marti.'

'My future?'

'Yes. It is important that you have a structured career plan and I want you to feel that you can rely upon me absolutely, to assist you.' He rested his hand lightly on top of hers. 'You know, you will be the youngest member of the IDE. I am afraid that it will cause some resentment. There will be those who feel they are more entitled to become an option bearer. So you must look upon me as your mentor, Marti. Now, what are your plans?'

She went to open her mouth, but he continued speaking.

'I think you should renew your contract as a consultant with James Wu. We at the IDE are expecting great things from you both.' He leaned across the table. 'May I speak in confidence to you, Marti?'

'Please do.'

'We are proposing to accept membership of the Chinese into the IDE.' He gave her a stern look. 'I repeat that this is strictly confidential. It will mean, of course, that Hong Kong will become an extremely important trading base.'

Her eyes widened. That was a true understatement. 'What about after 1997?'

He gestured with his hand. 'Even more so, wouldn't you say?'

The waiter reappeared with their drinks. He removed the empty glasses and placed fresh drinks on the table in one smooth operation. Marti watched his silent movements. If what Christian said was true, Hong Kong could be where she could definitely make her mark. Selling the Cambodian diamond had been purely a one-off thing. It was already stale news.

'What do you think, Marti?'

She looked up at Christian. 'Sorry, I was thinking over what you have just said. I would like to go back to work in Hong Kong, but that will depend upon James. He may not wish to renew my contract.'

He gave a faint sigh. 'It really is unnecessary to keep up this pretence. I know full well that the termination of your contract was a very naughty ploy on the part of both you and James to get around the IDE's ban. I have, Marti, forgiven you both, but just this once mark you.'

She picked up her glass and took a sip. It was the sale that had changed Christian's mind. She would not be sitting opposite him, if she had not had the courage to sell the Cambodian diamond. 'You know, there really isn't anything you have to forgive.'

Christian leaned back in his chair. Women always insisted upon being proved right. It was why he had never allowed a woman into the IDE before. He looked across at her. 'I consider that there is, but we have more important matters to discuss. I have spoken to James and he is more

than anxious that you rejoin his company. I understand
from him that you both get on well together, so he is
proposing to offer you a partnership in six months' time.
Now, may I suggest, Marti, that say within twelve months
you apply to the Hong Kong Diamond Merchants' Association for full membership. It would, of course, be a for-
mality. As an option bearer and a partner in James Wu,
there would be no reason for them to refuse such an
application.'

She sipped her drink. She was just beginning to see
where the conversation was leading. He was quietly
manipulating her and James to the IDE's advantage. 'Do
you play chess, Christian?'

'Sorry?'

'Do you play chess?'

He stared at her in complete bemusement. 'As a matter
of fact I don't.'

'I think you would be very good at it.'

'I suppose I am expected to ask why?'

She laughed. He leaned across the table again. 'You are,
if I may say, Marti, a very attractive young lady, but I
shall not find you so attractive if you insist upon these
obscure conversations.'

'Sorry. The thought occurred to me that as you are so
clever at manoeuvring people, you would make a good
chess player.'

He gave a faint smile. 'Diplomacy, Marti, not
manoeuvring. Manoeuvring is a word I do not like.'

'Why do you want me in Hong Kong?'

'Did I say that?'

'No, but it comes across loud and clear.'

'I want you in Hong Kong, because that is where I want
you to be.'

She looked at him quickly. It would be foolish to ignore
the steeliness of his voice.

'May I remind you, Marti, that the governing committee is considering your application for option-bearer status, purely on my recommendation.'

She picked up her glass. 'Have you ever been to Hong Kong?'

'No.'

'You should. It is a fascinating place. It takes a little getting used to, but an interesting place none the less. I am quite looking forward to returning.'

His eyes held hers for a moment. 'I am glad we understand each other, Marti.'

She took a sip of vermouth. Not half as glad as she was. 'When I do get back, I must make an effort to learn Cantonese. I am completely lost unless I am with someone who speaks English.'

'I think you will find it more useful in the future to learn Mandarin.'

She nodded. Again there was an edge to his voice that demanded compliance. 'That's the official language in China isn't it?'

'In Beijing certainly. It is impossible to have any meaningful negotiations unless you speak some Mandarin.'

'Who are you negotiating with in Beijing?'

'A man called Pa Jiaming. He's very good. More Westernised than he appears.'

She thought for a moment. 'That name sounds familiar. Isn't he the head of MOSAC?'

He stared at her in surprise. 'You know him?'

'No, but an acquaintance of mine does.'

'Who is the acquaintance?'

'Erwin Klein. He is a consultant for German interests out there. I think he does a lot of negotiating in Beijing.'

He raised an eyebrow. 'Then a very useful man to know.'

'That's what I thought.'

He laced his fingers together and rested them on the table. 'The Chinese are very strange. I see negotiating with them as a very stimulating challenge. It is difficult to categorise them, you know. Our representative in Beijing says it is rumoured that Pa is also head of the Central Military Commission for Scientific Advancement.'

'Difficult to see the connection between the military and diamond mining.'

'Quite.'

'Erwin says never bother talking to anyone in Beijing unless they wear an expensive suit and have a big chauffeured limousine.'

He looked at her quizzically. 'You appear very impressed with this Erwin Klein. I do not wish to interfere in your personal life, but –'

She laughed. 'Don't jump to conclusions, Christian. He is sixty and a grandfather.'

'Ah, I see. How did you meet?'

'At a party given by a British couple in Hong Kong.'

His face grew still, as if displeased by the news. 'I think it would be better, Marti, if you kept your distance from the British. You understand me?'

'Perfectly. I didn't much like them anyway. The husband is a business colleague of Beni Yasim's. Beni gave me an introduction to them when I first went out there.'

'What is good for Beni, is not always good for others, Marti. I don't know what his interests are in Hong Kong, but presumably he finds them lucrative.'

'I gather he's asset-stripping Paulinson Pacific.'

'Did he tell you that?'

'No. Erwin Klein did.'

'Interesting piece of news, and all the more reason to keep your distance from the British. The Chinese are very sensitive about what happens in Hong Kong. It would be unwise to blot one's copy book, so to speak.'

'I know.'

'May I ask a favour?'

'Yes.'

'You will keep me informed of any news you hear about Pa Jiaming? It could prove very useful. Intelligence gathering is a vital prerequisite to negotiating.'

'I understand.'

He smiled. 'I think you are going to be a great asset to the IDE, Marti.'

She took another sip of her drink. She couldn't afford not to be.

Pa Jiaming turned around to the woman standing behind him in the queue at the airport check-in desk. 'Please, go ahead of me.' He gestured with his hand to make his message clear. The woman gave him a grateful smile as she patted and soothed the wailing baby in her arms.

The man at the check-in desk handed Pa his pass. 'I hope you have enjoyed your visit to Vienna, Mr Wu.'

Pa smiled politely. 'I have enjoyed it very much. Thank you.' He followed the trail of people heading in the direction of the hand-luggage checkpoint. He looked around him with interest. He had enjoyed his visit very much indeed. Martina Van den Fleet had proved to be a most trustworthy servant. The proceeds of the Cambodian diamond, as the stupid *gweilos* had called it, were deposited in his bank account, exact to the last dollar.

The woman to whom he had given his place in the queue turned round and smiled gratefully at him. Pa smiled back and nodded. He gazed at the baby's face as it lay asleep on its mother's shoulder. There were just two further matters of business to be attended to. He transferred his folded raincoat from one arm to the other. Matters which would be concluded by the time he reached Beijing.

Chan Chunling parked in the car park next to the apartment block where he lived. He carefully locked the driver's door and turned to walk the few short yards to the entrance to the apartments. He whirled round as rough hands grasped both his arms and pinned them back. A card was held in front of his face.

'PSB. Come with us immediately.'

Chan stared at the card in fright. 'What is the matter? What have I done?'

'You are to be questioned. Come with us.'

He obeyed the invisible voice and allowed himself to be led away.

The car followed the flow of traffic along the Bund, without any apparent haste. Chan stared miserably ahead of him, confused thoughts whirling around in his head. Professor Li said they would be free. They would not be called upon again. The car swung off on to the Zhonghua–Renmin ring road.

Chan shivered as the car pulled up in the old quarter of Shanghai. He was ordered out of the car and again his arms were pinned to his sides, as he was hustled along the dark, narrow street. They turned into a cobbled alley. A voice instructed him to walk up to the door on the left and knock twice. Chan tried to turn his head to make one last appeal. 'I had to sell them. I had to. He said I would be shot if I didn't sell the diamonds.' He almost stumbled, as his arms were released and he was pushed on his way. He took a few steps forward and glanced back, but was commanded to go on. As he reached the door, a single shot rang out. He gave a shrill cry and slumped to the ground. One of the men walked up and bent down to examine him. He looked up and nodded to his companion.

Marti wrapped her hair in a towel and went to sit on the edge of the bed. She stared around the hotel bedroom. New York could be a very lonely place. She held her head down and rubbed at her hair. It had prompted her to call up Tony Bergman and get herself re-invited to dine with him and his wife. She smoothed her hair back from her face. Now should be a good time to call Hendrik. She dialled the number and braced herself for the housekeeper's monologue. 'Oh, Hendrik, hello. It's me, Marti.'

'I would never have guessed.'

'How is Father?'

'OK. Went to the hospital today for a check-up. Everything's fine.'

'Oh, I am pleased. Has Christian rung you?'

'What about?'

She grimaced. Hendrik's voice had sharpened. That meant trouble. 'Is Father there with you?'

'No.'

'It's just that Christian is coming to Europe and he wants to arrange a luncheon party for Father. I think it's a rather nice idea. What do you think?'

'Yes, very generous.'

'It's supposed to be a surprise, so don't say anything to Father about it.'

'OK.'

'Do you want to hear the other surprise?'

'What's that?'

'I have been elected as an option bearer. The governing committee met today and approved it.' She waited as the silence on the other end of the line deepened. 'Hello, Hendrik?'

'Is this a joke?'

'No.'

'Well, I suppose I should congratulate you, then. How did you manage to beat Christian into submission?'

She laughed. 'I didn't have to. I think he has finally found a use for me.'

'What are you going to do?'

'I am going back to Hong Kong to work with James Wu.'

'Oh, I see.'

She gave a wry smile at the relief in his voice. 'Don't worry, Hendrik, we shan't be getting into each other's hair any more.'

'I wasn't thinking that. If you're happy out there, good luck to you. How's business?'

'Very quiet. I spoke to James earlier on. He says it's so quiet, he's thinking of having the offices redecorated.'

Hendrik gave a sharp laugh. 'Might do the same here.'

'Things should pick up when the tears for happiness campaign gets underway. People will be falling over themselves to get small roughs.'

'I hope so. This ban on the Japanese is a real problem.'

'Well, let me know what you arrange with Christian about Father's luncheon party. I would like to attend.'

'OK, and congratulations again.'

'Thanks.' She put the telephone down and smiled to herself. Hendrik still sounded as if he had been hit on the head by a blunt instrument.

She switched on the hair-dryer and ran her fingers through her hair. Not even Hendrik's less than enthusiastic response could dim her excitement. It was like the thrill of expectancy she always felt on New Year's Eve. She turned her head to one side and fluffed out her hair. Except, in the past, each New Year had turned out to be exactly the same as the previous one. Beni had seen what she had not. She had been living under her father's shadow. She still loved him dearly, but he had always been a domineering man, even with her mother. She switched the dryer off and smoothed her hair into shape. The change she had feared so much had brought her freedom from that.

Professor Li made his way to the Second City Reception Centre. He pulled his jacket closer about him as protection against the chill wind. He did not normally notice his surroundings, but Lhasa was a place of exile. A cold, impoverished land. His lodgings at the Second City Reception Centre was a cubicle with an iron bed and a small stove that must not be lit until six o'clock. He rubbed his hands together. He should have remembered to bring his gloves.

As he turned the corner of the street, two men fell into step either side of him. He glanced at them then decided to ignore them. He did not know either of them. As he crossed the entrance to a small alleyway he found himself suddenly pushed into it. He let out a startled cry as his arms were pinned to his sides.

'PSB, Professor Li, we have orders to arrest you.'

He made an attempt to struggle free, but hard bodies were pressing against his sides, squeezing the very breath out of him. Chen. His eyes rolled in terror. Chen had sent them. 'Please, listen to me. I was forced to denounce him. They made me. They tortured me.'

A rag was stuffed into his mouth and he was propelled forwards. Half-way down the alley he was pushed through a doorway. He stumbled forward into the stable. His fingers clawed at the air as a wire was drawn tightly around his neck. The man behind him let him slowly sink to the ground. Li's body twitched, then lay still. The man bent down and removed the wire from around Li's neck. He looked up at his companion. 'What do we do with him?'

'It's been left to us. Let's take him up to the monastery and let the crows finish him off. It's the custom around here.'

Christian laced his fingers together. He looked across at George Forrester. 'What do you think?'

'There is very little that you can or should do, Christian. I think the governing committee did the right thing in merely fining Van den Fleet's for accounting irregularities. Evidence of illegal trading was not conclusive.'

'Mmm.'

'And you didn't help your case by having to admit that you did ask Hendrik Van den Fleet to drop everything and go to Geneva.'

Christian nodded. 'You know, George, I never thought

I would ever say this about a Van den Fleet, but I am not sure I trust Hendrik now.'

'Yoshino backs up the date of the transaction.'

'Yoshino would back up anything, if it served his purpose. What we need is to get hold of Duiss. He is the key here, I think.'

'He will surface sooner or later, Christian. Just a question of time.'

'Quite, although I shall not let this matter rest. I intend to keep a very close watch on young Mr Van den Fleet. Now, George, on to slightly more pleasant matters. If I may ask a favour of you. Will you stay for a few minutes? I am expecting Martina Van den Fleet at any moment. I thought a little welcoming committee would be appreciated. We had a most useful discussion last night over dinner. You know, she really is a most sensible girl. Utterly charming, too.'

'What did she agree to, Christian?'

Christian stared at him with a shocked expression. 'Whatever can you be implying, George?'

George smiled to himself. 'You mentioned the business about Van den Fleet's to her?'

'Yes, of course. She said Hendrik was crazy, but not that crazy.'

'Did you believe her?'

'I understand there is no love lost between her and her brother. She could have taken advantage of the situation, but seemed genuinely shocked at the suggestion that he would do anything illegal.'

Margaret opened the door a fraction. 'Mr Debilius, Miss Van den Fleet is here.'

'Do show her in right away, Margaret.'

Christian got to his feet and walked swiftly to the door. 'Martina.' He bent to kiss her cheek. 'I think I am entitled. I remember you when you were a little girl and wore braces on your teeth, you know.'

Marti smiled politely. She slipped her bag off her shoulder and tucked it under her arm. Christian definitely had a way with women. He took her arm. 'Let me introduce you to our legal guru, George Forrester.'

'How do you do, Mr Forrester.'

George held out his hand. 'Miss Van den Fleet.' He gazed at her curiously. She was attractive, but not outrageously so. He decided it was the eyes. The frank and level gaze held a hint of something. He wasn't quite sure what, but whatever it was, it was very interesting. Christian beckoned to Margaret. 'Drinks, please, Margaret. What would you like, Martina?'

'Vermouth, if you have it.'

'Margaret, can we manage that?'

'Yes, Mr Debilius.'

Margaret brought a tray of drinks and set them on the desk. 'Miss Van den Fleet, your vermouth. Mr Forrester. Mr Debilius.' She gave a friendly smile in Martina's direction. 'Will there be anything else, Mr Debilius?'

'Not for the moment, thank you, Margaret.'

Christian picked up his glass. 'A toast to the first woman option bearer of the International Diamond Exchange.' He raised his glass to Marti's. 'Martina Van den Fleet.'

George smiled and did the same.

Christian put his glass down and went to his desk. He withdrew a small packet from the drawer. 'Before I forget, Martina, your badge, as it were, of honour.'

She took the packet and opened it. She carefully removed a gilded badge and pinned it on the lapel of her suit.

'Wear that with pride, Martina.' Christian spoke sternly. 'Many women will envy you.'

'But not for long, Christian. Many more will follow me.'

Christian gave a quiet laugh. 'Let us not take things too quickly, Martina.'

'A time and a place, Christian?'

Christian smiled then furrowed his brow. He had heard that expression before, but couldn't quite place it. George's eyes strayed to Marti's. They sparkled back at him. He stared down at his drink. He had a strong suspicion that Christian had got himself more than he had bargained for. Martina Van den Fleet was no bimbo. Christian stared at his chair then pushed it up close to his desk, as if fearful someone might sit in it without his noticing.

Marti stepped out of the elevator and walked across the main hall. As she passed a security guard he addressed her by name and wished her a pleasant evening. She looked about her. Everywhere was decorated in black and white, the monochrome colours relieved only by the expanse of grey carpet. She smiled to herself. Very understated. Very Christian. She inhaled as if breathing in the quiet aura of power.

There were still a few remaining members of staff on the premises. The man on the reception desk eyed her for a moment, then turned his back and picked up a telephone. Marti was conscious of male eyes discreetly watching the IDE's token woman. Some curious. Some suspicious. She held her head higher. She would not remain token for very long. As she passed the reception desk, the man wished her good evening and told her that her limousine was waiting outside for her. She looked perplexedly at him for a moment. She hadn't ordered a cab, but decided perhaps Christian had. He seemed to rather enjoy making gentlemanly gestures.

As Marti stepped out on to the street, a chauffeur leapt from the limousine and opened the rear door. He touched the side of his cap. 'Miss Van den Fleet.'

She hesitated for a moment then walked slowly towards the limousine. As she stopped and paused at the open door, a hand reached out to her. She felt a small jolt of surprise. She would recognise that signet ring anywhere. She got in and turned to stare at Beni. He smiled and took her hand.

'What on earth are you doing here?'

'Waiting for you.'

'Why?'

'We were both a little angry with each other the last time we were together. I think we need to talk, Marti.'

She settled back into the seat. Perhaps they did. She glanced out of the window, as the limousine pulled away from the kerb and threaded its way into the evening traffic on Madison. 'Where are we going?'

'Newport.'

She stared in astonishment at him again. 'Newport?'

He raised her hand to his mouth. 'As you hate hotels so much, I have rented a house for the weekend, but you must promise not to take business calls in bed.'

She raised her fingers to the side of his face and he drew her to him.

Pa Jiaming poured himself a measure of brandy and switched on the television. He sat down in the armchair and lit up a cigarette. The newscaster smiled brightly back at him and announced that she would now be reading news from around the world.

The first item came from the USA, the centre of the world's diamond market. Pa leaned forward in his chair when a photograph of Marti appeared on the screen. Brief details were given of the first woman to be elected as option bearer with the International Diamond Exchange, then the photograph was exchanged for one showing the Cambodian diamond. The voice-over revealed that it had been sold in the West for $6 billion by Martina Van den Fleet, on behalf of an unknown and mysterious client. As if to emphasise the absurdity of Western obsessions, it was pointed out that the price represented the annual wage of twenty million people in the PRC. The image faded and was replaced by an aerial view of New York, then a close-up shot taken inside Tiffany's. As the camera slowly panned displays of diamond jewellery, the newscaster announced that the IDE had made sales totalling more than $10 billion the previous year.

A photograph of Christian Debilius appeared on the screen and a note of solemnity crept into the newscaster's voice as she gave details of the historic agreement between the Chinese People's Republic and the IDE. The agreement, granting full status to the PRC, would be signed in Beijing at the end of the month. A team of experts from the IDE were already on their way to the PRC to assist in the upgrading of existing diamond production and the future development of new mines. Pa drew on his cigarette and blew a perfect smoke ring.

More Thrilling Fiction from Headline

B.J.ROCKLIFF

CRACKERJACK

AN EXPLOSIVE FINANCIAL THRILLER SET IN LONDON, TOKYO AND CANADA

One of the most successful City lawyers in London, Meryl Stewart finds herself the reluctant heiress to her estranged father's Canadian petro-chemical empire. But Tundra Corporation is faced with a formidable takeover bid, staged by her father's oldest rival, and Discus Petroleum is perilously close to achieving control.

With her first-hand knowledge of international business, doubledealing and corruption, Meryl is prepared to fight for her inheritance against the takeover merchants. But when it appears that Tundra controls rights in a revolutionary processing technique that will change the face of the petrochemical industry, what had been a straightforward corporate battle becomes a situation as explosive as any high-octane petrol. And to survive, Meryl must look for friends where she can find them – and for enemies where she least expects them . . .

Crackerjack hurtles the reader from the boardrooms of London and Tokyo to the heart of the Canadian wilderness in a breathtaking story of one woman's struggle for corporate and personal survival.

'Tough and tender is our heroine, Meryl, and I'd put my money on her any day' *Woman's World*

Don't miss PAYDIRT by B.J. Rockliff, also from Headline

FICTION/THRILLER   0 7472 3174 5   £2.99

A selection of bestsellers
from Headline

FICTION

TALENT	Nigel Rees	£3.99 ☐
A BLOODY FIELD BY SHREWSBURY	Edith Pargeter	£3.99 ☐
GUESTS OF THE EMPEROR	Janice Young Brooks	£3.99 ☐
THE LAND IS BRIGHT	Elizabeth Murphy	£3.99 ☐
THE FACE OF FEAR	Dean R Koontz	£3.50 ☐

NON-FICTION

CHILD STAR	Shirley Temple Black	£4.99 ☐
BLIND IN ONE EAR	Patrick Macnee and Marie Cameron	£3.99 ☐
TWICE LUCKY	John Francome	£4.99 ☐
HEARTS AND SHOWERS	Su Pollard	£2.99 ☐

SCIENCE FICTION AND FANTASY

WITH FATE CONSPIRE The Destiny Makers 1	Mike Shupp	£3.99 ☐
A DISAGREEMENT WITH DEATH	Craig Shaw Gardner	£2.99 ☐
SWORD & SORCERESS 4	Marion Zimmer Bradley	£3.50 ☐

All Headline books are available at your local bookshop or newsagent, or can be ordered direct from the publisher. Just tick the titles you want and fill in the form below. Prices and availability subject to change without notice.

Headline Book Publishing PLC, Cash Sales Department, PO Box 11, Falmouth, Cornwall TR10 9EN, England.

Please enclose a cheque or postal order to the value of the cover price and allow the following for postage and packing:
UK: 60p for the first book, 25p for the second book and 15p for each additional book ordered up to a maximum charge of £1.90
BFPO: 60p for the first book, 25p for the second book and 15p per copy for the next seven books, thereafter 9p per book
OVERSEAS & EIRE: £1.25 for the first book, 75p for the second book and 28p for each subsequent book.

Name ....

Address ....

....

....